Transnational Organized Crime in Latin America and the Caribbean

Security in the Americas in the Twenty-First Century

Series Editor: Jonathan D. Rosen

Countries throughout the Americas face many challenges in the twenty-first century such as drug trafficking, organized crime, environmental degradation, guerrilla movements, and terrorism among many other major threats. In this series, titled Security in the Americas in the Twenty-First Century, we invite contributions on topics focusing on security issues in specific countries or regions within the Americas. We are interested in approaching this topic from a political science and international relations perspective. However, we invite manuscript submissions from other disciplines. The aim of this series is to highlight the major security challenges in the twenty-first century and contribute to the security studies literature. We invite both policy-oriented and theoretical submissions.

Titles in the Series

Transnational Organized Crime in Latin America and the Caribbean: From Evolving Threats and Responses to Integrated, Adaptive Solutions, by R. Evan Ellis

Cooperation and Drug Policies in the Americas: Trends in the Twenty-First Century, edited by Roberto Zepeda and Jonathan D. Rosen

Reconceptualizing Security in the Americas in the Twenty-First Century, edited by Bruce M. Bagley, Jonathan D. Rosen, and Hanna S. Kassab

Prisons in the Americas in the 21st Century: Human Dumping Ground, edited by Jonathan D. Rosen and Marten W. Brienen

Decline of the U.S. Hegemony?: A Challenge of ALBA and a New Latin American Integration of the Twenty-First Century, edited by Bruce M. Bagley and Magdalena Defort

Colombia's Political Economy at the Outset of the 21st Century: From Uribe to Santos and Beyond, edited by Bruce M. Bagley and Jonathan D. Rosen

The Obama Doctrine in the Americas, edited by Hanna S. Kassab and Jonathan D. Rosen

Linking Political Violence and Crime in Latin America: Myths, Realities, and Complexities, edited by Kirsten Howarth and Jenny H. Peterson

Organized Crime, Drug Trafficking, and Violence in Mexico: The Transitiona from Felipe Calderón to Enrique Peña Nieto (2006–2015), edited by Jonathan D. Rosen and Roberto Zepeda

U.S.–Cuba Relations: Charting a New Path, edited by Jonathan D. Rosen and Hanna S. Kassab

Fragile States in the Americas, edited by Jonathan D. Rosen and Hanna S. Kassab

Culture and National Security in the Americas, edited by Brian Fonseca and Eduardo A. Gamarra

Energy Security and Environmental Sustainability in the Western Hemisphere, edited by Remi B. Piet, Bruce Bagley, and Marcelo Zorovich

Transnational Organized Crime in Latin America and the Caribbean

From Evolving Threats and Responses to Integrated, Adaptive Solutions

R. Evan Ellis

LEXINGTON BOOKS
Lanham • Boulder • New York • London

Published by Lexington Books
An imprint of The Rowman & Littlefield Publishing Group, Inc.
4501 Forbes Boulevard, Suite 200, Lanham, Maryland 20706
www.rowman.com

Unit A, Whitacre Mews, 26-34 Stannary Street, London SE11 4AB

Copyright © 2018 by The Rowman & Littlefield Publishing Group, Inc.

All rights reserved. No part of this book may be reproduced in any form or by any electronic or mechanical means, including information storage and retrieval systems, without written permission from the publisher, except by a reviewer who may quote passages in a review.

British Library Cataloguing in Publication Information Available

Library of Congress Cataloging-in-Publication Data Available

ISBN 978-1-4985-6796-1 (cloth : alk. paper)
ISBN 978-1-4985-6797-8 (electronic)
ISBN 978-1-4985-6798-5 (pbk. : alk. paper)

∞™ The paper used in this publication meets the minimum requirements of American National Standard for Information Sciences Permanence of Paper for Printed Library Materials, ANSI/NISO Z39.48-1992.

Printed in the United States of America

Contents

PREFACE vii

1 Introduction 1
2 The Geography of Transnational Organized Crime 13
3 Transnational Organized Crime Groups 51
4 Comparative Solutions 103
5 The Path Forward 173

Bibliography 189
Index 215
About the Author 223

PREFACE

From February 2009 through August 2014, I worked as a professor with the Center for Hemispheric Defense Studies, a US Department of Defense school formed to provide strategic level education and outreach to personnel in the defense and security sector in Latin America and the Caribbean. One of my principal responsibilities at the center was to design and implement exercises and wargames for personnel from our partner nations. The planning phase of these exercises involved a dialogue with our partners to identify the security topics of greatest importance to their countries and institutions, to build the activity around those themes, in order to ensure that it was of greatest possible relevance and value to them.

In virtually every event that I developed and executed with our partners, the theme chosen was either humanitarian assistance and disaster response, or transnational organized crime. Within the latter category, the particular focus varied by country, from issues of cartels in Mexico, to violent street gangs in Central America, to posses and garrison community gangs in Jamaica, to terrorist and criminal groups in Peru. That experience, and my complimentary research and publications in the field, impressed on me the centrality of public insecurity and the struggle against transnational organized crime as a key security question for our Latin American and Caribbean partners.

In virtually all of the region, the challenge of transnational organized crime and associated public insecurity has evolved beyond what can be readily solved by repressive measures or actions against the leadership of criminal groups alone. Indeed, in many cases, such approaches have proven counterproductive, unleashing a wave of violence that expands, rather than controls the problem. The challenge of transnational organized crime requires addressing a host of interrelated challenges in a coordinated fashion, going beyond attacking criminal organizations and their leaderships, but also strengthening the economic, social, and governmental institutions of the host societies whose weakness and corruption create an environment in which criminality can spread, feeding off of and ultimately corrupting and destroying those very structures.

As my colleagues in government and academe who have confronted this challenge well know, it is easy to talk of the importance of internationally coordinated, whole-of-government solutions against transnational organized crime, but enormously difficult to formulate and apply such concepts. The challenges are not only mutually reinforcing, but also often so deeply embedded and of such magnitude that the resources available to confront them are insufficient to produce significant short-term results, even when those resources are supplemented by a benefactor such as the United States.

My thinking about the challenge of transnational organized crime has also been shaped by my work since 2014 as the Latin American studies research professor at the US Army War College. The position has truly been a blessing, allowing me to significantly expand my interactions with the security forces of our partners in the region in support of a broad range of other Department of Defense organizations like US Army South, US Southern Command, the Joint Special Operations University, and Special Operations Command South, among others.

My motivation to write this book was further reinforced by the 2016 US presidential elections, and the significant change in US policy and tone by President Donald Trump toward Latin America and the rest of the world. While President Trump's harsh rhetoric toward US neighbors such as Mexico, and initiatives to withdraw the US from trade treaties such as the Trans Pacific Partnership and the North American Free Trade Accord (NAFTA), seemed to cut US ties with other nations, the early emphasis of his administration on immigration and terrorism ironically also highlight just how much conditions in the hemisphere directly affect the security and prosperity of the US.

The present work on transnational organized crime calls attention how US security and prosperity is intimately connected to the hemisphere in which our nation is located, through flows of goods and money, both licit and illicit. Just as US demand for people, drugs, and illicit goods feeds the criminal economy and associated challenges to governance in the region, poor conditions in the region undermine commerce with the US, bring drugs and criminal groups to our territory, create refugee flows, and facilitate weakly governed spaces and illicit networks through which other types of threats may harm the US. This book is about working together with our partners in the region to find collaborative solutions to shared problems, emphasizing how US security depends on security, prosperity, and good governance in the regional "neighborhood" in which we live.

The present work is not designed to be a scholarly or theoretical treatise. Many of the observations and arguments that I make herein come from interviews and interactions with military and law enforcement practitioners in the region that I have had the fortune to interact with. In those interactions, I have been gratified to see that the concept of "whole of government" approaches, and the inclusion of international cooperation as part of a multidimensional, holistic orientation toward combatting organized crime has gained wide acceptance, yet the ability to coordinate the diverse resources that governments offer varies widely by country.

In my experience, the difference between success and stagnation in combatting organized crime is also the ability to develop and implement strategies that deploy the state and society's limited resources in the most effective way in a fashion that is not only simultaneous and coordinated, but also persistent, adaptive, and effectively sequenced. No government, even with the help of partners such as the United States, has the resources to simultaneously attack the challenge of transnational organized crime, in all of the myriad of social, economic, institutional, and other aspects that must be addressed, with sufficient force to decisively eliminate the problem in the near term. The effective strategist fighting counter-organized crime as a system must pick his or her points of intervention intelligently, and understand how to shift the focus of those efforts as the problem evolves. This is not a proscriptive work, but one that respectfully offers ideas to my fellow academics, government team members, and colleagues of the region, regarding how to combat the shared challenge that is collectively undermining security, governance, and prosperity in the region that we share.

As with any work of this nature, there are many people to thank.

I am most appreciative toward my leadership at the US Army War College, who has consistently given me the support and latitude over the years to engage in the travel and other activities to have the first-hand interactions in the region that have made this work possible. In this regard, I would particularly like to thank the head of the Strategic Studies Institute (SSI), Doug Lovelace, as well as Coronel Todd Key, his predecessors Coronel Tom Clady and Coronel Mark Hinds, and Coronel Tom Kardos, who have provided both their support and intellectual engagement that have supported the development of this work. Within the Army War College, I would also like to thank Carol Kerr and our provost, Jim Breckenridge, as well as now-departed members of the Army War College team Lance Betros, Robert Balcavage, and Ambassador Daniel Shields for their constant support for, and encouragement of, my travel, publication, and research.

I would like to thank my research assistant, Gadiel Rosenblut, whose work contributed to this product.

I would also like to further thank the US and foreign strategic research project students with whom I have had the honor of working during my time at the Army War College, and whose own work helped to inspire my thinking. These include Coronels Dan Morgan, Joey Palanco, Raul Torres, Rick Gonzalez, Franklin Gavarette, Fernando Farfan, Mariano Fuenzalida, Carlos Urrutia, Frank Melgarejo, Asirel Loria, Eliott Caggins, Ron Fitch, Juan Solari, Victor Orellana, Victoria Kinsey, Rod Arce, Michael Crawford, Luis Fuchu, Omar Noriega, Paul Vera, and Bosbeli Recinos.

Beyond the War College, I would like to thank US Southern Command, US Army South, US Special Operations Command South, and

Joint Special Operations University (JSOU). In this regard, I would like to specially thank Lieutenant General Joseph DiSalvo and Major General K. K. Chinn, as well as Marv Loera, Rocky Burrell, Jose Gutierrez, and many others who have helped me in my research activities, but who I cannot name here.

Outside my US military community, I would like to recognize the Colombian Army, EAFIT University, the German Institute of Global Affairs (GIGA), Mexico's Technical Institute of Monterrey, Mexico City Campus, the Beneficent Autonomous University of Puebla, Mexico, Brazil's Navy War College, and Army War College Strategic Studies Center (CEEEx) among others, for hosting me as a presenter, and providing the opportunities for important dialogues within the region.

I would like also to specifically thank the colleagues, experts, and senior personnel who generously contributed their time to help me with this work, including:

In the US, Patrick Duddy, Sergio de la Peña, Richard Millett, Maria Velez de Berliner, Brian Fonseca, Jonathan Rosen, Frank Mora, Randy Pestana, Felipe Trigos, Roger Noriega, Miguel Solis, and David Spencer, among others.

In Argentina, Fabian Calle, Andrei Serbin Pont, Gustavo Javier Vidal, Juan Calvo, Leonardo Orlando, Guillermo Rodriguez Conte, Jorge Malena, Augustin Romero, Martin Vermer Pedro de la Fuente, and Nicholas Rodriguez.

In Brazil, Marcio Magno de Farias Franco, William Felippe Abrahão, Anisio David de Oliveria Junior, Luiz Rocha Paiva, Claudio Rogerio de Andrade Flor, Claudio Rodrigues Correa, Marcelo Santiago Villas-Bôas, and Valerio Lange.

In Colombia, Roman Ortiz, Juan David Escobar, Jose John Maralaunda, Hugo Rodriguez Duran Gustavo Rosales Ariza, Ricardo Rubianogroot, Juan David Escobar, Luz Marta Melo Rodriguez, and Rocio Pachon.

In El Salvador, Maria Jose Sanabria, Ricardo Gomez Hecht, and Calixto Hernandez.

In Guatemala, Brigadier General Juan Manuel Perez Ramirez and the Guatemalan Defense Staff, Diego Solis, and Guillermo Pacheco, as well as the team in the office of the technical secretary of the Guatemalan National Security Council, and the Guatemalan Planning and Consulatory Commission.

In Mexico, Adalberto Arauz, Iñigo Guevara, Mario Vela Domínguez, José Ricardo Gómez Meillón, among others.

In Peru, Jorge Robles, Jorge Serrano Torres, Ernesto Morales, Pedro Yaranga, and Enrique Obando.

In Trinidad and Tobago, Anthony Bryan, Archilus Phillips, Dax Driver, Serena Joseph-Harris, Sheridon Hill, Calvin Wilson, Lloyd McAlpin, and Randy Seepersad.

There is a larger list of people whose contributions, for discretion, or speaking off the record, I cannot publicly acknowledge. But please know that you have my sincere thanks.

ONE
Introduction

OVERVIEW

On February 9, 2017, US president Donald Trump issued an executive order to "strengthen enforcement of Federal law in order to thwart transnational criminal organizations" threatening the security of the United States.[1] The order came just days after President Trump's January 25 executive order authorizing construction of a new wall along the US-Mexican border and expanded actions to control illegal immigration. The president justified the measures, in part, by arguing that "transnational criminal organizations operate sophisticated drug- and human-trafficking networks and smuggling operations on both sides of the southern border, contributing to a significant increase in violent crime and United States deaths from dangerous drugs."[2]

While President Trump's policy initiatives have been controversial in both the US and Latin America, they have highlighted the degree to which transnational organized crime activities, particularly in Latin America and the Caribbean, represent a serious challenge to US national security in a manner that resonates deeply with Americans, and with the new Trump administration, they are receiving attention at the highest level. The heightened attention to transnational organized crime in Latin America and the Caribbean with the election of President Trump is paradoxical. Seldom has there been an issue which has resonated so deeply with US voters as a threat, yet has received so little attention as a national security issue.

Transnational organized crime is arguably one of the greatest challenges to an international system in which US citizens and our neighbors can live under conditions of security, prosperity, dignity, and rule of law. It is a cancer on the increasingly interconnected and interdependent global economy. It is enabled by that interconnectivity and associated flows of people, money, information, and material across the globe,[3] yet it perverts the functioning of that system to reproduce violence and corruption which ultimately erodes the governance and trust upon which that system depends. As transnational organized crime destroys and spreads among the societies which are its host, its bi-products include poor governance, weak states, expanded poverty and inequality, a loss of faith in democratic institutions, an erosion in values, environmental degradation, and expanding spaces in which the other maladies of the contemporary world can thrive including exploitative authoritarian governments, terrorism, and the advance of global actors which indeed present existential threats to the United States and the rest of the world community.

It is perhaps ironic that in the US national security discourse, transnational organized crime is often presented as competing with other challenges for resources and the attention of policymakers. Although seemingly counterintuitive, virtually every significant non-state national security concern for Americans today, from terrorism to the challenges posed by US global rivals, to global warming and environmental degradation, is enabled or made worse by transnational crime.

Transnational organized crime is, almost without exception, a key source of funding for global terrorism. Its global networks are a necessary enabler for the laundering of money, the recruitment of people, the acquisition of arms, and the movement of goods for terrorist groups of all varieties. As the head of US Southern Command, Admiral Kurt Tidd, put it, "These networks are efficient, adaptive, innovative, and exceptionally ruthless. They will transport anything or anyone—cocaine, heroin, weapons, people, even wildlife—if they believe the potential profit is greater than the potential risk."[4]

The weak governance, economic needs, degradation of values, and culture of ignorance and resentment propagated by transnational organized crime is the cauldron in which terrorist groups thrive, prepare, and act, contributing to the destructive cycle, which tears apart their societies. As the dynamics of transnational organized crime undermine the faith of populations in democratic institutions and market economies to deliver dignity and prosperity, it also fuels political instability and populist regimes, creating opportunities for geopolitical challengers to the US and Western institutions, such as China, Russia, and Iran.[5]

Finally, transnational organized crime undermines the physical health of the globe and its population. Practices of transnational organized crime groups such as illegal mining leach toxic chemicals into the soil and groundwater, poisoning both the people and wildlife of the region. Illegal logging and the clearing of trees to grow illicit crops are significant contributors to deforestation, as is the crime-related economic need and displacement of people from their homes due to violence, generating refugees that expand the agricultural frontier in places like the Amazon.

Within the Western Hemisphere, transnational organized crime is widely recognized as the principal security challenge of the region. In a 2016 posture statement of US Southern Command before the US Congress, for example, Admiral Kurt Tidd stated that for Latin America and the Caribbean, "the principal challenge remains transnational criminal networks, which are well-organized, well-financed, well-armed, and technologically advanced."[6] This fact is commonly juxtaposed with the correct but misleading assertion that the hemisphere is generally free of more traditional threats by which the US has measured its security, such as state adversaries with large militaries or weapons of mass destruction, or terrorist groups actively launching attacks against US targets from the region.

Yet while the principal security challenge of the region is commonly characterized as "just" transnational organized crime, the strategic threat that it represents to the US is little understood and undervalued. There is no other region of the world more directly linked to US prosperity, security, and the ability of the US to operate as a global power than is Latin America and the Caribbean.[7] There is no other region of the world, including Asia, with which the United States has a stronger bilateral trade relationship, from which it imports more necessities such as food, and in which it has more sunk investments and financial interdependencies than the region. Nor is there any other region of the world to which the United States is physically bound by land borders and critical maritime approaches than Latin America and the Caribbean. Nor, with 17 percent of persons living in the United States claiming some Latin American or Caribbean ethnicity, is there any region in the world to which the United States is more bound by ties of family. Problems in Latin America affect the US economy not only through its companies and investors, but also through flows of refugees, and through the US citizens and other residents who call residents in the region "family."

With respect to geography, if governance in Latin America deteriorates to the point of permitting credible terrorist threats from the region or violence and chaos in US neighbors, as rapidly occurred in the Middle East with the December 2010 to mid-2012 events of Arab Spring, or if a geopolitical rival of the US is able to threaten the country from the region, the emergent threat from Latin America would quickly undermine the ability of the US to project power and influence globally, particularly in the current era of enormous public debt and limited resources.

Although the present work focuses on Latin America and the Caribbean because of its importance to the US and the need to advance contemporary thinking regarding its strategic value, there is no inherent geographic division between the region as a site for transnational criminal activities, versus other parts of the world. Indeed, as this book highlights, although an important part of illicit flows through the region are destined for the United States, and while weapons, cash, and other items of value in the criminal chain flow from the US back to the region, other continents such as Asia, Africa, and Europe are increasingly important and inseparable parts of transnational criminal dynamics in Latin America and the Caribbean. In light of the importance of the region, the concentration on this book on Latin America and the Caribbean allows it to focus on a broad yet manageable subset of cases with respect to patterns of activities, individual groups, government approaches to the problem.

DEFINING TRANSNATIONAL ORGANIZED CRIME

The United States National Security Council (NSC) defines *transnational organized crime* as: "those self-perpetuating associations of individuals who operate transnationally for the purpose of obtaining power, influence, monetary and/or commercial gains, wholly or in part by illegal means, while protecting their activities through a pattern of corruption and/ or violence, or while protecting their illegal activities through a transnational organizational structure and the exploitation of transnational commerce or communication mechanisms. There is no single structure under which transnational organized criminals operate; they vary from hierarchies to clans, networks, and cells, and may evolve to other structures. The crimes they commit also vary."[8]

The definition, although tautological in its use of "transnational," highlights the fact that the "transnational" character of the group may refer not only to the physical location of its core structures in multiple countries, but also to its operations across international boundaries, or use of international infrastructures to pursue its objectives or protect itself. Yet such multiple options for displaying "transnational" character also highlights the difficulty of establishing at what point a criminal organization can or should be considered international. By an extreme version of the above definition, any group of criminals that uses an international phone line, internet connection, or ATM card to support their illicit activities is a "transnational organized crime" group.

The present work does not seek to resolve the question of "how much transnational character is sufficient to qualify for the category?" but rather focuses on those groups which are generally recognized as important transnational criminal actors. Importantly, however, this work will include both groups whose physical presence and operations are substantially international in scope, such as the Mexico-based Sinaloa Cartel, as well as those which operate principally in one country, but which operate as an important part of a transnational criminal network, and whose ongoing criminal activities require their coordination with others outside that country.

Beyond the question of "transnational" character, the White House definition also highlights that the pursuit of power or influence may be the goal of transnational criminal groups, rather than just financial or material benefits. This caveat thus emphasizes the difficulty in distinguishing between groups traditionally referred to as guerillas or freedom fighters, who are considered to pursue material gains for ultimate political ends, versus groups which seek power or influence as a means to, or inseparable component of, their pursuit of material objectives. Indeed, the definitional challenge highlights an important policy debate regarding whether groups such as the National Liberation Army (ELN) in Colombia or the *Shining Path* in Peru (which are sustained principally by criminal activities and do not have a realistic chance of attaining political power) should be considered insurgent or terrorist groups, transnational criminal organizations, or both.

The White House definition highlighted in this chapter further suggests that a necessary characteristic of the organization is that it be "self-perpetuating," rather than strictly maintained by an external organization such as a foreign government, although some criminal organizations may be self-perpetuating even if part of their resources come from religiously or ideologically based support from foreign people, groups, or governments. Importantly, the definition highlights that such groups inherently pursue an interdependent mixture of licit and illicit activities.

Finally, the definition highlights that the organization of groups and their sources of revenue vary greatly and change over time in response to opportunities, the actions of governments, and other aspects of the environment. This concept of variability and mutability of transnational organized crime groups is an important characteristic which is highlighted throughout this work. Some groups, such as Mexico's Sinaloa Cartel, operate in numerous countries throughout the globe, with vast albeit federated structures to conduct their global activities from drug trafficking to money laundering. Others, such as the familial-based criminal clans found in Peru and the "transportistas" groups that move drugs and other contraband goods through Central America are transnational only within the sub-region in which they operate, and in terms of their contacts with larger cartels. Still others, such as the Mara Salvatrucha and Barrio 18 street gangs, are primarily local organizations focused on extorting money and selling drugs in the local neighborhoods in which they operate, and yet certain parts of the organization may have limited international networks for moving drugs to the United States. Even within categories, such as Mexico's cartels, some groups such as the Sinaloa organization actively manage global narcotics supply chains and may concentrate predominantly on the international drug trade, while others, such as Los Zetas, focus on extorting money from those who conduct both legal and illegal activities within the territory under their influence, including informal mining and human smuggling, as well as narcotics.

If there is one almost universal characteristic of criminal organizations in the region, it is that they seldom persist in one form for more than a few years. In Mexico, cartels such as the Arellano Felix, Carrillo Fuentes, and Beltrán-Leyva organizations, Knights Templar, and *La Familia Michoacána* have all splintered or substantially reduced in capabilities, even though their names persist. Intermediary organizations smuggling drugs and other goods in Central America such as the Cachiros and Valle Valle clans in Honduras, or the Mendoza, Lorenzana, Leon, and Lopez Ortiz families have lost substantial portions of their leadership structures. In the Northern Triangle region, the Barrio 18 and Mara Salvatrucha street gangs have come to own and operate legitimate businesses such as bus and taxi companies and nightclubs, as a complement to extortion and drug sales as their traditional sources of income. In Colombia and Peru, the relative importance of illegal mining and vice narcotrafficking has changed as the price of metals such as gold and coltan has fluctuated on international markets. Yet there is little evidence that government strategies and the distribution of effort evolve in response to progress against groups or the evolution of the situation, so much as to perceived failure and/or political change in the societies impacted by that crime.

THE REGIONAL RESPONSE

While it is debatable whether the response of Latin American and Caribbean governments to the transnational organized crime challenge is as adaptable as the threat groups, the governments of the region have shown signs of adopting new policies, strategies, concepts of organization, tactics, and institutional reforms to combat the organized crime challenge in their midst. Encouragingly, such strategies are increasingly multi-dimensional, incorporating a range of government organizations, elements of society, and international cooperation, although some such strategies are decidedly more effectively coordinated than others.

In recent years, the term *whole-of-government* has increasingly come in vogue in approaches to combat transnational organized crime in the region.[9] The 2011 White House strategy to combat transnational organized crime mentions, from the outset of the document, that the strategy will be implemented in a "whole-of-government" fashion[10] (although President Trump's Federal Executive Order on enforcing federal laws against transnational organized crime remarkably does not mention the term).[11]

Whole-of-government at a conceptual level, recognizes the importance of not simply operating against the leadership and individual members of criminal groups, but also seeking solutions to address the range of enabling conditions for their activities, as well as resolving institutional weaknesses that impair the fight against them. These include working to address the poverty and inequality of the youth and members of communities vulnerable to join street gangs or criminal organizations, working with communities to strengthen relationships, building trust in neighborhoods, and establishing the presence of the state in areas in which it has not been perceived to have a strong role. They also include various concepts for using military forces to supplement civilian law enforcement organizations, the formation of new interagency task forces including prosecutors, investigators, and special judges in some cases, and reforms of existing law enforcement institutions, including administrative changes and technical means to root out corruption.

There has also been innovation in the use of assets, and intelligence, including cooperation with foreign partners such as the United States, other neighbors, regional structures, the Central American Integration System (SICA), the Conference of Central American Armed Forces (CFAC), and the Conference of American Armies (CAA), as well as international organizations such as Interpol to work against organized crime. New structures and collaboration in targeting the financial dimension of those criminal activities, and the use of extradition to the United States and supranational organizations such as the International Commission against Impunity in Guatemala (CICIG) have proven to be important tools, particularly in countries of the region in which domestic judicial institutions are weak and penetrated by corruption.

Despite such innovation, the quality of the response to organized crime among the countries of the region is decidedly uneven at best. While the concept of "whole-of-government solutions" appears to be well accepted, the quality of those solutions appears to depend all too often on the management quality and dedication of attention by senior level leadership. Positive results have proven possible where capable leaders are dedicated to innovative, well-considered strategies, and have the authority, political latitude, and managerial capabilities to implement them. Unfortunately, such cases have been distressingly few, yet where they have been successful, such as the strengthening of governance in Colombia under Álvaro Uribe, such cases have served as an inspiration for others in the region.

THE IMPORTANCE OF A SYSTEM-ORIENTED APPROACH

Transnational organized crime may be understood as a complex, interdependent system, involving sometimes complimentary and other times competing criminal actors, as well as the physical, financial, and human infrastructures on which they depend, in interaction with, affecting, and affected by the economies and societies in which they operate. Organized crime groups themselves are effectively systems within systems. Their ability to function, evolve, and grow, at one level, reflects not only the discrete actions of individual leaders, but also the construction and maintenance of organizations, and an ongoing economic enterprise with production, logistics, and financial dimensions of their illicit activities. Each of these is, in effect, a system which interfaces with the broader systems of the societies in which they are embedded. Their members come from those societies, including both formal members of the organization, and others employed to provide services. Their systems for the generation of income draw on national transportation infrastructures to move people, drugs, mining products, and contraband goods, among other items. From their leadership to the tactical level, their organizations depend on communication infrastructures to manage their international operations. They depend on financial infrastructures to move, store, and hide their ill-gotten wealth. Organized crime groups thus transform, and are transformed by, the infrastructures of the societies in which they operate.

Beyond their internal workings and resources, the ability of transnational organized crime groups to prosper is a function of a myriad of interrelated conditions within the societies in which they operate. These include the functionality of judicial and penal institutions, law enforcement, and intelligence systems, levels of corruption within law enforcement, government, and the business community, the willingness of citizens to cooperate with government and/or to aid the criminals, values in the society, from attitudes toward government authority, to concepts of morality, family structures to guide youth, and relative economic opportunities, among other factors.

This work argues that the collaborative approach to fighting transnational organized crime in Latin America and the Caribbean must begin with understanding the dynamics of that crime, within the societies that it operates, as a complex, interdependent system. Instead of attacking symptoms, as will be explained later, policymakers must focus on the relationships between phenomena in that system, (e.g., between poverty and crime, or between corruption and citizen alienation) and how to selectively intervene to affect those relationships in a constructive fashion.

That analysis of such relationships leads to a focus on systemic "centers of gravity. Like centers of gravity in traditional military parlance, these are elements of the system which, if impacted, are believed to have the most significant effect on the dynamics of the system. Like traditional military centers of gravity in the physical battlefield, these are not necessarily the easiest to effect, and indeed, may require an indirect approach to impact them. But like their traditional military battlespace counterparts, impacting them promises to significantly affect the system.[12]

The three main centers of gravity in the fight against transnational organized crime are (1) the money of the groups involved, (2) corruption and impunity, and (3) political will. Virtually every aspect of transnational criminal actors depends on the flow and legitimation of resources from recruiting people and maintaining organizations to buying arms, to bribing officials, to purchasing factor inputs for drugs, to operating logistics systems, to more people and contraband products. Corruption and perceived impunity is an insidious phenomenon undermining the effectiveness of efforts against organized crime at levels from conducting operations and obtaining intelligence, to collaboration between government security organizations and international partners to work together, to the government's ability to obtain cooperation from citizens and respect for the right of the government to administer and make rules on the territory under its jurisdiction, which are together the key for the operation of law enforcement. Within organizations such as the police, judicial institutions, military, and other parts of the bureaucracy, the perception of corruption by the organization's members fuels even more corruption by suggesting that such practices both are socially acceptable and will not be punished.

With respect to political will, as seen from the violence unleashed in Mexico by the frontal attack on organized crime by the regime of President Felipe Calderón, or the economic costs of taking down key financial actors such as Jaime Rosenthal and Grupo Continental in Honduras, addressing transnational organized crime often not only is expensive in terms of resources often desperately needed in other parts of society, but also imposes significant negative consequences for the governments and societies that undertake the fight. In the face of such incentives, generally all too well understood by the politicians and other leaders in the region who undertake them, the temptation is to implement policies that seek to minimize the symptoms of the problem, such as high-profile violence and street crime, or worse yet, not taking on the problem at all.

As suggested previously, effective strategic concepts must be complemented by points of intervention to impact them. Too often, what a specific country or ministry does, as part of a coordinated, multidimensional strategic concept, is based on its assets and the functions it has traditionally performed. While these are often relevant, it is critical for those developing counter-transnational organized crime strategies to ask "how could my organization's capabilities contribute to impacting this center of gravity?" and then work together with others at the table to devise a plan to combine resources to do so, rather than just replicating the ministry's functions as lines of action.

Finally, good strategic concepts, rooted in well-understood centers of gravity and points of intervention, alone are not enough. Those designing and implementing the strategy must devise appropriate measures for monitoring the effects of their intervention, and how the system is evolving, to determine when and how to shift efforts to manage it.

ORGANIZATION OF THIS WORK

This work is divided into five chapters, including the present one.

Chapter 2 characterizes the "anatomy" of organized crime in Latin America and the Caribbean in terms of countries and sub-regions which are principally "sources" versus "transit zones." In the process, it provides a panorama of the interconnected dynamics of transnational organized crime in the region.

Chapter 3 describes key organized crime groups in the region according to a loose typology of regionally based "cartels," intermediary groups, ideologically oriented groups, and gangs.

Chapter 4 comparatively examines government initiatives against organized crime across the region within nine specific areas: (1) coordinated, whole-of-government solutions, (2) interdiction of criminal flows, (3) the targeting of transnational criminal organization group leaders and other high-value-added targets, (4) the use of the military in a domestic law enforcement context, (5) integrating intelligence against organized crime across government institutions, (6) institutional reform within law enforcement, (7) targeting the financial resources of transnational organized crime, (8) prison control and reform, and (9) binational and multinational cooperation against organized crime.

Finally, chapter 5 makes specific recommendations for policymakers in the region, as well as those in the US.

NOTES

1. "Presidential Executive Order on Enforcing Federal Law with Respect to Transnational Criminal Organizations and Preventing International Trafficking," The White House, February 9, 2017, https://www.whitehouse.gov/the-press-office/2017/02/09/presidential-executive-order-enforcing-federal-law-respect-transnational.

2. The White House, "Executive Order: Border Security and Immigration Enforcement Improvements," January 25, 2017, https://www.whitehouse.gov/the-press-office/2017/01/25/executive-order-border-security-and-immigration-enforcement-improvements.

3. Moises Naim, *Ilicit: How Smugglers, Traffickers, and Copycats Are Hijacking the Global Economy*, (New York: Anchor Books, 2005).

4. "Posture Statement of Admiral Kurt W. Tidd, Commander, United States Southern Command, before the 114th Congress Senate Armed Services Committee," March 10, 2016, http://www.southcom.mil/newsroom/Documents/SOUTHCOM_POSTURE_STATEMENT_FINAL_2016.pdf.

5. Douglas Farah, "Transnational Organized Crime, Terrorism, and Criminalized States in Latin America: An Emerging Tier-One National Security Priority" (Carlisle Barracks, PA: US Army War College Strategic Studies Institute, August 2012), http://strategicstudiesinstitute.army.mil/pubs/display.cfm?pubID=1117.

6. "Posture Statement."

7. See R. Evan Ellis, "The Strategic Importance of the Western Hemisphere—Defining US Interests in the Region," Testimony to the Subcommittee on the Western Hemisphere, US House of Representatives Foreign Affairs Committee, February 3, 2015, http://docs.house.gov/meetings/FA/FA07/20150203/102885/HHRG-114-FA07-Wstate-EllisE-20150203.pdf.

8. "Strategy to Combat Transnational Organized Crime: Definition," The White House, Official Website, accessed September 6, 2016, https://www.whitehouse.gov/administration/eop/nsc/transnational-crime/definition.

9. Farah, "Transnational Organized Crime."

10. See *Strategy to Combat Transnational Organized Crime: Addressing Converging Threats to National Security*, The White House, July 2011, https://www.whitehouse.gov/sites/default/files/microsites/2011-strategy-combat-transnational-organized-crime.pdf.

11. "Presidential Executive Order on Enforcing Federal Law with Respect to Transnational Criminal Organizations and Preventing International Trafficking," The White House, Official Website, February 9, 2017, https://www.whitehouse.gov/presidential-actions/presidential-executive-order-enforcing-federal-law-respect-transnational-criminal-organizations-preventing-international-trafficking/.

12. For a good discussion of centers of gravity in conventional military thought, see Antulio J. Echevarria II, "Clausewitz's Center of Gravity: Changing Our Warfighting Doctrine—Again!" (Carlisle Barracks, PA: US Army War College, 2002), http://www.strategicstudiesinstitute.army.mil/pdffiles/PUB363.pdf.

TWO

The Geography of Transnational Organized Crime

OVERVIEW

Just as the cultures and the patterns of economic activity in Latin America and the Caribbean are defined by its physical geography, the activities of organized criminal groups in the region can also be understood through interrelated, often overlapping flows from one part of the region to another. The patterns of transnational organized crime in Latin America and the Caribbean (not just for narcotrafficking) may be loosely defined in terms of "demand" and "source" zones, and the "transit" zones that connect them. The characterization is useful, albeit imperfect given that the range of products and services encompassed by organized crime means that countries that principally demand one product or activity can be sources or transit zones for others, although in general, it is the wealthier countries which are primarily the sources of demand.

With respect specifically to narcotrafficking, the position of a country as a source zone versus a transit zone versus a consumption zone for one drug, such as cocaine, is not necessarily the same as its position for another, such as heroine or synthetic drugs. The matter becomes even more complex when other illicit activities are included, such as illegal mining, timber, contraband goods, human trafficking, human smuggling, arms, and money flows.

Some types of organized crime activity such as extortion may sometimes be realized entirely within a particular country or area, yet in other instances, such as the extortion by groups controlling territory of others moving drugs through it, a type of criminal activity confined to one country (such as extortion in the previous example) may depend on a broader transnational flow and be affected by changes in it. Indeed, the evolution of transit routes, new sources of demand, or new sources of supply means that the specific role of a country or area in the geography of transnational organized crime the region may be in flux. Yet despite such imperfections in the categorization scheme, it nonetheless has some utility in loosely categorizing the region in terms of clusters of countries which have similar characteristics and associated challenges.

Beyond narcotrafficking, source zone countries generally serve as points of origin of raw materials for drugs (sometimes including laboratories for their transformation). They also commonly contain the terrain from which mining sector products and timber are illegally extracted. Source zone countries are, ironically, seldom the recipients of the majority of profits from those activities, and contrary to conventional wisdom, often atomized with respect to the structure of the groups which conduct their illicit activities. They are recipients of only some of the repatriated profits from armed groups, and often recipients of only a portion of illegal arms. Source zones are often simultaneously points of origin for people to be smuggled or exploited through human trafficking (although "transit zone" countries may also be important sources of human capital, owing in part to the violence generated by their activities as transit zones).

The transformation of illicit material may take place in either transit or source zone countries. Such transformation includes drug laboratories, but also encompasses operations where illegal mining products are consolidated with others to launder or legitimize the metals before selling them to consumption zone countries. Transit zone countries may be dominated by a series of intermediate groups who move drugs and other illicit products for others. Ironically, because of the violence occasioned by the competition for routes or territorial control to tax transit activities, transit zones may actually be a more important source of people being displaced toward consumption zones, than are pure source zones.

With respect to the movement and exploitation of people, experts make a distinction between human smuggling, in which the people are moved voluntarily, and trafficking, in which people are being exploited as a commodity.[1] Yet there is almost always an element of deception and exploitation in any smuggling operation. Immigrants smuggled through the Americas, for example, are often obliged to transport drugs across the border. Asian immigrants passing through Central America and the Caribbean en route to the United States are often obliged to work for little or no wages in stopping points along the way to help pay for their passage. While no good data is available on the number of Chinese immigrants passing through Latin America, Chinese trafficking organizations are believed to earn between $50,000 and $70,000 per person trafficked, producing $750 million per year in illicit earnings for smuggling immigrants into the United States, often through the region.[2]

Such trafficking and smuggling also feed an array of other criminal enterprises, including the personnel who act as guides and facilitate passage, to the cartels and gangs who may rob the immigrants (who traditionally carry cash for transactions on the journey to their new destination), charge for their safe passage, or both. While, as seen above, some transit zones also have features of source zones, others have features of consumption zones. Indeed, many of these countries are the most violent and problematic of the categories of countries examined in this book. In general, the evolution of demand for illicit products in transit zones developed through schemes involving payment in kind of drugs by transnational organized crime groups moving or transforming them in the territory, as well as a middle class with the resources to purchase drugs.

Ironically the competition for both markets and transit routes that make "transit and human source zones" highly violent also makes them significant markets for arms, which ironically, generally come in part from consumption zone countries (because of their advanced manufacturing capabilities), although also from others. In general, transit zone countries are significant consumers of contraband, owing to their status as middle-income economies, whose residents have some income to purchase such goods, yet not sufficient income to pay a premium for the actual name-brand products for which the contraband items are often a substitute. Finally, pure consumption zones are characterized by the end use of illicit products and services, including drugs, timber and mining products, people, and contraband goods. These countries generate the majority of earnings for criminal groups, which must subsequently be laundered. Yet because of the level of control associated with the sophisticated financial infrastructures of demand zone economies like the US, and the relative absence of an informal sector, the money generated is rarely laundered there. Ironically, as noted previously, although consumption zones are also major sources for arms, violence in consumption zones is typically well controlled, and the power of criminal groups is limited by functional, well-institutionalized legal systems.

Within such broad categories, the specific routes, criminal approach, and mixture of activities by criminal groups evolve over time in response to patterns of law enforcement, emerging opportunities (such as permissive political conditions in a particular country), and characteristics of the criminal groups and relationships between them. Such dynamics have been referred to as the "balloon effect" but are more complex than the simple geographic displacement of criminals and drug flows from one area to another, often associated with the term.

While this work focuses on the Western Hemisphere, the categories discussed here also may be applied to other regions. Similarly, the relationships between consumption, transit, and source zones may also apply across regions, such as drugs from source zone countries in Latin

America flowing through African transit zone countries to consumption zone countries in Europe.

UNITED STATES

Working loosely from the north to the south of the region, the United States may be considered as the principal "consumption zone" country of the region. According to the United Nations Office on Drugs and Crime, over 100,000 people in the US were in treatment for cocaine addiction in North America in 2016, versus approximately 32,000 in Latin America and the Caribbean.[3] The 2016 United States-Mexico Bi-National Criminal Proceeds study calculated that US drug demand alone channels $19 billion to $29 billion annually to Mexican organized crime groups.[4]

With respect to narcotics, the market for cocaine in the United States has been decreasing since approximately 2006, although it still remains substantial, and recent declines have not been as significant as earlier ones. On the other hand, the market for heroine in the United States is expanding, partly as a substitute for synthetic painkillers such as OxyContin, whose use has also expanded;[5] and Mexico has become one of the principal suppliers. On the other hand, China has become the major supplier of the synthetic drug fentanyl, which has played a major role in the opioid crisis in the United States.[6]

Marijuana use in the United States has also expanded, arguably fueled by the legalization of its use in eight states and Washington DC,[7] and the perception of decreased enforcement against its use under the US administration of Barrack Obama.

The relatively strong economy of and perceived prosperity in the United States and Canada make the region an attractive destination for migrants, particularly those fleeing violence in Mexico and the Northern Triangle nations of Central America. In the first half of 2015, for example, US authorities detained some 70,400 non-Mexican migrants at the US-Mexican border (mostly from Central America) while Mexican authorities detained an additional 93,000.[8] Such migration became a central theme in the presidential candidacy, and subsequently the presidency, of Donald Trump.

While the United States is commonly regarded as a destination for drugs and people, its importance as a source for firearms contributes to the dynamics of transnational organized crime in Mexico and elsewhere in the region.[9] An estimated 70 percent of the firearms seized from organized crime groups in Mexico, for example, come from the United States.[10] According to a 2015 study by the Mexican government, an estimated two thousand arms enter the country from the US each day.[11]

While the unlicensed export of weapons in the US is illegal, the ability to purchase them in a range of venues from shopping centers to gun shows facilitates their export to Latin America and the Caribbean. Nonetheless, weapons do come from other sources, with the black market for arms in the region including weapons acquired from the civil wars in Central America in the 1980s and 1990s, as well as from other parts of the world.[12]

With respect to financial flows, the US market for drugs and other criminal activities is an important source of earnings for transnational organized crime groups in the region. Such activities often generate bulk cash earned in the US, which must be either smuggled across the border or repatriated.

MEXICO

Mexico, largely because of its geography, is a major transit zone country that also has characteristics of a consumption zone. During the 1980s and 1990s, Mexico was the quintessential transit country for US-bound drugs. During the 1980s, US attempts to stop cocaine flows from Colombia through the Caribbean to Miami forced narcotraffickers to begin smuggling it through Mexico, converting Mexican smugglers into associates of the Colombians, with the Mexicans coming to collaborate in an association that came to be known as the Guadalajara Cartel.[13]

The murder of DEA agent Enrique Camarena in 1985 led to US pressure on the Mexican government to act more forcibly against the drug traffickers operating within its territory, eventually splintering the organization into the Arellano Felix, Carrillo Fuentes, and Sinaloa organizations, in addition to the already independent Gulf Cartel, some of the original key actors in Mexican narcotrafficking today. By 2006, cartel violence in Mexico was spiraling out of control, including a struggle for territory between a new group, *La Familia Michoacana*, *los Zetas*, which had begun as the armed wing of the Gulf Cartel.

Mexico's current "war against the cartels" began with a request from the governor of Michoacán for assistance to Mexico's newly elected president, Felipe Calderón, and Calderón's deployment of 6,700 federal troops to Michoacán in December 2006,[14] leading to an escalation of violence and the fragmentation of the criminal landscape in Mexico into more than fifty factions, gangs, and other criminal entities.

As of early 2017, some of the areas of Mexico most fiercely contested by the cartels include states of the central-west such as Michoacán and parts of Guerrero and Jalisco, known as *"tierra caliente."* The area around Mexico City is also, however, becoming increasingly subject to battles for control between drug groups, including the State of Mexico, and Morelos. In the east of the country, the Yucatan peninsula has historically been one entry point into Mexico for drugs coming from the Caribbean, including the important port of Veracruz, which has been subject to multiple struggles between drug organizations and the Mexican state in recent years.[15] Beyond Veracruz, the Yucatan peninsula has been relatively peaceful, although nonetheless important for the movement of drugs and other criminal activities. In early 2017, a series of violent incidents in and around Cancun suggested that a struggle between criminal groups may be emerging in this area as well.[16]

Beyond the drug wars, Mexico has also been significantly impacted by a host of other criminal activities, enabled in part by the weakness of the Mexican state in the face of well-financed criminal groups. In the state of Michoacán, for example, illegal mining has prospered, taxed by groups such as the Knights Templar organization, which effectively controlled the area, with the proceeds purchased by Chinese and other intermediaries.[17] Although there are no good estimates for the value of illegal mining goods exported from Mexico, the quantity of mining exports to China from the port of Lazaro Cardenas in Michoacán is believed to have quadrupled from 2008 to the first part of 2013 when the criminal organizations La Familia and Knights Templar controlled the state and the port. Indeed, Mexican authorities acknowledge that the illegal mining trade through the port was one of the factors that obliged them to take control of it. From 2010 to 2013, Mexican authorities received reports of illegal mining not only in Michoacán, but also in Jalisco and Colima. During the period authorities denied minerals export licenses to thirteen firms because they could not prove the legitimate origins of the minerals they were seeking to export.[18]

Mexico has also been a transit zone for US- and Canada-bound migrants, coming not only from its own territory, but also from Central America and points further south. This human capital has contributed to the difficult situation in the country, with persons accumulating south of the Mexico-US border, looking for opportunities to cross, becoming vulnerable to criminal groups preying on their need to charge them to cross, to rob them, or to obligate them to smuggle their narcotics across the border. Such migrants have also included those from other regions, such as the Chinese, who followed traditional immigration routes through Central America, among others, crossing into Mexico at Frontera Corozal, among other places, and obtaining new documents in Tapachula, before continuing to move north.[19] Such migrant flows also contributed to make the Mexican resort city of Cancun, in the Yucatan peninsula, an important hub of human trafficking, including forced prostitution and other forms of exploitation.[20]

As the migrant problem has become more acute for the Mexican government, Mexico has also increasingly collaborated with the US to increase controls over its southern border, as well as the US/Mexico border, forcing Central American and other immigrants to other routes.

CENTRAL AMERICA

As in Mexico, the imperatives of geography have made Central America and the Caribbean complements to Mexico as an important transit zone for US-bound drugs, other illicit substances, and persons.[21] From the 1970s and before, Honduras served as an important "bridge" between source zone countries such as Colombia and the United States.[22] The narcotrafficker Juan Ramon Matta, for example, famously used Honduras as an intermediate point in moving cocaine acquired in Colombia from Pablo Escobar's Medellin Cartel to Mexico for the Guadalajara Cartel.[23] During the 1980s, air and maritime routes directly through the Caribbean were the principal method for moving cocaine from Colombia and Peru to the United States, although such flows were significantly curtailed by increased collaboration with US partners in the region, and the establishment of Joint Interagency Task Force South (JIATF-S), further increasing the use of land routes for the final leg of the journey to the United States through the northern triangle countries Honduras, Guatemala, and Salvador, then through Mexico.

The increased use of land routes through the northern triangle by narcotraffickers was initially very successful due to a combination of complex terrain and weak state presence in the region, particularly in the areas outside of the principal cities. Honduras's and Belize's Atlantic coasts, in particular, are characterized by numerous small islands and inlets which facilitate the hiding of small boats and the fuel to refuel them. The distance of Honduras's relatively unpopulated eastern coast from the principal cities in the west of the county, and the lack of good roads, similarly has impeded the government from sustaining an effective presence in the territory, including difficulty in sustaining an adequate number of naval bases to cover national waters in remote areas.

The use of Central America as a transit zone also substantially contributed to the corruption of already weak institutions in the region, particularly in the northern triangle. Public corruption and associated ineffective governance played a role in the parallel growth of a separate, but related, challenge in the region: the rise of violent street gangs such as Mara Salvatrucha and Barrio 18. Although these groups had their origins in the expansion of deportations of Central American immigrants from the United States after 1996 with the with the passage of the Illegal Immigrant Reform and Immigrant Responsibility Act (IIRIRA),[24] taxing the flow of drugs through areas under gang control came to complement extortion and petty crime as sources of income for the gangs. The groups, principally Mara Salvatrucha (MS-13) and Barrio-18 (B-18), received drugs as payment in kind for allowing drugs to pass through their territories, and other activities in support of the narcotraffickers. Their sale of these drugs to those living in the neighborhoods under their control, in turn, contributed to local drug demand and conflict, furthering the cycle of violence and other problems in those areas, and increasing the flight of the population from the region to the United States and elsewhere.[25] Those immigrants, in turn, as they migrated through Central America and Mexico toward the United States, generated business opportunities for the human traffickers who would exploit them, and the thieves and other criminals who would prey on them in the journey.

In recent years, Central American governments, with US support, have expanded efforts to control these remote territories, yet the region has continued to be a leading transit route for US-bound narcotics.[26] Nonetheless, enforcement efforts appear to have impacted the way in which drugs and other illicit goods are moved through Central America. As an example, improved radar coverage, coordination between the US and partners in the region, and the pursuit of new laws for "shooting down" narco-flights (even without actually shooting down any aircraft) caused the number of suspect air tracks transiting the region to fall 53 percent from 2015 to 2016 alone.[27]

Another important change in patterns of narcotrafficking through Central America has been the increase in the use of the Pacific coast of the continent. Indeed, by 2016, US Southern Command estimated that some 68 percent of drugs passing through the region were using the Pacific Ocean.[28] Notable quantities of drugs transit the Pacific Coast of Guatemala, sometimes landing on the Guatemalan coast and, from there, moving by land to the Guatemala-Mexico border, in the Department of San Marcos, or at points more inland. The problem of human trafficking and human smuggling through the region complements narcotrafficking and other flows. In June 2016, for example, Central American authorities broke up a ring for smuggling migrants through the region that was bringing people from outside the region through Brazil, Colombia, Central America, and Mexico to the United States.[29]

A principal driver of refugees leaving from the nations of Central America toward the United States is the previously mentioned challenge of violent street gangs. For many residents of the northern triangle, the urban street gangs, and particularly Mara Salvatrucha and Barrio 18, are more serious problems than drug trafficking. The problem of extortion of local businesses and the transport sector has become particularly severe. In Honduras, in the first seven months of 2016, for example, criminal elements burned thirty urban and inter-city buses and killed sixty-three public transport workers, presumably for not paying the extortion demanded of them.[30] In Guatemala, between 2013 and April 2016, one study found 10,664 extortion complaints, concentrated in three heavily urban departments with a high concentration of street gangs: Guatemala, Mixco, and Villa Nueva.[31]

Honduras

While the relatively uninhabited eastern portion of Honduras was long an important area for narcotransits, its role as a narco corridor dramatically expanded in 2009 when the forced removal of Honduras's president, Manuel Zelaya,[32] led to the suspension of security assistance and other forms of cooperation with the country by the US and other members of the international community.[33] Taking advantage of the situation, criminal groups quickly expanded the use of Honduran territory for US-bound narcotics shipments,[34] with an estimated 80 percent of US-bound narcoflights landing in Honduras during that period.[35]

The election of Pepe Lobo as president of Honduras in a 2009 special election, and his subsequent replacement by Juan Orlando Hernandez, paved the way for renewed cooperation with Honduran authorities by the US and the rest of the international community, helping to reduce the use of Honduras as the preferred intermediate stop for drug flights.[36] In the process, however, the expanded enforcement efforts in and off the coast of Honduras drove narcotraffickers to shift to other routes, including greater use of the Pacific Coast, and routes involving stops in or transits through Costa Rica and Panama.

Although most cocaine moves through Honduras as a finished product, some drug laboratories have been discovered near major sea and highway logistic routes. One such facility, for example, was discovered in 2011 in the Merendon mountain area near the Guatemalan border. A second was found approximately forty kilometers from La Ceiba, and the third was discovered in the vicinity of the village of Omoa, also close to Guatemala.[37]

Guatemala

Because of its location straddling both the Atlantic and Pacific coasts of Central America, Guatemala has historically played a key role as a transit country for drugs. Following the end of the Guatemalan civil war in 1996, the budget and manpower of the armed forces were significantly reduced, undercutting the ability of the military to maintain an effective presence across the national territory. Military funding and manpower reductions reached their low point in 2004 under President Oscar Berger, with a defense budget of only .15 percent of GDP.

At the same time, per the peace accords, Guatemala's national police was disbanded and replaced by a new one, based on a new model derived from the Spanish *Gendarmerie*, yet the transition was beset by significant problems.[38] The combined effect of dramatic reductions in military capabilities and difficulties with the creation of a new police force, was that neither the armed forces nor the police could adequately control the national territory.

The relatively inaccessible and sparsely populated Petén region in the north, during this time, was heavily used as a waypoint for narcoflights, although expanded enforcement actions under the Guatemalan government of Álvaro Colom and increasing opportunities to use Honduras for drug transits reduced the role of the Petén region, in favor of eastern Honduras Nonetheless, by July 2016, evidence of expanded illegal forest clearance for the construction of clandestine runways for narco-flights suggested that traffickers were returning to the use of the region, to some degree, for such transits.[39]

With respect to overland routes, with expanded enforcement along the Honduran border into the Guatemalan provinces of Izabal, Zacapa, and Chiquimula, narcotraffickers are believed to have expanded their use of the border with El Salvador, moving drugs into the Guatemalan province of Jutiapa. Similarly, although Guatemalan narcotraffickers traditionally moved drugs into Mexico across the border from the Guatemalan provinces of San Marcos and Huehuetenango, they have also increasingly used more northerly routes through the country to cross drugs into Mexico from the Petén, taking advantage of the Guatemalan government's limited ability to control the rivers in that state, including that forming its border with Mexico.

The Pacific coast of the country has also been an important waypoint for the movement of drugs toward the United States, including the use of boats, towed buoys, and narcosubmarines which often originate in Ecuador or Colombia, stopping in coastal villages such as Champerico and Quetzal, Guatemala's only Pacific-coast commercial port, to either offload their cargo to continue overland, or refuel before continuing on toward Mexican ports such as Acapulco.

One major trafficker captured in April 2016, Marlon Monroy Meoño (*El Fantasma*) reportedly used contacts in the military to move drugs from Colombia and Ecuador to the Pacific coast of Guatemala, then on to Mexico and the United States.[40]

Although Guatemala is principally a transit zone, it is also a source for heroin to supply the US and other markets. Most such heroin is derived from poppies grown in the mountainous and difficult to access terrain of San Marcos, bordering Mexico.[41] As in Honduras, Guatemala has also been the site of a modest number of drug laboratories. These have been located in areas relatively off the beaten path, yet accessible by major logistics routes, including methamphetamine labs in the departments of San Marcos and El Progresso.[42]

El Salvador

El Salvador's small size has historically limited its role in the flow of drugs through Central America. Nonetheless, efforts to control drug flows through neighboring Honduras, and El Salvador's relatively good highway infrastructure, have led criminal organizations to move a growing quantity of drugs through the country. Traditionally, such flows have been dominated by two smuggling organizations: Los *Perrones* and the *Texis* Cartel (discussed in greater detail in the next chapter). El Salvador's two dominant gangs, Mara Salvatrucha and Barrio 18, have principally extorted money from smugglers transporting drugs through zones that they control and providing protection and other "services" to the smugglers. In recent years, however, select suborganizations of Mara Salvatrucha with ties to the United States, including the "Program" *Fultones Locos*, have become more active in physically moving drugs through the country, with the acquisition of properties on the country's Pacific coast to support such efforts.[43]

With respect to Mara Salvatrucha and Barrio 18, El Salvador is arguably the northern triangle country with the largest number per capita of gang members, and in which the gangs have most severely challenged the state. In March 2012, the violence spawned by the clash between Mara Salvatrucha and Barrio 18 led the government and the Catholic church to informally mediate a truce between them, later joined by smaller gangs Mao Mao, La Maquina, and Mirada Loca.[44] Within the first several months following the implementation of the truce, the number of murders fell by almost half.[45] Yet critics of the agreement worried that the relative peace was providing cover for the gangs to consolidate their control over territory, while continuing to extort the population and engage in other criminal enterprises.[46]

By 2014, murders had reached and surpassed their previous level. In January 2015, a the newly elected government of Salvador Sánchez Cerén announced that he would not continue to support the truce, and took a series of actions demonstrating a more uncompromising posture toward the gangs, including returning senior gang leaders to the maximum-security prison Zacatecoluca, from which they had been transferred as part of the previous government's negotiations.[47]

By 2016, El Salvador's violence had become the highest in all of Central America, and the highest for any country in the world not in an active war zone.[48] Beyond gang-on-gang violence, during 2015, attacks against police personnel expanded rapidly, with four hundred attacks recorded against the Salvadoran National Police in 2014 compared to 140 in 2013. During 2015, gangs attacked police stations with grenades,[49] and even attempted to detonate a car bomb in front of the Salvadoran treasury building in San Salvador in September 2015.[50] By early 2017, a combination of new government initiatives (discussed in chapter 4), and initiatives by the gangs themselves to restrain their members, had reduced violence, yet nonetheless left the extortion and violence of the gangs as the country's principal security challenge.[51]

Costa Rica and Panama

Further to the south, counterdrug enforcement actions by the US and local authorities in the northern triangle has induced narcotraffickers to increasingly use routes that make stops in, or transit through, Costa Rica and Panama.

With respect to moving drugs by air, between November 2015 and March 2016, Costa Rican authorities identified thirty-five clandestine airstrips on the Pacific coast of the country.[52] One factor in Panama's role in narcotrafficking is that it adjoins Colombia, one of the region's principal source zones for narcotrafficking, and home to numerous powerful criminal groups. In addition to the powerful Colombian Gulf Cartel, involved in criminal activities in Panama, the remnants of the 57th front of the Fuerzas Armadas Revolucionarios de Colombia (FARC) are involved in moving narcotics from Colombia across the Panama border toward the north. Panamanian authorities worry that the demobilization of the FARC, as part of the organization's November 2016 peace agreement with the neighboring government of Colombia, will transform the remnants of the 57th front into a more explicitly criminal organization, as well as expanding the ranks of the *Gulf Clan* and other groups using Panama for criminal purposes.[53]

The use of Panama by transnational organized crime is compounded by its role as an international hub for commerce, maritime logistics, and finance. A portion of the narcotics going through Panama come by sea from Peru and Ecuador, transiting the Panama Canal with ultimate destinations in Europe, as well as in the US.[54] The expansion of the Panama Canal, inaugurated in June 2016, will likely expand opportunities to use the country as a regional and global center for illicit goods and money laundering. Expanded commercial opportunities with the People's Republic of China following Panama's diplomatic recognition of the country in June 2017 is likely to have a similar effect, particularly to the extent that the new ties expand the number of flights and cargo ships visiting the country, as well as expanding the role of Chinese banks in the country.[55]

With respect to money laundering, the potential for illicit activities arising from Panama's role as an international hub was highlighted by the international scandal in 2016 regarding politicians and wealthy businessmen with clandestine bank accounts in Panama, set up by the financial firm Mossack Fonseca.[56]

THE CARIBBEAN

The geographic location of the Caribbean makes it a natural maritime transit zone for drugs and people bound for the United States, although drugs and people also pass through the region for Europe and other destinations. As noted previously, the establishment of joint task forces in the region to combat drug flows, and the merger of two previous task forces to create Joint Interagency Task Force South (JIATF-S) in Key West, Florida, in 1999, played an important role in reducing the movement of people, drugs, and other illicit goods through the region.

In recent years, however, the deterioration of law enforcement control in Venezuela, including the collaboration of some Venezuelan law enforcement and military authorities in transnational criminal operations,[57] has complimented the traditional flows of illicit goods from Colombia to cause the Caribbean to re-emerge as a significant route for drugs.[58] According to the US Drug Enforcement Administration (DEA), in the three years from 2011 to 2014, the portion of cocaine bound for the US going through the Caribbean more than tripled from 5 to 16 percent.[59]

Beyond drugs, with "fiscal paradises" such as the British Virgin Islands and Cayman Islands, and cash-intensive businesses such as casino gambling, the region is also an important money laundering hub, used by not only criminal groups based in the Western Hemisphere, but also those in Europe and Asia, among others.

Dominican Republic

The 2015 National Drug Threat Assessment identifies the Dominican Republic as one of the principal transit countries for US-bound drugs moving through the Caribbean.[60] The country has also become a site for some groups to store narcotics, waiting for the right moment to move shipments on to the next destination. Two major narco laboratories have been discovered in the country in recent years, in the mountainous region near the southern coast. In 2008, a small laboratory was discovered in Peralta, in the department of Azua. In 2013, a much larger one was discovered in San Cristobal.[61]

Part of the drugs coming into the Dominican Republic arrive by air.[62] Narcotraffickers reportedly take off from Colombia or Venezuela and fly north until reaching the southern edge of Dominican airspace, but without entering. One technique is reportedly to approach Isla Barta in the extreme south of the country and drop the cocaine in the proximity of fishing vessels, which move into international waters to pick it up.[63]

In general, it is believed that most drugs coming into the Dominican Republic arrive by sea, sent by Colombian groups such as the Gulf (formerly Úsuga) clan, as well as Venezuelan cartels associated with that nation's military and government. Mexico's Sinaloa Cartel is believed to be one of the principal clients, although Dominican groups also play a key role in distributing drugs in the US.[64]

Part of the drugs moving through the Dominican Republic are believed to be smuggled via container ships, with cocaine concealed inside false-bottom shipping containers manufactured in "metalworking facilities" located throughout the island. Often, such cocaine is introduced into containers as ships come from the US through the Dominican Republic bound for Europe. In addition to the country's other commercial ports, the Dominican port of Manzanillo is believed to play an important role for drugs being shipped to the United States, as well as legitimate products, providing a direct sea route from the port to US ports in Florida, as well as to Europe.

Although the Dominican Republic is principally a drug transit country, as in other parts of the region, a portion of the drugs flowing through the country stay there, contributing to a growing drug market in Santo Domingo, among other places.[65]

Jamaica

The 2016 International Narcotics Control Strategy Report lists Jamaica as principally a transit country for US-bound drugs, but also notes that it is the principal supply country for marijuana to the US from the Caribbean.[66] As in Central America, Jamaica's role as a transit country has also empowered once marginal criminal groups, with highly negative effects on governance. Money from drugs, as well as other activities such as the internationally famous, Jamaica-based "Lottery Scam,"[67] has helped to transform local gangs into powerful local players with influence in Jamaica's political system, as well as international reach. Indeed, the telephone-based fraud scheme, directed principally at persons in the United States, is estimated to net over $300 million per year for Jamaican gangs.[68]

With respect to narcotrafficking, In 2011, Dudus Coke, a particularly powerful local drug lord with connections in the Jamaican communities in New York and Miami, was caught in a standoff with Jamaican authorities in which he demonstrated his local influence and the power of his group, the Shower Posse, by holding off the Jamaican police and Jamaica Defense Force for days in an active series of gun battles, while spawning supporting riots in marginalized neighborhoods throughout the capital of Kingston.[69]

Following the confrontation between Coke's Shower Posse and the Jamaican government, such groups have maintained a lower profile in smuggling narcotics, and focused on the equally or more lucrative business of the lottery scam. While a transit zone for cocaine and other substances coming through South America, the Caribbean is also a minor source zone for people.[70]

SOUTH AMERICA

As noted previously, South America is a complex and evolving mixture of source, transit, and consumption countries. With respect to drugs, Colombia, Peru, and Bolivia are important sources of cocaine exported to the US, Europe, Asia, and the rest of the world. Yet while these Andean countries receive much attention in popular culture references to drugs in the US, other countries play equally important roles in the criminal economy of the region. These include the emergence of Brazil and Chile as important consumers of illicit drugs in the region, and the increasingly important roles of Bolivia, Paraguay,[71] Argentina, and Uruguay as transit countries supporting markets in Europe and South America itself.

Colombia

Colombia has long been an important source zone country for cocaine in the hemisphere. Its drug cartels and criminal bands (BACRIM) have consistently been among the region's most powerful criminal actors, conducting operations and interacting with other criminal organizations throughout the world, including the Caribbean, Central America, Mexico, and elsewhere in South America.

Colombia's civil war, which began in 1964, exacerbated problems with an already weak state presence in the countryside. The emergence of the country in the 1980s as an important source zone country for coca production, principally destined for the United States, fueled the rise of two powerful criminal cartels, initially the Medellin Cartel, led by famous drug kingpin Pablo Escobar, and later the Cali Cartel. Initially, these groups sourced much of their cocaine from Peru, but the emergence of the Sendero Luminoso guerilla movement in the highlands of the Peruvian Andes, and the corresponding efforts of the Peruvian government to assert greater control over Peruvian territory, led the Colombian cartels to increasingly grow the coca in their own territory. This created a need for the cartels to protect the drug operations in the countryside against the guerillas that operated there, given the insufficiency of the military and other government forces to do so. To protect their operations, the Colombia cartels contracted private security forces on a large scale, who later became involved themselves in narcotrafficking. At the same time, in other parts of the territory, the rebel groups, such as the FARC, became involved in extorting payment from coca growing and narcotrafficking operations in areas under their control, sometimes involving themselves directly in such activities. Such activities contributed greatly to the revenue of these initially ideologically based organizations, contributing to both their wealth and the increasingly criminal component of the character of some of the guerilla organizations. With the decapitation and subsequent collapse of the Medellin and Cali cartels in the mid-1990s, many of the former security organizations, which evolved into a diverse array of different types of territorial militias, themselves became involved in the drug trade, giving rise to a complex but productive criminal economy. Other more ideologically oriented groups in Colombia, such as the ELN, focused more on kidnapping and extortion of companies operating in areas under their influence.

The criminal economy in Colombia evolved significantly during the first decade of the twenty-first century. On one hand, through a military campaign focused mostly against the FARC, and associated "whole-of-government" actions, the government substantially weakened the FARC and reasserted control over much of the national territory. The campaign was largely paid for by the Colombian government, to include a significant increase in taxes to cover the expansion of the military. Nonetheless, beginning in 2000, the country also received significant financial, material, training, and intelligence support from the United States in a plan initially focused against the drug problem, known as "Plan Colombia," which totaled approximately $10 billion by 2015.[72]

Aside from US support through Plan Colombia, the Colombian government's campaign was never designed to attack criminality, but rather, the political challenge to the state in the form of the guerillas.

In 2005, the Colombian government reached an agreement to demobilize the country's territorially based militias, leading to a proliferation of new groups as parts of some groups refused to give up criminal activities and metamorphized into new groups, while some "demobilized" former fighters returned to criminal activity. As a result, the number of criminal groups in the country leapt to thirty-two, referred to collectively as criminal bands, or "BACRIM." Narcotrafficking and other forms of transnational criminal activity continued through these groups, as well as through the activities of the FARC.

In addition to drugs, Colombia has also been an important source zone for illegal mining, including the extraction of gold and coltan. Indeed, one authority estimates that 88 percent of the product of Colombia's mining sector may be illegal.[73] Much of the product of the industry passes from the eastern plains of Colombia into the interior of Venezuela and Brazil through the Amazon river system, as discussed later.

Colombia's cocaine production has expanded significantly with the May 2015 end of aerial spraying of the drug glyphosate[74] due to concerns regarding the health risks of the chemical,[75] including arguments by the World Health Organization that it might cause cancer.[76] In 2016, the US government estimated that the area under cultivation for coca in Colombia had tripled to 159,000 hectares, a 44 percent increase over the previous year,[77] representing 40 percent of all coca production in the world.[78]

Although the Colombian government attempted to compensate for the end to aerial spraying through manual eradication of coca plants, the manual process was far less efficient, with the results inhibited by the government's limited number of eradication teams and protests blocking eradication in the areas where it was to be performed.[79] In addition, while the Colombian government signed agreements with families in coca growing areas to substitute legitimate crops for growing coca, as of the end of the year, funds available for such programs were only a fraction of the amount required based on the commitments made to the coca growers by the government.

As of 2017, the principal source of instability in the Colombian criminal economy was the peace agreement finalized in November 2016 between the government and the FARC. While, at the end of 2017, the smaller guerilla group, the ELN, had committed to a ceasefire with the government, analysts worried that demobilized guerillas would simply pass into the hands of the criminal bands, as had occurred with demobilized militias after the 2005 accords with those groups.[80]

Venezuela

The permeation of corruption to the highest levels of government in Venezuela, in combination with the deteriorating economic and political situation in the country,[81] has transformed that nation into an important transit zone for narcotics, people, and illicit goods.[82] During the regime of Hugo Chavez in Venezuela, and continuing with his successor, Nicholas Maduro, the country became a haven for a variety of terrorists and criminals, including Colombia-based criminal bands,[83] terrorist organizations such as the FARC and ELN,[84] and a range of others.

Members of Venezuela's security forces and government are believed to profit from the flows of drugs and contraband goods across Venezuela's territory, with the principal criminal organization in the country referred to as the "Cartel of the Suns," after the rank insignia of Venezuelan generals, denoting the involvement of its highest military leadership in such criminal enterprises (see chapter 3).[85]

A significant number of Venezuela's highest officials are also believed to be involved in narcotrafficking and other forms of organized crime, including the nation's current vice president, Tarik al-Aissami,[86] former head of the Interior Ministry Nestor Reverol,[87] and former head of the Venezuelan National Assembly Diosdado Cabello, named as head of the "Cartel of the Suns."[88]

With respect to involvement of the military in such activities, Venezuelan businessman Walid Makled, who was arrested in 2011 for having shipped up to ten tons of cocaine per month from Colombia through Venezuela, claimed to have Venezuelan army generals on his payroll.[89] The conviction in the United States of the nephews of Venezuelan first lady Cecilia Flores for cocaine trafficking illustrates the penetration of criminal activities to the highest levels of government.[90] Other Venezuelan officials who have been publicly named in criminal indictments for narcotrafficking, under the US Kingpin act, include Pedro Luis Martin Olivares, the head of finance for the nation's Intelligence Service (SEBIN), former senior anti-drug official Jesus Alfredo Itriago, former minister of defense Henry Rangel Silva, governor of Guárico state Ramón Emilio Rodríguez Chacín, Major General Cliver Antonio Alcalá Cordones, and deputy head of the National Assembly Freddy Alirio Bernal Rosales, among others.[91]

Within the country, high levels of corruption and impunity have also fueled the rise of violent gangs, such as the "Tren de Aragua," who concentrate on extortion, robbery, and other forms of criminality within the broader criminal landscape of the country.[92]

Beyond criminal violence, the deteriorating economic situation and political crisis in Venezuela have also made the country an increasingly significant exporter of people, feeding illicit human smuggling and trafficking networks in the region, with destinations from neighboring Colombia and Trinidad and Tobago, to Miami. Indeed, Venezuela, along with its neighbor, Suriname, were the only two countries in the Western Hemisphere designated by the US State Department as "Tier 3" on its human trafficking watch list, reserved for countries which do not meet its minimum standards for combatting human trafficking, nor are considered to be adequately working to remedy the situation.[93]

Guyana, Suriname, French Guyana

Although often neglected in analyses of the region, the countries of the Guyanese shield—Guyana, Suriname, and French Guyana—also play a role in the panorama of organized crime in the region. The relative isolation of these countries from major economic or population centers in the region restricts their role as transit zones for narcotics or people. Nonetheless, some such flows do occur. In 2014, then-leader of Guyana's political opposition, and currently president, Brigadier David Granger, spoke of the narcotrafficking routes being established in the country.[94] With respect to human trafficking and smuggling, a significant number of Chinese immigrants entering the Guyanas, often to support construction projects, work in the country for some time and ultimately move on to developed countries such as the United States.[95]

Beyond the limited role of the subregion as a transit zone, its timber, gold, and other mineral resources make it an important source zone country for such goods, which are then often shipped out to the coast, or south, through Brazil. Indeed, the extraction of gold through unauthorized informal mining in the interior of Guyana and Suriname prompted leaders of both countries to meet in February 2013 to collaborate against the threat.[96]

Ecuador

In the strategic landscape of organized crime in the region, the small nation of Ecuador finds itself with the challenge of being located between two of the region's most important drug source zone countries: Colombia and Peru. In addition, Ecuador's access to the Pacific Ocean makes it attractive for commerce in illicit goods, while its use of the US dollar as its currency makes it an attractive country for criminal groups to launder proceeds from drug sales and other criminal activities realized in the US.

To date, Ecuador has not become a significant producer of drugs. The near absence of coca cultivation in the north of the country contrasts dramatically with the significant production in Colombia just across the Putumayo river, although some residents on the Ecuadoran side reportedly grow small quantities of coca near the border and transport the coca leaves across the Putumayo river to Colombia to sell to the 48th Front of the FARC. With the agreement between the government and FARC in neighboring Colombia, some in Ecuador worry that coca production and other types of criminal activity will expand as demobilized guerillas cross the border from Colombia to begin or continue their criminal activities in Ecuador.

Beyond drug production, Ecuador's position on the Pacific between Colombia and Peru give it a minor role as a transit country. Some drug shipments which originate in Peru transverse Ecuador or its coastal waters, en route north, with the Mexico-based Sinaloa Cartel playing an important role in organizing and financing the traffic. Correspondingly, the quantity of drugs intercepted on Ecuador's Pacific coast has steadily increased since 2013. In addition, officials have also begun to find clandestine narco airstrips in the country, including one discovered on the central coast, in the province of Los Rios, supporting a narcotics operation linked to a former Ecuadoran military officer.[97]

In a similar vein, the north coast of the country has become an important launching point for narcosubmarines smuggling cocaine toward the United States. As of mid-2016, Ecuador had discovered seven such vessels, all built by Colombians.[98] Within Ecuador itself, as in other drug transit countries, there are some indications of growing drug consumption, particularly in major cities such as Quito, Guayaquil, Cuenca, and Ambato. To date, however, such internal consumption principally appears to involve marijuana from Colombia, rather than cocaine from Peru.

Beyond drugs, Ecuador has become a transit country for Chinese immigrants. Ecuador has twice in recent years dropped its visa requirements for visitors arriving from China. In 2008, after the first time that it did so, the number of Chinese visitors exploded from 339 recorded entries for the entire previous year, to almost ten thousand.[99] Indeed, the flood of Chinese through Ecuador forced the government to re-impose the visa requirement, but not before the matter received significant attention in the media.[100] In May 2016, the government of Rafael Correa once again dropped the visa requirement for tourists, setting the stage for a new wave of human smuggling and trafficking of Chinese through the country.[101]

With respect to money laundering, the amount of bulk cash seized by Ecuadoran authorities increased almost four-fold between 2008 and 2012.[102]

Peru

Peru has been one of the most important source countries in South America for both cocaine and illegal mining products, as well as an important source of outbound immigrants feeding trafficking and smuggling groups.

With respect to narcotics, as of late 2014, Peru was estimated to produce more than two hundred tons of cocaine per year,[103] and by some estimates, ranked above Colombia with respect to the area of coca under cultivation.[104] By contrast to Colombia, the production and transportation of cocaine in Peru reflects the activities of a myriad of small entities. Multiple groups are involved in the importation of precursor chemicals, control of important ports, coordinating with local farmers to harvest and transport coca leaves, and moving the goods out of the country through a combination of means including individuals carrying small amounts of product out of growing areas on foot via backpack (*mochileros*), as well as smuggling overland by truck and watercraft, and via small aircraft. Those groups also include the remnants of the *Shining Path* terrorist/insurgent organization which fought a bloody civil war in remote mountains of Central Peru such as the Upper Huallaga valley (UHV) and the Apurimac, Ene, and Mantauro River valleys (VRAEM), and later taxed and became involved in drug-related operations under their control. Yet as of 2017, *Shining Path* had been reduced to a presence of no more than several hundred persons, confined largely to the VRAEM, albeit with rumored presence in other areas.

Beyond Sendero Luminoso, the majority of narcotrafficking activities in Peru are conducted by relatively small family-based clans. While such groups occasionally compete, such as over the control of key ports such as Callao, near Lima, the activities of multiple illicit chemical suppliers, farmers, collectors of the harvest, transporters, and others are surprisingly coordinated by forces of the illicit market. While major groups outside Peru such as Mexico's Sinaloa Cartel purchase the product and occasionally provide financing and coordination, drug production in Peru is less of a directed activity than an emergent behavior of multiple groups collaborating and responding to market signals, making the narcotrafficking landscape in the country stubbornly adaptable to government efforts to restrict it.

Peru's illicit mining industry appears similarly atomized, with collaborating groups of people who sell chemicals, work the individual mines, purchase the ore at the local level, transport it, and sell and provide services to those who work in the mining camps.

With respect to narcotics, while the Peruvian state has made significant progress in recent years controlling coca production in the Upper Huallaga Valley, one of the country's two traditional coca growing areas, coca growing has recently expanded along the Putumayo River, Peru's northern border with Colombia and Ecuador, and the eastern side of the Andean mountain range, which runs north to south through the middle of the country, separating its arid coast from its jungle interior. New coca crops have been also reported north of the VRAEM in Pichis Palcazu, in the south in Madre de Dios, and even near Oxapampa just 243 kilometers east of Lima.[105] Although the growing conditions in some of the lower lying areas are not as favorable for the growth of coca, they have the advantage of relatively less attention from the government.

With respect to the export of narcotics, there are multiple avenues and methods by which drugs leave the country, supporting multiple markets. By contrast to Colombia, whose cocaine has principally been exported to the US, a substantial portion of the drug produced in Peru goes to Europe or major South American population centers in Brazil, Chile, and Argentina. A portion of the cocaine produced in Peru is smuggled by family clan-based criminal operations to ports on the nation's Pacific coast such as Paita, Chimbote, and Piura, then northward, often to destinations in Europe.[106] The sophistication of smuggling operations from Peru's coast were illustrated in September 2014, with the discovery by authorities of a factory operation near the coastal port of Trujillo, inserting cocaine into blocks of coal to be shipped from Peruvian ports of to Spain and Belgium.[107]

The important role of Peru's major commercial ports has made them the focus of struggle between criminal entities. Indeed, the nation's principal port of Callao has been the subject of fights between narcotraffickers, vying to control the narcotics going through the port, including a struggle between groups led by Gerald Oropeza and Gerson Gálvez Calle (*Caracol*) escalating violence in the city in late 2015, leading the government to declare martial law and deploy military forces to restore order.[108]

Beyond and supporting drug exports from the ports, the movement of cocaine through a combination of overland and river routes, and by small aircraft through Bolivia to Brazil, has become increasingly important. In remote mountain valleys, such as those in the VRAEM, smugglers use clandestine runways, often "rented" from local landowners,[109] to move the cocaine out. As of mid-2015, an estimated six to ten flights per day were departing from the area.[110] In some cases, the product is flown directly to Brazil, including airdrops near the Peru-Brazil jungle border, in coordination with smugglers on the ground, who pick it up and continue its movement across the country. In other cases, cocaine is moved north out of the VRAEM and adjacent valleys, up Peru's Amazonian river system, past Iquitos, to enter Brazil near the tri-border area of Leticia (Colombia)-Tabatinga (Brazil)-Cabalococha (Peru).[111]

In addition to the two routes mentioned above, a portion of Peru's cocaine also is exported to markets in Chile and Asian countries such as Japan, Australia, Singapore, and China. Indeed, while not widely recognized outside the region, Chile's relatively high per capita income has made it a significant consumer of cocaine.[112]

With respect to illegal mining, Peru, like Colombia, is an important source of illegal products. Significant quantities of gold are illegally produced in the department of Madre de Dios although in recent years, illegal mining have also spread to neighboring departments such as Junin and Cusco.[113] On the other hand, the expanded efforts by Peru's government to control illegal mining have led traffickers to expand use of neighboring Bolivia and Ecuador as markets for purchasing such products, including legitimate mines where illegally obtained gold is blended with that obtained illicitly to disguise its illicit origin.

As a compliment to the illicit production of goods such as drugs or precious metals, groups operating in Peru also earn revenue by extorting legitimate companies operating there in sectors such as oil and mining. The group Sendero Luminoso, for example, extorts petroleum operators working with the Camisea pipeline.[114]

Brazil

Particularly in the last decade, Brazil has emerged as an important drug transit and consumption country. Initially, cocaine from source zone countries such as Peru and Bolivia passed through Brazil, Uruguay, and the north of Argentina, en route to Africa, with an ultimate destination of Europe or Russia.[115] A significant portion of the cocaine going from Latin America to Europe travels through the Brazil's largest port, Santos,[116] as well as Argentine ports such as Rosario and Buenos Aires, or the Uruguayan port of Montevideo.

With time, Brazil's large population, in conjunction with the substantial throughput of Europe-bound drugs, made Brazil an important consumer market for cocaine.[117] Demand was particularly significant in prosperous coastal zone including the large cities of Rio de Janeiro and Sao Paolo. With time, a market has also emerged in the northeast of the country, and even in Manaus, in the Amazon.

Beyond cocaine, consumption a less refined, cheaper, but more lethal and highly addictive form, "crack," has become widespread in the slums or "favelas" of Brazil's major urban centers. Brazil also has an estimated 1 million users of this substance; favelas where the drug is widely consumed are referred to as "cracolandia."[118]

As a complement to cocaine, Brazil also consumed increasing quantities of marijuana. The supply principally comes from Paraguay, although some also comes from the Brazilian amazon.

The expansion of the drug market in Brazil has been driven by, and has enabled, the growth of powerful urban gangs. The oldest of these, the *Red Command* (CV), was established in the 1970s, although the First Capital Command (PCC) has arguably been the most successful, with an estimated twenty-one thousand members across Brazil, and a presence in Bolivia and Paraguay. These gangs, and others, including the mafia-like *Amigos do Amigos*, and the *Third Pure Command*, play an important role in selling drugs in the areas that they control, and conducting other criminal activities. The relationship between the drug flows, the gangs, and the poor neighborhoods that they dominate, has been the subject of much scholarship, including works by Enrique Arias[119] and Benjamin Lessing,[120] among other authors.

Brazil is also an important destination as well as a source country for human trafficking, including the international sex trade,[121] as well as a market for contraband goods from China and other countries. The county's Amazon basin and the system of rivers that feed it have also become an important transit route for extracting mining products from the interior of Bolivia, Peru, Colombia, Venezuela, Guyana, and Suriname, to markets in Europe and the United States.[122]

Beyond drugs and mining, the sparsely populated, vast Amazon jungle region has become an important area of multiple types of criminal activity, including marijuana and coca production and illegal logging. Brazil's principal city in the Amazon, Manaus, has become an important center of organized crime.[123] The challenge in the Amazon has been further augmented by the entry of migrants from Venezuela into the Brazilian state of Roraima,[124] and the displacement of FARC and ELN guerillas, and members of other criminal bands from Colombia.[125]

Bolivia

Bolivia is a source zone country which is increasingly also becoming a transit country, not only for drugs, but also for minerals and people. With respect to drugs, Bolivia is becoming an important transit country for cocaine from Peru being smuggled to Europe, as well as to Brazil, Argentina and Uruguay. In the three years from 2013 to 2016, Bolivia's counterdrug service FELCN reported to have found over one thousand clandestine airstrips, principally supporting narcoflights from Peru.[126] Important drug transit routes through Bolivia include from Puerto Quijaro, in the province of Santa Cruz, to the Brazilian port of Santos,[127] as well as from

Santa Cruz across the Argentine border to the ports of Rosario and Buenos Aires in Argentina, and Montevideo in Uruguay.

Bolivia is also becoming increasingly important for transforming coca into cocaine, because it is reportedly easier to import precursor chemicals into Bolivia than into neighboring Peru. The province of Beni, in Bolivia's east, is the host to numerous cocaine production laboratories.[128] Similarly, Bolivia is becoming an important transit zone, as well as a source zone, for illegally mined gold and other metals, because controls over the sector are reportedly more lenient than in neighboring Peru.[129]

Bolivia is a significant human trafficking area, include prostitution and forced labor in the mining and drug production sector.[130] A 2016 report by the Global Initiative Against Transnational Organized crime noted that child prostitution and force labor around illegal mining areas was a particular problem.[131] In addition. As a source zone country for human trafficking, Bolivians are smuggled not only north toward the United States, but also south toward Argentina and Chile.[132]

Paraguay

Paraguay is principally a transit country for cocaine and other drugs moving from Peru and Bolivia, although also a source zone for marijuana, for which the country is the largest producer in the hemisphere, with significant output in the east of the country near the border with Brazil,[133] and estimated annual revenues of $1 billion.[134] The drug trade in the region is reportedly dominated by Brazilian gangs, including the First Capital Command (PCC), and to a lesser extent, the *Red Command* (CV). A study by a Paraguayan development organization estimated that as much as 40 percent of Paraguay's GDP could come from illicit sources.[135]

Paraguayan towns along the porous land border with Brazil, including Pedro Juan Caballero, have become major drug trafficking centers. While some of the drugs flow east into Brazil, some are transported south down international waterways to Argentine and Uruguayan ports. Although Uruguay in 2013 moved to legalize marijuana for domestic consumption, as of 2016, 90 percent of the marijuana consumed in Uruguay came from Brazil.[136]

Beyond drugs, the country is also principally a source zone for human trafficking supplying Brazil and other markets, although forced labor and prostitution within Paraguay is a problem as well.[137]

Argentina

Argentina, like Brazil, is a transit country for drugs and, like Brazil, driven by consumption in its principal cities, has increasingly become a destination country. It has also become a destination for migrants from its poorer neighbors, including Peru, Bolivia, and Paraguay.

With respect to narcotrafficking, drugs, mostly cocaine, principally follow two routes through Argentina. Some are moved across the relatively porous Argentine-Bolivia border and accumulated on the Argentine side, before being shipped south down highways to the country's major international ports, including Rosario and Buenos Aires. From there, the drugs are loaded onto oceangoing container ships and other vessels crossing the Atlantic to Africa, and eventually to Europe.

In addition, as noted previously, drugs also enter Argentina via a route that begins near the river port of Pedro Juan Caballero, Paraguay. From there, they are loaded onto barges and other watercraft, then smuggled down the Parana river to the same Argentine ports of Rosario or Buenos Aires for their trans-Atlantic journey.

The status of Rosario as a major drug port, as well as a commercial port for the export of soy and other agricultural goods to Europe and Asia, has made it, and the surrounding province of Santa Fe, one of the most dangerous parts of the country.[138] In some cases, drug enforcement has also displaced narcotraffickers to use other ports, such as Bahia Blanca, further to the south, as well as Montevideo, Uruguay, whose government has fewer resources to guard the port against narcotrafficking.[139]

Beyond these routes, as elsewhere, the use of aircraft to smuggle drugs through Argentina has become a growing challenge. Argentine authorities have identified over 1,400 irregular airstrips in the country used to support such flights.[140] In 2015, Argentine radar detected over 450 unauthorized flights transiting the national airspace. Critics believed that there were many more, since the radars detecting the flights generally function for a limited number of hours on a regular schedule that can be anticipated by narcotraffickers.[141]

In part as a consequence of such drug transits, major urban areas such as Buenos Aires, Rosario, and Cordoba have become significant drug consumption centers. Especially in lower income neighborhoods, the scourge includes widespread consumption of a relatively cheap, highly addictive crack-like substance known as "paco,"[142] as well as low-quality cocaine and other drugs. By one estimate, the consumption of paco has doubled in recent years.[143] The neighborhoods where paco consumption is highest, such as the Buenos Aires suburbs of Bajo Flores and Villa Zavleta, have experienced high rates of crime and violence, are correspondingly known as "paco villas."

While the country has a relatively significant chemical industry, centered near Cordoba, relatively strict controls mean that Argentina has not become a significant source of precursor chemicals.

Because of Argentina's relatively high per capita income, the country has further become a center for the consumption of synthetic drugs such as methamphetamines. Although the government has uncovered a small number of laboratories in the greater Buenos Aires area for the fabrication of such drugs, the majority are believed to be imported from Europe in finished form.[144]

With respect to human trafficking, the ability to enter the United States from Argentina without a visa prior to 2002[145] made the country, for a time, a strategically important destination in US-bound human smuggling networks. At the same time, Argentina's relatively high per capita income has also made it a destination country. As noted previously, Argentina has been a destination for migrants being smuggled or trafficked from Peru, Bolivia, Paraguay, and China, among other destinations. In addition, in 2016, Argentina began to receive a significant influx of immigrants from Africa, with a particularly large number coming from Senegal.[146]

Uruguay

Like Argentina, Uruguay has become both a consumer and a transit country, with significant amounts of cocaine and other drugs passing through the country. Uruguay's principal port of Montevideo has become a hub for Europe-bound cocaine,[147] smuggled from the interior of the continent down the Paraguay and Parana rivers, as well as over land routes.

In addition to cocaine, Uruguay's 2013 law legalizing the consumption of marijuana has increased criminal activity associated with that drug as well.[148] Although Uruguayan authorities had hoped that legalization would replace marijuana smuggled into the country with marijuana legally grown locally, full implementation of the new system was delayed, increasing demand, but also black-market supply. From 2015 to 2016, seizures of marijuana expanded from approximately 2,500 kilograms in 2015 to 4,300 in 2016.[149] Uruguay has also become a modestly important destination, and to some degree a source and a transit country, for human smuggling.[150]

With respect to money laundering, Uruguay's traditional role as safe place for residents of neighboring Argentina to keep their money safe, and hold it in US dollars as a hedge against inflation, has had the side effect of making the country's banking system attractive for organized crime. Although Uruguay's banking system thus offers numerous options for depositing dollars, in recent years, controls over foreign deposits in Uruguayan banks have increased.[151]

Chile

Like Argentina and Uruguay, Chile is both a consumer and a transit country for narcotics. Chile's geographic position as a gateway to Asia for South America makes its ports both a point of departure for drugs crossing the Pacific, as well as a point of entry for contraband goods from

China and other Asian countries. The northern Chilean port of Iquique is particularly vulnerable in this regard as a port of entry for contraband goods destined for poorer markets in neighboring Bolivia and Paraguay.[152] At the same time, Chile's wealth has made the country the number 1 per capita consumer of drugs in the continent.[153]

Finally, Chile's prosperity has made it an attractor for human trafficking and smuggling from both its northern neighbors Peru and Bolivia, as well as the PRC and other Asian countries. Indeed, as of 2009, Chile had the fastest-growing immigrant population of any nation in South America.[154]

EXTRA-HEMISPHERIC AREAS

As noted previously, transnational organized crime is a global phenomenon. As such, it is important to consider changing patterns of supply and consumption, and other dynamics beyond Latin America and the Caribbean that affect the region.

Europe

Europe, like the United States, is an increasingly important partner for Latin America with respect to illicit flows of drugs, people, money, and goods. With respect to narcotics, Europe is the second largest market for Latin American cocaine after the United States.[155] Although an imprecise measure, the United Nations estimated that almost eighty thousand people in Europe were in drug treatment for addition to cocaine, by contrast to just over 100,000 in the United States.[156] Nonetheless, in Europe, the consumption of opioids such as heroin, versus cocaine, is a much larger fraction of drug consumption than it is in the Western Hemisphere.[157] Although the amount of cocaine consumed in Europe grew four-fold between 1998 and 2006, consumption has since leveled off.[158] Similarly, opiate consumption in Europe has generally been steady or declining, although within the category, consumption of heroin has risen slightly.[159] Europe also leads the world in demand for marijuana, although because the value-to-weight ratio for marijuana is lower than for synthetic drugs and cocaine, the majority of marijuana consumed in Europe comes from north Africa, not the Western Hemisphere.[160]

As with the United States, Europe is a significant attractor of migrants from Latin America and the Caribbean, and with it, opportunities for the exploitation of those persons by transnational organized crime groups. As of 2014, for example, the Economic Commission for Latin America and the Caribbean (ECLAC) estimated that Spain alone was home to 2.4 million persons from the region.[161]

Asia

Among the important extra-hemispheric zones relevant to Latin America, it is important to mention China and other nations of Asia. With the expansion of trade and other commercial interactions between Asia and Latin America, illicit interactions have expanded as well. From Latin America's perspective, Asia is primarily a consumer of drugs and goods from the illicit mining trade, but also a supplier of precursor chemicals, contraband goods, and persons who principally transit through Latin America and the Caribbean.

With respect to drugs, Chinese companies have also become important suppliers of precursor chemicals for synthetic drugs such as methamphetamines. Both the Mexico-based cartels *Sinaloa* and *Jalisco Nueva Generación* have substantial relationships with counterparts in Asia, including Chinese triad organizations, for sourcing precursor chemicals such as ephedrine and pseudoephedrine to produce the synthetic drug.[162] The arrest of Sinaloa Cartel boss El Chapo Guzman in February 2014 highlighted the extent of such ties.[163] The same Mexican groups also sell narcotics to Asian markets, including Japan, Hong Kong, Macau, Singapore, and the coastal provinces of China, among others.[164]

Beyond drugs, the PRC is also an important source of illegal migrants. These persons are often brought from the PRC through the region with the US or Canada as an ultimate destination. Moving these persons requires the participation of not only Chinese and other gangs, but also local collaborators, such as the Chinese shopkeepers in the region who provide boarding and employment for the migrants in transit, in return for their labor.

Asia also contributes to the transnational organized crime dynamic through the supply of contraband merchandise, as well as by purchasing metals obtained from the informal mining sector of the region. In 2010, for example, Chinese companies were regular purchasers of illicit iron, exported from Michoacán, Mexico, then under the control of the cartel *La Familia Michoacana*.[165]

Beyond illicit flows of goods and people, the expansion of commerce and banking ties between Latin America and the region, and particularly with the PRC, have expanded opportunities for money laundering. In 2015, for example, the US government exposed an operation in which a Colombian criminal network had leveraged banks, money exchange houses, and goods purchased in the PRC to launder more than $5 billion.[166]

Although the volume of transpacific organized crime remains limited, it is an emerging threat, insofar as Latin American law enforcement lacks the contacts and capabilities to effectively combat the problem. Vulnerabilities include a lack of Latin American security personnel who can speak Chinese dialects such as Cantonese and Hakka, or personnel who are ethnically able to penetrate Chinese communities in the region.[167] Such transpacific organized crime is a significant concern not only because of its potential to grow, but also because, through protracted contact, the currently limited relationships between Asian and Latin American organized crime groups could grow into something much more threatening to authorities on both sides of the Pacific.

CONCLUSIONS

Several conclusions can be drawn from the patterns of transnational organized crime across the region described in this chapter.

First, while the activities manifest considerable complexity and heterogeneity, there is a general pattern of criminal products and services moving from the center of the region, particularly South America, toward multiple in-region and extra-regional sources of demand. These include not only the US and Canada, but also Europe and Russia, and to a growing degree, Asia.

Second, the diversity of criminal activities in the countries of the region highlight the importance of not limiting an analysis of criminal patterns in the region to the movement of cocaine, or even narcotrafficking in general. Indeed, the criminal activities in the region, such as contraband goods, illegal mining, timber, weapons, and money laundering, reinforce each other in important ways. Each depends on and contributes to the corruption and dysfunctionality of the state, creating a reinforcing mechanism which keeps the state weak and its population poor, ensuring a constant supply of persons among them with the need and willingness to participate in organized crime activities.

Third, the emergence of demand for products like drugs in middle-income countries such as Brazil, Argentina, Uruguay, Chile, and Mexico has arguably made the dynamics of those parts of the region more complex. It also highlights the over-simplicity of the "source zone" "transit zone," "consumption zone" construct and its ability to evolve over time.

Fourth, the nature of transnational organized crime activities crosses borders, going beyond separate challenges of individual groups operating in individual nations. By implication, isolated actions by each state are generally inadequate to combat the problem. In addition, significant changes in one country, such as the significant erosion of governability in Venezuela, have spillover effects for the country's neighbors and the rest of the region.

Finally, there is an array of criminal groups, of varying sizes and capabilities, operating within the national territory, and across its boundaries. The goal-seeking behavior of each, including both cooperation and competition, is shaped by the opportunities of the criminal landscape, but at the same time, shapes that landscape as the groups involved fight, are broken up, or change their strategies. It is to the actions and perspectives of those individual groups that we turn in the next chapter.

NOTES

1. See "Human Trafficking & Migrant Smuggling: Understanding the Difference," US Department of State, July 27, 2015, http://www.state.gov/j/tip/rls/fs/2015/245175.htm.
2. Rachel Brown, "The Boom in Chinese Smuggled Across the US Border," *Newsweek*, July 24, 2016, http://www.newsweek.com/boom-chinese-smuggled-across-us-border-483262.
3. "Global Overview of Drug Demand and Supply," *World Drug Report, 2017* (New York: United Nations Office on Drugs and Crime, 2017), https://www.unodc.org/wdr2017/field/Booklet_2_HEALTH.pdf.
4. *United States of America-Mexico Binational Criminal Proceeds Study* (Washington D.C.: Department of Homeland Security, 2016), https://www.ice.gov/doclib/cornerstone/pdf/cps-study.pdf.
5. *World Drug Report, 2014* (New York: United Nations Office on Drugs and Crime, 2014), http://www.unodc.org/documents/wdr2014/World_Drug_Report_2014_web.pdf.
6. See, for example, Sui-Lee Wee, "China Deflects Blame for Opioid Crisis as Trump Visit Nears," *The New York Times*, November 3, 2017, https://www.nytimes.com/2017/11/03/world/asia/china-opioid-fentanyl-trump.html.
7. Melia Robinson, "It's 2017: Here's Where You Can Legally Smoke Weed Now," *Business Insider*, January 8, 2017, http://www.businessinsider.com/where-can-you-legally-smoke-weed-2017-1.
8. "Central America's Unresolved Migrant Crisis," *New York Times*, June 16, 2015, http://www.nytimes.com/2015/06/16/opinion/central-americas-unresolved-migrant-crisis.html?_r=0.
9. James C. McKinley, "US Is Arms Bazaar for Mexican Cartels," *New York Times*, February 5, 2009, http://www.nytimes.com/2009/02/26/us/26borders.html.
10. . Ed Payne, "Report: Many weapons used by Mexican drug gangs originate in US," *CNN*, June 4, 2011, http://www.cnn.com/2011/US/06/14/mexico.guns/index.html.
11. David Gagne, "2000 Illegal Weapons Cross US-Mexico Border Per Day: Report," *Insight Crime*, January 22, 2015, http://www.InsightCrime.org/news-analysis/2000-illegal-weapons-cross-us-mexico-border-every-day.
12. "Firearms in Central America," United Nations Office on Drugs and Crime, Accessed October 14, 2016, https://www.unodc.org/documents/toc/Reports/TOCTA-SouthAmerica/English/TOC-TA_CACaribb_firearmssmuggling_within_CAmerica.pdf.
13. Guillermo Valdés Castellanos, *Historia del Narcotrafico en Mexico* (Mexico City: Penguin-Random House, 2015).
14. Daniel Hernandez, "Calderon's War on Drug Cartels: A Legacy of Blood and Tragedy," *Los Angeles Times*, December 1, 2012, http://articles.latimes.com/2012/dec/01/world/la-fg-wn-mexico-calderon-cartels-20121130.
15. Noe Zavaleta, "Espiral de violencia en Veracruz: Narcofosas, balaceras, secuestros . . . ," *El Proceso*, July 4, 2014, http://www.proceso.com.mx/376645.
16. Zorayda Gallegos, "Un policía y tres atacantes mueren en un tiroteo contra la Fiscalía de Cancún," *El País*, January 18, 2017, http://internacional.elpais.com/internacional/2017/01/18/mexico/1484696156_746631.html.
17. "Mexican Drug Gangs Expand into Illegal Mining," *Reuters*, October 4, 2010, http://www.reuters.com/article/us-mexico-mining-idUSTRE69D04U20101014.

18. Mark Stevenson, "Mexican Drug Cartels Are Now Involved in Lucrative Illegal Mining Operations," *Business Insider*, November 29, 2013, www.businessinsider.com/mexican-drug-cartels-mining-2013-11.

19. R. Evan Ellis, "Chinese Organized Crime in Latin America," *Prism* 4, no. 1 (2012): 67-77.

20. Natasha Bertrand, "This Mexican Town is the Sex-Trafficking Capital of the World," *Business Insider*, February 10, 2015, http://www.businessinsider.com/this-mexican-town-is-the-sex-trafficking-capital-of-the-world-2015-2.

21. Claire Rebando Seelke, Liana Sun Wyler, and June S. Beittel, "Latin America and the Caribbean: Illicit Drug Trafficking and US Counterdrug Programs," Congressional Research Service, April 30, 2010, http://fpc.state.gov/documents/organization/142364.pdf.

22. "Cocaine from South America to the United States," *United Nations Office on Drugs and Crime*, http://www.unodc.org/documents/toc/Reports/TOCTASouthAmerica/English/TOCTA_CACaribb_cocaine_SAmerica_US.pdf.

23. See, for example, "Trial of Honduran Drug Kingpin Matta Opens," *Los Angeles Times*, October 6, 1990, http://articles.latimes.com/1990-10-06/local/me-1378_1_drug-kingpin.

24. Al Valdez, *Gangs: A Guide to Understanding Street Gangs* (San Clemente, CA: Law Tech Publishing Company, 2000). See also Sonja Wolf, "Mara Salvatrucha: The Most Dangerous Street Gang in the Americas?" *Latin American Politics and Society* 54, no. 1 (2012): 65-99. See also Sonja Wolf, "Street Gangs of El Salvador," in *Maras: Gang Violence and Security in Central America* (2011): 43-70. See also José Miguel Cruz, "Central American Maras: From Youth Street Gangs to Transnational Protection Rackets," *Global Crime* 11, no. 4 (2010): 379-398.

25. Claire Ribando Seelke, "Gangs in Central America," (Washington D.C.: Congressional Research Service, August 29, 2016), 1.

26. "2016 Seizures Suggest CentAm Still Top Drug Corridor to US," *Insight Crime*, July 26, 2016, http://www.InsightCrime.org/news-briefs/2016-drug-seizures-suggest-centam-still-top-trafficking-corridor.

27. "Posture Statement."

28. "Posture Statement."

29. David Gagne, "CentAm Authorities Break Up Massive Migrant Smuggling Ring," *Insight Crime*, June 30, 2016, http://www.InsightCrime.com/news-analysis/centam-authorities-break-up-massive-migrant-smuggling-ring.

30. Luis Fernando Alonso, "30 Buses Burned in Honduras This Year as Result of Extortion," *Insight Crime*, August 25, 2016, http://www.insightcrime.org/news-briefs/30-buses-burned-in-honduras-this-year-as-result-of-extortion.

31. Luis Fernando Alonso, "Guatemala Struggles to Prosecute Extortion in Capital," *Insight Crime*, June 28, 2016, http://www.InsightCrime.com/news-briefs/guatemala-struggles-to-prosecute-extortion-in-capital.

32. Helene Cooper and Marc Lacey, "In a Coup in Honduras, Ghosts of Past US Policies," *New York Times*, June 29, 2009, http://www.nytimes.com/2009/06/30/world/americas/30honduras.html?_r=0.

33. Ginger Thompson, "US Suspends $30 Million to Honduras," *New York Times*, September 3, 2009, http://www.nytimes.com/2009/09/04/world/americas/04honduras.html.

34. See R. Evan Ellis, "Honduras: A Pariah State, or Innovative Solutions to Organized Crime Deserving US Support?" US Army War College Strategic Studies Institute, June 2016, http://www.strategicstudiesinstitute.army.mil/pubs/display.cfm?pubID=1315.

35. See "Victims Caught in Honduras Drugs Crossfire," *BBC*, July 16, 2012, http://news.bbc.co.uk/2/hi/programmes/hardtalk/9737563.stm.

36. "Honduras ha reducido un 98.11% aterrizaje de avionetas con droga en 5 años," *El Nuevo Diario*, October 1, 2015, http://www.elnuevodiario.com.ni/internacionales/372236-honduras-ha-reducido-98-11-aterrizaje-avionetas-dr/.

37. Ellis, "Honduras: A Pariah State."

38. R. Evan Ellis, "The Struggle Against Organized Crime in Guatemala," *Latin America Goes Global*, November 10, 2016, http://latinamericagoesglobal.org/2016/11/struggle-organized-crime-guatemala/.

39. Deborah Bonello, "Criminal Activity Spreading Fire in Guatemala's Maya Reserve," *Insight Crime*, July 1, 2016, http://www.InsightCrime.com/news-briefs/criminals-spread-fire-in-guatemala-maya-reserve.

40. Steven Dudley, "Guatemala Authorities Capture Ex-Military Turned Drug Trafficker," *Insight Crime*, May 2, 2016, http://www.InsightCrime.com/news-briefs/guatemala-authorities-capture-ex-military-turned-drug-trafficker.

41. Elyssa Pachico, "Guatemala Military Brigade to Fight Poppy Production Near Mexico," *Insight Crime*, January 3, 2013, http://www.InsightCrime.org/news-briefs/guatemala-military-poppy-production-mexico.

42. Ellis, "The Struggle Against Organized Crime in Guatemala."

43. Interview with Salvadoran security official, San Salvador, El Salvador, May, 2016.

44. R. Evan Ellis, "The Gang Challenge in El Salvador: Worse Than You Thought," *War on the Rocks*, December 16, 2015, http://warontherocks.com/2015/12/the-gang-challenge-in-el-salvador-worse-than-you-can-imagine/.

45. "El Salvador cerrará 2012 con mitad de homicidios por tregua," *La Prensa*, December 12, 2012, http://www.prensa.com/mundo/Salvador-cerrara-mitad-homicidios-tregua_0_3546395343.html.

46. Claire Ribando Seelke argues that the truce allowed the gangs to consolidate their position and become stronger. Seelke, "Gangs in Central America," 2016.

47. Suchit Chávez and Nelson Rauda, "Traslados de pandilleros por atentados contra policías," *La Prensa Grafica*, January 20, 2015, http://www.laprensagrafica.com/2015/01/20/traslados-de-pandilleros-por-atentados-contra-policias#sthash.VAYic3DN.dpuf.

48. Ellis, "The Gang Challenge in El Salvador."

49. "Nuevos ataques con granadas en puestos de la PNC," *La Prensa Grafica*, March 31, 2015, http://www.laprensagrafica.com/2015/03/31/nuevos-ataques-con-granadas-en-puestos-de-la-pnc-1.

50. Irvin Alvarado, "Fiscalía: 'Sabemos quién es el responsable de este atentado,'" *La Prensa Grafica*, September 11, 2015, http://www.laprensagrafica.com/2015/09/11/fiscalia-sabemos-quien-es-el-responsable-de-este-atentado?rel=HomePrincipales#sthash.u01uAIIF.dpuf.

51. Carlos Martinez and Roberto Valencia, "MS-13 pide diálogo al gobierno y pone sobre la mesa su propia desarticulación," *El Faro*, January 9, 2017, http://elfaro.net/es/201701/salanegra/19747/MS-13-pide-di·logo-al-gobierno-y-pone-sobre-la-mesa-su-propia-desarticulaciÛn.htm.

52. Pablo Rojas, "Cierran pistas ilegales para frenar 'fiesta' narco," *Costa Rica Hoy*, July 7, 2016, http://www.crhoy.com/archivo/cierran-pistas-ilegales-para-frenar-fiesta-narco/nacionales/.

53. Interview with Latin American security official, February 2016.

54. Conversation with Panamanian police official, September 2016.

55. . See, for example, R. Evan Ellis, "What Panama's Recognition of China Means for America's Backyard," Interview, *World Politics Review*, October 5, 2017, https://www.worldpoliticsreview.com/trend-lines/23316/what-panama-s-recognition-of-china-means-for-america-s-backyard.

56. David A. Graham, "What Is Mossack Fonseca, the Law Firm in the Panama Papers?" *The Atlantic*, April 4, 2016, http://www.theatlantic.com/international/archive/2016/04/panama-papers-mossack-fonseca/476727/.

57. See Jose de Cordoba and Juan Forero, "Venezuelan Officials Suspected of Turning Country into Global Cocaine Hub," *Wall Street Journal*, May 18, 2015, https://www.wsj.com/articles/venezuelan-officials-suspected-of-turning-country-into-global-cocaine-hub-1431977784.

58. "Venezuela," *2016 International Narcotics Control Strategy Report*, US Department of State, 2016, https://www.state.gov/j/inl/rls/nrcrpt/2016/vol1/253323.htm.
59. Maye Primera, "El tráfico de cocaína hacia EE UU y Europa se hace fuerte en la ruta del Caribe," *El Pais*, April 15, 2014, http://internacional.elpais.com/internacional/2014/04/15/actualidad/1397517496_768647.html.
60. "Dominican Republic," *2016 International Narcotics Control Strategy Report*, US Department of State, 1 (2016), https://www.state.gov/j/inl/rls/nrcrpt/2016/vol1/253257.htm.
61. . "Descubren en República Dominicana un gran laboratorio soterrado de drogas," *El Mundo*, September 1, 2013, http://www.elmundo.es/america/2013/09/01/noticias/1378063613.html.
62. Teresa Casado, "Autoridades indagan sobreprecio Super Tucano y montos seguros La Procuraduría investiga a varios legisladores que supuestamente habrían recibido dinero," *El Dia*, August 19, 2016, http://eldia.com.do/autoridades-indagan-sobre-precio-super-tucano-y-montos-seguros/.
63. Interview with senior military officer from the Dominican Republic, Bogota, Colombia, September 2016.
64. 2015 National Drug Threat Assessment Summary, US Drug Enforcement Administration, 2015, https://www.dea.gov/docs/2015%20NDTA%20Report.pdf.
65. Ezra Fiezer, "Drug Use Soars in Dominican Republic," *The Star*, August 24, 2011, https://www.thestar.com/news/world/2011/08/24/drug_use_soars_in_dominican_republic.html.
66. "Jamaica," *2016 International Narcotics Control Strategy Report*, Department of State, 2016, https://www.state.gov/j/inl/rls/nrcrpt/2016/vol1/253277.htm.
67. Wayne Drash, "Driven to Death by Phone Scammers," *CNN*, October 7, 2015, http://www.cnn.com/2015/10/07/us/jamaica-lottery-scam-suicide/index.html.
68. Karyl Walker, "Lotto Scammers Living Large," *Jamaica Observer*, May 13, 2012, http://www.jamaicaobserver.com/news/Lotto-scammers-living-large_11448148.
69. "Nation Was Fortunate Security Forces Repelled the Shower Posse," *Jamaica Gleaner*, April 14, 2015, http://jamaica-gleaner.com/article/news/20150414/nation-was-fortunate-security-forces-repelled-shower-posse-attack-ellington.
70. "Jamaica Pushes Back Human Trafficking," *Jamaica Gleaner*, July 21, 2013, http://jamaica-gleaner.com/gleaner/20130721/focus/focus6.html.
71. Pablo Ferri and Jose Luis Pardo, "Paraguay's Marijuana Trade: The Bitter Green Smell of the Red Land," *Insight Crime*, August 4, 2014, http://www.insightcrime.org/news-analysis/inside-paraguay-marijuana-trade-to-brazil.
72. For a detailed discussion, see Jonathan Rosen, *The Losing War: Plan Colombia and Beyond* (Albany, NY: SUNY University Press, 2014).
73. "El 88% de la producción de oro de Colombia es ilegal, alertan," *Newsweek en Espanol*, August 2, 2016, http://nwnoticias.com/#!/noticias/el-88-de-la-produccion-de-oro-de-colombia-es-ilegal-alertan-mineros.
74. William Neumann, "Defying US, Colombia Halts Aerial Spraying of Crops Used to Make Cocaine," *The New York Times*, May 14, 2015, https://www.nytimes.com/2015/05/15/world/americas/colombia-halts-us-backed-spraying-of-illegal-coca-crops.html?_r=0.
75. "Es oficial: termina era del glifosato en fumigaciones en Colombia," *El Tiempo*, May 15, 2015, http://www.eltiempo.com/politica/justicia/colombia-dejara-de-fumigar-con-glifosato/15757420.
76. "Roundup Weedkiller 'Probably' Causes Cancer, Says WHO Study," *The Guardian*, March 21, 2015, https://www.theguardian.com/environment/2015/mar/21/roundup-cancer-who-glyphosate-.
77. Nick Miroff, "Colombia Is Again the World's Top Coca Producer. Here's Why That's a Blow to the US," *The Washington Post*, November 10, 2015, https://www.washingtonpost.com/world/the_americas/in-a-blow-to-us-policy-colombia-is-again-the-worlds-top-producer-of-coca/2015/11/10/316d2f66-7bf0-11e5-bfb6-65300a5ff562_story.html?utm_term=.4707114c9d4c.

78. "Coca in the Andes," Office of National Drug Control Policy, US Department of State, Accessed October 13, 2016, https://www.whitehouse.gov/ondcp/targeting-cocaine-at-the-source.

79. Mimi Yagoub, "Colombia Protests Bad Sign for Post-Conflict Coca Reduction," *Insight Crime*, August 24, 2016, http://www.InsightCrime.org/news-analysis/colombia-protests-cast-doubts-over-post-conflict-coca-reduction.

80. R. Evan Ellis and Roman D. Ortiz, "Un acuerdo entre interrogantes," *Foreign Affairs Latinoamérica* 17, no. 1 (2017): 93–100. Available at www.fal.itam.mx.

81. R. Evan Ellis, "Anticipating the Collapse of Venezuela," *Latin America Herald Tribune*, May 8, 2016, http://laht.com/article.asp?CategoryId=13303&ArticleId=2411674.

82. "Smuggling Soars as Venezuela's Economy Sinks," *Reuters*, January 20, 2016, http://www.reuters.com/article/us-venezuela-smuggling-insight-idUSKCN0UY1IT.

83. "US Requests Colombia Urabenos 'Gang Leader' Extradition," *BBC*, December 29, 2012, http://www.bbc.com/news/world-latin-america-20862023.

84. "Colombian Farc Rebels' Links to Venezuela Detailed," *BBC*, May 10, 2017, http://www.bbc.com/news/world-latin-america-13343810.

85. Brenda Fiegel, "Venezuela, Military Generals, and the Cartel of the Suns," *Small Wars Journal*, June 27, 2015, http://smallwarsjournal.com/jrnl/art/venezuela-military-generals-and-the-cartel-of-the-suns.

86. Scott Zamost, Drew Griffin, Kay Guerrero, and Rafael Romo, "US Calls Venezuela's Vice President an International Drug Trafficker," *CNN*, February 13, 2017, http://www.cnn.com/2017/02/13/world/us-sanctions-venezuela-vice-president/.

87. Nathan Crooks, "Venezuela Shakes up Cabinet, Appoints Drug-Indicted General," *Bloomberg*, August 2, 2016, https://www.bloomberg.com/news/articles/2016-08-03/venezuela-s-maduro-replaces-perez-abad-as-his-economy-czar.

88. Kjal Vyas and John Forero, "Top Venezuelan Bodyguard Defects to US," *Wall Street Journal*, January 27, 2015, https://www.wsj.com/articles/top-venezuelan-bodyguard-defects-to-u-s-1422406536.

89. Benedict Mander, "Venezuela Accused of Becoming 'Narco State,'" *Financial Times*, April 12, 2011, https://www.ft.com/content/85701a1c-652d-11e0-b150-00144feab49a.

90. Daniel Uria, "Venezuelan First Lady's 'Narco Nephews' Jailed for Drug Trafficking," *UPI*, December 14, 2017, https://www.upi.com/Top_News/World-News/2017/12/14/Venezuelan-first-ladys-Narco-Nephews-jailed-for-drug-trafficking/4611513304357/.

91. "Venezuela." *2016 International Narcotics Control Strategy Report*, U.S. Department of State, 2016, https://www.state.gov/j/inl/rls/nrcrpt/2016/vol1/253323/htm.

92. "PJ denunció utilización del 'Tren de Aragua' para sabotear las primarias," *El Nacional*, September 12, 2017, http://www.el-nacional.com/noticias/politica/denuncio-utilizacion-del-tren-aragua-para-sabotear-las-primarias_203200.

93. *Trafficking in Persons Report*, US Department of State, June 2016, http://www.state.gov/documents/organization/258876.pdf.

94. Seth Robbins, "Guyana Is Becoming a 'Narco-State': Ex-Military Commander," *Insight Crime*, April 10, 2014, http://www.insightcrime.org/news-briefs/guyana-is-becoming-a-narco-state-ex-military-commander.

95. See, for example, R. Evan Ellis, "Suriname and the Chinese: Timber, Migration, and the Less-Told Stories of Globalization," *SAIS Review* 32, no. 2 (Summer-Fall 2012): 85–97.

96. "Guyana, Suriname Discuss Gold Smuggling, Exploitation of Natural Resources," *Kaieteur News*, February 13, 2013, http://www.kaieteurnewsonline.com/2013/02/13/guyana-suriname-discuss-gold-smuggling-exploitation-of-natural-resources/.

97. Interview with senior Ecuadoran security official, Bogota, Colombia, September, 2016.

98. Five fully submersible vehicles were discovered in the north, near the Colombian border in the province of Esmeraldas. Two, which were semi-submersibles, were

discovered further to the south in the province of El Oro, in Isla Puna, bound for Peru. The Ecuadoran government has also discovered towed torpedoes and buoys with geolocation devices, allowing the boat towing them to simply cut the line if they encounter a patrol boat, and return for them later. Based on an interview with senior Ecuadoran security official, Bogota, Colombia, September 2016.

99. "Ecuador, escala en tráfico de indocumentados chinos," *El Universo*, December 12, 2008, http://www.eluniverso.com/2008/12/12/1/1360/40F307FB4904484381C8C0F32D1FE45C.html.

100. "China complacida por lucha del tráfico de personas en Ecuador," *El Universo*, November 14, 2008, http://www.eluniverso.com/2008/11/14/0001/626/77D77D68D2D646D091AF366AB0CD8B67.html.

101. "Ecuador y China eliminan visa para turismo," *El Universo*, June 14, 2016, http://www.eluniverso.com/noticias/2016/06/14/nota/5636385/ecuador-china-eliminan-visa-turismo.

102. Steve Bargeant, "Ecuador Bulk Cash Smuggling Reflects New Laundering Trend," *Insight Crime*, April 11, 2013, http://www.insightcrime.org/news-analysis/rise-in-ecuador-cash-smuggling-reflects-wider-crime-trends.

103. Loren Riesenfeld, "Peru Shoots Down Narco Plane Heading to Bolivia," *Insight Crime*, March 2, 2015, http://www.InsightCrime.org/news-briefs/peru-shoots-down-narco-plane-heading-to-bolivia.

104. *Perú: Monitoreo de Cultivos de Coca 2012*, United Nations Office on Drugs and Crime, September 2013, http://www.unodc.org/documents/crop-monitoring/Peru/Peru_Monitoreo_de_Coca_2012_web.pdf.

105. R. Evan Ellis, "New Developments in Organized Crime in Peru," *The Cipher Brief*, May 20, 2016, https://www.thecipherbrief.com/column/strategic-view/new-developments-organized-crime-peru-1091.

106. See, for example, R. Evan Ellis, "The Evolving Transnational Crime-Terrorism Nexus in Peru and Its Strategic Relevance for the US and the Region," *PRISM*, 5, no. 4 (2016): 189–205, http://cco.ndu.edu/Portals/96/Documents/prism/prism_5-4/Evolving%20Transnational%20Crime-Terrorism.pdf.

107. "Urresti presentó 7.6 toneladas de cocaína incautadas en Trujillo," *Peru21*, September 1, 2014, http://peru21.pe/actualidad/droga-cocaina-dirandro-daniel-urresti-policia-nacional-trujillo-2197279.

108. Ellis, "Organized Crime in Peru."

109. While *Sendero Luminoso* reportedly accepts payment from farmers in coca leaves, and has operated a small number of its own sites for transforming the coca leaf into intermediate products, there is little evidence to suggest that members of the group are directly engaged in either growing coca or producing cocaine on a significant scale.

110. Ellis, "Crime-Terrorism Nexus in Peru."

111. See R. Evan Ellis, "The Evolution of Transnational Organized Crime in Peru," *Latin America Goes Global*, May 4, 2017, http://latinamericagoesglobal.org/2017/05/evolution-transnational-organized-crime-peru/.

112. Ricardo Muga M., "In Chile, Cocaine Consumption Is on the Rise," *Santiago Times*, April 25, 2010, http://santiagotimes.cl/2010/04/15/in-chile-cocaine-consumption-is-on-the-rise/.

113. Ellis, "Organized Crime in Peru."

114. See, for example, "VRAEM: Ataque terrorista a base temporal deja un militar herido," *Peru.com*, November 18, 2014, http://peru.com/actualidad/nacionales/vraem-ataque-terrorista-base-temporal-deja-militar-herido-noticia-301927.

115. *World Drug Report, 2016* (New York: United Nations Office on Drugs and Crime, 2016), http://www.unodc.org/wdr2016/, 37–39.

116. Lloyd Belton, "Report Spotlights Drug Traffic at Santos Port, Brazil's Drug Policies," *Insight Crime*, July 20, 2016, http://www.InsightCrime.org/news-analysis/report-spotlights-drug-trafficking-at-santos-port-brazil-drug-policies.

117. *World Drug Report, 2014*, xi.

118. Stephanie Nolan, "Crack Cocaine Is King in Brazil: What Sao Paulo Is Doing about It," *The Globe and Mail*, April 26, 2014, http://www.theglobeandmail.com/news/world/crack-is-king-in-brazil-what-sao-paulo-is-doing-about-it/article18232957/.

119. See, for example, Enrique Desmond Arias, *Drugs and Democracy in Rio de Janeiro: Trafficking, Social Networks, and Public Security* (Chapel Hill, NC: University of North Carolina Press, 2009). See also Enrique Desmond Arias, "Faith in Our Neighbors: Networks and Social Order in Three Brazilian Favelas," *Latin American Politics and Society* 46, no. 1 (2004): 1–38. See also Enrique Desmond Arias, "Trouble en Route: Drug Trafficking and Clientelism in Rio de Janeiro Shantytowns," *Qualitative Sociology* 29, no. 4 (2006): 427–445.

120. Benjamin Lessing, *The Logic of Violence in Criminal War: Cartel-State Conflict in Mexico, Colombia, and Brazil* (Berkeley: University of California, 2012).

121. "Brazil," *Trafficking in Persons Report 2016*, US Department of State, 2016, https://www.state.gov/documents/organization/258878.pdf, 104–108.

122. See, for example, R. Evan Ellis, "Brazil: Between Cooperation and Deterrence," *Global Americans*, December 18, 2017, https://theglobalamericans.org/2017/12/brazil-cooperation-deterrence/.

123. Dom Philips, "With Nearly 100 Dead in Prison Riots, Brazil's Government Faces Crisis," *New York Times*, January 8, 2017, https://www.nytimes.com/2017/01/08/world/americas/brazil-prison-riots-michel-temer.html?_r=0.

124. Sabrina Martin, "Brazil Evaluates Measures against Influx of Venezuelan Refugees," *PanamPost*, October 16, 2016, https://panampost.com/sabrina-martin/2016/10/20/brazil-evaluates-measures-against-influx-of-venezuelan-refugees/.

125. "Brazil, Colombia Warn FARC Renegades Could Fuel Crime," *Yahoo*, January 31, 2017, https://www.yahoo.com/news/brazil-colombia-warn-farc-renegades-could-fuel-crime-002149583.html.

126. Marilyn Choque, "La FELCN encontró 1.000 pistas clandestinas en los últimos tres años," *La Razon*, June 5, 2016, http://www.la-razon.com/nacional/seguridad_nacional/FELCN-encontro-pistas-clandestinas-ultimos_0_2503549647.html.

127. See, for example, "Incautan 37,5 kilos de cocaína en Quijarro," *El Deber*, June 26, 2015, http://www.eldeber.com.bo/santacruz/incautan-37-kilos-cocaina-quijarro.html.

128. Conversation with Peruvian law enforcement official, Lima, Peru, July 2015.

129. "ENFOQUE-Lucha contra minería ilegal de oro en Perú crea nueva ruta de contrabando por Bolivia," *Reuters*, November 25, 2014, http://lta.reuters.com/article/topNews/idLTAKCN0J91WL20141125?pageNumber=1&virtualBrandChannel=0.

130. "Bolivia," *Trafficking in Persons Report 2016*, US Department of State, 2016, https://www.state.gov/documents/organization/258878.pdf, 99–102.

131. Anastasia Moloney, "Sex Trafficking 'Staggering' in Illegal Latin American Gold Mines: Researchers, *Reuters*, March 30, 2016, https://www.reuters.com/article/us-latam-trafficking-mines/sex-trafficking-staggering-in-illegal-latin-american-gold-mines-researchers-idUSKCN0WW21U.

132. Carlos Granada, "Los Invisibles de la Quiaca," *Foro de Periodismo Argentina*, September 5, 2016, http://www.investigacionesfopea.com/trata-personas-jujuy/#11. See also Tristan Clavel, "Bolivian Children Sold for $300 on Argentina Border," *Insight Crime*, September 7, 2016, http://www.InsightCrime.org/news-briefs/bolivian-children-sold-for-300-on-argentina-border.

133. "Paraguay," *2016 International Narcotics Control Strategy Report*, US Department of State, 2016, https://www.state.gov/j/inl/rls/nrcrpt/2016/vol1/253299.htm.

134. "Economia Subterranea: El Caso de Paraguay," *ProDesarollo Paraguay*, 4th Edition, November 2016, http://www.pro.org.py/wp-content/uploads/2016/11/ECONOMIA_SUBTERRANEA_2016.pdf.

135. "Economia Subterranea."

136. Aaron Daugherty, "Murder Draws Attention to Paraguay-Uruguay Marijuana Trade," *Insight Crime*, February 11, 2016, http://www.insightcrime.org/news-briefs/murder-draws-attention-to-paraguay-uruguay-marijuana-trade.

137. "Paraguay," *Trafficking in Persons Report 2016,* US Department of State, https://www.state.gov/documents/organization/258881.pdf, 302–304.
138. "A Lethal Location," *The Economist,* September 17, 2016, http://www.economist.com/news/americas/21707244-how-argentine-port-became-gang-war-zone-lethal-location.
139. Laura Ávila, "Brazil Gang in Uruguay Shows Country's Growing Role in Drug Trade," *Insight Crime,* January 27, 2017, http://www.InsightCrime.org/news-briefs/brazil-gang-uruguay-shows-growing-role-drug-trade.
140. "Lucha contra el narcotráfico y derribo de aviones," *La Nacion,* February 9, 2016, http://www.lanacion.com.ar/1869405-lucha-contra-el-narcotrafico-y-derribo-de-aviones.
141. "Lucha contra el narcotráfico."
142. See, for example, Maria Paz Paniego, "El paco avanza: En las villas, ya lo consumen desde los 10 años," *La Nacion,* August 11, 2016, http://www.lanacion.com.ar/1926815-el-paco-avanza-en-las-villas-ya-lo-consumen-desde-los-10-anos.
143. James Bargent, "Argentina Drug Law Reforms Target Cocaine Paste," *Insight Crime,* January 9, 2017, http://www.insightcrime.com/news-briefs/argentina-drug-law-reforms-target-cocaine-paste.
144. Interview with Argentine counternarcotics expert, Buenos Aires, Argentina, December 2016.
145. Maia Jachimoowicz, "Argentina's Economic Woes Spur Emigration," *Migration Policy Institute,* July 1, 2003, http://www.migrationpolicy.org/article/argentinas-economic-woes-spur-emigration/.
146. Interview with Argentine security official, December 2016.
147. Ávila, "Brazil Gang in Uruguay Shows Country's Growing Role in Drug Trade," 2017.
148. For further details, see María Fernanda Boidi, Rosario Queirolo, and José Miguel Cruz, "Cannabis Consumption Patterns among Frequent Consumers in Uruguay," *International Journal of Drug Policy* 34 (2016): 34–40.
149. "Traficantes cambian la ruta de la marihuana," *El Pais,* January 17, 2017, http://www.elpais.com.uy/informacion/traficantes-cambian-ruta-marihuana-narcotrafico.html.
150. "Uruguay," *Trafficking in Persons Report 2016,* US Department of State, 2016, https://www.state.gov/documents/organization/258882.pdf, 393–395.
151. Fermin Koop, "Argentine Cash Deposits in Uruguay Grow 13%," *Buenos Aires Herald,* http://www.buenosairesherald.com/article/187215/argentine-cash-deposits-in-uruguay-grow-13.
152. See, for example, "Iquique como puedo pasar contrabando a Peru," *La Primera,* July 5, 2012, https://www.diariolaprimeraperu.com/online/entrevista/contrabando-el-enemigo-economico-peru-114732/.
153. Bruce Bagley, *Drug Trafficking and Organized Crime in the Americas: Major Trends in the Twenty-First Century* (Washington D.C.: The Woodrow Wilson Center for International Scholars), https://www.wilsoncenter.org/sites/default/files/BB%20Final.pdf, August 2012, https://www.wilsoncenter.org/sites/default/files/BB%20Final.pdf.
154. "Chile Has Fastest Growing Immigrant Population in South America," *Mercopress,* May 26, 2009, http://en.mercopress.com/2009/05/25/chile-has-fastest-growing-immigrant-population-in-south-america.
155. *World Drug Report, 2014.*
156. "Global Overview of Drug Demand and Supply," in *World Drug Report 2017,* United Nations Office on Drugs and Crime (New York: United Nations 2017), 18.
157. *World Drug Report 2016,* United Nations Office on Drugs and Crime, 2016, http://www.unodc.org/doc/wdr2016/WORLD_DRUG_REPORT_2016_web.pdf, 9.
158. *World Drug Report 2016,* 38.
159. *World Drug Report 2016,* 27.
160. *World Drug Report 2016,* xiv.

161. Jorge Martínez Pizarro, Verónica Cano Christin, and Magdalena Soffia Contrucci, "Tendencias y patrones de la migración latinoamericana y caribeña hacia 2010 y desafíos para una agenda regional," New York: Economic Commission for Latin America and the Caribbean, October 2014.

162. Ellis, "Crime-Terrorism Nexus in Peru."

163. Peter Shadboldt, "Philippines Raid Reveals Mexican Drug Cartel Presence in Asia," *CNN*, February 25, 2014, http://www.cnn.com/2014/02/24/world/asia/philippines-mexico-sinaloa-cartel/index.html.

164. "Mexican Cartel Smuggling Cocaine into Hong Kong amid Booming Demand for Drugs," *South China Morning Post*, February 2, 2014, http://www.scmp.com/news/hong-kong/article/1418852/mexican-cartel-smuggling-cocaine-hong-kong-amid-booming-demand-drugs.

165. "Mexican Drug Gangs."

166. "Colombian Drug Cartels Used Hong Kong Banks to Launder More Than US$5bn," *South China Morning Post*, September 12, 2015, http://www.scmp.com/news/hong-kong/law-crime/article/1857155/laundering-ring-pumped-billions-drug-money-through-hong.

167. Ellis, "Chinese Organized Crime."

THREE
Transnational Organized Crime Groups

OVERVIEW

There is significant variety in the transnational organized criminal groups operating in Latin America and the Caribbean, as well as evolution in the activities in which they are engaged, their relative power, and a continuing process of the emergence of new groups, and the disappearance of old ones.

The groups discussed in this chapter come in a wide range of sizes, with different cultures, objectives, sources of income, and other characteristics. Some may have explicitly political objectives, such as overthrowing a government or its underlying socioeconomic or political system, while others are more transparently interested in material gain.

Sources of income may include various roles in the production of illicit products and services, as well as activities such as contraband, extortion, kidnapping, human trafficking and smuggling, and arms trafficking. In some cases, group earnings may come from operating a criminal value chain, such as the production, transformation, transport, and/or selling of narcotics or illegal mining. In other cases, earnings may come from extorting money from the legal or other activities in geographic areas under the group's influence, or simply taking money through robbery or kidnapping.

In general, transnational organized crime groups rely on a combination of formally legal income sources mixed with others outside the law. Legitimate businesses both contribute to the resources of the group, and help to launder the earnings from illicit sources.

This chapter organizes the myriad of transnational organized crime groups operating in the region into a loose and overlapping typology of cartels, intermediary groups, ideologically oriented groups, and gangs, and discusses some of the principal entities operating in the region,[1] as well as the shifting mixture of activities undertaken by the entities, including drug trafficking, mining, human smuggling and trafficking, kidnapping, extortion, robbery, arms trafficking, and money laundering.

It is of note that, with the exception of gangs, the preponderance of the entities discussed in this section have their origins in, or have metamorphized through their role in, the narcotics trade. This reflects the enormous contribution of the money from narcotrafficking to the capabilities of criminal groups, as well as the fact that groups specializing in other activities are often smaller and less publicly known. Nonetheless, this chapter is a discussion about organized crime groups broadly, and not simply narcotrafficking organizations.

CARTELS

The term *cartel* refers to a group whose control over supply or demand allows it to have a significant impact on price in the market; it is used in this chapter to group organizations whose operations span multiple types of criminal activities, often including, but not limited to, multinational production and movement of drugs.

Mexico-Based Groups

The fact that the principal groups discussed herein are Mexican in their origin, and secondarily, Colombian, highlights the historical importance of the Colombia-Mexico narcotrafficking axis in the evolution of organized crime in the region. The criminal landscape in Mexico is a topic that has received considerable attention from scholars, including David Shirk,[2] John Bailey,[3] Jorge Chabat,[4] and Nathan Jones,[5] among others.

Although the landscape of Mexican cartels has evolved significantly over time, during the decade following the entry of the Mexican army into Michoacán in 2006, seven groups arguably dominated the criminal landscape: *Sinaloa, Jalisco Nuevo Generación (CGNG)*, the *Gulf Cartel, Los Zetas*, the Arellano Felix organization (*Tijuana Cartel*), the Carrillo Fuentes organization (*Juarez Cartel*), and the *Beltran-Leyva* organization. Nonetheless, when the splintering of groups over time, the emergence of new groups, and the role of cartel-affiliated gangs is included, the number of quasi-independent entities is at least forty.[6] In 2012, Mexico's attorney general reported the existence of as many as eighty criminal entities operating in the country.[7] One analysis, presented by the mayor of San Pedro, Nuevo Leon, argued that as of July 2017, as many as 280 distinct criminal entities were operating in Mexico.[8]

Such fragmentation is arguably a natural tendency of the fight between modern transnational criminal organizations and the state. On the one hand, large groups, especially high-profile ones, are arguably more vulnerable to the targeting of their leadership and operations. On the other hand, in the modern interconnected global economy, the movement of illicit goods from source zones to consumption zones does not require centralized control. Rather, such flows can "emerge" as a result of a large number of individual groups responding to supply and demand signals within the broader illicit economy. When law enforcement breaks up groups, it unleashes a dynamic of uncertainty and rivalry that stimulates further violence and inhibits the formation of new, large groupings. Because the criminal economy can continue to function through the interaction of smaller groups, in a manner that is less vulnerable to state intervention, the tendency over time is toward a criminal economy featuring a larger number of smaller groups.

Much, but not all, of the activities of Mexico's principal cartels initially centered on narcotrafficking. With time, however, some, such as Los Zetas, have come to make even more money from "taxing" or become directly involved in other criminal activities in the areas under their influence. As a product of the central role of drugs in the evolution of the cartels, however, much of the struggle between them has centered on the fight to control key routes to move those drugs (as well as people) north to the United States and Canada. Strategic points along these routes are referred to as "plazas."

Mexico's cartels have fought each other, collaborated in a complex and shifting series of alliances, although the majority of the violence has occurred between affiliated gangs and enforcer groups. The efforts of the Mexican government against individual criminal entities and their leaders has indirectly contributed to the violence by creating succession struggles within the groups whose leader has been arrested or killed, or tempting a group to encroach on the territory of a rival who is perceived to have been weakened by such developments.

As of early 2017, the three most significant and troubling trends within Mexico's shifting criminal landscape were the continuing splintering of the cartels into numerous smaller, loosely affiliated bands and gangs, the expanding power of one aggressive and internationally well-connected cartel, *Jalisco Nueva Generación* (CJNG), and the emergence of a loose alliance between CJNG and an array of other groups, to chip away at the territory and power of the most wealthy and internationally connected Sinaloa Cartel, whose traditional leader, Joaquín *"El Chapo"* Guzmán Loera, was extradited to the United States in January 2017.[9] The combination of these events threatened to unleash a new wave of violence in Mexico at the end of the presidential term of Enrique Peña Nieto, in the context of a challenge to the economic and security relationship with Mexico's closest partner, the United States.

Sinaloa

Until 2017, Sinaloa had arguably been the largest and most internationally connected of the Mexican cartels, reportedly operating in as many as fifty countries.[10] Overall, the Sinaloa Cartel was believed to be one of the wealthiest, if not the wealthiest cartel in Mexico, with estimated annual earnings of $3 billion.[11] A significant portion of the Sinaloa Cartel's income comes from producing and transporting drugs, including affiliated distribution networks in the United States, as well as supply and distribution points as far away as Europe and China. The organization is believed to be the most important player in the drug routes from Andean source zone countries, to the United States, acting as the key contractor for shipments through intermediary groups in Central America.

The Sinaloa Cartel has its roots in the role of its home region in growing poppies for the production of heroin to supply the US during World War II, and later marijuana and cocaine for the US market. Following the murder of DEA agent Enrique Camarena in 1985, US pressure led to a stepped-up campaign by the Mexican government against narcotrafficking organizations in the country, leading to the arrest of Rafael Caro Quintero, leader of the Guadalajara Cartel, which previously dominated drug smuggling routes through the center and west of Mexico into the United States. Quintero's arrest caused the organization to splinter into three organizations: the Arellano Felix organization (*Tijuana Cartel*), the Carrillo Fuentes organization (*Juarez Cartel*), and the Sinaloa organization, led by El Chapo.

Numerous key narcotrafficking figures in Mexico trace their ties to the Sinaloa organization, including Hector, Alfredo, and Arturo Beltrán-Leyva, who broke from the organization in 2008 to form the Beltrán-Leyva organization (BLO), as well as Ismael Zambada Garcia (*El Mayo*) and Juan José Esparragoza Moreno (*El Azul*), who allegedly died from a heart attack in 2014.

Sinaloa is rumored to have powerful connections within the Mexican government,[12] as well as other national governments.[13] Indeed, some suggest that relative to other cartels, the Mexican government has favored it because it has been less violent than the others in conducting its criminal activities.

While Sinaloa maintains significant international supply networks, it generally has not conducted significant operations under its own name outside of Mexico, but rather, has worked through allied or contracted groups.

The cartel's principal leader, El Chapo, was captured by authorities in 1993, but escaped from jail in 2001, then was captured again in 2014, only to escape from Mexico's highest security prison in 2015 with the help of associates who tunneled underneath the walls to briefly free him, before he was recaptured yet again. The federated nature of the cartel, and the role of others such as *El Azul* in running the affairs of the cartel while El Chapo was in prison, leads many who follow Mexico's criminal panorama to believe that even by the time of his 2015 escape, El Chapo's real authority within the organization had eroded greatly, and arguably fell precipitously with his January 2017 extradition to the United States.[14]

The "old guard" of the Sinaloa Cartel is believed to have brokered deals with some of the key organizations with which they previously competed, including the Tijuana and Juarez Cartels, and more recently the cartel *Jalisco Nuevo Generación*. With El Chapo now in prison in the United States, tension appears to have emerged between the old guard and others with aspirations to a leadership role, including El Chapo's son, Jesus Alfredo Guzman. The kidnapping of El Chapo in August 2016 from a nightclub in Puerto Vallarta[15] was regarded as an indication of the potential collapse of previously reached accords, as well as the willingness of Sinaloa's increasingly powerful rival, *Jalisco Nueva Generación*, to take advantage of Sinaloa's weakness. Further evidence that El Chapo's rivals are moving against him came in February 2017, with another attack against El Chapo's sons and former lieutenant, *El Mayo* Zambada.[16]

With the deportation of El Chapo, a grouping of its former associates, including the remnants of the Beltran-Lleyva, Arellano Felix, and Carillo Fuentes organizations (discussed below), in combination with the cartel *Jalisco Nuevo Generation*, have combined forces to challenge the dominance of Sinaloa, pushing it out of positions in a number of Mexican states over the course of 2017.

Jalisco Nuevo Generation

The Jalisco Nuevo Generation Cartel (CJNG), although not new to Mexico, has newly emerged as one of the most powerful and aggressively expanding of Mexico's cartels.[17] It both has ties to the Sinaloa Cartel, and competes with it.

CJNG has its roots in the Milenio Cartel, which arose in the 1970s in the Mexican states of Jalisco and Michoacán as a provider of marijuana and opium poppies for other traffickers. Importantly, Milenio developed ties both with Colombian narcotraffickers in Medellin for the supply of cocaine, as well as with Asian providers of precursor chemicals for methamphetamines, such as Zhenli Yi Gon. The Milenio Cartel, with these contacts and capabilities, were incorporated into the Sinaloa Cartel federation in 2003, but the group divided in 2009 following the capture of its leader, Oscar Nava Valencia (*El Lobo*), and the death of its Sinaloa Cartel overseer, Ignacio Coronel Villarreal (*El Nacho Coronel*). CJNG, under the leadership of Nemesio Oseguera (*El Mencho*) was one of the factions to emerge from the split of Milenio, with the other being La Resistencia, under Ramiro Pozos (*El Molca*). From the time of the split until the present, CJNG and other smaller factions of the former Milenio Cartel allied with Sinaloa, while *La Resistencia* allied with Sinaloa's rival, Los Zetas.

In this fashion, CJNG inherited from the Milenio Cartel parts of its Asian and Colombian narcotrafficking connections, which proved useful for CJNG in expanding its own narcotrafficking activities, even though its history was also shaped by its longstanding alliance with the Sinaloa Cartel, which helped CJNG to survive.

Although CJNG has thus been a part of the Sinaloa federation, as the group has grown in power, CJNG has adopted a posture increasingly independent of Sinaloa, as well as more bellicose toward both other cartels and the Mexican government. Indeed, CJNG's emergence into national prominence in 2015 involved a series of high-profile violent actions, including blockading the important Mexican city of Guadalajara in April, with roadblocks created by setting trucks and other vehicles on fire.[18] It then ambushed a convoy of Mexican police vehicles when they attempted to respond, killing fifteen officers.[19] The following month, CJNG downed a Mexican Army helicopter with a rocket-propelled grenade.[20]

In the months that followed, CJNG rapidly expanded its influence across the country, including extending its presence beyond Jalisco into Mexico City and at least seven other states: Colima, Michoacán, Guanajuato, Nayarit, Guerrero, Morelos, and Veracruz, threatening the territories of the other cartels.[21]

As noted previously, CJNG not only is expanding into the territory of rivals such as Los Zetas, but also has allied with other groups such as remnants of the Carrillo Fuentes, Arellano Felix and Beltran Leyva organization to challenge the territory of its former ally, the Sinaloa Cartel, particularly in the major Mexico-US border towns. In Tijuana, remnants of the Arellano Felix organization, backed by CJNG, appear to be taking on the Sinaloa Cartel in the area for control of that strategic entry point into the United States, including a shootout between members of the two groups in the city in December 2016.[22] Similarly in Juarez, as of the end of 2016, gunmen affiliated with the remnants of the Carrillo Fuentes clan, but backed by CJNG, were fighting against Sinaloa for control of that entry point into the US.[23]

Gulf Cartel

The Gulf Cartel is one of Mexico's oldest, tracing its roots back to a smuggling group set up by Juan Nepomuceno Guerra in the Mexican state of Tamaulipas, operating near the US border to smuggle alcohol into the US during Prohibition. After the end of Prohibition, Guerra established the Matamoros Cartel, which engaged in car theft, prostitution, and other illicit activities.

In 1984, Juan Garcia Ábrego established the contemporary version of the Gulf Cartel to smuggle cocaine into the US along routes similar to those used by the Matamoros Cartel during prohibition. The location of Tamaulipas was strategic in this regard, both bordering the United States and providing access to the Caribbean Sea.

The Gulf Cartel worked with the then-powerful Cali Cartel in Colombia, bringing cocaine from Peru and Colombia through the Caribbean and the east coast of Mexico, to the United States.

Following the kidnapping and death of US DEA agent Enrique Camarena in 1985, as noted previously, US pressure led the Mexican government to step up its activities against the leadership of drug trafficking organizations operating in Mexico, including not only the Guadalajara Cartel, but also the Gulf Cartel. As part of that campaign, in 1996, Ábrego was captured by Mexican authorities and extradited to the United States, leading to a prolonged succession struggle until Osiel Cardenas Guillen emerged as the Gulf Cartel's sole leader, after murdering his partner, Salvador Gómez Herrera (*El Chava*), with whom he shared power over the group, thus earning the name "He who kills friends" (*El quien mata amigos*).

As perhaps his most impactful achievement as head of the Gulf Cartel, in 1999, Guillen created *Los Zetas*, an elite paramilitary organization to fight for the organization, recruited largely from active duty and retired members of the Mexican Army Air-Mobile Special Forces (GAFE), and known for its extremely violent tactics.[24]

By 2002, under Guillen, the Gulf Cartel had grown in power, and was divided into three groups: one led by "*El Lazca*" Lazcano ("Z-3"), one by Ezequiel Cárdenas Guillén (*Tony Tormenta*), and one by Jorge Eduardo Costilla Sanchez (*El Coss*). In March 2003, Guillen was captured by the Mexican Army, following a confrontation in Matamoros, and in 2007, was extradited to the US, leaving leadership of the organization in the hands of his three lieutenants. After Guillen's fall, the Zetas also became increasingly important and powerful within the Gulf Cartel, conducting activities such as collecting extortion fees in areas under Gulf Cartel control, and eliminating Gulf Cartel. The most significant of these confrontations occurred in Nuevo Laredo, where Los Zetas confronted and badly defeated one of Sinaloa's own armed organizations, *Los Negros*, which Sinaloa had largely created to confront Los Zetas.

In 2010, the Zetas turned on their creators, the Gulf Cartel, who in turn, turned to their former rivals the Sinaloa Cartel and *La Familia Michoacana* to try to put the Zetas down. The Zetas, in turn, allied with the Beltrán-Leyva organization, the Juarez Cartel, and the Tijuana Cartel, leading to a bloody series of confrontations, including in Tamaulipas along the US border, an area which previously had been relatively peaceful. Also in this year, splits began to appear between organizations within the Gulf Cartel, including a fight between the "Metros" faction and "Rojos" faction over selection to a leadership position in the cartel, further weakening the embattled organization.

In November of 2010, Gulf Cartel leader Tony Tormenta was killed in a large-scale confrontation with the Mexican military in Matamoros, leaving *El Coss* in charge of the group. The confrontation also publicly highlighted a new paramilitary organization created by the Gulf Cartel, the "Scorpions," who were believed to have protected the Gulf leader during the firefight.[25] As a product of its battle with the Zetas, and enforcement actions by the Mexican authorities, the Gulf Cartel has since fragmented into at least twelve distinct groups, focused in part on narcotrafficking, and in part on extortion and other activities in the areas that they control.

Los Zetas

Los Zetas were once one of the most feared and publicly visible of the Mexican cartels. As noted in the previous section, the group was created by the head of the Gulf Cartel, Osiel Cardenas Guillen, as an elite paramilitary force to protect the Gulf Cartel and fight its battles, particularly against the latter's principal rival (at the time), the Sinaloa Cartel. Their founding members were recruited from active duty and retired members of the Mexican Army Special Forces Organization (GAFE). These included Arturo Guzmán Decena (Z-1), who defected from the Mexican military to the Gulf Cartel in 1997 and worked with Guillen to set up Los Zetas, Heriberto Lazcano Lazcano (Z-3, or *El Lazca*), who later became the leader of Los Zetas, and Miguel Treviño Morales (Z-40), who mounted the Zetas' previously mentioned defense against an attempt by the Sinaloa Cartel to invade the territory of the Gulf Cartel in eastern Mexico.

Among their other activities before turning on their creators, Los Zetas provided military training to other groups in support of the Gulf Cartel, including *La Familia Michoacana* (discussed below). By 2010, the Zetas were believed by some to have amassed a sizeable army of affiliated gangs and forces that one author estimated to number ten thousand persons.[26]

By contrast to the other Mexican cartels, which have maintained a presence outside Mexico principally through representatives and intermediaries, during the period of their most significant expansion in 2008, the Zetas sought to work with disaffected Guatemalan criminal groups to establish a physical presence in that country, principally concentrated on strategic corridors for moving drugs to Mexico.

In 2010, as noted previously, the Zetas turned against their founder, the Gulf Cartel, to carve out their own territory in the drug business and other aspects of international crime, leading to a conflict with the Gulf Cartel focused in Tamaulipas and the frontier with the US. By contrast to groups such as Sinaloa and CJNG, Los Zetas have generally made money less from moving drugs and operating other illicit businesses, and more from controlling territory and extorting other criminal organizations, as well as legitimate businesses, for the money-generating activities that occurred on that territory.

The Zetas suffered an important loss when Miguel Trevino was arrested by Mexican authorities. He was later extradited to the United States in December 2017 to face charges.[27]

Beyond Trevino's arrest and extradition, the Zetas organization has been significantly reduced through its conflict with the Gulf Cartel and other rivals, as well as the targeting of the Zeta leadership by Mexican security forces. More recently, its territory has come under attack from CJNG.[28] The group is currently splintered into at least thirteen organizations, concentrated principally in Tamaulipas and Quintana Roo, although there have been rumors of attempts by the group to unify its factions and reconstitute itself. In January 2017, a series of attacks for which the Zetas claimed credit in the tourist zone of the state of Quintana Roo[29] raised concern about a new wave of violence driven by the ongoing conflict between the Zetas, the Gulf Cartel, and *Jalisco Nuevo Generación*, in the zone.

Arellano Felix Organization

The Arellano Felix organization, also known as the "Tijuana Cartel," for the area in which its operations are centered, is one of Mexico's oldest narcotrafficking organizations. It was born from the disintegration of the Guadalajara Cartel, following the previously mentioned arrest of that organization's head Rafael Caro Quintero, and its founding leader, Miguel Angel Felix Gallardo, in 1989.

The activities of the Arellano Felix organization were based principally on the organization's control of the drug trafficking route through the Western Mexican state of Baja California, including the city of Tijuana, a strategic gateway into the United States. In its heyday in the 1980s, the group was considered one of the country's most powerful cartels. It persisted in a loose federation with the Juarez-based Carrillo Fuentes organization and the Sinaloa Cartel, until the death of Armando Carrillo Fuentes in 1992.

The organization engaged in a rivalry with the Sinaloa Cartel for control of the Tijuana corridor, which it substantially lost in 2006. Its position was further undermined by the arrest of leader Javier Arellano Félix during the same year and the deployment of the Mexican military to Tijuana in January 2007 in "Operation Tijuana."

In 2008, a bitter and violent rivalry emerged within the cartel itself, in Tijuana, between one group led by Luis Fernando Sánchez Arellano (*El Ingeniero*), who preferred to focus on drug trafficking, and another, under Teodoro García Simental (*El Teo*), who preferred kidnapping as a revenue stream. Thanks in part to the continuing activities of Mexican armed forces in the area through "Operation Tijuana," *El Teo's* faction was largely eliminated, leaving *El Ingeniero* to continue drug trafficking, in a renewed alliance with Sinaloa, with the combination of the end of the rivalry and the new cooperation with Sinaloa significantly decreasing violence in the area. The June 2014 capture of *El Ingeniero* by Mexican security forces left the organization decimated. By 2016, the remnants of the group had affiliated with CJNG, calling themselves *"Tijuana Nueva Generación,"* and beginning to challenge Sinaloa for control of the Tijuana corridor.[30]

Carrillo Fuentes Organization

The *Carrillo Fuentes* organization, also known as the *Juarez Cartel*, is centered in Ciudad Juarez, another strategic point of entry for northbound drugs, people and contraband goods entering the US. As with the Arellano Felix organization, the *Juarez Cartel* was born from the disintegration of the Guadalajara Cartel. Following that disintegration, its leader, Amado Carrillo Fuentes, arguably emerged as the most powerful narcotrafficker in Mexico, referred to as *"El Senior de Los Cielos"* (the boss of the skies") for his use of aircraft to smuggle drugs into the United States.

During the heyday of the cartel in the 1980s and 1990s, and after the imprisonment of El Chapo Guzman allowed the *Carrillo Fuentes* organization to become the dominant member of the collaborating groups, the *Carrillo Fuentes* organization maintained a loose federation with the Sinaloa Cartel and the Tijuana-based *Arellano Felix* organization.

In 1997, near the height of his power, Amado Carrillo Fuentes was killed in a botched plastic surgery, and his brother Vicente assumed the leadership of the organization, working with his other brother, Rodolfo, and in alliance with other established narcotraffickers such as Juan José Esparragoza Moreno (*El Azul*), as well as El Chapo Guzman (after he escaped from prison in 2001).

Despite such collaboration, the Sinaloa Cartel eventually presented the *Carrillo Fuentes* organization with its most bloody and damaging struggle. After El Chapo escaped from Mexican federal prison in 2001, he began rebuilding his organization, in part by recruiting members of the Juarez Cartel to defect from their organization to his, creating tension between the groups. In 2004, Rodolfo Carrillo Fuentes was killed in a hit allegedly ordered by El Chapo, provoking Vicente Carrillo Fuentes to reciprocate by ordering the murder of El Chapo's brother, then in prison. The murders ignited a bitter two-year war between the *Carrillo Fuentes* and *Sinaloa* organizations for control over the Juarez corridor into the United States. The struggle greatly weakened the Carrillo Fuentes organization, although Sinaloa was forced to suspend the struggle in 2005, due to its more demanding war against the Gulf Cartel in the east. The war heated up again in 2008, when the *Beltran-Leyva* organization joined *Car-*

rillo Fuentes in a new alliance against Sinaloa, but without ultimately changing the status quo, and leaving the *Carrillo Fuentes* organization in control of the Juarez corridor.

As noted previously, by 2017, the rising power of CJNG, and the vulnerability of Sinaloa with the re-arrest and extradition of El Chapo, appeared to tempt the *Carrillo Fuentes* organization to engage in yet another alliance against Sinaloa, this time with CJNG. With the latter's backing, the armed band created by *Carrillo Fuentes*,, "La Linea," has expanded the struggle for control over Juarez, contributing to a new spike of violence in the long-troubled city.[31]

Beltrán-Leyva Organization

The Beltrán-Leyva organization (BLO) was part of the first generations of narcotraffickers in Mexico. The Beltrán-Leyva brothers (Alfredo, Arturo, Carlos, Héctor, and Mario Alberto) initially formed part of the Sinaloa Cartel, later playing a key role on behalf of Sinaloa in its struggle with the Gulf Cartel for territory and routes in the east of the country. Despite this collaboration, the January 2008 arrest of Alfredo Beltrán-Leyva provoked a series of reprisals, including the assassination of Mexico's police commissioner (seen as responsible for the action) by a group of "special forces" loyal to Alfredo's brother Arturo, and later, the assassination of the son of El Chapo Guzman, who was thought to have played a role in the arrest.

The assassination of El Chapo's son broke the Sinaloa-BLO alliance, and in 2008, as noted in the previous section, BLO joined the Carrillo Fuentes organization in the latter's fight against Sinaloa for control of the Juarez corridor. In 2010, BLO joined another anti-Sinaloa coalition, this time allying with *Los Zetas* against Sinaloa, the Gulf Cartel, and *La Familia Michoacana* for control of the similarly strategic plaza of La Reynosa in the state of Tamaulipas.

The downfall of BLO occurred principally during 2014–2015, including the October 2014 arrest of the group's leader, Hector (*El H*) Beltrán-Leyva. The organization subsequently split into factions, including *Los Rojos* and *Guerreros Unidos*, among others, fighting for territory in the key narcotrafficking area of Mexico's Guerrero state.

While these groups have contributed significantly to the conflict in Guerrero and neighboring states, the organization as a whole has lost significant presence as an international narcotrafficking organization. As noted previously, as of the end of 2017, the remnants of BLO had joined the CJNG in an emerging new fight against Sinaloa.

La Familia Michoacana / Knights Templar

La Familia Michoacana (LFM) was an organization born out of the Milenio Cartel in Michoacán. Initially established in the 1990s by Nazario

Moreno González (*El Chayo*), *La Familia* worked with the Gulf Cartel as its armed wing in the state, trained by the Gulf Cartel's principally paramilitary organization Los Zetas, to help the former fight against the presence of the Sinaloa organization, then dominating Michoacán, although in 2006 it turned against Los Zetas, launching a bloody war for control of Michoacán.

The leader of *La Familia*, *El Chayo*, used quasi-religious principles to guide the cartel, including a book of his own sayings, as well as a series of strict practices including forbidding the members of his own organization to use drugs.

La Familia came into the public spotlight in 2006 through a violent action in a nightclub in the city of Uruapan, Michoacán. In a public statement against the presence of *Los Zetas* in the state (whom *La Familia* had recently turned against, its members tossed severed heads of members of *Los Zetas* whom it had executed onto the dance floor of the club, which *Los Zetas* were known to frequent.

Over the next years, the organization used violent tactics to fight against *Los Zetas* and other rival organizations in Michoacan. Indeed, as noted previously, it was this violence, and the associated plea for help by Michoacán's governor, PRD politician Lázaro Cárdenas Batel, that helped to convince incoming Mexican president Felipe Calderón to deploy Mexican security forces into the state in November 2006,[32] launching the war against the cartels.

With time, La Familia became as thoroughly involved in criminal activity as the organizations that it had displaced, including extortion of both legitimate and illegitimate businesses operating in the state.[33] In November 2010, La Familia's leader, *El Chayo*, was believed to be killed in a confrontation with police, leading to a division in the organization between rivals vying for leadership. One of the contenders, Servando Gómez Martínez (*La Tuta*), went on to form a rival organization, the *Knights Templar* organization, leaving the remainder of *La Familia* in the hands of José de Jesús Méndez Vargas (*El Chango*), although with both external challenges and internal infighting, by 2014, *La Familia* had largely ceased to exist.

Under *La Tuta*, Gómez, the *Knights Templar* organization gradually assumed control of most of what had previously been the territory of *La Familia* in Michoacán, including establishing an armed group of hitmen, *La Resistencia*, targeting the cartel's arch-rival in Michoacán, Los Zetas. In February 2015, the group's leader, *La Tuta*, was arrested by Mexican police. In part as a consequence of such blows, both the *Knights Templar* and *La Resistencia* have been largely, but not completely, disarticulated.[34]

Colombia-Based Groups

During the mid-1990s, the nation of Colombia hosted some of the most powerful transnational groups in the region, with truly transhemispheric reach, including the Medellin and Cali Cartels, and later the *Norte de Valle* Cartel. The demise of the first two and the partial disintegration of the third, in part through the efforts of the Colombian government, contributed to the assumption of a more significant role in the drug trade by Mexican cartels, as discussed in the previous section.

Complicating matters, as discussed in the previous chapter, the expansion of coca growing and its transformation into cocaine on Colombian territory, often in areas under the influence of the nation's two principal guerilla/terrorist groups, the *Fuerzas Armadas Revolucionarios de Colombia* (FARC) and the *Ejercito de Liberación Nacional* (ELN), led them to become involved in taxing such activities in the areas they controlled, and often to become directly involved with it. In a similar fashion, they also became involved in illegal mining, kidnapping, and extortion in areas under their influence. Driven in part by the challenge presented by such groups, large landowners and business groups (often with criminal ties themselves) hired security guards and created militias to protect themselves. Criminal groups such as the Medellin Cartel, for example, came to employ militias to protect themselves against the FARC rebels in the areas in which they operated.[35]

In times, these militias also came to be involved in organized criminal activities. In the decade following the fall of the Medellin and Cali drug cartels in Colombia, many of the militias came to battle the FARC and other ideologically oriented groups for control over coca growing and mining areas, and areas to conduct other illicit activities. The collapse of the Medellin and Cali cartels, the emergence of a larger number of smaller criminal groups involved in drug production and other illicit activities in the countryside, and the increasing involvement of both individual guerilla fronts and militias in these activities, gave rise to a complex new criminal economy in the Colombian countryside.[36]

In 2006, when the Colombian government of Álvaro Uribe signed a peace deal with the self-defense groups, a total of more than thirty-two thousand militia members demobilized.[37] Unfortunately, many, instead of integrating into the formal economy, joined criminal bands, or formed new ones, swelling the ranks of criminal organizations in the countryside, and the associated criminality.[38]

Within two years of the peace deal, over thirty major organized criminal groups were operating in Colombia, collectively referred to as "criminal bands" or "Bacrim."[39] The struggle between these groups unleashed new criminal violence between them in which the numerous groups eventually consolidated down to four, of which the one which emerged dominant was known as the *Urabeños*, subsequently renamed to the

Úsaga clan, then renamed a second time as the "Gulf" clan, since the prior names were considered affronts to both residents of Urabá and those with the last name Úsaga.

The November 2016 agreement between the Colombian government and the FARC has led many to be concerned about a new flood of recruits into the hands of the criminal bands, producing expanded criminality as well as violence as the leading BACRIM suppress emerging new rival organizations.[40]

Gulf Clan

As of early 2017, the *Gulf Clan* was arguably the most powerful in Colombia, operating throughout the national territory. The group was one of many born out of the previously mentioned demobilization of the United Self-Defense Groups of Colombia (AUC) in 2006. Their predecessor organization within the AUC was the *Centaurios block*, which, prior to demobilization, had become one of the wealthiest of the self-defense organizations, principally through narcotrafficking in Colombia's eastern plains. Their leader, Daniel Rendón Herrera (*Don Mario*), had worked as the finance chief of the Centaurios block, and with the demobilization of the AUC, used that knowledge to become head of the *Gulf Clan*.

Don Mario not only continued his criminal activities, but also began actively recruiting members from other AUC groups which were demobilizing, as well as from the defunct *People's Liberation Army* (EPL) in the department of Urabá (giving rise to the group's initial name, "Urabeños").

The main revenue-earning activity of the *Gulf Clan* under Don Mario was smuggling cocaine from Colombia through the Gulf of Mexico. By 2008, its illicit activities had transformed it into the wealthiest criminal organization in the country, with an estimated three thousand members.[41] In May 2009, Don Mario was arrested on a farm in Urabá, leaving two lieutenants and former paramilitaries, Juan de Dios and Dario Antonio Úsuga David (*Otoniel*), to take control of the organization. In January 2011, however, Juan de Dios Úsuga was killed by authorities in the department of Choco during a police raid, leaving Otoniel in charge of the organization. The latter made a name for himself by terrorizing the country, publicly offering $1,000 for every police officer killed in the department of Antioquia as a reprisal for his brother's death.

In 2011, the *Gulf Clan* came increasingly into direct conflict with the Rastrojos, one of the other leading groups to emerge successfully from the post-AUC demobilization struggle for power. Among other issues, the Rastrojos and *Gulf Clan* fought over the control of illicit activities in the Medellin area, with the *Gulf Clan* ultimately prevailing and thus becoming the undisputed most powerful criminal band in Colombia.

Reflecting its power and the focused efforts of the Colombian government against it, the *Gulf Clan* is the only criminal entity beyond the FARC and the ELN to have been explicitly targeted by the nation's military, which bombed one of its encampments in November 2015.[42] Further highlighting the emphasis the Colombian government has put on it, in 2016, the Gulf Cartel was listed by the government as an "Organized Armed Group," a new classification of entities which the Colombian government maintains are sufficiently powerful, and have characteristics sufficient to permit them to be legitimately subject to military action under the principles of international law.

Since 2014, with the implementation of Operation Agamemnon, the Colombian government has focused particular attention against the *Gulf Clan*, targeting its leadership and structures. The operation has led to the detention or killing of several of them and has arguably been key in forcing the group to cede control of its strategically important core territory in the Eastern plains.

As of early 2017, *Gulf Clan* seemed positioned to be one of the principal beneficiaries of the demobilization of Colombia's FARC rebels under the terms of the November 2016 peace accords, just as the group had initially been created, and its ranks swelled by, the results of the 2003–2006 AUC demobilization. Indeed, as the peace accords were ratified in November 2016, the Colombian government believed that the *Gulf Clan* was actively recruiting FARC members, in an attempt to take control of coca production and the criminal economy in territory that the FARC was withdrawing from.[43]

Nonetheless, despite the opportunity that the accords with the FARC seemed to offer the group, during 2017, the Colombian government was able to achieve a considerable number of successes against it and its leadership. In August 2017, Colombian police and military forces killed "Gavilan" the group's second in command, in a military operation in Úraba.[44] In November, they arrested his successor, "Inglaterra,"[45] even while the group's leader, Dairo Antonio Úsuga, was negotiating surrender and the group's demobilization with Colombian authorities.[46]

Rastrojos

The *Rastrojos* was formed in 2004 by Wilber Varela *(El Jabón)*, a dissident leader of the once powerful *Norte del Valle* Cartel, with his ally Diego Rastrojo, who became the single leader of the group. The Rastrojos became completely independent of the *Norte del Valle* Cartel (a powerful narcotrafficking organization itself descended from the Cali Cartel) after Wilber Varela was killed in Venezuela in 2008, leaving leadership firmly in the hands of Diego Rastrojo.

The *Rastrojos* inherited a significant network of armed enforcers from the Norte del Valle organization, as well as infrastructure for producing and transporting cocaine. Their organization leveraged these assets to generate significant earnings acquiring coca from Colombia, principally in territory controlled by the *ELN*, subsequently transforming it into cocaine and transporting it through Central America and the Caribbean to sell it to Mexican cartels and other buyers. The group also reportedly traffics in heroin and engages in kidnapping. In the process, for a time, they became one of the wealthiest and most powerful narcotrafficking groups in Colombia.

The *Rastrojos'* principal trafficking routes in Colombia include both the Pacific coast and the border region with Venezuela, which became an increasingly lucrative area as law and order in the latter began to disintegrate. As noted previously, the group suffered a significant series of blows in 2011, when it engaged in a struggle with the larger and more powerful *Gulf Clan* for control of criminal activities in the territory around Medellin. Its decline was accelerated when, in May 2012, its leader, Javier Antonio Calle Serna (*Comba*), surrendered to US authorities. In June of the same year, authorities also captured Diego Rastrojo, and in October, arrested Comba's brother, Luis Enrique Calle Serna.

Despite such evidence of the group's demise, the position of part of the group in the Catatumbo, along the frontier with Venezuela, provided an opportunity for the organization to partially reconstitute itself,[47] taking advantage not only of drug production on the Colombian side of the border and its smuggling into Venezuela for transit out of the region, but also of the considerable contraband trade along the border, including tens of thousands of desperate Venezuelan refugees crossing the border in areas under Rastrojo influence.

Los Puntilleros

This small group operates in the relatively unpopulated but strategically important eastern plains of Colombia, on the border with Venezuela, the site of operations of both the FARC and the ELN. While criminal operations in the region have long benefitted from the traditional absence of the Colombian government in the area, the collapse of governability in neighboring Venezuela from the mid-2000s has created even more opportunities, increasing the importance of the area in which Los Puntilleros operated as a corridor for the movement of drugs from Colombia through Venezuela, as well as for contraband supplying desperate persons inside the latter. In addition, the area is also rich in the valuable substance coltan and other minerals and precious metals such as gold.

Los Puntilleros is a relatively new group, with its name taken from the criminal name of its leader, Oscar Mauricio Pachón Rozo (*Puntilla*), who amassed power through narcotrafficking and other illicit activities in the region as the Colombian acted against rival organizations operating in the area, including the *Gulf Clan* and the "Colombian Revolutionary Anti-Subversive Army" (*ERPAC*).[48]

As with many other Colombia-based groups described in this chapter, the Puntilleros were born out of the 2003–2006 AUC demobilization. ERPAC dominated Colombia's eastern plains under its founder and leader, Pedro Oliverio Guerrero (*Cuchillo*). He was killed in a confrontation with the government in 2010, leading ERPAC to splinter into the *Meta Block* and the *Libertadores de Vichada*, both of which survived the formal disbanding of ERPAC in 2011.[49]

The *Libertadores de Vichada*, under Martín Farfán Díaz González (*Pijarbey*), came to dominate the eastern plains from 2010 through 2015, until *Pijarbey* also was killed. Remaining elements of both the *Libertadores de Vichada* and the *Meta Block*, in turn, joined together to form the *Puntilleros*, in the process resisting attempts by the *Gulf Clan* to assert its own domination of the region. Despite such advances, in February 2016, the group's leader, *Puntilla*, was arrested, leaving the fate of the group, and control of the strategically important criminal terrain it occupies, uncertain.[50]

INTERMEDIARY GROUPS

Although there is no firm division between "cartels" and "intermediary groups" for the purpose of this work, intermediary groups may be thought of as those which principally facilitate the transnational criminal economy through providing illicit services, such as the production and smuggling of drugs, mining products, weapons, and other contraband goods. Intermediary groups may also include those which facilitate financial transactions and/or money laundering. While intermediary groups generally have business relationships that span national boundaries, and may have personnel operating in multiple countries, their role as "facilitators" is often concentrated in a particular country.

In many of the cases, the activities of intermediary groups in criminal endeavors such as narcotrafficking have evolved from participation in lower-level illicit activities, such as smuggling, within their country of origin as opportunities for criminal enrichment have evolved. Many, but not all, such groups tend to be family-based, yet not exclusively so.

Particularly in Central America, there is a synergistic relationship between intermediary groups, and gangs such as Mara Salvatrucha and Barrio 18, which dominate many of the neighborhoods in which the intermediary groups must operate. In terms of manpower, intermediary groups are generally far smaller than the gangs which may, at times, provide them services. By contrast to intermediary groups, gangs typically focus more on controlling territory, and have far larger formal memberships.

There is often a synergy between gangs and intermediary groups in countries in which the two cohabitate. Particularly in Central America, the intermediary groups will often pay local gang members for the right to pass through their territory, and in some cases, will contract them to act as guards, or to carry out assassinations and other targeted actions.

In general, the intermediary groups provide the "within country" logistics networks by which foreign-based cartels (often the Mexicans or Colombians) move narcotics and other goods and people through the country. The cartels may provide advance financing to the intermediary groups for the movement of products, and may send representatives into the country to supervise shipments, or take delivery at the final point of departure from the country, but with few exceptions (such as the entry of *Los Zetas* into Guatemala), the cartels generally leave their business within those countries to the intermediary groups, who act as their agents.

As with the cartels, there has also been considerable change among intermediary groups operating in the region over time, particularly since 2014. Such change reflects successful enforcement efforts against intermediary group leadership, often with US and other international help, in the process, creating a more fractionalized and uncertain strategic environment, just as actions against cartel leaders have done in Mexico.

Such actions have driven a reshuffling of relationships between cartels and intermediary groups, as the cartels work to forge new relations with a larger number of smaller entities who once worked for the intermediary groups, whose leaders have been arrested or killed. Further adding to uncertainty, the cartels which previously maintained the relationships, such as Sinaloa, are themselves coming under attack, creating the need to forge new relationships on both sides.

Venezuela: Cartel of the Suns

Although multiple groups are believed to be operating in Venezuela, the Cartel of the Suns both has received the most media attention and is arguably the most powerful, given the alleged participation of senior Venezuelan defense and other government officials in the organization. The organization's rise was the environment of permissiveness toward corruption of the "Bolivarian socialist" government of Hugo Chavez beginning in February 1999, as well as the government of Nicolás Maduro, who succeeded Chavez in 2013.[51]

The organization's rise was due in part to the evolving role of personnel in the Venezuelan government, military, and national guard under the Bolivarian socialist government, from receiving income for allowing illicit activities such as narcotrafficking to occur in territories under their control, to groups actively performing such activities, and coming to more directly organize and engage in those activities. Although there was evidence of the expanding involvement of Venezuelan government and military personnel with organized crime throughout the presidency of Hugo Chavez and his successor, Nicolás Maduro, some of the most authoritative evidence of their role emerged in 2008, when the US Office of Foreign Assets Control (OFAC) announced sanctions against Hugo Carvajal Barrios (then director of military intelligence), Henry Rangel Silva (then general-in-chief and subsequently defense minister), and Ramon Rodriguez Chacin, former minister of the interior and justice,[52] among others.

As noted in the previous chapter, the organization is believed to be headed by the speaker of the Venezuelan parliament, Diosdado Cabello, with the participation of former head of the Venezuelan National Guard and now interior minister, Nestor Reverol, and other key National Guard personnel.[53]

Currently the elements of the Venezuelan military and National Guard believed to be most deeply involved in criminal activities are those along the border with Colombia in the Venezuelan states of Apure, Zulia, and Táchira, due to their control of road checkpoints between the two states, as well as airports and ports such as Puerto Cabello.[54] The partial and later total closure of the Venezuelan border from August 2015 through August 2016 further contributed to opportunities for the Venezuelan military units controlling those checkpoints to enrich themselves by accepting payments to permit the passage of contraband goods.

The relative lack of functionality of law enforcement against politically connected personnel within the national territory, and the significant contraband activities arising from state control of the economy and scarcity of basic goods, have each contributed to the organization's power.[55] Despite such enablers, the ability of the organization to operate has been curtailed by significant attention from US and other law enforcement organizations, and the defections of a number of key personnel to the US, now presumably collaborating with US authorities to provide information on the group. In January 2015, for example, Diosdado Cabello's personal bodyguard defected to the United States, publicly accusing his former boss of being the head of the Cartel of the Suns.[56] In November 2016, the nephews of Hugo Chavez were arrested in Haiti and extradited to the US on charges of trafficking cocaine to the United States, providing further evidence of high-level involvement.[57]

Honduras-Based Transportistas

Until their recent demise, the two main criminal intermediary groups in Honduras were the Cachiros and the Valle Valles. They have traditionally operated in the departments of Copan, Olancho, and Gracias a Dios, leveraging an available informal sector labor force in those areas where other economic opportunities are scarce, as well as deriving protection from a political class thoroughly compromised by drug money and a judicial system where, until recently, impunity approached 100 percent.[58] The Barrio 18 and Mara Salvatrucha street gangs are also key parts of the criminal landscape in Honduras, but are discussed later in this chapter under the section on gangs.

Cachiros

Even prior to their involvement in narcotrafficking, the family-based Cachiros group had a long history of smuggling of goods through Honduras, operating principally on the northeastern coast in the province of Colon, with a territory estimated to span from the department of Gracias a Dios in the east of the country, to San Pedro Sula in the West and Olancho in the south.[59]

As Mexican and Colombian narcotraffickers increasingly looked to Honduras as a key node for smuggling narcotics overland through Central America to the United States, the Cachiros made use of their established logistics networks for small-scale smuggling to support the movement of cocaine and other drugs through the region. The isolation of Honduras from the international community following the ouster of its president Manuel Zelaya in June 2009[60] created an opportunity for the group to significantly expand their narcotics smuggling, and with it, their associated wealth. Among its other activities, the group received small planes loaded with drugs from Colombia and other points of origin, and smuggled the cargo through the country, and across the Honduras-Guatemala border. Based on this business, according to a calculation by the US Treasury Department, by 2013, the Cachiros operated 90 percent of the clandestine airstrips in Honduras.[61]

As the Cachiros grew in power, they worked with powerful political allies for protection, as well as with well-connected Honduran businessmen such as the Continental financial group of Jaime Rosenthal to finance their operations and launder money.[62]

In January 2015, the two principal leaders of the Cachiros family clan, Javier Eriberto Rivera Maradiaga (Javier Cachiro) and his brother Deves Leonel Rivera Maradiaga, fled to the Bahamas, where they turned themselves over to US authorities, in an apparent effort to avoid incarceration in Honduran jails.[63] Their detention led to the substantial disintegration of the organization. The Mexican cartels that they had previously supplied, in turn, begin working directly with Cachiro sub-organizations to continue moving narcotics through the country.

The story of the Cachiros also illustrates how the take-down of an important gang leader (if not killed) may open the door for a broader series of actions against organized crime in a country, and often associated controversies. During his trial in New York in March 2017, for example, Devis Leonel Rivera Maradiaga testified to criminal collaboration with Fabio Lobo, son of ex-president of Honduras Pepe Lobo, attempted bribery of President Lobo himself, and illicit dealings with the brother of Honduras's current president, Juan Orlando Hernandez,[64] accusations which may have influenced the outcome of December 2017 national elections, in which Hernandez sought re-election.

Valle Valles

The Valle Valles, like the Cachiros, were a family-based clan based in Honduras, dedicated to smuggling and other licit and illicit activities. Like the Cachiros, the Valle Valles leveraged their logistics networks, connections, and experience with smuggling to expand their wealth moving narcotics for drug trafficking organizations such as the Sinaloa Cartel. Indeed, in 2013, the leader of the Sinaloa Cartel, Joaquim "El Chapo" Guzman, was reported to have spent time in a residence of the Valle Valles in the Honduran town of "El Paraiso."[65]

As with the Cachiros, the Valle Valles greatly expanded their drug smuggling business during the international isolation of Honduras following the 2009 ouster of President Manuel Zelaya. The principal area of operations for the Valle Valles has been somewhat to the northwest of the routes used by the Cachiros, concentrated along Honduras's border with Guatemala.

As a compliment to their narcotrafficking activities, the Valle Valles have also been significantly involved in the real estate and other businesses, particularly in their center of operations, the provincial capital of Copan.[66] Among other techniques, the group reportedly used persons with adjoining property on both sides of the Honduras-Guatemala border to smuggle drugs and persons across, avoiding established border checkpoints.[67]

As with the Cachiros, the majority of the leadership of the Valle Valles was dismantled through collaborative efforts between the United States and the Honduran governments, with a key breakthrough being work with Digna Valle Valle, formally arrested in July 2014.[68] In October 2014, Honduran authorities arrested group leaders Miguel Arnulfo and Luis Alonso Valle Valle, extraditing them in December of the same year,[69] as well as younger brother Jose Inocente Valle Valle.[70] The operations effectively crippled the organization as a transporter group in Honduras.

The dismantling of the leadership of both groups beginning in 2014 helped to pave the way for smaller groups, which used to work for each, to begin working directly with Mexicans and other criminal counterparts to move drugs and other illicit goods through the region.

Other Honduras-Based Groups

Within Honduras, a number of other organizations have historically operated to move drugs and conduct other operations with varying levels of affiliation with, or subordination to, the Cachiros and Valle Valles, including the "Olancho Cartel" (operating in the department of Olancho), the "Southern Valley" Cartel (operating principally around Choluteca, a strategic point where Nicaragua, Honduras, and El Salvador converge in the Gulf of Fonseca), *Los Pintos* (operating primarily in the south),[71] the "AA Brothers" organization, and "14e," a shadowy umbrella organization rumored to coordinate the organized crime activities of the fourteen leading families in San Pedro Sula.[72]

As noted in the previous paragraph, with the dismantling of the leadership of the Cachiros and the Valle Valles, such groups are believed to have begun working more directly with the Mexicans and other cartels to fill the void. Indeed, in May 2015 the Honduran newspaper *El Heraldo*, reported an alleged meeting between ranchers in Olancho and members of Mexico's Juarez Cartel to discuss such collaboration.[73]

By October 2016, the media was also reporting the presence of new groups, including the *Atlantic Cartel*, which reportedly operated in the Department of Gracias de Dios, with ties to other groups such as the AA Brothers operating to the West in areas such as Copan.[74] The identity and status of such groups continue to evolve as they become the focus of enforcement actions by Honduran and other law enforcement authorities. Members of the Saramiento family reportedly fled to Nicaragua in response to actions by the Honduran government in the July 2015 period against the Olancho Cartel.[75] Similarly, the mayor of El Paraiso and suspected boss of the AA Cartel, Alexander Ardon, was arrested in November 2015.[76] In November 2016, in "Operation Sultan," Honduran authorities moved against the relatively unknown group "Los Pintos."[77]

Guatemala-Based Transportistas

In Guatemala, like Honduras, the principal transnational organized criminal groups in the country have been the street gangs and smuggling organizations moving narcotics and other contraband goods through the country. As in Honduras, the movement of narcotics through Guatemala has been done by a limited number of small, family based organizations, of which the most prominent have been the Mendoza, Lorenzana, Leon, and Lopez Ortiz families, as well as an increasingly important group known as the Huistas. As in Honduras, with the exception of the Huistas, the leadership of virtually all of these organizations has been decimated in recent years through the action of authorities, in collaboration with the United States, giving rise to a larger group of smaller competing organizations, and greater uncertainty.

Mendozas

The Mendozas are a politically well-connected smuggling family with operations based in the family hometown of Morales in the Guatemalan department of Izabal. Their activities have been concentrated in the Petén region of Guatemala near the Mexican border. By contrast with many transportistas groups who deal primarily with the Sinaloa Cartel, the geographic orientation of the Mendozas has contributed to their relationship with Mexico's Gulf Cartel, which would take delivery of narcotics from the group and continue moving them from the Petén border across Mexico's Yucatan peninsula, and up the eastern (Gulf coast) side of Mexico. The Mendozas also had a reputation for robbing drug shipments from other transportistas groups and selling them back to the cartel from whom it was robbed, or to the highest bidder. The incursion of the Mexican narcotrafficking organization Los Zetas into Guatemala from 2008 to 2011 forced most of the Mendoza family to flee the country. Yet with the decline of the Zetas in Guatemala after 2011, the Mendozas were reportedly able to continue their narcotrafficking business, albeit in a weakened state.[78] Further debilitating the group, the suspected head of the group, Haroldo Mendoza Matta, was arrested in November 2014 by Guatemalan security forces.[79] In April 2016, Walter Mendoza, who had reportedly become the clan's leader, was also arrested, as part of a series of raids conducted against the group in the states of Petén and Izabal.[80]

Lorenzanas

The Lorenzanas were once one of the key transportistas groups moving narcotics and other contraband goods through Guatemala for Mexican organized crime families. They reportedly moved much of their drugs through the department of San Marcos, with Mexico's Sinaloa Cartel as their principal client.[81] As with the other intermediary organizations discussed in this chapter, the Lorenzanas were both politically well-connected at senior levels in Guatemala, and backed within the poorer communities that they supported, and which provided manual labor for their operations. Due to law enforcement actions against the group's leadership, the Lorenzana organization is now believed to be largely disarticulated. Following the election of Otto Perez Molina as president of Guatemala in 2011, family patriarch Waldemar Lorenzana was arrested, as well as his sons Eliu and Waldemar. The father was subsequently extradited to the United States in March 2014 and pleaded guilty to narcotrafficking charges.[82] The remaining brother, Haruldo (considered by Guatemalan analysts to be less capable than his other brothers),[83] was left to carry on the family business.[84]

Leones

The Leon family, like many of the other intermediary organizations discussed in this chapter, began as smugglers of cattle and small-time thieves. The contemporary focus of the group has been drug smuggling, with operations concentrated on Guatemala's border with El Salvador.

The Leones were aligned with Mexico's Gulf Cartel, generally against their established Guatemalan rivals, the Mendozas and Lorenzanas, often stealing their drug shipments.

The strength of the Leones was significantly reduced after a March 2008 gun battle with the Mexican organization *Los Zetas*. The casualties from the fight included the leader of the Leones, Juan (*Juancho*) Leon Ardon. Indeed, some analysts believe that that the Mendozas and Lorenzanas may have brought the Zetas into Guatemala, wholly or in part, to eliminate the Leon clan for stealing their narcotics shipments.[85]

Lopez Ortiz Family

Prior to his capture in 2011, Juan Alberto (*Juan Chamale*) Lopez Ortiz was considered one of the most important traffickers in Guatemala. Juan Chamale smuggled cocaine from Guatemala's Pacific coast through the province of San Marcos, across the Mexican border, delivering it principally to Mexico's Sinaloa Cartel. He also reportedly was involved in smuggling heroin produced in San Marcos into Mexico.

Huistas

In the shadows of the previously mentioned Guatemalan intermediary groups, the family-based clan known as the "Huistas" (for their geographical location in the Guatemalan department of Huehuetenango) has come to play an increasingly important role in drug smuggling through the country.

The Huistas benefitted from the strategic location of their department, which, like San Marcos, is located in the mountainous west of the country, positioning the group to smuggle cocaine and other drugs across the border into Mexico, selling them principally to Mexico's Sinaloa Cartel. Indeed, part of the business niche of the Huistas was reportedly to purchase drugs for a relatively low price near Guatemala's border with El Salvador and Honduras, then move it across the country and sell it for a profit at the border with Mexico.

The security of the operations of the Huistas has been assisted by the complex geography of the department of Huehuetenango, with each of the department's valleys a relatively isolated and often ethnically and linguistically distinct enclave, benefitting the personal relationships and working knowledge that the Huistas have reportedly built with the residents of each over the years, and making it difficult for the state to surreptitiously penetrate the zone and gain the trust of local residents to work against the group.

El Salvador–Based Transportistas

Like Honduras and Guatemala, the principal transnational organized crime groups in El Salvador are the street gangs and drug smuggling groups. The small size of the country and its relatively good transportation infrastructure has limited opportunities for intermediary groups focused on narcotics smuggling, although two such organizations can be identified in the country: the *Perrones* and the *Texis* Cartel.

Perrones

The *Perrones* are one of the two main family-based intermediary groups operating in El Salvador, believed to be responsible for moving substantial amounts of narcotics and other illicit substances through the country. As with other intermediary groups in Central America, the origins of the *Perrones* go back many years to smuggling other goods, such as cattle, which subsequently afforded them the personnel and logistics connections they needed to move narcotics through the region.[86] Indeed, the *Perrones* were once called the "cheese cartel" for their role in smuggling cheese from Honduras in a prior era, motivated by attempting to avoid import taxes on the product.

As with many of the other intermediary organizations in Central America, *Los Perrones*' principal client for the cocaine that they smuggle has been Mexico's Sinaloa Cartel, although they reportedly work with the Gulf Cartel as well.[87] The group is reportedly active not only in El Salvador but also throughout Central America from Panama to Guatemala.[88]

Since 2014, the *Perrones* have suffered a number of important losses, including the 2014 assassination of one of their leaders, Jose Natividad Luna Pereira (*Chepe Luna*), in Honduras, presumably at the hands of a rival,[89] as well as the capture of three of its key leaders, Daniel Quezada, Reynerio Flores, and Juan Colorado.[90] Nonetheless, the May 2017 arrest of José Carlos Ramírez Umanzor, mayor of Pasaquina, on drug trafficking charges involving the Perrones, illustrated that the group was still active in smuggling. Moreover, the affiliation of Umanzor with the opposition ARENA party and personal ties to previous Salvadoran presidents and other figures, highlights the high-level reach of the *Perrones* within the country.[91]

Texis Cartel

The *Texis* Cartel, like the *Perrones* is an El Salvador-based intermediary group focused on the movement of drugs through the country. By contrast to the *Perrones*, the *Texis* Cartel has maintained a lower profile, and is regarded to be somewhat better connected politically. Indeed, in 2016 El Salvador's vice president, Óscar Ortiz, was discovered to have jointly formed a real estate company, *Montecristo*, together with the head of the *Texis* Cartel, Adán Salazar Umaña (*Chepe Diablo*).[92] Similarly senior leader Umaña Samoya is the mayor of the Salvadoran town of Metapan.

The *Texis* Cartel reportedly operates principally in the northern part of El Salvador, smuggling cocaine across El Salvador's border with Honduras, then through the northeast part of the country near Metapan, and then into Guatemala.[93] Thanks, some believe, to the *Texis* Cartel's high-level connections, to date the Salvadoran government has had difficulty in prosecuting those who are believed to be the leaders of the cartel, including Chepe Diablo, Umaña Samayoa, and Roberto Herrera.[94] Nonetheless, at the end of 2016, Salvadoran attorney general Douglas Melendez, opened a long-postponed investigation against Chepe Diablo,[95] and in April 2017, he was arrested in El Salvador and charged with money laundering,[96] representing an important blow against the leadership of the group. In a demonstration of the senior-level contacts the Texis Cartel had in the Salvadoran government, the vice president of El Salvador, Oscar Ortiz, was a business partner in the company used by Chepe Diablo for his alleged money laundering activities.[97]

IDEOLOGICALLY ORIENTED GROUPS

Traditionally, scholars have treated ideologically motivated groups seeking political change in the region differently from criminal groups focused more explicitly on profit. With time, however, ideologically motivated groups in Latin America and the Caribbean have increasingly leveraged their control of territory and resources to commit violence, to raise money for their organizations through illicit activities. These include taxing groups engaged in the production of or movement of narcotics through the territory under their control, illegal logging and mining, and extorting money from legitimate companies operating in that territory in commercial sectors such as petroleum and mining. With time, some such as *Shining Path* and the *Revolutionary Armed Forces of Colombia (FARC)*, have participated directly in the production and movement of narcotics, kidnapping, and a range of other illicit businesses.

This work treats ideologically oriented groups as actors within the broader transnational criminal economy. Yet it acknowledges that their interest in overthrowing the government of the territory in which they operate (a more important and realistic goal for some groups than for others) makes their motivations, and sometimes their behaviors, different than those of other transnational criminal groups.

The current section focuses on the criminal activities of groups seeking, or recently seeking, to overthrow the state through violent means, however realistic or unrealistic such efforts may be. Although only a subset of all such groups in the region, it includes a discussion of the

FARC and the *National Liberation Army* (ELN) of Colombia, and *Shining Path* of Peru.

Revolutionary Armed Forces of Colombia (FARC)

Since its establishment in 1964, the FARC has been the principal armed group explicitly seeking the overthrow of the Colombian government, prior to signing an agreement with the Colombian government on November 24, 2016, committing to end its struggle.[98]

Although the FARC had been involved in narcotrafficking activities in areas under their control for some time, in the 7th Congress of the FARC in 1982, the group more fully embraced the use narcotrafficking as a revenue stream, significantly deepening its involvement in the business and permitting the expansion of its membership from six thousand fighters to twenty thousand in the years that followed, but for some, subverting the ideological goals of the organization with the search for profit.[99]

By the time of the peace accord with the Colombian government, according to one estimate, the FARC controlled as much as 70 percent of the coca crops in the country, as well as a significant portion of the capabilities in the region for converting coca leaf into coca base.[100] As of 2016, the group had 6,300 persons in its ranks,[101] and a total of twenty thousand when including persons affiliated with or supporting the organization,[102] when its leader Timoleón (*Timochenko*) Jiménez led the organization into a negotiated peace with the Colombian government.

On November 24, 2016, the FARC and the Colombian government signed a peace accord ending more than half a century of armed struggle (although Colombian voters had rejected a similar agreement just two months before).[103] The demobilization and disarmament process began in January 2017.[104] Among its other terms, the agreement promised to put an end to the FARC as an insurgent group and transnational criminal organization and enlist the organization's help in combatting coca growing and other illicit activity in areas previously under its control.[105] Although the FARC also committed to hand over its assets to a fund to compensate victims of the war, and the Colombian government seized approximately $100 million in FARC assets in February 2017,[106] the organization insisted that it had almost no funds, leaving unaccounted for almost $10 billion that some estimated the group had accumulated in illicit earnings.[107]

As of November 2017, there were an estimated seven hundred to one thousand dissident elements of the FARC who did not concur with the peace accords, concentrated principally in the country's most lucrative coca growing and illegal mining areas, to include Norte de Santander, Guaviare, and Nariño.[108] Such dissidents included members of the organization's Southern Block.[109] The dissidents not only were reportedly being pursued by Colombian authorities, but also had engaged in military skirmishes with their own organization.[110]

While the FARC were successfully united in concentration zones around the country, disarmed and demobilized by June 2017,[111] concerns persisted in Colombia that they had not turned over all of their arms or money. The inability of the Colombian Congress to pass all of the legislation required to implement the peace accords prior to the expiration of the period in which the Congress had special "fast track" legislative authority to do so created concern that some of the guerillas might remobilize.[112] Indeed, even prior to the implementation of the agreement, some of the FARC members were believed to be passing into the hands of their fellow guerilla group, the *Ejército de Liberación Nacional* (although by the end of 2017 the ELN had engaged in a cease fire with the government working toward its own peace accord), while others were being recruited by criminal bands who hoped to take over the criminal economy in territory that they were ceding.[113] A December 2017 clash in the western department of Chocó between dissident factions of the FARC and ELN illustrated that elements of both groups continued to act as combatants.[114]

National Liberation Army (ELN)

The National Liberation Army (ELN) is the smaller of Colombia's two principal remaining guerilla groups, with an estimated two thousand fighters. As of September 2017, when it engaged in a cease-fire as part of peace talks with the Colombian government,[115] it operated in ten of Colombia's thirty-two departments,[116] principally in the Pacific coast of the country in the departments of Nariño and Cauca, the north in Antioquia, Santander, and Norte de Santander, and the northeast, in Arauca. The ELN was formed during the political turmoil in Colombia of 1964 which also gave birth to the FARC, and formally launched in 1965 when the group overran the village of Simacota in Santander. The group is considered somewhat more ideological than the FARC, with roots in both the Maoist concept of popular war and liberation theology, as manifested in one of its early leaders, the priest Camilo Torres (who died in 1966 in his first battle).

With respect to involvement in criminal activity, the group's current and longstanding leader, Nicolás Rodríguez Bautista (*Gabino*), focused the group on kidnapping as a key source of revenue. Indeed, in the group's more than fifty years of existence, its most spectacular attacks include the kidnapping of 186 people from a church in Cali Colombia in May 1999,[117] and the hijacking of a flight by Colombia's national airline, Avianca, the same year.[118]

The ELN and FARC have coexisted, with relatively similar ideologies and sources of criminal income, in a number of parts of Colombia. Indeed, one analysis identified some sixty zones in Colombia where the FARC and ELN cohabit territory,[119] creating a concern that the demobilization of the FARC per the November 2016 peace accord would displace some of its former members to the ELN, prompting an expansion of ELN criminal activity, as well as terrorism, in the zones that they occupy.[120]

By mid-2016, the ELN was reportedly reasserting a presence in areas in which it had occupied in the 1990s, but from which it had been pushed out by the Colombian military and private militias, such as in the east of the department of Boyacá, and in Casanare.[121] During the second half of 2016, the government detected an increase in the strength of the ELN in at least nine of Colombia's thirty-two departments, including Antioquia, Nariño, Santander, Amazonas, Cauca, Tolima, Guaviare, Caquetá, and Putumayo.[122] Indeed, in the lead-up to the October 2 vote, the ELN was reported to expand in areas with strong FARC presence, such as Catatumbo and Tumaco as the FARC began to stand down from its activities there in September 2016.[123]

While the government and ELN began negotiations in Ecuador for a peace agreement in 2016 and reached a temporary cease-fire in September 2017, the decentralized nature of the ELN and the more extensive nature of its demands[124] will still make it difficult for such talks to produce a permanent agreement.[125]

Shining Path

Shining Path is a rural guerilla group principally operating in the relatively isolated Andean highlands of eastern Peru. The group derives the majority of its income from extorting peasants and criminal family clan organizations which grow coca and produce drugs in areas under its influence.[126] Its current strength is estimated at not more than several hundred people.[127]

The group was formed in the 1960s and 1970s in the Peruvian highlands by philosophy professor Abimael Guzman, espousing an ideology inspired by the revolutionary doctrine of Chinese leader Mao Zedong. *Shining Path* publicly launched its armed struggle against the Peruvian state on May 17, 1980, burning ballot boxes in the town of Chuschi, Ayacucho. From its launch, until substantially defeated by the Peruvian armed forces in the 1990s under the government of Alberto Fujimori, *Shining Path* waged a guerilla war against the Peruvian state which cost an estimated sixty-nine thousand lives.[128] At its height, the organization may have had as many as ten thousand followers.[129]

The imprisonment of Guzman in 1992, and his negotiation of a peace accord with the Peruvian state in 1993, prompted a division between remnants of the group who followed the "Guzman" line of thinking, led by Forindo Eleuterio Flores Hala (*Comrade Artemio*), concentrated in the Upper Huallaga Valley, versus the more pragmatic Quispe Palomino faction, concentrated in the Apurimac, Ene, and Mantaro river valleys (VRAEM). The latter rejected the truce with the Peruvian state agreed to by Guzman while in prison, as well as parts of his ideology. Although the Artemio faction in the upper Huallaga was the first to tax coca growing in the area under his influence as a source of revenue, it was ultimately the Quispe Palomino clan in the VRAEM that most fully exploited the drug business, and through it, grew to be the militarily more powerful of the two.[130]

By 2014, Peruvian government efforts had largely disarticulated the Artemio-led organization in the Upper Huallaga Valley, and to a lesser extent, reduced the strength of the Quispe Palomino faction in the VRAEM. Key milestones against the group include the September 2012 killing of its principal sharpshooter, Victor Hugo Castro Ramírez (*Comrade William*), in Huanta,[131] and the August 2013 killing by the government of VRAEM-based leaders Alexandro Broda Casafranca (*Comrade Alipio*) and Martin Quispe Palomino (*Comrade Gabriel*).[132]

While many of *Shining Path*'s remaining members were believed to be hiding in the inaccessible terrain of Vizcatán, there were indications that the organization was seeking to expand into the east to the province of La Convención, in an attempt to position itself to exploit petroleum companies operating the Camisea pipeline and gas fields there.[133] Its growing presence in La Convención was brought to national attention by the April 2013 kidnapping of thirty-six workers of the petroleum service company Skanska in Cusco, and a badly-executed attempt by the government to rescue them.[134]

While the deployment of the 33rd Counter-Terrorist Brigade of the Peruvian Military in La Convención in 2016 largely neutralized *Shining Path*'s advance there, some analysts believed that the organization was also attempting to expand into the adjacent province of Ucayali, a site of increasing flights carrying cocaine to neighboring Brazil.[135]

In the south of the country, a May 2016 attack by *Shining Path*, on the eve of Peru's national elections, highlighted that the group continued to have the capability to commit terrorist acts.[136] Similarly, in March 2017, the group reminded the country of its continuing presence in the VRAEM with the ambush of a patrol of soldiers near the counternarcotics base at Palmapampa.[137]

GANGS

Through the territory that they control and the manpower that they may make available to other criminal actors such as the cartels and intermediary groups, gangs in Latin America and the Caribbean play a fundamental role in the criminal economy of the region. It is a role that is continuously evolving. Although there are a variety of gangs throughout the region, this section concentrates on those in Central America, the Caribbean, and Brazil, where gangs have arguably played the most significant role in the criminal landscape.

Central American Gangs

As noted previously, Central America is dominated by two principal street gangs, Mara Salvatrucha and Barrio 18. Both have their roots in migration from the region, fleeing the violence and lack of economic opportunity associated with civil wars in El Salvador and Guatemala. During the 1980s and 1990s, many of those refugees settled in economically marginal urban neighborhoods of Los Angeles. There, as their parents or guardians often worked long hours, the children were lured to form or join street gangs as a form of solidarity and protection against the other (mostly Mexican) gangs already in the area.

Beginning in the mid-1990s, US authorities began increasing deportations of undocumented immigrants who had incurred criminal convictions during their time in the United States. Those deported arrived where they had few if any family or support networks,[138] pushing many to turn to the same gang structures that they had created in the US as an alternative form of family and support. These gangs brought to their new environment a greater level of violence and more sophisticated arms than that of the existing groups they found there. They rapidly dominated the other gangs to play a major role in the major urban areas where they established themselves. Expanded deportations from the US thus helped to transplant the MS-13 and Barrio 18 street gangs into the urban centers of Central America.[139]

A combination of factors reinforced the rapid growth of the gangs in the region. In an environment in which economic opportunity was scarce, the gang members were role models for youth of the neighborhoods; in an environment of poverty, they were the ones with fancy clothing and shoes, nice cars, and attractive women. The gangster rap culture that the *maras* brought from the United States further added to their appeal for youth seeking to express their frustration with and alienation from societies that did not seem to provide them with opportunity.[140]

The attraction of the gangs was reinforced by broken family structures in the region, with many parents having immigrated to the United States, making gang membership an alternate source of family for the youth they left behind. Once having joined the gangs, however, getting out was virtually impossible. On one hand, attempting to leave risked death or other severe retaliation by other gang members against the defectors and his or her family members. In addition, the process of joining the gang typically included initiation rites, often including committing a serious criminal act (including murder in some cases), which made the gang member feel that there was no possible return to civil society. Even for those who could overcome such obstacles to leave, gang members are often regarded as social outcasts for whom securing legitimate employment to sustain themselves outside the gang is virtually impossible.

Both Mara Salvatrucha and Barrio 18 lived principally off of extorting business owners and bus and taxi companies in neighborhoods that they dominate, as well as selling drugs there, often received for services rendered to other criminal organizations in the area, such as allowing narco-traffickers and other smugglers to move products through the area the gang controlled.[141]

Over time, the gangs have evolved in important ways. In reaction to government policies which criminalized gang membership, many of the second and third generation gang members do not use visible tattoos or other gang symbols, as their predecessors had, or they display those symbols in less visible locations such as in eyebrows or on the inside of their lip. Over time as well, as gangs expanded and acquired commercial establishments as a product of prolonged interactions with the businesses that they were extorting, gangs began sending selected members to college to study for careers in areas such as law and business, to serve the gangs in defending their organizations and running the newly acquired businesses. In some cases, those gang members also attempted to enter police academies and the military.[142] In other cases, members of the armed forces joined the gangs after getting out, or were paid or intimidated into working with the gangs to train their members in military tactics and the use of military-grade firearms. Yet despite stories about the gangs receiving paramilitary training in rural camps,[143] the level of military sophistication of most gang cells remains modest.

The evolving capabilities of the gangs, and their potential ties to both transnational organized crime and terrorist groups, is of concern. Operations by a small number of cells of Central American street gangs that demonstrate familiarity with military tactics, plus indications that some have sought and received training in military tactics and the use of military-grade arms, has drawn the attention of authorities.[144]

There is also some evidence of cooperation between the gangs and the radical islamic group Hezbollah to launder money, as well as at least one meeting between gang members and the terrorist group al Qaeda,[145] although there is a vigorous dispute between scholars regarding the existence of such ties.[146]

Estimates of the size of the gangs in the Northern Triangle relative to the population vary among the three nations of the region. In 2012, the United Nations Office on Drugs and Crime (UNODC) estimated conservatively that El Salvador had twenty thousand gang members, Honduras had twelve thousand, and Guatemala had twenty-two thousand, yet El Salvador was estimated to have the worst gang problem relative to the size of its population, with an estimated 323 gang members per 100,000 people.[147] In Honduras and Guatemala, the situation is particularly grave in the major urban areas of those countries, including Tegucigalpa-Comayagüela San Pedro Sula and Guatemala City.

Within the Northern Triangle, the situation of the gangs vis-à-vis other groups differs by country. In Salvador, the gangs are generally considered to be more powerful than the local intermediary groups, whereas in Guatemala, the narcotraffickers have largely managed to keep the maras under control, save for the impoverished urban areas around the capital where the majority of their membership resides.

In the case of both Mara Salvatrucha and Barrio 18, the basic gang structure is the local clique (*clica* in spanish), of which there are an estimated 560 in Salvador alone, although the way that those clica were integrated into higher-level organizations was different for each gang. In Salvador, for example, as of 2016, MS-13 was believed to be divided into 360 clicas, organized into ninety-six "programs," while the two hundred clicas of B-18 clicas are organized as thirty-five "tribes."[148]

Although MS-13 and B-18 also operate in other Central American countries including Nicaragua, Costa Rica, and Panama, they are far less prevalent there. The difference, in part, is because these countries sent only a limited number of refugees to the United States, and thus were less affected by the deportations of undocumented immigrants with criminal records in the 1990s and 2000s. In the case of Costa Rica and Panama, the two countries are relatively more prosperous, and did not suffer civil wars like their counterparts to the North.[149] In the case of Nicaragua, the relatively greater degree of social control that the communist Sandinistas imposed on the neighborhoods of the country is also believed to have played a role.

Given that the spread of both MS-13 and B-18 throughout the Northern Triangle was fueled in part by the expanded deportation of Central American immigrants from the United States in the early 2000s, the new wave of expanded deportations initiated under the Trump administration in the US, in combination with the termination of "Temporary Protected Status" allowing some 260,000 Honduran and Salvadoran immigrants to live and work legally in the country, creates the danger of a further expansion of a wave of new recruits for the maras in the region.

Mara Salvatrucha

Of the two major street gangs in the northern triangle, Mara Salvatrucha (MS-13) has shown itself to be somewhat more sophisticated and unified than its counterpart, Barrio-18, at least in El Salvador. Indeed, in October 2012, reflecting the growing capability and international sophistication of some parts of MS-13, the US Treasury Department Office of Foreign Assets Control (OFAC) designated Mara Salvatrucha as a transnational criminal organization.[150]

In the neighborhoods that it dominates in Salvador and Honduras, Mara Salvatrucha reportedly concentrates its extortion on the bus and taxi companies, to minimize alienation of the residents of the neighborhoods. The group is also reportedly more disposed than its rival Barrio 18 to allow police and others to enter those neighborhoods without resistance, helping it to avoid unnecessary conflict with authorities.[151]

The MS-13 organization is divided up into a series of "programs," below which fall the basic gang unit, the "clicas." While the clicas are guided by the gang leadership, they may exercise considerable autonomy on day-to-day issues. Within the clicas, MS-13 members are referred to as "soldiers," highlighting their aspiration in at least some respects, to the group's distorted concept of military life.

Within El Salvador, MS-13 is comprised of fifty-eight programs, organized by four territorial divisions: the western, central, paracentral, and eastern. There is considerable variation among these entities, with fifteen reported to have "transnational character" (e.g., conducting international narcotrafficking operations) and the other forty-three having a more "national" character.[152]

In El Salvador, most of the gang's top leaders are reportedly in prison, although their lieutenants on the outside (known as *"ranfleros libres"*) continue to coordinate with them to conduct gang business.

A limited number of clicas of Mara Salvatrucha have become directly involved in the international drug business, including some shipments of drugs between El Salvador and the United States by clicas affiliated with the Normandie and Fulton programs. As of 2017, members of the Fulton program were reportedly involved in moving drugs along El Salvador's Pacific coast. Indeed, some analysts are concerned that in El Salvador, Mara Salvatrucha is reaching the level of sophistication in the drug trade that it is reaching out to the Mexican cartels to transport drugs through the region, rather than limiting itself to interactions with the local smuggling groups. It was arguably no coincidence that the two Mara Salvatrucha programs that had become wealthy and independent through their involvement in narcotrafficking (Fullton and Normandie) were the principal actors behind an initiative to launch a new gang faction, the "MS-503" (named for the telephone area code of the country).[153]

Mara Salvatrucha has also shown willingness to use terrorist tactics to intimidate businessmen and government officials. In September 2015, for example, members of the gang rigged an explosive to detonate outside the Salvadoran finance ministry.[154] Members of the gang have also been accused of meeting with members of Islamic terrorist organizations, including one believed meeting between MS-13 leaders and al Qaeda operative Adnan El Shukrijumah in July 2004 in Honduras,[155] although evidence that such contacts occur on a significant, ongoing basis is limited.

In El Salvador, following an explosion of gang-related violence in 2015 and 2016, a new strategy by the government to counter the gangs, and evidence of expanded assassinations of gang members by "death squads," Mara Salvatrucha, along with the Sureños faction of Barrio 18, expressed an interest in negotiating with the government to dismantle its organization in the country, in exchange for economic and social benefits for its members,[156] but as of early 2017, such talks had not gone forward.

In El Salvador, Mara Salvatrucha is almost twice the size of Barrio 18. In Guatemala and Honduras, by contrast, Barrio 18 is somewhat bigger than Mara Salvatrucha.

Barrio 18

Like Mara Salvatrucha, Barrio 18 is concentrated principally in the states of the Northern Triangle, and earns its revenues principally through extortion, and secondarily, the sale of drugs and other criminal activities.

The organization of Barrio 18 is somewhat simpler than that of MS-13. At the top is a leadership group known as "the wheel" or "the 12 apostles." Below these, it is organized into "tribes," which are divided into "canchas," (the equivalent of clicas), which like their counterparts in MS-13, are comprised of "soldiers."

In the case of El Salvador, but not the other nations of the Northern Triangle, Barrio 18 is split into two factions, the *Revolucionarios* and the *Sureños*. The split was reportedly caused by an incident which occurred in 2013 in a San Salvador nightclub, "Caesar's Palace," as well as a dispute regarding the distribution of the earnings of the group by its leadership.[157]

By contrast to Mara Salvatrucha, Barrio 18 is reportedly more disposed to extort protection money from local businesses, although both regularly extort taxi and bus companies whose vehicles transit the areas they control. It is also reportedly more likely to violently resist attempts by police and other government authorities to enter the neighborhoods that it dominates.

In March 2016, the growing capabilities of Barrio 18 were highlighted by their use of a small remotely detonated explosive device on an inner-city bus in Guatemala City, killing five people, presumably for a failure to pay the extortion routinely demanded of the operators of such buses.[158]

The use of the device, remotely detonated by a cell phone, also highlighted the diffusion of such dangerous, yet relatively easy-to-acquire technology, into the hands of the gangs. Indeed, the March 2016 remotely detonated bus bomb was not the first time the maras had used such devices. In 2010, also in Guatemala, Barrio 18 used a remotely detonated device to blow up a car in an administrative building of a prison facility. In El Salvador, in 2011, another bomb, also believed to have been detonated remotely, exploded in a public bus.[159]

Panama Groups

By contrast to the Northern Triangle, in both Panama and Costa Rica, the criminal landscape features a relatively large number of smaller gangs, without a significant presence of Mara Salvatrucha or Barrio 18.[160] Nonetheless, the growing international reach of Panama's gangs, and their role in transnational criminal activities, merits discussion.

In Panama, as of mid-2016, the national police had identified 204 gangs, divided into two loose federations: *Bagdad*, and *Calor Calor*.[161] The two groupings are believed to be relatively similar in size, with a total of eight hundred members in each. Both federations feature some specialization among members, with some gangs focused more on kidnapping, others on moving or selling drugs within the areas they control, and others on extortion. The Bagdad federation is believed to be a more hierarchical organization, with one leader on top and more pronounced functional and territorial divisions between member gangs. By contrast, *Calor Calor* has a flatter organization, with constituent gangs sometimes competing with each other in the same geography.[162]

As in other parts of Central America, the majority of the gang leaders in both federations have been put in jail, yet doing so has not decisively impeded the functioning of the groups.

As with Mara Salvatrucha in Salvador, with the shifting narcotrafficking landscape in the region, including the expanded use of the southern part of Central America to move drugs, Panamanian gangs are increasingly becoming involved in narcotrafficking.[163] As of late 2016, however, their role still centered on selling drugs and taxing the movement of drugs through areas under their control.[164]

Caribbean Groups

In the Caribbean, the gang scene has not yet become dominated by a small number of powerful groups, as has occurred in the Northern Triangle. As in the Northern Triangle, however, Caribbean gangs are generally connected to transnational organized crime through selling drugs in areas under their control, and in some cases, providing criminal services to transnational criminal organizations such as smuggling drugs and people.

In the Caribbean, as in Central America, connections to communities of co-nationals living in the United States has facilitated some transnational drug connections from those countries to the US, particularly in cities with large populations from the Caribbean, including New York City and Miami.

Jamaica

In Jamaica, as in the south of Central America, there are a relatively large number of gangs, each engaged in a range of criminal activities, from narcotrafficking to the "lottery scandal" targeting the US market.[165] There are reportedly over 270 gangs in Jamaica's neighborhoods. Significant groups include the Stone Crushers,[166] the Clansmen, and One Order, a gang with origins in a failed messianic attempt to unify all gangs in the country.[167]

In Jamaica, the gangs have a longstanding linkage to politics which is relatively unique to the region. Politicians from the nation's two post-independence parties, the Jamaica Labor Party (JLP) and the People's National Party (PNP), historically funded affiliated community leaders in the nation's poor neighborhoods to deliver votes for them. Those "bosses," in turn, created organizations which became involved in narcotrafficking and other organized crime activities.[168]

The group that is perhaps best known outside Jamaica is the now-defunct "Shower Possie," whose leader Dudus Coke, came to have a powerful narcotrafficking operation from the neighborhood that he was "boss" of, Tivoli Gardens, with linkages to fellow gang members in New York and Miami, among other places. The extent of his power and control over the local community was demonstrated in May 2010 when gunmen loyal to Coke attacked police stations throughout Kingston to protest an attempt to arrest and extradite Coke to the United States on drug charges. The crisis devolved into a siege of Tivoli Gardens by supporters of Coke, with his supporters barricading the neighborhood to fight off authorities, as well as orchestrating supporting uprisings in multiple other neighborhoods outside Tivoli Gardens.[169] Following Coke's arrest and extradition, his group, the Shower Possie, was disbanded by authorities, and similar groups around Jamaica sought to lower their profile.[170]

Dominican Republic

In the Dominican Republic, as in Jamaica, there are a relatively large number of smaller gangs, including some transplanted from major urban areas in the United States such as New York, where large numbers of Dominicans live. These include groups such as the Bloods, Crypts, Folk, and Latin Kings. In addition, there are a number of locally grown Dominican gangs, including Los Dorados or Los Cielos. As with gangs in Central America and other parts of the Caribbean, the criminal activity of gangs in the Dominican Republic principally concentrates on extortion, petty crime, and selling drugs within the areas under their control.[171] Yet as in Jamaica, the connection between the Dominican Republic and the Dominican diasporas in Miami and New York facilitate linkages used by

Dominican Republic-based gangs to smuggle drugs into the United States.

Brazilian Groups

As demand for drugs in Brazil has expanded, thanks to that nation's position as a transit route to Europe and its growing prosperity, gangs in the nation's major cities, particularly Rio de Janeiro and São Paolo, have come to occupy a role similar to that of urban street gangs in the Northern Triangle, exercising de facto control over the slums (*favelas*) of Brazilian cities, and through that control, selling drugs and conducting other illicit business.

By contrast to gangs of the Northern Triangle, the most powerful of the Brazilian gangs, including the First Capital Command (PCC), have developed international criminal operations, particularly smuggling drugs and money laundering. Nonetheless, despite having some characteristics of cartels, they are nonetheless included in the present section on gangs.

First Capital Command

The First Capital Command (PCC) is one of South America's largest criminal organizations, with an estimated twenty thousand members and annual earnings of $40 billion.[172] Although the organization is centered in São Paulo, it has some presence in all of Brazil's twenty-seven states, and is reportedly expanding across the northeast,[173] and into other parts of the country. Indeed, a substantial part of the violence in the favelas of Rio de Janeiro in 2017 was related to the expansion of the PCC, including "wars" to control turf between its surrogate groups, and those of its rivals.[174]

The *PCC* was formed by prison inmates in Carandiru prison in São Paulo, initially as a self-defense and advocacy organization in response to conditions leading to the murders of over one hundred prisoners in the facility in October 1992. The formation of the *PCC* was also inspired by the formation of the group *Red Command* in Rio de Janeiro in the 1970s. *Red Command* became powerful both inside and out of prison, emerging into the public light in 2001 with a coordinated prison riot, forcing the shutdown of twenty-nine prison facilities across São Paulo state. The group further demonstrated its power and captured international attention in May 2006 when it launched a coordinated series of two hundred and fifty attacks inside seventy prisons across São Paulo state, including the taking of hostages, and ultimately resulting in 115 deaths before Brazilian authorities were forced to negotiate with the gang's imprisoned leadership to bring the violence under control.[175] Arguably the wave of violence within Brazilian prisons in January 2017 reflected a breakdown in a de facto truce between the PCC and its rival, Comando Vemehlo, and the surrogates of both groups, within Brazilian prisons.[176]

Beyond its activities in Brazil, the PRC is also one of the South American groups with the greatest international reach, with significant operations in Paraguay, Bolivia, and Peru, as well as Brazil. Reflecting the increasing importance of drug routes from Peru through the Brazilian Amazon, by 2017, the *PCC* reportedly had a presence in seven states in the region.[177] The *PCC* imports marijuana into Brazil from Paraguay, and imports coca from Bolivia to Brazil, before shipping that which is not consumed locally onto Europe.

Beyond narcotrafficking, the *PCC* is also arguably the most advanced of the Brazilian groups with respect to money laundering, with international ties that include the radical Shia Islamic organization Hezbollah,[178] as well as to Chinese banks.[179]

As of early 2017, most of the group's foundational leaders were in prison, although believed to continue to manage their organization from behind bars. Nevertheless, one, Fabiano Alvez de Souza (*Paca*), is at large, thought to be working out of the Paraguayan city of Pedro Juan Caballero, on the border with Brazil.[180]

Red Command

The *Red Command* (CV) is the oldest of Brazil's major gangs. It had its origin in the 1970s in cells of communists within prisons in Brazil's Rio de Janeiro state which organized as a left-wing militia within the Candido Mendes prison, but later abandoned most of its ideology to focus on organized crime. By 1979, the group was operating in the slums of Rio de Janeiro and elsewhere in the country.

As with gangs in Central America counterparts, the ability of *Red Command* to continue to operate over the long term was a function of the ability of gang leaders in prison to maintain a communication with and discipline over members both inside and outside. As with the gangs of Central America, *Red Command* sells cocaine and other drugs in slums under its control, principally in Rio de Janeiro. As the demand for drugs in Brazil grew, the group's dominance of the narcotics markets in Rio was challenged by various breakaway factions and emergent groups: initially by the *Third Command* in the mid-1980s, and later by Friends of Friends (*Amigos dos Amigos*) in the 1990s.[181] As with the First Capital Command, the group is involved in narcotrafficking and other activities in neighboring Paraguay and Bolivia. *Red Command*'s presence in the latter was highlighted in September 2015, when two of its members were caught attempting to take off for Brazil from a clandestine airstrip near Santa Rosa, Bolivia with 400 kilograms of cocaine hydrochloride.[182] Red Command is believed to have a relatively decentralized structure. Prominent leaders include Luiz Fernando da Costa (*Fernandinho Beira-Mar*)[183] and Luis

Claudio Machado *(Marreta)*, who was captured in December 2014 in Paraguay by the Paraguayan Anti-Drug Secretariat (SENAD).[184]

Third Pure Command

The Third Pure Command (TCP) is a Rio de Janeiro-based street gang focused principally on drug sales and extortion in the territory which it controls. As of 2017, the group is loosely aligned with the *Red Command*, and opposed to *Amigos dos Amigos*. The group's current alliances reflect its origins in the mid-1980s: The group *Third Command* split from *Red Command* and became its rival for control of the drug market in Rio de Janeiro. In 2002, TCP, under Nei da Conseicao Cruz *(Facão)*, split from *Third Command*, creating *Third Pure Command,* loosely aligned with *Red Command* opposing both Third Command and *Amigos dos Amigos*. Facão was captured and put in prison in 2009, with leadership eventually assumed by Fernando Gomes de Freitas *(Fernandinho Guarabu)*.[185]

Friends of Friends

The group Friends of Friends *(Amigos do Amigos,* in Portuguese) is principally based in Rio de Janeiro, with a focus on drug trafficking and sales. It was established in 1998 as a by Celso Luis Rodrigues *(Celsinho da Vila Vintem)* and Ernaldo Pinto de Medeiros *(Ue)* as a faction breaking away from *Third Command*, just as *Third Command* itself had split from the *Red Command* in the mid-1980s. In both cases, the act of breaking away reflected the ambitions of junior leaders within the larger group who saw an opportunity to establish a niche in supplying the expanding Brazilian narcotics market on their own.

Friends of Friends captured national attention in October 2009 when it engaged in a gun battle with its rival the *Red Command* over the *Morro dos Macacos* favela of Rio de Janeiro, leading to the crash of a police helicopter.[186] The principal leader of the group, Antonio Francisco Bonfim Lopes *(Nem)*, reportedly was the principal authority in the slum of Rocinha in his heyday,[187] but was arrested in November 2011, and has been in prison since that time.[188]

Friends of Friends is believed to have approximately three hundred members, concentrated principally in the favelas of the north and west of Rio, including Rocinha. Despite the incarceration of *Nem*, the persistent influence of the group in Rocinha was dramatically illustrated in October 2017, when one of Nem's previous lieutenants, *Rogerio 157*, defected to rival group Comando Vemehlo,[189] setting off a battle for control, and obliging the Brazilian military to deploy almost one thousand troops to the favela.[190]

As with other gangs, the group maintains some influence in the slums in which it operates by using part of its narcotics income to provide some social services, as well as throwing parties for residents. *Friends of Friends* is not, however, as international in its activities as the *PCC*.[191]

CONCLUSIONS

This chapter highlights a number of patterns and common elements among the transnational organized crime groups in the region.

First, not only do such groups rely on a combination of legitimate and illicit earnings, but also in some cases, such as with *Mara Salvatrucha* and *Barrio 18*, engagement in some illicit activities, such as extortion, increases the group's portfolio of legitimate economic activities, as the extorting groups inherit the companies that could not pay, and become the operators themselves.

Second, whatever the official posture of the group, its objectives are often a mixture between pure revenue seeking, and other goals, and that mixture tends to evolve with and shape the group.

As seen in the discussion of the FARC and ELN, as well as *Shining Path*, groups that nominally pursue ideological goals are generally tempted or forced to seek illicit financing, which changes the orientation of the group itself over time. The involvement of the Quispe Palomino faction of *Sendero Luminoso* in narcotrafficking, for example, made it militarily stronger than its counterpart in the Upper Huallaga Valley which had chosen to follow the ideological line of Abimael Guzman, and that addiction to drug money, in turn, made it more independent from its ideological base. Similarly, the decision by the FARC in the 7th Party Congress in 1982 to become involved in narcotrafficking arguably freed it, in part, from having to develop, and be influenced by, the positions of its followers.

To some degree, the reverse of the transformation of ideologically oriented groups by money may also occur. Pure money-making groups seek political power, either to protect their operations and earnings, or as a reflection of the personal ambition of the leader and desire for legitimization that comes with wealth.

Third, this chapter suggests that both the goals and culture of the group help to determine the business model it adopts. Some, such as the FARC, ELN, or Sendero Luminoso, engage in extortion because their political ambitions drive them to seek to influence territory, naturally extorting those who live within that territory as a revenue stream. On the other hand, groups such as Mara Salvatrucha and Barrio 18 also use extortion as a principal money earning scheme, not because they have political goals, but because their tradition of occupying and dominating neighborhoods leads them to extortion as a tool for raising money in the areas that they control. Reciprocally, intermediary groups, whose origin is in smuggling, may be more inclined to move and transform illicit products, rather than threatening local populations, as their key revenue source, although each of these imperatives may evolve, with changes in the power, leadership, and culture of the group over time.

Fourth, the ideological character of some criminal groups is not necessarily related to the realism of the goals. While some groups, such as the FARC, have had, during periods of their existence, somewhat realistic hopes of overthrowing the governments to which they were opposed, others, such as the EPP and ACA in Paraguay or the EZLN and EPR in Mexico, have never had more than a tiny number of followers, making such goals unrealistic at best. Nonetheless, these groups cling on to these goals, however unrealistic, because it legitimizes their existence, and the conduct of illegal activities in support of those goals.

Finally, with the increasing effectiveness of governments in the region against transnational criminal groups, there is a discernable tendency toward a greater number of smaller groups. The ability of modern law enforcement to identify and target the heads of large, multinational organizations, and the interest of both internal and external rivals to challenge those leaders if they appear weakened by state action against them, all work against the persistence of large hierarchical organized crime groups for long periods of time. On the other hand, modern communication technology, including the ability to globally transfer money and coordinate the movement of goods, makes it ever easier for small organizations to work together to sustain complex illicit supply chains, such as smuggling drugs or people, simply by following profit signals, even without an overarching authority to manage the activity. Indeed, the idea that a rational criminal economy can emerge from many small groups each pursuing their own profit in an information-rich environment suggests that combatting international illicit flows will become ever more challenging for states. It will become ever less about taking down kingpins, and ever more about disrupting networks, suggesting the need for a shift in strategy.

Equally worrying, empirical evidence to date suggests that a larger number of smaller criminal entities means greater uncertainty and competition between groups, and on average, less experienced leaders more disposed to violence and error. In short, the criminal economy in the region may be evolving in a way that renders old leadership-targeting strategies ever less effective, while generating tendencies for ever more violent, chaotic outcomes.

NOTES

1. This chapter recognizes the applicability of the categorization scheme to extra-regionally based groups, but will treat them separately.
2. David A. Shirk, *The Drug War in Mexico: Confronting a Shared Threat* (New York, Council on Foreign Relations, 2011).

3. John Bailey, *The Politics of Crime in Mexico: Democratic Governance in a Security Trap* (Boulder, CO: Lynne Rienner, 2014).
4. John Bailey and Jorge Chabat, Eds., *Transnational Crime and Public Security: Challenges to Mexico and the United States* (Boulder, CO: Lynne Rienner, 2002).
5. Nathan P. Jones, *Mexico's Illicit Drug Networks and the State Reaction* (Washington D.C.: Georgetown University Press, 2016).
6. Interview with Mexican security official, Mexico City, February 2016.
7. E. Eduardo Castillo, "Reportan hasta 80 carteles del narco en México," *Yahoo*, December 18, 2012, https://www.yahoo.com/news/reportan-hasta-80-carteles-del-narco-en-m-175244606.html.
8. Luciano Campos Garza, "Hay 280 organizaciones criminales en México," *Proceso*, July 24, 2017, http://www.proceso.com.mx/496191/280-organizaciones-criminales-en-mexico-revela-alcalde-san-pedro-nl.
9. Phil Gast, Catherine E. Shoichet, and Evan Perez, "Extradited 'El Chapo' Guzman Arrives in US; Hearing Set for Friday," *CNN*, January 20, 2017, http://www.cnn.com/2017/01/19/us/el-chapo-guzman-turned-over-to-us/index.html.
10. Christopher Woody, "'El Chapo' Guzmán's Key Role in the Global Cocaine Trade Is Becoming Clearer," *Business Insider*, August 6, 2015, http://www.businessinsider.com/the-sinaloa-cartel-and-colombian-cocaine-2015-8.
11. Madison Park, "Mexico's Most Notorious Drug Cartels," *CNN*, August 18, 2016, http://www.cnn.com/2016/08/18/americas/mexican-drug-cartels/.
12. Patrick Woody, "There's a Sinister Theory for Why the Mexican Government Can't Take Down Fugitive Drug Lord 'El Chapo' Guzmán," *Business Insider*, December 21, 2015, http://www.businessinsider.com/mexican-government-sinaloa-cartel-cooperation.
13. Interview with Mexican security official, Mexico City, February 2016.
14. Patrick J. McDonnell, Kate Linthicum, and Del Quentin Wilber, "Drug Lord 'El Chapo' Extradited to the United States, *Los Angeles Times*, January 19, 2017, http://www.latimes.com/world/la-fg-el-chapo-extradition-20170119-story.html.
15. Emanuella Grinberg and Rafael Romo, "Official: Son of 'El Chapo' Has Been Kidnapped," *CNN*, August 17, 2016, http://www.cnn.com/2016/08/16/americas/el-chapo-son-kidnapped-official-says/index.html.
16. "Report: 'El Chapo' Guzman's Sons Wounded in Cartel Attack," *ABC News*, February 9, 2017, http://abcnews.go.com/International/wireStory/report-el-chapo-guzmans-sons-wounded-cartel-attack-45363829.
17. "Treasury Sanctions Five Businesses Supporting Cartel De Jalisco Nueva Generacion," US Department of the Treasury, Official Website, September 17, 2015, https://www.treasury.gov/press-center/press-releases/Pages/jl0168.aspx.
18. Veronica Calderon, "Una ofensiva del narco en México derriba un helicóptero militar," *El Pais*, May 2, 2016, http://internacional.elpais.com/internacional/2015/05/01/actualidad/1430505154_355398.html.
19. "México: Matan a 15 policías en una emboscada en Jalisco," *BBC*, April 7, 2015, http://www.bbc.com/mundo/ultimas_noticias/2015/04/150407_ult-not_mexico_policias_mueren_emboscada_bd.
20. "Derriban helicóptero de Sedena en Jalisco; mueren 3 militares," *Nacional*, May 1, 2015, http://diario.mx/Nacional/2015-05-01_7cfde641/derriban-helicoptero-de-sedena-en-jalisco-mueren-3-militares/.
21. Ruben Mosso, "Invade cartel de Jalisco ocho estados y el DF," *Milenio*, April 20, 2015, http://www.milenio.com/policia/PGR-predominante_cartel_de_Jalisco_Nueva_Generacion-carteles_del_narcotrafico_0_503349665.html.
22. Bernardo Cisneros, "Pugna entre cartels de Jalisco y Sinaloa deja 5 muertos en Tijauana," *Milenio*, December 13, 2016, http://www.milenio.com/policia/muerte_tijuana-baja_california-cartel_sinaloa-jalisco_nueva_generacion-milenio_0_865113674.html.

23. "As Cartels Renew Battle, Violence in Border City of Ciudad Juarez Spikes Again," *Fox News*, November 4, 2016, http://www.foxnews.com/world/2016/11/04/as-cartels-renew-battle-violence-in-border-city-ciudad-juarez-spikes-again.html.

24. Guadalupe Correa-Cabrera, *Los Zetas Inc.: Criminal Corporations, Energy, and Civil War in Mexico* (Austin: University of Texas Press, 2017).

25. "Los Escorpiones, terrible escolta de Tormenta," *El Universal*, November 5, 2010, http://archivo.eluniversal.com.mx/notas/721570.html.

26. Ioan Grillo, *El Narco: En el corazón de la insurgencia criminal Mexicana* (Mexico City: Tendencias, 2012).

27. "Former Mexican Drug Cartel Leader Extradited to US: Justice Department," *Reuters*, December 19, 2017, https://www.reuters.com/article/us-usa-mexico-drugs/former-mexican-drug-cartel-leader-extradited-to-u-s-justice-department-idUSKBN1EE01B.

28. Andre Valencia, "Cartel Jalisco Nueva Generación va por 'territorios' de Los Zetas en Tamaulipas ante caída del Z42," *Blog del Narco*, March 2015, http://www.blogdelnarco.mx/2015/03/cartel-jalisco-nueva-generacion-va-por.html.

29. Sergio Caballero, "En narcomantas, Los Zetas se atribuyen ataque al Blue Parrot," *El Proceso*, January 17, 2017, http://www.proceso.com.mx/470454/en-narcomantas-los-zetas-se-atribuyen-ataque-al-blue-parrot.

30. Cisneros, "Pugna entre cartels."

31. "As Cartels Renew Battle."

32. Alejandro Dominguez, "Estrategias en Michoacán comenzaron en 2006 y siguen," *Milenio*, January 13, 2014, http://www.milenio.com/politica/seguridad-estrategias_Michoacan-Calderon_Michoacan-Pena_Nieto_Michoacan-violencia_0_226177863.html.

33. William Finnegan, "Silver or Lead: The Drug Cartel La Familia Gives Local Officials a Choice: Take a Bribe or a Bullet," *The New Yorker*, May 31, 2010, http://www.newyorker.com/magazine/2010/05/31/silver-or-lead.

34. "'El cártel de Los Caballeros Templarios está totalmente desmembrado'," *Univision*, March 8, 2015, https://www.univision.com/noticias/noticias-de-mexico/el-cartel-de-los-caballeros-templarios-esta-totalmente-desmembrado.

35. Laura Ávila, "AUC," *Insight Crime*, https://www.insightcrime.org/colombia-organized-crime-news/auc-profile/.

36. For a good discussion of the evolution of Colombia's militias following the takedown of the Medellin and Cali cartels, see Sarah Zukerman Daly, *Organized Violence after Civil War* (New York: Cambridge University Press, 2016).

37. "Country Fast Facts: Colombia," *CBS News*, September 17, 2007, http://www.cbsnews.com/news/country-fast-facts-colombia-3268352/.

38. An excellent discussion of this phenomenon is provided by Daly, 2016.

39. Jeremy McDermott, "Colombia's BACRIM Count More Than 3400 Fighters," *Insight Crime*, September 8, 2014, http://www.insightcrime.org/news-briefs/colombia-bacrim-count-more-than-3400-fighters.

40. Ellis and Ortiz, "Un acuerdo entre interrogantes."

41. David Gagne, "Who Are the Urabeños Leaders Indicted by the US?," *Insight Crime*, June 24, 2015, http://www.insightcrime.org/news-analysis/us-indicts-17-leaders-of-urabenos.

42. "Primer bombardeo directo a banda criminal: mueren 12 del 'clan Úsuga,'" *El Tiempo*, November 3, 2015, http://www.eltiempo.com/politica/justicia/clan-usuga-bombardeo-en-choco/16419814.

43. "Clan del Golfo recluta a guerrilleros de las Farc por $1,8 millones: Fiscal General," *El Heraldo*, January 25, 2016, http://www.elheraldo.co/colombia/clan-del-golfo-recluta-guerrilleros-de-las-farc-por-18-millones-fiscal-general-322884.

44. Eduardo Garcia, "Abatido alias Gavilán,segundo al mando del Clan del Golfo," *El Heraldo*, August 31, 2017, https://www.elheraldo.co/colombia/abatido-alias-gavilan-segundo-al-mando-del-clan-del-golfo-398185.

45. "Colombia: Abatieron a Luis Orlando Padierna Peña alias 'Inglaterra,' el número dos del Clan del Golfo," *InfoBae*, November 23, 2017, https://www.infobae.com/america/colombia/2017/11/23/colombia-abatieron-a-luis-orlando-padierna-pena-alias-inglaterra-el-numero-dos-del-clan-del-golfo/.

46. "Alias 'Otoniel' y otros 1.500 hombres del Clan del Golfo se someterían a la justiciar," *Caracol*, September 11, 2017, https://noticias.caracoltv.com/colombia/alias-otoniel-y-otros-1500-hombres-del-clan-del-golfo-se-someterian-la-justicia.

47. "Los Rastrojos se están fortaleciendo en territorio venezolano, alerta la FIP," *El Espectador*, July 16, 2017, https://www.elespectador.com/noticias/judicial/los-rastrojos-se-estan-fortaleciendo-en-territorio-venezolano-alerta-la-fip-articulo-703454.

48. Aaron Daugherty, "Has Colombia's Next Narco Boss Emerged?" *Insight Crime*, November 2, 2015, http://www.InsightCrime.org/news-briefs/colombia-next-narco-boss-puntilla-pachon.

49. Frédéric Massé, "La entrega del Erpac," *El Espectador*, December 21, 2011, https://www.elespectador.com/noticias/judicial/entrega-del-erpac-articulo-318004.

50. Mimi Yagoub, "Colombia's Eastern Plains Up for Grabs after Drug Lord Capture," *Insight Crime*, March 1, 2016, http://www.InsightCrime.org/news-briefs/colombia-eastern-plains-up-for-grabs-after-drug-lord-capture.

51. See, for example, Quenton King, "$350 Billion Lost to Corruption in Venezuela: Expert," *Insight Crime*, March 22, 2016, http://www.insightcrime.org/news-briefs/350-billion-lost-to-corruption-venezuela-official.

52. "Cartel de los Soles," *Insight Crime*, accessed August 30, 2016, http://www.InsightCrime.org/venezuela-organized-crime-news/cartel-de-los-soles-profile.

53. Manuel Rodriguez, "Ex-agente de la DEA: Reverol es líder en el Cártel de los Soles," *Noticias Venezuela*, August 2, 2016, http://noticiasvenezuela.org/2016/08/02/ex-agente-de-la-dea-reverol-es-lider-en-el-cartel-de-los-soles/.

54. "Cartel de los Soles."

55. "Venezuela."

56. Vyas and Forero, "Top Venezuelan Bodyguard."

57. Kay Guerrero, Claudia Dominguez, and Catherine E. Shoichet, "Venezuelan President Nicolas Maduro's Family Members Iindicted in US Court," *CNN*, November 12, 2015, http://www.cnn.com/2015/11/11/americas/venezuela-president-family-members-arrested/index.html.

58. Ellis, "Honduras: A Pariah State."

59. "Cachiros," *Insight Crime*, accessed August 30, 2016, http://www.InsightCrime.org/honduras-organized-crime-news/cachiros.

60. Cooper and Lacey, "In a Coup in Honduras."

61. "Treasury Targets Los Cachiros Drug Trafficking Organization in Honduras," US Department of the Treasury, September 19, 2013, https://www.treasury.gov/press-center/press-releases/Pages/jl2168.aspx.

62. "Continental hipotecó bienes de Los Cachiros," *El Heraldo*, October 19, 2015, http://www.elheraldo.hn/pais/892193–214/continental-hipotec%C3%B3-bienes-de-los-cachiros.

63. Hondurans consulted for this study believe that the men believed that they would have a higher probability of survival within the US justice system, than facing justice in Honduras.

64. Ana Melgar, "Narcotraficante hondureño señala a hermano de presidente Juan Orlando Hernández," *CNN*, March 17, 2017, http://cnnespanol.cnn.com/2017/03/17/narcotraficante-hondureno-senala-a-hermano-de-presidente-juan-orlando-hernandez/.

65. See, for example, Jacobo G. Garcia, "'El 'Chapo Guzmán' podría encontrarse en Honduras'," *El Mundo*, November 20, 2013, http://www.elmundo.es/internacional/2013/11/19/528bbd5261fd3d914e8b457a.html.

66. "Valles," *Insight Crime*, accessed August 30, 2016, http://www.InsightCrime.org/honduras-organized-crime-news/lvalles.

67. Ellis, "Honduras: A Pariah State."

68. "Digna Valle, la mujer que pone en jaque al cartel de Sinaloa," *La Prensa*, October 7, 2014, http://www.laprensa.hn/inicio/755263-417/digna-valle-la-mujer-que-pone-en-jaque-al-cartel-de-sinaloa.

69. . "Leaders of Honduran Drug Cartel Face Federal Drug and Money Laundering Charges in the Eastern District of Virginia," Federal Bureau of Investigation Official Website, December 19, 2014, https://www.fbi.gov/washingtondc/press-releases/2014/leaders-of-honduran-drug-cartel-face-federal-drug-and-money-laundering-charges-in-the-eastern-district-of-virginia.

70. "Autorizan extradición a EUA de José Inocente Valle y esposa," *La Prensa*, November 13, 2014, http://www.laprensa.hn/inicio/767394-417/autorizan-extradición-a-eua-de-josé-inocente-valle-y-esposa.

71. "Ministerio Público pone en marcha la Operación 'Sultán,'" Ministerio Publico, Official Website, November 28, 2016, https://www.mp.hn/index.php/author-login/48-noviembre/1019-ministerio-publico-pone-en-marcha-la-operacion-sultan.

72. Ellis, *"Honduras: A Pariah State."*

73. "Carteles mexicanos en labores de reclutamiento en Honduras," *El Heraldo*, May 29, 2015, http://www.elheraldo.hn/alfrente/844491-209/carteles-mexicanos-en-labores-de-reclutamiento-en-honduras.

74. "EUA tras cartel formado por jueces, militares, alcaldes y policías," *La Prensa*, October 11, 2016, http://www.laprensa.hn/honduras/1007292-410/eua-tras-cartel-formado-por-jueces-militares-alcaldes-y-polic%C3%ADas.

75. See, for example, Sam Tabory, "Arrests Add to Murky Picture of Crime-Politics Links in Honduras," *Insight Crime*, August 19, 2015, http://www.InsightCrime.com/news-briefs/arrests-add-murky-honduras-picture-crime-political-relationship.

76. "Cabecilla del cartel de los AA está enmontañado," *El Heraldo*, November 5, 2015, http://www.elheraldo.hn/pais/898146-466/cabecilla-del-cartel-de-los-aa-est%C3%A1-enmonta%C3%B1ado.

77. "Operación 'Sultán.'"

78. Elyssa Pachico, "Guatemala Arrests Alleged Leader of Mendoza Criminal Clan," *Insight Crime*, April 6, 2016, http://www.InsightCrime.com/news-briefs/guatemala-arrests-alleged-leader-of-mendoza-criminal-clan.

79. "Mendozas," *Insight Crime*, accessed August 30, 2016, http://www.InsightCrime.org/guatemala-organized-crime-news/los-mendoza.

80. "Capturan a Walter Mendoza, presunto líder de estructura criminal," *La Hora*, April 6, 2016, http://lahora.gt/capturan-walter-mendoza-presunto-lider-estructura-criminal.

81. "Guatemala decide extraditar a veterano narcotraficante a EEUU," *Reuters*, August 6, 2012, http://lta.reuters.com/article/domesticNews/idLTASIE87600320120807.

82. "Lorenzanas," *Insight Crime*, accessed August 30, 2016, http://www.InsightCrime.org/guatemala-organized-crime-news/los-lorenzana.

83. Interview with Guatemalan security official, Guatemala City, October 2016.

84. Julie Lopez, " Los Lorenzana se quedan sin Patriarca. ¿Quién tomará su lugar?" *Soy502*, March 18, 2014, http://www.soy502.com/articulo/extraditan-waldemar-lorenzana-quien-era-y-quien-lo-sucedera.

85. "Leones," *Insight Crime*, accessed August 30, 2016, http://www.InsightCrime.org/guatemala-organized-crime-news/los-leones.

86. Juan Carlos Pérez Salazar, "Los *Perrones*, el poderoso grupo criminal que pocos conocen," *BBC*, August 28, 2014, http://www.bbc.com/mundo/noticias/2014/08/140820_el_salvador_perrones_transportistas_cocaina_jcps.

87. Julieta Pelcastre, "Los *Perrones* collaborate with 'El Chapo' in Central America," *Dialogo*, September 26, 2013, https://dialogo-americas.com/en/articles/los-perrones-collaborate-el-chapo-central-america.

88. "Perrones," *Insight Crime*, November 7, 2015, http://www.insightcrime.org/el-salvador-organized-crime-news/perrones-profile.

89. "Matan a 'Chepe' Luna; caen 4 de los sicarios y dos mueren," *La Tribuna*, June 27, 2014, http://www.latribuna.hn/2014/06/27/matan-a-chepe-luna-caen-4-de-los-sicarios-y-dos-mueren/.
90. "Perrones."
91. Héctor Silva Ávalos, "El Salvador Mayor's Arrest," *Insight Crime*, June 1, 2017, https://www.insightcrime.org/news/brief/shadow-perrones-looms-el-salvador-mayor-arrest/.
92. Héctor Silva Ávalos and Suchit Chávez, "Montecristo, la sociedad que unió a un capo y al vicepresidente Ortiz," *Factum*, April 5, 2016, http://revistafactum.com/montecristo-la-sociedad-unio-capo-al-vicepresidente-ortiz/.
93. Sergio Arauz, Óscar Martínez, Efren Lemus, "El Cartel de Texis," *El Faro*, May 16, 2011, http://elfaro.net/es/201105/noticias/4079/?st-full_text=0.
94. Arauz, et al., *"El Cartel de Texis."*
95. Héctor Silva Ávalos, "In About-Face, El Salvador Govt Reopens 'Chepe Diablo' Case," *Insight Crime*, December 7, 2016, http://www.insightcrime.org/news-analysis/in-about-face-el-salvador-govt-reopens-chepe-diablo-case.
96. Bryan Avelar, "Fiscalía: Óscar Ortiz participó en "métodos de lavado," *Factum*, April 17, 2017, revistafactum.com/fiscalia-oscar-ortiz-participo-en-metodos-de-lavado-en-caso-chepe-diablo/. See also Bryan Avelar, "El Salvador Vice President Engaged in 'Money Laundering Methods': Prosecutors," *InsightCrime*, April 18, 2017, https://www.insightcrime.org/news/analysis/el-salvador-vice-president-engaged-money-laundering-methods-prosecutors/.
97. Avelar, "Fiscalía: Óscar Ortiz."
98. Nicholas Casey, "Colombia and FARC Sign New Peace Deal, This Time Skipping Voters," *New York Times*, November 24, 2016, https://www.nytimes.com/2016/11/24/world/americas/colombia-juan-manuel-santos-peace-deal-farc.html.
99. John Otis, "The FARC and Colombia's Illegal Drug Trade," The Wilson Center, November 2014, https://www.wilsoncenter.org/sites/default/files/Otis_FARCDrugTrade2014.pdf.
100. Jeremy McDermott, "What Does Colombia Peace Deal Mean for Cocaine Trade?" *Insight Crime*, August 24, 2016, http://www.InsightCrime.org/news-analysis/what-does-colombia-peace-deal-mean-for-cocaine-trade.
101. "Colombia FARC Rebels Start Demobilization Process," *Yahoo News*, January 31, 2017, https://www.yahoo.com/news/colombia-farc-rebels-start-demobilization-process-160029284.html.
102. See R. Evan Ellis, "Colombia: Preparing for the Post-Agreement,' Not the 'Post-Conflict,'" *Latin America Goes Global*, March 15, 2016, http://latinamericagoesglobal.org/2016/03/2755/.
103. Christopher Woody, "Colombia Has a New Deal to End a 52-Year War, but Violence and Uncertainty Still Loom over It," *Yahoo*, November 25, 2016, https://www.yahoo.com/news/colombia-deal-end-52-war-211559588.html.
104. "Colombia FARC Rebels Start."
105. "Colombia to Crack Down on Coca Crops," *BBC*, January 28, 2017, http://www.bbc.com/news/world-latin-america-38769685.
106. "Colombia Freezes FARC Assets under Peace Deal," *Yahoo News*, February 23, 2017, https://www.yahoo.com/news/colombia-freezes-farc-assets-under-peace-deal-212015308.html.
107. "FARC Denies Having Billions of Dollars, Colombia Has No Proof," *Telesur*, April 29, 2016, http://www.telesurtv.net/english/news/FARC-Denies-Having-Billions-of-Dollars-Colombia-Has-No-Proof-20160429-0026.html.
108. "FARC Dissidents Face Full Force of Colombia Military: President," *Reuters*, November 23, 2017, https://www.reuters.com/article/us-colombia-peace/farc-dissidents-face-full-force-of-colombia-military-president-idUSKBN1DN24A.
109. Matthew Bristow, "Colombia Hunts 300 FARC Dissidents Doing 'Pure Organized Crime,'" *Bloomberg*, January 26, 2017, https://www.bloomberg.com/politics/articles/2017-01-26/colombia-hunts-300-farc-dissidents-doing-pure-organized-crime.

110. "Renegade Colombia FARC Rebels in Deadly Clash," *The Guardian*, January 18, 2017, https://guardian.ng/news/renegade-colombia-farc-rebels-in-deadly-clash/
111. "Colombia's FARC Has Completed Disarmament, UN Says," *BBC*, June 27, 2017, http://www.bbc.com/news/world-latin-america-40413335.
112. "In Colombia, Peace Remains Elusive One Year On," *Deutsche Welle*, November 23, 2017, www.dw.com/en/in-colombia-peace-remains-elusive-one-year-on/a-41372941.
113. "Clan del Golfo recluta a guerrilleros de las Farc por $1,8 millones: Fiscal General," 2016.
114. Gimena Sánchez-Garzoli, "December Update: Colombia Social Leaders Face Imminent Security Threat from Illegal Armed Groups," *Washington Office on Latin America*, https://www.wola.org/analysis/december-update-social-leaders-face-imminent-security-threat-illegal-armed-groups/.
115. Florencia Trucco and Alanne Orjoux, "Colombia's Government Reaches Ceasefire Deal with ELN," *CNN*, September 4, 2017, www.cnn.com/2017/09/04/americas/colombia-eln-ceasefire/index.html.
116. Fabio Andres Diaz, "Will Colombia's Most 'Stubborn' Rebel Group Agree to Peace?," *Huffington Post*, February 7, 2017, http://www.huffingtonpost.com/the-conversation-global/will-colombias-most-stubb_b_14634604.html.
117. "Rebel Leader Apologizes for Colombian Church Kidnapping," *CNN*, June 7, 1999, http://www.cnn.com/WORLD/americas/9906/07/colombia/.
118. "Terror on Flight 9463," *The Guardian*, April 27, 1999, https://www.theguardian.com/theguardian/1999/apr/28/features11.g23.
119. McDermott, "Colombia Peace Deal."
120. Ellis and Ortiz, "Un acuerdo entre interrogantes."
121. Interview with Colombian security expert, September 2017, Bogota, Colombia.
122. Interview with Colombian security official, November 2017.
123. David Gagne, "Despite Colombia Accord, a New Rebel Threat Emerges," *Insight Crime*, September 14, 2016, http://www.InsightCrime.org/news-analysis/despite-colombia-accord-new-rebel-threat-emerges.
124. Florence Panoussian, Colombia Seeks 'Complete Peace' at ELN Talks, *Yahoo News*, February 7, 2017, https://www.yahoo.com/news/colombia-seeks-complete-peace-eln-talks-022328664.html.
125. "Colombian ELN Rebels 'Regret' Journalists' Kidnap," *BBC*, May 30, 2016, http://www.bbc.com/news/world-latin-america-36412101.
126. R. Evan Ellis, "El nexo evolutivo entre el crimen transnacional y el terorismo en Peru, y su importancia estratgica para EE.UU y la region," *Academia de Guerra Naval*, March 7, 2016, http://www.acanav.mil.cl/agn/documentos/temas_seleccionado/2016/Tema_Seleccionado_01.pdf
127. "Peru Comes out Strong in Fight against Shining Path," *Dialogo*, February 3, 2014, https://dialogo-americas.com/en/articles/peru-comes-out-strong-fight-against-shining-path.
128. Truth and Reconciliation Commission, *Final Report*, August 28, 2003, http://www.cverdad.org.pe/ingles/ifinal/index.php.
129. Ellis, "Crime-Terrorism Nexus in Peru."
130. Ellis, "Crime-Terrorism Nexus in Peru."
131. "Cómo murió 'William,'" *IDL Reporteros*, September 6, 2012, https://idl-reporteros.pe/como-murio-william/.
132. "Tras muerte de 'Alipio' y 'Gabriel': ¿Qué otros cabecillas tiene Sendero?" *El Comercio*, August 12, 2013, http://elcomercio.pe/peru/lima/muerte-alipio-ygabriel-que-otros-cabecillas-tiene-sendero-noticia-1616591.
133. In October 2012, *Sendero Luminoso* destroyed three helicopters in Cusco belonging to Camisea oilfield contractors Helisur and Los Andes, allegedly for not having paid protection money to the organization. See "Helicopters Face High Risk of Attack in Peru's VRAEM Region," *IHS Jane's Intelligence Weekly*, October 29, 2014, http://

www.janes.com/article/45176/helicopters-face-high-risk-of-attack-in-peru-s-vraem-region.

134. "Gustavo Gorriti: El drama de Kepashiato muestra la compleja y vulnerable situación del VRAE," *La Republica*, April 13, 2012, http://www.larepublica.pe/13-04-2012/gustavo-gorriti-el-drama-de-kepashiato-muestra-la-compleja-y-vulnerable-situacion-del-vrae.

135. Mimi Yagoub, "Peru's Shining Path Is Making a Comeback, Analyst Says," *Insight Crime*, August 25, 2016, http://www.InsightCrime.org/news-briefs/peru-shining-path-making-a-comeback.

136. "Se confirma muerte de 10 personas en ataque terrorista en Vraem," *El Comercio*, April 11, 2016, http://elcomercio.pe/sociedad/vraem/vraem-confirman-muerte-diez-personas-ataque-terrorista-noticia-1893147.

137. Jacqueline Fowks, "Tres policías peruanos mueren en una emboscada de narcoterroristas," *El Pais*, March 18, 2017, https://elpais.com/internacional/2017/03/18/america/1489871093_445014.html.

138. See, for example, Steven C. Boraz and Thomas C. Bruneau, "Are the Maras Overwhelming Central America?" *Military Review*, November–December 2006, http://usacac.army.mil/CAC2/MilitaryReview/Archives/English/MilitaryReview_20061231_art007.pdf.

139. For a good account, see Ana Arana, "How the Street Gangs Took Central America," *Foreign Affairs*, May/June 2005, https://www.foreignaffairs.com/articles/central-america-caribbean/2005-05-01/how-street-gangs-took-central-america.

140. See Alejandro Jacky, "Hip Hop Is Not Dead: The Emergence of Mara Salvatrucha Rap as a Form of MS-13 Expressive Culture," *Alternativas*, Spring 2014, http://alternativas.osu.edu/en/issues/spring-2014/essays1/jacky.html.

141. See Alessandro Solis Lerici, "Detrás de la economía de las maras salvadoreñas," *Nacion*, January 15, 2017, http://www.nacion.com/ocio/revista-dominical/Detras-economia-maras-salvadorenas_0_1609839033.html

142. Jaime Lopez, "Maras intentan infiltrar PNC, Academia y Ejército," *El Salvador.com*, February 4, 2017, http://www.elsalvador.com/articulo/sucesos/maras-intentan-infiltrar-pnc-academia-ejercito-140038.

143. Martin Movilla, "MS-13 habría recibido entrenamiento militar en El Salvador," *Radio Canada Internacional*, March 17, 2014, http://www.rcinet.ca/es/2014/03/17/ms-13-habria-recibido-entrenamiento-militar-en-el-salvador/.

144. See, for example, "Desmantelan campamento de pandillas en manglares," *La Prensa Grafica*, January 12, 2015, http://www.laprensagrafica.com/2015/01/12/desmantelan-campamento-de-pandillas-en-manglares.

145. "Al Qaeda Seeks Tie to Local Gang," *Washington Times*, September 28, 2004, http://www.washingtontimes.com/news/2004/sep/28/20040928-123346-3928r/.

146. Juan José Martínez D'Aubuisson, "International Terror and the Gangs of Douglas Farah," *Insight Crime*, February 26, 2016, https://www.insightcrime.org/news/analysis/international-terror-douglas-farah-gangs-ms13-barrio18/.

147. U.N. Office on Drugs and Crime (UNODC), Transnational Organized Crime in Central America and the Caribbean: A Threat Assessment, September 2012, http://www.unodc.org/documents/data-and-analysis/Studies/TOC_Central_America_and_the_Caribbean_english.pdf.

148. Ellis, "The Gang Challenge in El Salvador."

149. Seelke, "Gangs in Central America."

150. Seelke, "Gangs in Central America."

151. Interview with Salvadoran security officials, San Salvador, El Salvador, July 2015.

152. Conversation with Salvadoran security official, San Salvador, El Salvador, July 2015.

153. "Dissident Faction Splits with El Salvador's Notorious MS-13 Gang," *Telesur*, May 2, 2017, https://www.telesurtv.net/english/news/Dissident-Faction-Splits-with-El-Salvadors-Notorious-MS-13-Gang-20170502-0015.html.

154. "Fiscalía: 'Sabemos quién es el responsable.'"
155. "Al Qaeda Seeks Tie."
156. Tristan Clavel, "Barrio 18 Wants to Join Possible Talks with El Salvador Govt: Report," *Insight Crime*, January 17, 2017, http://www.InsightCrime.org/news-briefs/barrio-18-wants-to-join-possible-talks-with-el-salvador-govt-report.
157. Interview with a Salvadoran security official, San Salvador, El Salvador, July 2015.
158. Claudia Palma, "Guatemala. Ministerio de Gobiernación vi desafío en ataque de las maras," *Kaosenlared*, March 15, 2016, http://kaosenlared.net/guatemala-ministro-de-gobernacion-ve-desafio-en-ataques-de-marasministro-de-gobernacion-ve-desafio-en-ataques-de-maras/.
159. "Penas de 500 años a pandilleros por atentado," *La Prensa Grafica*, February 2, 2014, http://www.laprensagrafica.com/2014/02/12/penas-de-500-aos-a-pandilleros-por-atentado.
160. See José Arcia, "'Maras no operan en territorio panameño,'" *La Estrella de Panama*, July 15, 2016, http://laestrella.com.pa/panama/politica/maras-operan-territorio-panameno/23951030.
161. Ismael Gordón Guerrel, "Informe de Fiscalía reporta unas 204 pandillas en Panamá," *La Estrella de Panama*, April 7, 2016, http://laestrella.com.pa/panama/nacional/informe-fiscalia-reporta-unas-204-pandillas-panama/23932442.
162. Interview with senior Panamanian security official, Bogota, Colombia, September 2016.
163. "Principal narcotraficante do Panamá é capturado, diz polícia," *Globo*, September 6, 2016, http://g1.globo.com/mundo/noticia/2016/09/principal-narcotraficante-do-panama-e-capturado-diz-policia.html.
164. Interview with senior Panamanian security official, Bogota, Colombia, September 2016.
165. "Lottery Scam Taskforce Being Reintroduced," *Jamaica Observer*, September 26, 2016, http://www.jamaicaobserver.com/news/Lottery-Scam-Taskforce-being-reintroduced.
166. Barbara Gayle, "Stone Crusher Gang Leader Bailed," *Jamaica Gleaner*, March 9, 2012, http://jamaica-gleaner.com/power/35795.
167. "Dangerous 'One Order' Concept Spreading, Says Senior Cop," *Jamaica Observer*, January 20, 2010, http://www.jamaicaobserver.com/news/One-order-concept-Wed--Jan-20--2010_7340287.
168. See, for example, Ioan Grillo, "Jamaican Organized Crime after the Fall of Dudus Coke," *Combatting Terrorism Center*, January 15, 2014, https://www.ctc.usma.edu/posts/jamaican-organized-crime-after-the-fall-of-dudus-coke.
169. Grillo, "Jamaican Organized Crime."
170. Grillo, "Jamaican Organized Crime."
171. Interview with senior Dominican Republic security official, Bogota, Colombia, September 2016.
172. "Narcos brasileños usan Uruguay de trampolín," *El Pais*, January 24, 2014, http://www.elpais.com.uy/informacion/narcos-brasilenos-uruguay-trampolin-crimen.html.
173. Interview with Brazilian security official, Bogota, Colombia, September 2016.
174. See, for example, Michael Royster, "Opinion: Rio's Evil Export," *The Rio Times*, January 6, 2017, http://riotimesonline.com/brazil-news/opinion-editorial/opinion-rios-evil-export/.
175. Paulo Prada, "5 Days of Violence by Gangs in São Paulo Leaves 115 Dead Before Subsiding," *New York Times*, May 17, 2006, http://www.nytimes.com/2006/05/17/world/americas/17brazil.html?_r=0.
176. "Dozens Killed in Gang Violence at Brazilian Jail," *Reuters*, January 2, 2017, https://www.theguardian.com/world/2017/jan/02/dozens-killed-in-gang-violence-at-brazilian-jail-manaus.

177. David Gagne, "Lucrative Cocaine Trade Fuels Gang Presence in Brazil's Amazon," *Insight Crime*, January 13, 2017, http://www.insightcrime.com/news-briefs/lucrative-cocaine-trade-fuels-gang-presence-brazil-amazon.

178. Francisco Leali, "Polícia Federal aponta elo entre facção brasileira e Hezbollah," *O Globo*, September 11, 2014, http://oglobo.globo.com/brasil/policia-federal-aponta-elo-entre-faccao-brasileira-hezbollah-14512269#ixzz4NjTVRVQf.

179. Bruno Ribeiro, "PCC envia dinheiro do tráfico para Estados Unidos e China," *O Estado de S. Paulo*, January 15, 2015, http://sao-paulo.estadao.com.br/noticias/geral,pcc-envia-dinheiro-do-trafico-para-estados-unidos-e-china,1619985.

180. Cándido Figueredo Ruiz, "Identifican a supuesto alto 'jefe' del PCC en Paraguay," *ABC Color*, August 3, 2014, http://www.abc.com.py/edicion-impresa/judiciales-y-policiales/identifican-a-supuesto-alto-jefe-del-pcc-en-paraguay-1272485.html.

181. "Red Command," *Insight Crime*, accessed November 30, 2016, http://www.InsightCrime.org/brazil-organized-crime-news/red-command-profile.

182. Ivan Condori, "Miembros del Comando Vermelho intentaron sacar droga de Bolivia," *La Razon*, September 4, 2015, http://www.la-razon.com/nacional/seguridad_nacional/Gobierno-miembros-Comando_Vermelho-intentaron-sacar-droga-Bolivia_0_2338566180.html.

183. "Red Command."

184. Iván Leguizamón, "Un 'general' del Comando Vermelho en Paraguay," *ABC Color*, December 29, 2014, http://www.abc.com.py/edicion-impresa/suplementos/judicial/un-general-del-comando-vermelho-en-paraguay-1320957.html.

185. For a good brief description, see "Pure Third Command," *Insight Crime*, accessed August 30, 2016, http://www.InsightCrime.org/brazil-organized-crime-news/pure-third-command.

186. "Helicóptero da PM cai durante operação em favela do Rio," *Globo*, October 18, 2009, http://g1.globo.com/Noticias/Rio/0,,MUL1344807-5606,00-HELICOPTERO+DA+PM+CAI+DURANTE+OPERACAO+EM+FAVELA+DO+RIO.html.

187. The criminal career of Nem and Amigos dos Amigos is documented in detail in Misha Glenny's book *Nemesis* (New York: Alfred A. Knopf, 2016).

188. "Single-Handed," *The Economist*, September 12, 2015, http://www.economist.com/news/books-and-arts/21664050-how-ant-nio-francisco-bonfim-lopes-better-known-nem-rocinha-took-over-brazilian.

189. Dom Phillips and Júlio Carvalho, "Brazil's Army Returns to Rio Favela amid Clashes between Gangs and Police," *The Guardian*, September 22, 2017, https://www.theguardian.com/world/2017/sep/22/brazils-army-deployed-to-rio-favela-amid-clashes-between-gangs-and-police.

190. "Brazil Army Deploys in Rio Slum as Drug-Related Violence Worsens," *Reuters*, September 22, 2017, https://www.reuters.com/article/us-brazil-violence/brazil-army-deploys-in-rio-slum-as-drug-related-violence-worsens-idUSKCN1BX2Z9.

191. "Amigos dos Amigos," *Insight Crime*, accessed August 30, 2016, http://www.InsightCrime.org/brazil-organized-crime-news/amigos-dos-amigos.

FOUR
Comparative Solutions

OVERVIEW

Virtually every country in the region has wrestled with the challenge of transnational organized crime and the best way to combat it, although their strategies, style of international cooperation, and use of particular institutions such as the armed forces have varied widely. In general, most have come to recognize (at least in their discourse) the importance of whole-of-government solutions and international cooperation. Most have similarly recognized the importance of strategies which both go after the criminal groups involved, reform and strengthen institutions, and address the underlying socioeconomic factors that contribute to the problem.

A key factor behind the specific challenges is the level of corruption and impunity that exists in many states in the region,[1] and the corresponding ability of criminal organizations to penetrate the apparatuses of government, both undercutting their effectiveness against transnational organized crime groups, and decreasing citizen willingness to collaborate with the government in that struggle.[2]

Despite such commonalities, the nature of the policies and strategies adopted by individual governments, and their relative successes and consequences, differs in important ways. These differences reflect national circumstances, institutional capabilities, and other factors.

This chapter makes a comparative examination of government initiatives against transnational organized crime across Latin America and the Caribbean in eight areas:

- Whole-of-government solutions;
- Interdiction of criminal flows;
- Targeting of transnational criminal organization leaders;

- Use of the military in a domestic law enforcement context;
- Institutional reform within law enforcement;
- Targeting the financial flows and resources of organized criminal groups;
- Prison control and reform, and;
- Binational and multinational cooperation against organized crime.

The objective of these comparisons is to highlight innovative solutions and pitfalls in the efforts of one country that may be usefully applied in a selective fashion in the national context of others.

COORDINATED, WHOLE-OF-GOVERNMENT SOLUTIONS

While the countries of the region differ in the effectiveness of implementing coordinated, multidimensional solutions to the challenge of organized crime confronting their nations, virtually all have, to some degree or another, come to recognize the efficacy of such an approach, combining elements of law enforcement, institutional reform, and addressing underlying socioeconomic contributors to the problem.

In reality, criticisms of the efforts of Latin American and Caribbean governments against transnational organized crime are often misleading. Few if any governments in the region have ever adopted a strictly military or security-oriented approach toward criminal groups, as for example, discussions of *"mano duro"* policies in El Salvador and Honduras[3] often imply. It is correct that the focus of early policies such as "mano duro" begun by Salvadoran president Francisco Flores in 2003 were ineffective, with the byproduct of actually increasing violence. Such shortcomings, many scholars believe, were due to the excess focus on detaining gang members, with insufficient coordination with the capabilities necessary to effectively prosecute those gang members, control them in prison, enable them to leave the gangs, or prevent other at-risk youth from joining the gangs.[4] Nonetheless, in recent years, most states in the region have rethought the appropriate balance between security, institutional reform, and addressing socioeconomic contributors to organized crime, and have sought to increase coordination across ministries, state and local governments, and public and private entities, as well as working more closely with international partners.

The rise of the "whole-of-government" discourse in Latin America was arguably driven, in part, by the perceived success of Colombia's government against the FARC, in combination with the perceived failure of law enforcement-dominated efforts by governments of the Northern Triangle during the same period against violent street gangs. Arguably, neither the nuances of the Colombian case, nor those of the Northern Triangle were fully understood by those drawing lessons from them to confront their own public security threats. Nonetheless, by the second decade of the century, virtually every government of the region was pursuing a policy that was "whole-of-government" to some degree, although the quality of the plan, the level of coordination, and the ability to adapt that coordination as conditions changed have varied widely.

Colombia

In Colombia, during the eight years from 2002 to 2010, the government of Álvaro Uribe reduced the FARC from a force controlling significant portions of the national territory and threatening to overthrow the national government, to a greatly reduced and dispersed group of fighters and sympathizers engaging in criminal activities and sporadic acts of terrorism.[5] The Uribe government's considerable success, which captured the imagination of many in the region, owed largely to an integrated strategy which emphasized the mutually reinforcing relationship between using the armed forces to defeat the FARC and ELN militarily in specific places, denying them control over territory, then using the displacement of the threat to rebuild the presence of the state in the area, and with it, to reconstruct the bond between the government and the residents of the territory. In the process, the Colombian state helped to enable non-criminal economic activities, and provided public services, both of which gave residents a stake in the legitimate economy and reinforced that government-society bond.

For Colombia, the progressive reassertion of state control over national territory also had the secondary benefit of reducing the space in which criminals could operate, furthering the bond with the population, and generating enthusiasm both at home and abroad. That success did not, however, fully address the criminality and corruption deeply rooted in Colombian society. To some degree, the international perception of Colombia's success was as important in its effect on the rest of the region as what was actually happening. Such perceptions were helped by articulate leaders such as the nation's president Álvaro Uribe, and then-ambassador to the US Luis Alberto Moreno, who presented those lessons in compelling terms. The understanding was further bolstered by a young and highly capable cadre in the Colombian military and government which presented the nation's progress to US and other audiences through quantitatively-oriented graphs and charts within compelling, high-quality presentations.

The perceived lessons were further shaped and magnified by a US policymaking community eager to trumpet the case of Colombia as an example of the success of US support in helping a country to rescue itself from the abyss. Under the administration of President Uribe's successor, Juan Manuel Santos, the Colombian government has replaced President Uribe's "Democratic Security Strategy" with the "Security Policy for a

New Century," developed by the Ministry of Defense, in coordination with other ministries.

Below the strategic level, the government has made important innovations in coordinating the security and socioeconomic dimensions of government engagement to deny the national territory to organized crime groups. One of Colombia's best-known tools for coordinating such efforts at the local level is its "Integrated Action" program (*Acción Integral*). During the war against the FARC and ELN, when the military defeated the enemy military threat and security forces took control of an area, the government began work there to strengthen the bond between local residents and the government through building or repairing infrastructure and public services, and by helping residents to create legitimate economic activities.

Initially, *Acción Integral* was conducted entirely within the military. In 2007, however, the government broadened the program by creating a new organization within the Ministry of Social Protection. Critics of the change argue that by transforming *Acción Integral* from a part of the military campaign to an instrument of social policy, it weakened the coordination between the security and socioeconomic dimensions of government engagement. Further compounding the problem, as the Colombian government signed a peace agreement with the FARC, the principal but not the only politically oriented criminal group in the country, it targeted *Acción Integral* for a significant budget reduction.

Despite such successes in restoring the presence of the Colombian state to the countryside and defeating the FARC on the battlefield, it is important to recognize that the US support for the country's efforts, best known as "Plan Colombia," initially began as a war on drugs in the US understanding, even while Colombia's leadership was principally focused on fighting an insurgency against Marxist guerillas who happened to be heavily involved in the drug trade. Indeed, scholars have been sharply critical of the lack of progress on this front,[6] to include dramatic increases in coca production in Colombia as the conflict with the FARC was formally concluded at the negotiating table.

Mexico

Mexico provides an example of both the adoption of "whole-of-government" strategies against organized crime by Latin American and Caribbean governments, and some of its limitations. In 2012, the incoming president, Enrique Peña Nieto, promulgated a National Development Plan for his period in office that emphasized a "multidimensional" approach toward security, highlighting the importance of integrating security and developmental goals and societal health.[7]

The government also developed a National Security Program aligned with the plan, covering both the Mexican Army and Navy (which, in

Mexico, are separate institutions).[8] The program includes a detailed breakdown of strategies and lines of action, although not indicating specifically which organizations have responsibility for which lines of action. The document was written by a committee drawing on the staffs and higher education institutions of the Mexican Army and Navy, although formally supervised by the Interior Ministry, with inputs from other ministries as well.[9]

The Mexican government also created individual sectoral programs for both the Army and the Navy, as well as for other ministries relevant to the multidimensional security concept, including the Ministry of Finance, the Foreign Ministry, and the Interior Ministry (which includes the national intelligence organization CISEN).

Beyond such plans, the Peña Nieto regime has also sought to improve interagency coordination through reorganization. At the beginning of his term in office, a major reorganization placed the national police, along with CISEN, under the Interior Ministry (*Gobernación*), with the official goal of improving coordination between the police and other elements of the government.[10]

The Mexican government has also more actively involved state-level governments in the security decision-making process, although the ability to do so is arguably facilitated by the fact that the majority of states in Mexico have historically been, and continue to be, governed by Peña Nieto's Institutional Revolutionary Party (PRI). As part of this effort, the president has actively coordinated with the influential council of governors, *CONAGO*,[11] as well as through the *National Council on Public Security*, a broadly inclusive albeit impractically large body that includes the country's governors and their security officials, some mayors and non-governmental organizations, the heads of both houses of the Mexican Congress, both of the nation's separate armed forces, and other organizations.[12]

To combat the economic dimension of organized crime, the Peña Nieto plan targeted five impoverished "special economic zones," principally in the south of the country, to receive special security and development assistance, including infrastructure projects.[13]

The US-funded Merida Plan, through which the US has provided Mexico with $2.8 billion in security and other assistance since 2008,[14] was also an important part of the country's whole-of-government effort against organized crime. In its initial phases, it concentrated mostly on combatting transnational organized crime groups and drug trafficking, although the focus arguably shifted over time.[15] Nonetheless, it is also important to recognize that the contributions of Plan Merida, although often receiving much focus by US scholars, made only modest contributions to Mexico's campaign against organized crime groups.

Guatemala

With the help of US government organizations such as the Defense Institutional Reform Initiative (DIRI), Guatemala has created a relatively sophisticated whole-of-government national security planning system. The system and associated activities reflect cumulative progress over multiple administrations, including the previous president, Otto Perez Molina, and continuing under the current administration of President Jimmy Morales.

As in Mexico, the Guatemalan system includes a National Security Council (NSC), convened by the president at least once a month, and which includes the ministers of defense, interior, and foreign relations, the attorney general, the secretary of national intelligence, and the vice president.[16] The work of the Guatemalan NSC is coordinated by a technical secretariat, and guided by a series of interrelated whole-of-government planning documents, including the government's strategic plan (the 2016–2020 plan was released in the summer of 2016), the "National Risk Agenda," the National Security Policy, and the Strategic Agenda for the Security of the Nation.[17]

At the operational level, in the fight against transnational organized crime, the government has also sought to achieve greater coordination between the national police and other relevant organizations by creating new interagency entities. Under Otto Perez Molina, the government created a series of functional task forces to facilitate coordination against particular criminal challenges, including entities to combat extortion, robbery of vehicles and cellular telephones, crimes against public transportation, and the murder of women, among others. The task forces were initially small groups of experts, coordinating across ministries (including the PNC, the public ministry, and the military, among others), to combat crime in the designated focus area.

With the government of Jimmy Morales, these "thematic" task forces have been disbanded, although some have been incorporated into new interagency-focused organizations as the anti-pandillas directorate (*DI-PANDA*) within the national police. DIPANDA earned favorable national and international attention in October 2016 by facilitating the capture of MS-13 leader José Alonso Marroquin, and his repatriation to El Salvador, his country of origin.[18]

Beyond thematic task forces, the Guatemalan government has also created interagency entities focused on specific geographic areas, principally urban zones. These include the task forces *Maya*, *Kaminal*, and *El Milagro* in Guatemala City.

Honduras

In Honduras, the most notable aspect of the government's interagency effort against transnational organized crime is the president's "Inter-Agency National Security Plan," and the inter-agency body which it guides, FUSINA. FUSINA integrates military, police, prosecutors, judges, and some special assets such as the military police. FUSINA's activities are guided by "Operation Morazán," the plan for operating against criminal organizations and insecurity across the national territory.[19]

FUSINA's integration of assets from multiple ministries for operational purposes is relatively unique in the region. The organization comes under the civilian control of the president and his national security council, but is run by a military officer, with an officer of the National Police as his second in command. FUSINA has been assigned part, but not all, of the national police and armed forces, as well as investigative personnel and some special judges. It is also supervised by an "executive board," of senior personnel from the different ministries from which FUSINA draws assets, facilitating access to special resources from those organizations when needed in specific operations.[20]

El Salvador

In El Salvador, the "whole-of-government" approach of the government of President Salvador Sánchez Cerén is defined by the administration's "Plan Secure Salvador," which contemplates $2.1 billion of spending, including resources for both social development programs and military ones, paid for by a tax on telecommunications.[21] While Salvadoran experts question the degree of coordination between the economic and security components of the program,[22] the concept illustrates the government's acceptance of a holistic approach. Below the national level, although the Salvadoran government did not create a national-level interagency force like FUSINA, it did create a number of joint units integrating military and police officers, and in some cases, prosecutors, discussed in subsequent sections.

Panama

In Panama, as in other states in the region, the administration's "whole-of-government" approach toward security is defined in its National Security Plan, whose current version was written in 2014 by the incoming president, Juan Carlos Varela. Similar to other countries discussed in this work, Panama coordinates the work of its ministries and organizations on a day-to-day basis through a National Security Council, which includes the president, the minister of foreign relations, the minister of public security, and an executive secretary, who facilitates the process.

At the operational level, the de facto lead organization in Panama's efforts against transnational organized crime is the Ministry of Public Security, which integrates the national police, the frontier service (*Senafron*), the air and naval patrol service (*SENAN*), and immigration, among other organizations.

The current government has implemented a program "secure neighborhoods" (*Barrios Seguros*), which provides a combination of community engagement and social benefits to those which abandon criminality,[23] leveraging the combined efforts of the Ministry of Public Security in coordination with the Ministry of Social Development and the Ministry of Labor to administer the promised benefits.

Peru

Peru, like most other countries in the region, generates a National Security Plan as its reference document to integrate the efforts of different government agencies against transnational organized crime and other challenges. The Ministry of Defense takes the lead in writing the document, but also coordinates with the economy, interior, and other ministries.

Below the national level, Peru has sought to integrate the efforts of multiple government entities in the fight against transnational organized crime in two troubled regions, the Upper Huallaga Valley and the Apurimac, Ene, and Mantauro river valleys (VRAEM), by setting up special administrative zones there where government organizations can work together to advance both security and development.

In the VRAEM, the 4th Division of the Peruvian Army and the Peruvian National Police were put under a unified military command, headquartered in the military base at Pichari, near the center of the zone. Since the establishment of the zone,[24] Peru's government has established some sixty temporary and permanent bases at strategically selected locations there.[25] In December 2015, the government proposed transferring administrative control of the VRAEM from the military to the Peruvian National Police.[26]

At the national level, security and development activities of different ministries are coordinated by a cabinet-level committee, called the CODEVRAEM. Yet the organization's ability to shape the priorities of the ministries involved is reportedly limited by a lack of staff, funding, and the relatively junior status of the official who leads it, below the cabinet ministers he or she must negotiate with.[27]

Under Peru's previous president, Ollanta Humala, the government implemented some development projects in the VRAEM, including building roads and bridges to connect the population to markets for their products, yet important projects such as a road from Quinua (Ayacucho) to San Francisco experienced delays. Moreover, as has occurred in many projects throughout the country, significant parts of development project budgets are consumed by corruption.[28]

Developing the VRAEM has further been hampered by difficulties in coordinating between local and national governments: The VRAEM is made up of relatively sparsely populated portions of five of Peru's twenty-five regions (Junin, Huancavelica, Ayacucho, Apurimac, and Cusco). Although the national government wishes to develop the VRAEM, regional governments often prefer to spend their limited resources on projects in the more urban parts of those regions, where their constituents are.[29]

The most successful application of a whole-of-government approach in Peru arguably came not in the VRAEM, but in the Upper Huallaga Valley, where the national police led the security effort, with the military in support, including a relatively successful eradication program for coca. The efforts benefitted from the relatively weaker presence of the *Shining Path* in the area. Yet the government did secure important victories in the Upper Huallaga Valley, capturing the principal leader of *Shining Path* in the zone, Artemio,[30] and going on to dismantle the *Shining Path* military organization there, while substantially reducing coca production there.

Beyond the VRAEM and the Upper Huallaga Valley, Peru has also begun to pursue integrated "whole-of-government" solutions with some success in the Amazon. Perhaps one of the most innovative under the government of Ollanta Humala was the "mobile state" initiative.[31] The project deployed riverboats in the Peruvian Amazon, populated by representatives from multiple government agencies and the private sector to bring services of the Peruvian state to remote difficult-to-reach areas, in order to strengthen the relationship between the state and society there. Such services included medical services, payment of teacher salaries, and public registries, among others. As of mid-2016, three such vessels were operating, built by the local Peruvian company SIMA-Iquitos, with plans to deploy three more by the end of 2016, with a total of twelve eventually envisioned.[32]

Although the Peruvian government has thus had mixed success with bringing security and development to the VRAEM, Upper Huallaga Valley, and Amazon, such efforts, at least, highlight the government's awareness of the importance of coordinated, whole-of-government approaches.

Ecuador

Ecuador emphasizes integration across ministries in its approach to security. Like Mexico, it has a national security plan that is derived from its national development plan. The latter, called "Living Well" (*buen vi-*

vir), was created in 2009 by the government of Rafael Correa. Reflecting the emphasis on a whole-of-government approach integrating law enforcement with the economic and social elements of security, it uses the term "Integral National Security Plan" (*Plan de seguridad nacional integral*).

By contrast to many other countries in the region, Ecuador also has a dedicated ministry to coordinate the efforts of other agencies of the government in that respect. That organization is responsible for writing the integral national security plan, as well as for ensuring that the supporting plans of each relevant ministry are consistent with it.

Argentina

Argentina's security planning is guided by the national policy directive for defense (*Directiva Politica Nacional de Defensa*), which is a document elaborated by the Ministry of Defense, albeit incorporating elements from other parts of the government. Complicating interagency planning efforts, the last edition of the document was written in December 2014 by the previous government, and focuses almost exclusively on combatting foreign state threats.[33]

INTERDICTION OF CRIMINAL FLOWS

Cutting illicit flows has been, and continues to be, a key element of the fight against transnational criminal groups across the region. While discussions of interdiction usually focus on the fight against narcotrafficking, blocking illicit flows of people, money, arms, and other restricted goods are also important elements.

Interdiction against criminal flows is a constantly evolving activity. Criminal groups not only vary their routes in response to interdiction efforts, but also vary the means of transportation (mixtures of air, land, and sea routes, the use of small craft versus smuggling in large vessels and container ships). Criminal groups also use an evolving range of technologies, to include submersible and semisubmersible craft, drones, and the use of human mules.

The challenge of interdiction involves both control over large, often remote areas, where the problem is adequately covering the geography, versus control over commercial chokepoints, such as major commercial ports and border crossings, where the challenge is identifying illicit cargoes amidst the large volume of legitimate goods that traverse a point. Such challenges are discussed, for example, by scholars such as Peter Andreas[34] and Ted Gallen Carpenter.[35]

Most governments spend a significant portion of their efforts against transnational organized crime on interdicting illicit flows. Such dedication of resources presumably owes, in part, to the fact that physically blocking or intercepting a flow which is prohibited is one of the most visible, tangible ways for a government to demonstrate that it is attacking the problem and producing results. Interdiction implicitly presumes that cutting supply will eventually impact demand, while critics of the approach often argue the opposite, that it is necessary to do more to attack demand, which will eventually affect supply.

The US has traditionally played a significant role in supporting interdiction efforts by governments in the region. These include the establishment of Joint Interagency Task Force South (JIATF-South) in Key West, Florida, and forward operating locations throughout the region such as Joint Task Force-Bravo in Honduras, Comalapa in El Salvador, and Aruba, in the Caribbean. From such facilities, and other locations, the US has deployed numerous assets, including US Coast Guard patrols to detect and intercept illicit goods—generally narcotics being smuggled by boat, aircraft, and in recent years, submarines.

Interdiction may be divided into naval, air, and land operations. This section gives special attention to interdiction at borders, although effective interdiction also requires control of the national territory, airspace, and waters more broadly. Control of official land border crossing points, ports, and airports is a special topic, and often more challenging than is commonly recognized, due to the quantity of people, goods, and money flowing through such points, within which the small portion of illicit traffic must be identified. Doing so requires not only physical controls and technology, but also intelligence regarding what is being moved and how.

Naval Interdiction

Naval interdiction in Latin America principally concentrates on drugs, although the entry of contraband goods into ports is also of concern. Some of the key trends in naval interdiction in the region include increasing use of the Pacific Ocean for moving drugs from Peru and Colombia, toward the US and Europe, as well as the resurgent use of Caribbean routes. The enormous amount of money involved in drug movements causes traffickers to continuously seek new ways to hide and move product, including the increasing use of submersible vehicles, semisubmersibles, and towed buoys with geolocation devices, as well as continuing innovations with respect to hidden compartments in boats and commercial containers, and new operations and tactics by various types of watercraft, in combination with aircraft and land operations.

Guatemala

With respect to the maritime domain, Guatemala faces a difficult challenge in covering the 200 nautical miles of waters which extend from its

Pacific Coast, using a very small number of small vessels with limited endurance. As of 2017, Guatemala had only nine small ocean-going Boston Whaler watercraft, plus several smaller go-fast boats (confiscated from criminals under the country's 2010 asset appropriation law [58–2010]), to patrol its large portion of the Pacific Ocean. Compounding the problem, Guatemala has only one Pacific Coast naval base, the port of Quetzal, to resupply those assets. The distance from the port to the remote parts of the ocean to be patrolled severely limits the time that the watercraft can remain on-station.

Although the Guatemalan Navy evaluated establishing a second naval base on its Pacific coast near the town of Champerico (close to the Guatemala-Mexico coastal border) the government was slow to pursue the option because the port required extensive dredging in order to be usable,[36] although as of the end of 2017, a port facility in the area was reportedly in the works.

To help the Guatemalan Navy meet the endurance challenge, in 2016, the US Navy donated a frigate-sized vessel, at a cost of $1.9 million, to be used as a "mothership" to refuel and resupply the limited endurance Guatemalan watercraft at sea. The mothership allows patrol craft to remain in their offshore patrol areas longer in support of their mission. Based on the initial success of the concept, the Guatemalan navy was reportedly considering acquiring a second such vessel with its own funds.[37]

Honduras

With respect to naval interdiction, Honduras has focused on improved coastal and riverine interdiction capability, working closely with the US Navy and Coast Guard to obtain upgraded assets and operational and support for those efforts.[38] A key aspect of Honduran efforts to protect its national waters against incursions by narcotraffickers and other criminal smugglers has been the establishment of new naval stations in remote areas in the east of the country, which traditionally suffered from limited state presence. Nonetheless, the ability of Honduras to conduct effective maritime interdiction there is limited by operational costs of maintaining that presence given the distance of the bases from major population centers for providing logistics support and rotating personnel.

Honduran efforts to control its waters are also complicated by the difficult topography of the north and east coast region, with a rugged coastline dotted by numerous small islands where narcotraffickers can hide and refuel. The multiple rivers flowing from the interior to that coast also present a challenge, allowing smugglers to rapidly bring goods from the ocean deep inland, with multiple options for offloading their goods from the rivers to land routes. Combatting such activities presents a challenge for the limited resources of the Honduran Navy, since the types of watercraft best suited for patrolling the coast are different from those used to patrol those rivers. To address the challenge of riverine interdiction, the Honduran Navy has been working with the United States in a program to convert boats seized from drug smugglers, in order to obtain more fast, flat-bottom boats suited for operating on rivers.[39]

Panama

Because the Panama Canal is a global logistics transshipment hub in which illicit flows are buried within an enormous volume of legitimate commercial activity, control of traffic transiting the canal and its ports on the Atlantic and Pacific side represent a disproportionate part of its maritime challenge. In just the month of January 2017, for example, 1,260 ships transited the canal,[40] including a large portion of container ships each carrying thousands of shipping containers.

Beyond the canal, control of Panama's national waters also continues to be a significant challenge. Improved control by Panama's government of over-land smuggling of people, drugs, and other illicit goods has displaced illicit flows into maritime routes,[41] while the expanded use of Pacific coast routes for northbound drugs leaving Colombia and Peru has increased the challenge for Panama's Coast Guard, *SENAN*.

In part, *SENAN* has managed this challenge through the assistance of and coordination with the US Coast Guard, although it has plans to procure eight interceptor aircraft and a multipurpose boat, in addition to other assets and naval facilities. It is also creating a new organization specialized in narcotics interdiction combining land, air, and ground assets, called the Special Anti-Narcotics Force (FEAN).[42]

Caribbean

Despite the increasing use of maritime drug routes through the Caribbean, most of the nations of the region are small island governments with relatively modest maritime interdiction capabilities. They thus rely principally on the US Coast Guard to help them stop narcotrafficking and other illicit flows through the region's waters.

The Dominican Republic has the largest maritime patrol fleet, with thirty-three watercraft of various sizes, including those used for both coastal and river patrol. Cuba has the second largest maritime force, with twenty-two vessels.

Peru

In Peru's unique geography, the challenge of patrolling its Pacific coastline are separate from the challenge of patrolling the rivers in the interior of the country, which almost exclusively feed into the Brazilian

Amazon, and not to the Pacific coast. With respect to coastal patrol, expanding commerce with Asia has increased the throughput of the nation's major commercial, fishing, and mining ports along the Pacific, as well as the associated burdens of port security. Part of the Peruvian government's response to the challenge of illicit flows has been to expand port security capabilities, such as scanners. It has also sought to increase the number of naval vessels for patrolling national waters. As of 2016, the Peruvian government had contracted with the local shipbuilder SIMA-Callao to purchase ten patrol vessels, with the option to acquire fourteen more. Yet according to Peruvian naval analysts, the acquisition would represent only a modest enhancement to the ability of the Peruvian Navy to guard its substantial coastline.[43]

Land Interdiction

The physical control of borders, which receive significant attention with respect to the movement of people, is also an important tool throughout the region for combatting the movement of drugs, contraband goods, arms, and bulk cash, not only at the US southern border, but also throughout the region. In controlling these borders, the use of physical barriers, personnel, technology, and tactics is constantly seeking to adapt to innovation of transnational organized crime elements to subvert such controls, using everything from bribery to creative concealment of contraband in products, to smuggling drugs in body cavities or inside people's bodies, to the use of technology such as UAVs to circumvent physical barriers.

Countries in the region regularly use military forces to assist in controlling their frontiers, although some, such as Panama, Chile, and Argentina, continue to use dedicated frontier forces, similar to the US Border Patrol, or other specialized organizations under the jurisdiction of the national police.

Particularly in Central America, countries of the region are increasingly collaborating along the frontiers, including joint forces, as well as committees to coordinate frontier control (*Combifrons*), bi-national forces to more effectively coordinate patrols and other activities on both sides of shared frontiers, and to facilitate regular meetings between armed forces units on the border, or between intelligence units of both nations, in the framework of organizations such as the Conference of Central American Armed Forces (CEFAC).

Guatemala

Guatemala has taken steps in recent years to increase coordination with its neighbors and exercise greater control over national territory against transnational criminal flows through the use of joint police-military task forces. As of early 2017, these included interagency task force *Tecun Uman* in San Marcos, near the border with Mexico (operating since October 2013) and *Chorti,* deployed in the Guatemalan departments of Chiquimula, Zacapa, and Izabal, near the border with Honduras (operating since October 2014). Guatemala's government is also creating a new interagency task force, *Xinca,* inaugurated in Jutiapa in August 2017,[44] with the objective of better controlling the border with El Salvador, and a proposed new task force which would operate in the west of the department of Petén, to more effectively control the border with Mexico.

In addition to these task forces, the Guatemalan government also exercises territorial control through the deployment of its armed forces throughout the national territory. In recent years, the Guatemalan Army has formed new brigades to augment its presence in areas of the country that present significant narcotrafficking challenges, including a new jungle brigade deployed in the western portion of Petén (including in the *Maya* Biosphere Reserve national park, where clandestine narco airstrips are a persistent problem).[45] Similarly, the Guatemalan military has established a "high mountain" brigade in the department of San Marcos, site of both significant narcotrafficking smuggling operations and drug laboratories. Unfortunately, severe budgetary limitations have prevented the Guatemalan military from having the resources necessary to properly equip either unit in a fashion corresponding to their special designations as "Jungle Brigade" and "High Mountain Brigade," undermining their ability to effectively control the difficult terrain to which they have been assigned.[46]

Beyond joint task forces and military units, Guatemala's Interior Ministry contributes contraband and immigration police within the Interior Ministry, DIPAFRONT, which works alongside the customs service (SAT), to control the nation's ports, airports, and official border crossings. DIPAFRONT has had some success seizing contraband goods coming through the country, although the informal crossings are left to the police and interagency task forces.

Despite some advances in supervision of ports and airports, the government continues to lack technology to help control its internal roadways. Indeed, as of late 2016, Guatemala reportedly had only one mobile scanning device for detecting contraband at established highway checkpoints, currently controlled by the counter-narcotics department of the Interior Ministry.[47]

Honduras

Under the presidency of Juan Orlando Hernandez, Honduras moved to exercise greater control over its territory, to include the relatively remote and sparely populated areas in the east of the country, such as the department of Gracias a Dios. A key tool for this effort has been the previously mentioned interagency organization FUSINA, which contributes police and military forces, as well as special prosecutors to control the national territory. Within FUSINA, the Military Police for Public Order (PMOP), and the elite police unit the Tigres are used to go after special criminal leadership targets, and to provide security in difficult urban areas.

The Honduran Armed Forces have also cooperated extensively with its neighbors to institute bi-national border patrol forces, such as the Honduran contribution of *Task Force Maya* to the previously mentioned joint task force *Maya Chorti*, which collaborates in patrolling the Honduras-Guatemala border. Similarly, Honduras has contributed the *Task Force Lenca* to the joint task force *Lenca Sumpul*, to patrol its frontier with El Salvador.

In addition, within the framework of the Conference of Central American Armed Forces (CFAC), Honduras has initiated a series of joint border control activities with its neighbor to the south, Nicaragua, called "Morazán-Sandino."[48]

El Salvador

In the case of El Salvador, a special military command, *Sumpul*, is assigned control the nation's frontiers with Honduras and Guatemala.

A second special command, *Zeus*, supports police in controlling territory and conducting operations inside the country against transnational organized crime groups, while *Eagle* Command protects schools and tourist sites. Both are backed by a special airmobile rapid reaction force, the *Thunder* Command.[49]

Zeus Command is the largest of the special commands, comprised of 3,100 soldiers deployed divided into eight task forces and deployed to thirty-one municipalities throughout El Salvador. Thirteen hundred troops have been deployed to 651 schools and tourist sites under Eagle Command, while three hundred and sixty personnel have been dedicated to the rapid response "Thunder Command."[50]

In 2016, the Salvadoran government of Sánchez Cerén also created two new interagency forces: The *Specialized Reaction Force of El Salvador (FERES)*, integrating police and military special forces, principally to go after organized crime leadership and other strategic targets, and the Interagency *Territory Recuperation Force* (FIRT), designed to occupy and recover municipalities occupied by criminal groups, such as violent street gangs.[51] *FERES* was originally composed of four hundred persons, divided into ten interagency units of forty people each, with each unit composed of twenty-four military personnel and sixteen police, drawn from elite-trained units on both sides. By contrast to other Salvadoran units that supported internal security missions such as *Zeus* Command, the police and the military in the FERES units actually trained together and worked the same hours to improve unit cohesion. FIRT was initially established in 2016, with an operating concept of recovering approximately ten municipalities at a time,[52] although as of 2017, the effort was reportedly going much slower.

Panama

Although Panama does not formally have a military to support government efforts to maintain territorial control against transnational criminal groups, its national police and other law enforcement organizations are of a size and capability, and operate with a level of professionalism, that compare favorably to both militaries and police forces elsewhere in the region.

In addition to the National Police, in 2008, the Panamanian government restructured their security organizations, combining the national air service and national maritime service into a new, ultimately more capable organization, the Air-Naval Service (*SENAN*). In addition, the Frontier Service was transferred from the police and made into an independent organization, *SENAFRONT*.[53]

With respect to border control, Panama's southern border with Colombia has historically presented more challenges than the northern border with Costa Rica. Efforts to controlling and interdicting illicit flows on that border involve not only traditional smuggling groups, but also the 57th front of the FARC in Colombia, including the threat that the group has presented in the past to towns on the Panamanian side of the border. At the height of power of the 57th Front, the Panamanian frontier forces had to divert significant resources from effectively controlling the national territory, to simply protecting Panamanian towns. In 2009, however, *SENAFRONT* launched "Plan Total Mobility," which improved the government's control of the area by using company-sized mobile forces, which allowed its forces to move beyond guarding border towns to project a more constant presence on the border.

Such advances notwithstanding, with the November 2016 peace accords in Colombia, Panamanian security forces worried about the remnants of the FARC front converting into criminal organizations, or passing into the ranks of established Colombian transnational groups already operating in the area such as the *Gulf Clan*.[54]

Peru

For Peru's security forces, territorial control to combat transnational organized crime is a multidimensional challenge, made more difficult by the size and diversity of the national territory and the number and different types of transnational criminal operations operating within it.

The land control challenges for Peruvian forces include the need to stop narcotraffickers transporting cocaine and other products through the national territory, often carried in vehicles with hidden compartments, or in backpacks by individuals traveling on foot (*mochileros*) from drug producing regions out of the country. Problem areas to be controlled include the *VRAEM*, previously the Upper Huallaga Valley (less a focus today than in the late 2000s), and (more recently) the eastern side of the Andes mountains. Reciprocally, Peruvian security forces must control the smuggling of dynamite and guns from Bolivia into Peru.[55]

Part of Peru's attempts at territorial control involves the deployment of military and other forces into problem regions such as those mentioned previously. In the VRAEM, which has arguably been the principal focus of such efforts in recent years, the Peruvian military has established approximately sixty permanent and temporary bases to control the terrain, particularly in areas where the *Shining Path* is believed to be operating.[56]

With respect to controlling the roads for moving illicit goods in the country, the efforts of the Peruvian authorities are limited by the number of scanners that the government has been able to acquire to deploy at checkpoints along the nation's fourteen principal land transport corridors, in order to examine the contents of trucks and containers passing through. Complicating matters, such scanners also break down frequently, in what is believed to be deliberate sabotage orchestrated by the smugglers.[57]

Brazil

In the case of Brazil, during the past decade, the country has significantly expanded its efforts to control its extensive land border, shared with ten countries. Such efforts include beginning to deploy a system of satellite observation and communication relays for monitoring the Amazon, *SIVAM* (*Sistema de Vigilância da Amazônia*), leveraging other systems, such as the CINDACTA-4 system of air control radars providing coverage in the region.[58] Even more importantly, Brazil is building a system for monitoring the nation's borders, *SISFRON* (*Sistema de Vigilância Integrada das Fronteras*),[59] although due to budget limitations, as of the end of 2017, only a prototype of the system was being deployed in the area along Brazil's border with Paraguay, and even this project was approximately two years behind schedule.[60]

The country is also deploying additional military forces into the 150-kilometer band of territory along its borders where the military is authorized special police powers.[61] Nonetheless, the need to dedicate forces to provide urban security in the favelas and other "Guarantee of Law and Order" missions has delayed such deployments to the border to some degree. In addition to long-term deployments, the military also regularly conducts exercises in the border region, including a major exercise in

November 2017 in the Brazil-Colombia-Peru tri-border area called Amazon Log.[62]

As Brazil has sought to expand coordination with its neighbors for improved cooperative security of those borders, its principal series of exercises focused on controlling organized crime activities on its borders is the Ágata series of exercise, initiated in 2011.[63] One such exercise was conducted in June 2016, featuring eleven thousand soldiers deployed in the border region from Roraima state (adjoining Venezuela and Guyana to the north), to Rio Grande do Sul in the south, and seizing over $200,000 in contraband merchandise.[64] In recent years, the Agata family of exercises has been restructured to permit greater flexibility in the scope and duration of each event, to increase effectiveness by making it more difficult for criminals to predict when the armed forces may be conducting a major operation in the area.[65]

Despite some progress, efforts to control the borders have been impeded by the vastness of the area to be controlled, Brazil's political, economic, and associated fiscal crises, and the lack of an interagency legal framework which facilitates coordination among multiple players at the federal and state levels.[66]

Beyond border control, the Brazilian military has occasionally been deployed to provide security against powerful delinquent groups in favelas such as Rocinha, Alemao, and Maré, particularly during important events such as the 2014 World Cup and the 2016 Olympics, and when the need has exceeded the capabilities of state and local law enforcement. In 2017, federal forces were deployed to provide territorial Control in the City of Vitoria, When Police Went on Strike There,[67] and later in Rio de Janeiro, when local security forces threatened to do so.[68]

Argentina

Because Argentina's 1988 defense law prohibits the military from involvement in internal security, the control of the national territory against overland smuggling and other criminal activity on the national territory is almost exclusively the responsibility of civilian organizations such as the national police, the *Gendarmerie* (elite police forces), and provincial-level police forces. The resources of these organizations have been stretched, particularly with the need to dedicate a greater number of forces, including the *Gendarmerie*, to combat insecurity in urban areas.

Because, as noted previously, Argentina has particular problems with the flow of drugs across of the north of the country from the Bolivian border to international ports in the province of Santa Fe, and near Buenos Aires, the Macri administration has established a series of interagency task forces focused on this region of the country. The first one was established in the province of Salta in late 2016, with the second one to begin functioning in the province of Misiones during 2017.[69]

Air Interdiction

Airspace control has been a particularly important focus for Latin American governments for controlling narcotrafficking and other activities by transnational organized crime groups in both source zone and transit zone countries. Governments have generally attacked illicit flows through the airspace through a combination of identifying and destroying clandestine airstrips, and attempting to stop smuggling flights themselves by improving radar coverage of the national airspace, deploying interceptor aircraft, and passing laws authorizing the forcing down (or shooting down, if necessary) of aircraft violating the airspace.

Thanks to interdiction efforts by the US, led by JIATF-South, in conjunction with partner nations across the region, the number of suspicious flights transiting the airspace of Latin American countries fell by 53 percent from 2015 to 2016.[70]

Attempts to attack the problem by acting against airstrips have been relatively unproductive, since these can be rebuilt (generally by paying workers from the local community) almost fast as they can be identified and destroyed.[71] Across the region, an increasing number of countries have sought to stop drug flights by asserting more positive control over their airspace through legal frameworks that allow them to shoot down unauthorized aircraft. Indeed, as of the end of 2016, Argentina, Bolivia, Honduras Paraguay, Peru, and Venezuela had all adopted such "shoot down" laws. Such laws have generally been accompanied by the purchase or upgrade of radar systems, interceptor aircraft, and other capabilities to make the assertion of control over the national airspace credible, although in practice, such acquisitions and the ability and willingness of the countries involved to intercept and force down aircraft varies greatly. During the US administration of Barrack Obama, the pursuit of "shoot down" laws created difficulties in the country's security cooperation relationship with the United States.

Guatemala

The ability of Guatemala to control its airspace has been limited by the absence of adequate interceptor aircraft, as well as lack of an integrated radar picture capable of integrating national radar assets and other feeds to identify and respond to unauthorized transits by suspected narcoflights.

The assets of the Guatemalan Air Force are limited to a small number of relatively slow, light helicopters and fixed wing planes which have been previously confiscated from criminals. These include a B-200 Beechcraft King Air, outfitted by the US with *Forward-Looking Infrared Radar* (*FLIR*) to detect targets at sea, as well as a Cessna Caravan which helps to identify narco landing strips in remote areas such as Petén, and three other similar small planes. Yet none of these have the speed, armament, or other attributes which would allow them to function effectively as interceptors.

Although Guatemala also has A-37 and Pilatus P-7 aircraft donated by the US, these are considered too expensive to repair and return to flight status. Similarly, the nation's five Bell UH-1H helicopters are unable to fly due to a need to overhaul their turbine engines, while the two Bell 212 helicopters owned by the Air Force are even more expensive to maintain.[72]

With respect to the ability to detect air targets, Guatemala currently has three primary (transmitting) radars, located in San Jose, Puerto Barrios, and Petén, as well as three secondary radar receivers, in San Jose, Petén, and Palermo. None of these, however, are directly linked to Guatemala's national command and control system, meaning that radar operators must manually report targets that they detect, creating delays and imprecision that decreases the likelihood of successfully intercepting the detected target.

Honduras

Honduras is one of the countries in the region which has most assertively taken action to control its airspace through a new combination of laws, radar coverage, and interception capabilities. In 2013, the Honduran government purchased three radars from Israel to provide it a capability for detecting and tracking aircraft entering its airspace.[73] In January 2015, the Honduran Congress passed a law authorizing its armed forces to force or shoot down aircraft making unauthorized transits.[74] Its actions reportedly raised concern in the US over the possibility of an accidental downing of an aircraft, leading the US to restrict types of military collaboration with the country that could support such a shoot-down, such as passing radar tracks.[75] Nonetheless, the program has led to a significant reduction in narcotraffickers using aircraft to smuggle drugs through Honduras,[76] even though, as of 2017, the Honduran government had not shot down any aircraft.

Panama

In the case of Panama, in 2012, the government began to acquire a system of radars to assert control over its airspace, but ran into difficulties with the procurement. It purchased nineteen radars for $25 million,[77] but the contract was only partially fulfilled due to cost overruns, generating a public scandal and charges of criminal wrongdoing.[78]

As a complement to the radars, *SENAN*, the previously discussed aeronaval service, has seven helicopters which provide a limited capability for aerial interception.

Dominican Republic

As noted in chapter 2, the airspace of the Dominican Republic is regularly challenged by narcoflights originating from Colombia and Venezuela, including planes which approach the edge of Dominican airspace and drop packages of drugs with locating devices to be picked up by boats that come from shore. In a small number of cases, narcotraffickers had become so bold as to fly into the nation's airspace and openly land their planes on the roads to transfer their cargo of drugs.

Partly in response to such incursions, in 2008, the country's military has acquired eight Brazilian "Super Tucano" interceptor aircraft,[79] complemented by a $34 million system of radars purchased from Israeli Aircraft Industries.[80] As of 2017, the Dominican government had not passed a law authorizing the interceptors to shoot down aircraft entering its airspace without authorization, but the ability to intercept and follow such flights nonetheless had some deterrent effect; in recent years, attempts to penetrate the national airspace have fallen 50–60 percent.[81]

Peru

Peru, like Honduras, has partially put into place a physical and legal framework for intercepting aircraft making unauthorized incursions into its airspace. In February 2015, the Peruvian government declared a "no fly zone" over the VRAEM.[82] In following month, the Defense Committee of the Peruvian Congress advanced a law legalizing the shoot-down of unauthorized flights through Peruvian airspace.[83] Nonetheless, consideration of the law caused significant concern within the United States during the Obama administration, particularly given the previous mistaken downing of a civilian aircraft by Peruvian authorities in 2001, in which the US had a supporting role in the interception.[84] In recognition of the sensitivity over the new law, the Humala government never called it for a vote before the full Peruvian Congress.[85]

With respect to the radars necessary to monitor Peruvian airspace against incursions, the Peruvian government reportedly visited multiple potential suppliers, yet was slow to make a purchase.[86] In addition, due to political sensitivities, final authority to shoot down an aircraft was initially vested in the president of the republic, making obtaining an authorization difficult. By the end of 2017, authority to shoot down an aircraft had been transferred to the Ministry of Defense, and the Peruvian armed forces had acquired the radars and other technical requirements to effectively respond to and force down unauthorized aircraft in Peruvian airspace. According to Peruvian sources consulted off-the-record for this work, by the end of 2017, the ability of the system to intercept aircraft had significantly reduced unauthorized air transits, yet the armed forces had not actually had to use the system to shoot down an aircraft.

Brazil

The government of Brazil has a relatively robust defense against narcoflights. This includes a system of radars for monitoring national airspace, CINDACTA, a relatively modern fleet of capable interceptor aircraft, and a law authorizing shoot-downs of aircraft making unauthorized transits of Brazilian airspace. Through the previously mentioned SIVAM system, soldiers on patrol on the ground are also able to relay the position of suspected narco aircraft passing overhead to air controllers. Nonetheless, the area encompassed by Brazil's border regions and the overlying airspace is enormous, making it difficult for Brazilian interceptors to respond to fleeting incursions of the nation's airspace, such as flights carrying drugs from Peru, before the aircraft can drop its cargo of drugs on the Brazilian side of the border to awaiting accomplices and return to the Peruvian side of the border.

Argentina

Argentina is arguably the most recent country in the region to begin using its armed forces to prevent narcoflights in the national airspace. In January 2016, the incoming administration of Mauricio Macri adopted Decree 228,[87] which declared a state of emergency and authorized the limited use of the armed forces in the fight against narcotrafficking. The decree empowered the military to protect the national airspace in the north of the country in support of the government's broader operation to control its borders against narcotraffickers, termed "Operation Northern Shield." Among its other provisions, Decree 228 authorized the military to shoot down suspected narco flights. Nonetheless, for some Argentine military officers, the number of their comrades-in-arms still in prison for having killed civilians during the country's "dirty war" against leftist insurgents in the 1970s makes them uncomfortable with the military's legal protections under the decree.[88]

In support of its new mission, the Argentine military has expanded radar coverage against drug flights by increasing the number of operating hours of radars positioned in the north, and deploying new radars to the north of the country (including those produced domestically by the government defense technology company INVAP).[89] Nonetheless, efforts by the Argentine government to expand radar coverage have reportedly been impeded by some provincial governments, such as that of Formosa, which reportedly has moved slowly in building the infrastructure necessary to deploy the radars.[90]

Complicating the military's ability to carry out the mission, the Argentine Air Force has a very limited number of aircraft suitable for use as interceptors, including domestically built Pucara and Pampa jets, and US-supplied A4s. The expanded pace of operations required to support

Operation Northern Shield, in combination with the age of the aircraft involved, has increased maintenance problems limiting the availability of the aircraft.[91] Indeed, in a speech to the nation in March 2016, President Macri highlighted military aircraft "incapable of flight" as a worrisome impediment in defending the national airspace against narcoflights.[92] Despite such challenges, and even without shooting down a single aircraft, the government's much-publicized decree and associated actions contributed to a 20 percent decrease in suspected narcoflights detected during 2016.[93]

THE TARGETING OF TRANSNATIONAL CRIMINAL ORGANIZATION GROUP LEADERS

In virtually every case in the struggle against organized crime groups, one early and repeated strategy of government forces has been to go after the leaders of the groups involved, through either killing or arresting them. Phrases in law enforcement discourse, such as the "kingpin strategy" are deeply rooted in the concept that taking down the head of the organization will cause the rest of the organization to fall.[94] In general, the governments of the region have succeeded in such endeavors, but in the process, have frequently expanded violence in the country and changed the pattern of criminal activities, without significantly impairing the quantity smuggling or other criminal activity.

The targeting of the leadership of transnational criminal groups arguably has its roots in traditional military thinking, in which targeting the leadership of an adversary's armed forces is an often an effective way of impairing its effectiveness or will to fight.[95] Such strategies are most commonly employed against hierarchically organized state opponents. Contemporary military doctrine acknowledges that in fighting dispersed, networked adversaries, leadership targeting is not always effective and sometimes counterproductive.[96]

Nonetheless, for Latin American politicians and leaders of military and law enforcement organizations, going after the leaderships of criminal groups is compelling because it can produce visible evidence of government accomplishments, even if broader effectiveness of the strategy is less certain and generates troubling side effects.

Mexico

From the beginning of the contemporary Mexican government campaign against the cartels when then-president Felipe Calderón ordered Mexican military forces into Michoacán in December 2006, the government identified and targeted the leaders of those groups as a core part of the national strategy. At the beginning of the Calderón *sexenio* (six-year period in office), the government published a list of its principal criminal targets,[97] and on March 23, 2009, the Mexican attorney general's office released its own list of the thirty-seven most wanted criminals in the country.[98] Over the years, during both the Calderón and Peña Nieto *sexenios*, the government repeatedly highlighted, with press conferences and official statements, its achievements against these leaders.

Notable examples of government successes against leaders of criminal groups in Mexico include the killing of Gulf Cartel leader Antonio Ezequiel Cárdenas Guillén (*Tony Tormenta*) in November 2010, the June 2013 arrest of senior Zeta boss Miguel Treviño Morales (*Z-40*) by the Mexican navy, the arrest of Hector Beltrán-Leyva (*El H*) in October 2014, the killing of Nazario Moreno González (*El Chayo*) of *La Familia Michoacana* in 2014, the February 2015 arrest of Knights Templar organization boss Servando Gómez Martínez (*La Tuta*) by the Mexican police, and the capture on multiple occasions of Sinaloa Cartel boss Joaquín Archivaldo Guzmán Loera (*El Chapo*), with the cycle of his repeated captures and escapes seeming to end with his January 2017 deportation to the United States.

As seen in chapter 3, although the government's strategy succeeded in significantly impairing, and often dismantling, the principal threats existing at the time, they also contributed significantly to violence in the country by provoking succession struggles and fights between rival groups over territory, following the weakening of one of the groups by a government operation against the other.

Central America

In Central America, by 2014, the government had begun to have some success in going after the leadership of intermediary groups which had long been moving narcotics and other illicit products through the region. While Central American governments also took action against the leaders of the Mara Salvatrucha and Barrio 18 and other street gangs, the more decentralized nature of these gangs, and the relative lack of control by the governments over their nations' penitentiaries limited the positive impact of such detentions, with gang leaders often continuing to control their organizations from within the prisons.

Guatemala

In Guatemala, as in Mexico and elsewhere in Central America, government efforts against high-value criminal targets (often supported by US intelligence collaboration and other forms of support) have contributed to successes against the leadership of the majority of Guatemala's narcotics smuggling families. As noted in chapter 3, such successes have included the arrests of Juan Alberto Ortiz Lopez (2011), Lorenzana family patriarch Waldemar Lorenzana and his sons Eliu and Waldemar

(2014), Mendoza family clan head Haroldo Mendoza Matta (2014), and Walter Mendoza (2016), among others.

As occurred in Mexico and elsewhere, these arrests and killings contributed to the fractionalization of the criminal landscape in the country, giving rise to a larger number of relatively smaller groups now working with the Mexican cartels and other organizations moving narcotics through the country. Indeed, one security official estimated that, by mid-2016, the number of criminal groups in Guatemala had risen to fifty-four, with many focused-on charging extortion or moving drugs relatively short distances from one side of the country to the other.[99]

As with other nations in the region Guatemala has relied on a combination of intelligence and financial cooperation with other countries, and elite units, to act against high-value criminal targets. Key units used include the Interagency task force against terrorism (*FIAT*). FIAT is comprised of PNC special forces (the *Halcones*) transported by the Guatemalan Air Force. In addition, the *Special Interdiction and Rescue Group* (*GEIR*) is also used against high-value criminal targets, leveraging Guatemala's elite military special forces units, the *Kaibiles*.

Honduras

In Honduras, in 2014 and 2015, with the help of the United States, the government successfully took down the leadership of the two major intermediary groups in the country: the Valle Valles (in October 2014)[100] and the Cachiros (the Javier and Leonel Rivera Maradiaga family organization) (in January 2015).[101] The Honduran government also began to pursue some of the smaller cartels, arresting Alexander Ardon of the "Ardon Brothers" in November 2015,[102] and going after the leadership of the organization *Los Pinto* through Operation Sultan in November 2016.[103] Yet while the decapitation of the leadership of such groups impaired narcotrafficking transit operations in the Honduras, it did not significantly impair organized crime. Indeed, deprived of their traditional leaders, the Mexican and other cartels working in the region began to construct ties with the new smaller groups left behind, changing the dynamics of, but not necessarily reducing, organized crime in the country.

With respect to actions against the leadership of street gangs by the Honduran government, during 2016, Honduran security forces conducted sixty raids in two waves in February and October 2016 as part of "Operation Avalanche," seizing almost sixteen hundred properties.[104] In the process, they demonstrated their willingness to go after the resources and leadership of the gangs (and not just the narcotraffickers). Nonetheless, while the level of homicides continues to fall in Honduras, it is not clear that this trend (which began far earlier with the establishment of the interagency organization FUSINA and the PMOP) is significantly driven by such leadership targeting efforts.

El Salvador

As in Guatemala and Honduras with the transportistas in those countries, the government of El Salvador has targeted the heads of that country's two major smuggling groups, the *Texis* Cartel, and the *Perrones*. As noted previously, in April 2017, the Salvadoran police successfully arrested Texis Cartel leader Chepe Diablo on money laundering charges. Previously, in July 2014, the government arrested twnety-nine members of the *Perrones* in July 2014,[105] Nonetheless, the most significant action against the leadership of the *Perrones*, the June 2014 murder in Honduras of the group's boss, Chepe Luna,[106] cannot be ascribed to government efforts.

With respect to actions by the Salvadoran government against the leadership of the gangs, as mentioned at the beginning of this chapter, from the beginning of its initial "heavy hand" (*mano duro*) response to the gangs, under Salvadoran president Francisco Flores in 2003,[107] it targeted their leaders, placing the majority of known MS-13 and Barrio 18 leaders in prison, but was unable to prevent them from continuing to manage the affairs of their organizations from behind bars. Indeed, El Salvador's relatively poorly controlled prisons arguably gave the gangs the opportunity to consolidate leadership over group members who found themselves inside Salvador's penitentiaries with those leaders.

Despite the shortcomings of such early efforts, when El Salvador launched a new series of actions against the gangs in April 2016, it chose, among its other activities, to target one hundred key gang leaders in the country not already in prison.[108] The Salvadoran government also used the previously mentioned FERES integrated military-police units to go after gang leaders, as well as relocating already incarcerated key gang leaders to maximum security prisons in an effort to impair their ability to control their organizations.[109]

Colombia

In Colombia, as in other countries in the region, the police, armed forces, and others have sought to take down high-value targets as part of their broader struggle against terrorist and criminal groups. The effort includes intelligence subcommittees, commonly referred to as "bubbles" (*burbujas*). The Colombian government reportedly has a two-tier system of high-value targets, with some considered more strategic and others more secondary. The number on the list has reportedly varied. In addition to the leadership of dissident FARC factions, BACRIM are significant targets.[110] The impact of the Colombia peace accord on high-value targeting is unclear, but presumably the signing of the accords required the removal of senior FARC operatives from the list.

Peru

In Peru, task forces such as those previously led by Ivan Vega have had considerable success in operations against leaders of the narcoterrorist group *Shining Path*. The organizations involved in such operation include the *Wolf Brigade* of the National Police, which played a key role against the organization when Vega was viceminister of the interior. Later, the *Combined Intelligence and Special Operations Command* (CIOEC) reportedly played an important role in such high-value targeting when Vega was Viceminister of Defense, although he resigned from the post in March 2013.[111] Successful actions against the *Shining Path* leadership using such organizations include the previously mentioned killing of Comrade William in Ayacucho in September 2012,[112] and the August 2013 killing of Comrades Alipio and Gabriel by *Operation Wolf*.[113] By contrast to the targeting of the leadership of *Shining Path*, there have been only a modest number of operations against the leaders of Peru's family clans, which are generally much smaller and more numerous, and which collectively control important parts of the nation's criminal economy.[114]

THE USE OF THE MILITARY IN DOMESTIC LAW ENFORCEMENT

In the majority of countries of the region, governments have concluded that in certain areas, the challenge of transnational organized crime requires the use of the military to supplement conventional law enforcement organizations. In most of Latin America, the question of using the military in the fight against organized crime is complicated by a twentieth century history of problems related to use of the military against other internal threats, leaving a legacy of mistrust among some sectors of the population regarding potential abuses by the armed forces in such a role, and often, legal and constitutional prohibitions against a military role in internal security. A number of scholars have also emphasized the distinct nature of the military from the police as institutions, with different fundamental purposes, tradition, training, and other attributes.[115]

The motivations for involving the military in the fight against organized crime are diverse. Military officials and others commonly argue that the constant contact of law enforcement personnel with populations engaged in criminal activity has made them vulnerable to both the resources of organized criminal groups and the ability of those groups to intimidate law enforcement members and their families. Another frequently offered reason for the need for military involvement is that conventional police lack the firepower, assets, advanced training, quantity, or quality of personnel to take on sophisticated, well-armed, and equipped criminal groups. In some cases, however, the impulse to use the military in the context of a significant threat to public order also reflects the self-image of the armed forces as the guardians of last resort of order in the country.

Such reasoning does not, however, always lead to a decision to involve the military in a major way in the fight against transnational organized crime. In Chile, for example, the combination of history of prior military involvement in internal affairs, laws clearly separating the role of the military from the police, viable options for confronting organized crime through conventional law enforcement, and the military's organizational pride regarding not involving itself in internal affairs, together has prevented them from assuming a significant role in the fight against transnational organized crime in their countries.

Mexico

In the contemporary struggle against organized crime in Latin America and the Caribbean, no other country in recent history has employed the military against transnational criminal groups on a greater scale than has Mexico. Although the deployment of the Mexican armed forces against criminal organizations in the country since 2006 is often characterized as an anomaly in current Mexican politics, in reality, its military has periodically played a role in maintaining internal order in the country since the Mexican Revolution, and before. The contemporary legal framework for the Mexican armed forces to conduct operations against narcotrafficking is the country's National Security Law, reformed in 2010,[116] and again in December 2017, to provide additional legal authority to govern the ongoing involvement of its military forces in operations against narcotrafficking.

Although the Mexican armed forces had previously conducted smaller-scale operations against organized crime groups in the country, their large-scale use against criminal groups in the contemporary context begun with the deployment of the Mexican army and navy to the state of Michoacán in December 2006, in response to extreme violence by transnational organized groups there including both the *Zetas* and the campaign of *La Familia Michoacana* against them, as discussed in chapter 3.

While the armed forces have coordinated with the national police in conducting operations, they have often maintained a distance from the country's state and municipal police forces due to concerns over corruption. Indeed, often military interventions, including the deployment of the Mexican Navy to Veracruz in 2011 to temporarily assume control over public security functions there, have been driven in part by the belief that state police forces are thoroughly corrupted.[117]

Within Mexico's two separate armed forces (the army and the navy), the deployment of the military has arguably had the most significant impact on the navy, whose pre-2006 role with respect to land forces was principally focused on ports and littoral areas, the protection of critical infrastructure such as petroleum assets in the Gulf of Mexico, and the preparation of naval special forces for operations where needed. Since the first major deployment of the navy, to Michoacán in 2006, that involvement has arguably contributed significantly to the refinement of doctrine regarding land operations by the Mexican naval infantry, as well as to greater coordination between the Mexican navy and Mexican army.

As of the time this book went to press, the Mexican army and navy together had approximately fifty-two thousand persons deployed across the country. As cartel violence continued to escalate at the end of the Peña Nieto sexenio, military deployments to individual crisis spots continued. In January 2017, for example, the government deployed five hundred soldiers to Ciudad Mier, in the state of Tamaulipas, along the US-Mexico border, in response to security challenges there.[118]

As has occurred in many countries in the region, the involvement by the military in operations on Mexican territory with Mexican nationals has led to concern regarding the adequacy of the legal framework in which the armed forces operate. As in other countries in the region, the ability to try Mexican military officers in civilian courts for activities not arising directly from their military duties has created discomfort among military officers. Such concerns have been heightened by numerous complaints against Mexican military officers,[119] as well as specific high-profile cases, such as an investigation into whether a June 2014 gun battle in Tlatlaya that killed twenty-two gang members was actually an execution by military forces,[120] or whether the military was involved in wrongdoing in the September 2014 deaths of forty-seven university students in the town of Ayotzinapa.[121] The passage of a law clarifying the role, responsibilities, and legal protections for the military in conducting domestic law enforcement operations in December 2017 was, in part, a response to the need for a clearer legal framework for the military to operate in, as highlighted by such cases.[122]

As in other parts of the region, extracting the Mexican military from its internal security role is regularly discussed, with little progress toward that goal. During Enrique Peña Nieto's campaign for the presidency in 2012, he proposed creating a new fifty thousand member militarized elite police force, the *Gendarmerie*, in order to replace the Mexican military in its operations inside the country. In the end, however, the *Gendarmerie*, was redefined as a much smaller, five thousand-person force, subordinate to the national police, and its creation did not substantially impact the use of the military within the country.[123]

Guatemala

Guatemala, like its Central American neighbors Honduras and El Salvador, has been forced to use the military in a security role. Yet Guatemala is arguably the Central American nation in which that role has been most restricted.

Although the Guatemalan military played a key role in the internal affairs of the country during the 1960–1996 Civil War, its size and budget were dramatically reduced pursuant to the 1996 peace accords ending that conflict. Indeed, the 1996 peace accords limited the size of the Guatemalan defense budget to a mere .33 percent of Gross Domestic Product and an end-strength of thirty-three thousand troops, down from fifty-four thousand during the war. Oscar Berger, who was President of Guatemala from 2004 to 2008, reduced the military budget and size of the armed forces even further, to just .17 percent of GDP and fifteen thousand persons, arguably impeding its ability to exercise effective control over national territory, although its funding has subsequently been restored to the level authorized under the 1996 Peace Agreement. Nonetheless, perhaps more than its other Northern Triangle counterparts, the Guatemalan armed forces face resistance from within segments of the society to its role in internal security, including insistence that its activities should always be in support of, rather than directing, civil authorities.

As significant cuts to the military created opportunities for the expansion of narcotrafficking and organized crime in the country in the mid-2000s, Guatemala's initial stopgap measure was to create a new civil force, drawing heavily on former military officers, to patrol the streets, called *Citizen Security Squadrons* (*Escuadrones de Seguridad Ciudadana*). As of late 2016, there were nine such squadrons of six hundred people each. They were principally used to patrol in the poorer, high-crime neighborhoods of the country's major cities, often in conjunction with regular police.[124]

The *Citizen Security Squadrons* have arguably been handicapped by their status as neither formally a military nor a police organization. On the one hand, they lack police authority, such as the ability to make arrests, as well as institutional legal protections against citizen complaints. On the other hand, they lack the capability of a traditional military organization, although as noted, many of their members have former military experience. In addition, as has occurred with the regular police, there is concern that regular contact with the population by the *Citizen Security Squadrons* in the areas being patrolled is beginning to involve the force in corruption.[125]

As of 2017, Guatemala's government was working to expand the national civil police force by six thousand persons, with the objective of eventually replacing the *Citizen Security Squadrons* with regular national police forces.[126] As an initial step, in January 2017, the government announced that the Citizen Security Squadrons would be removed from their current patrolling duties, with some to be redeployed to help the regular armed forces control territory in areas such as the remote *Maya Biosphere* in the north of the country.[127]

Apart from the *Citizen Security Squadrons*, perhaps the most significant use of the Guatemalan military in support of civil authorities to combat organized crime, as previously noted, is the creation of a series of interagency task forces focused on the nation's borders. These include the *Interagency Task Force Tecun Uman*, deployed in San Marcos since October 2013, focused on the border with Mexico, and the *Interagency Task Force Chorti*, deployed since October 2014, focused on the border with Honduras, including activities in the departments of Chiquimula, Zacapa and Izabal. In August 2017, the government inaugurated a third interagency task force, "*Xinca*," in Jutiapa, focused on the border with El Salvador, and planned to establish a fourth task force, "*Jaguar*," to operate in the west of Petén, focused on that department's border with Mexico.[128]

While the task forces have generally been well-regarded, there have reportedly been difficulties. Police units assigned to the task forces are criticized as being relatively disconnected from intelligence and support of the rest of the national police system (due in part to concerns of corruption within that police network). In addition, military officers have expressed frustrations over being subordinated to police commissars with much less experience than they have in commanding large units in the field.[129]

Beyond the interagency task forces, Guatemala has also incorporated the military in elite interagency units to act against criminals. These include the previously mentioned *GEIR*, which incorporates units from the elite special forces the *Kabiles* to operate against high-value criminal objectives. In the maritime domain, Guatemala has created a Naval Infantry Brigade (*Brigada de Infantería de Marina*), which it uses for law enforcement missions in its territorial waters and in its rivers. As part of this force, the navy's own elite special forces, the *FEN* (*Fuerzas Especiales Navales*), operate as an interdiction forces to realize operations against narcotraffickers on the open ocean and inland waterways, although representatives of the Guatemalan National Police participating in the group must still physically make the arrest.

El Salvador

In Salvador, as in Guatemala, the role of the military in the fight against organized crime is shaped by the legacy of the civil war in that country. As in Guatemala, following the end of the Salvadoran Civil War in 1992, the armed forces were cut in size from sixty-three thousand to thirty-two thousand, creating a power vacuum that was arguably an enabling factor in the expansion of violent street gangs across the country.

During the same period, the national police was restructured and rebuilt, using a quota system that ensured significant representation by the

FMLN in the force. Not only was the inclusion of the *FMLN* difficult for the armed forces, which had fought against the organization for twelve years in a war that cost the lives of seventy-five thousand Salvadorans, but also the quota system guaranteeing the representation of a specific number of *FMLN* within the reconstructed police, contributed to the perception among the military that the new body was both heavily shaped by its former enemy and filled with members who were not qualified to be police officers.

Nonetheless, in the context of the significant threat to law and order from violent street gangs, the Salvadoran police and military have worked through such sources of mistrust and bad feelings, to confront the common threat.

The Salvadoran military has supported the fight against transnational organized crime in the country through a series of special military commands, although always in support of civilian authorities, and always with the police retaining the principal authority make arrests. The original commands used by the Salvadoran military in this struggle, as noted previously, are *Zeus*, augmenting police in their realization of operations; *Sumpul*, protecting the nation's frontiers; *San Carlos*, helping to guard Salvadoran prisons alongside police and penitentiary system personnel; *Eagle Command*, providing military personnel to guard schools and tourist site; and *Thunder Command*, a rapid response force as needed to support other operations.

In addition, in early 2016, as noted previously, the Salvadoran military created a special reaction force, the *FERES*, to conduct operations against gang leaders and conduct forcible entry operations in gang-infested neighborhood. Going beyond the simple use of the military to complement the police, as seen in *Zeus* command, the FERES were designed as an integrated force of military and police special forces, initially comprised of ten sections of forty persons each (twenty-four military personnel and sixteen police), each divided into four squads of six military and four police.

As a compliment to the FERES, the Salvadoran government also created the previously mentioned *Intervention and Territorial Recuperation Force (FIRT)*, led by the police, but also leveraging military forces, to occupy and reestablish government control in dangerous neighborhoods across the country. The *FIRT* was launched, in April 2016, with mixed success, in the neighborhood of La Campañera,[130] although its use thereafter in other parts of the country has reportedly proceeded slowly.

Honduras

In Honduras, concerns about high levels of corruption in the police led President Juan Orlando Hernandez to create an elite police capability within the armed forces, the *Military Police for Public Order (PMOP)*, as a complement to the use of the regular armed forces in support of the police. The *PMOP* was legally authorized by the Honduran Congress in August 2013,[131] spearheaded by Juan Orlando Hernandez himself, as head of the Congress before assuming the Honduran presidency. *PMOP* was assigned wholly under the command of the previously discussed inter-agency force *FUSINA*.[132]

By contrast to other military forces conducting internal security missions in the region, the *PMOP* was given authority, under Honduran law, to perform police functions such as making arrests, with its members given substantial training in such activities. To date, it has been used principally to conduct law enforcement operations in difficult areas, such as imposing order in urban neighborhoods dominated by the maras, and conducting operations against both gangs and narcotrafficking organizations in the country. The PMOP has also been used to provide security for important public events and escorting high-profile criminals to detention facilities, or to the airport for extradition.[133]

As of 2017, the *PMOP* was comprised of six battalions of 524 persons each, deployed principally in the major urban areas of the country, Tegucigalpa, its sister city Comayagüela, and San Pedro Sula. The Hernandez administration ultimately aims for a ten-battalion force with a total compliment of compliment of 5,976 members.[134]

In addition to the training of its members in police operations, the *PMOP* uses a program of entry-level screening, and ongoing monitoring and confidence tests, including polygraphs approximately every six months, to avoid the corruption of its members.[135] Thanks in part to the *PMOP*, the murder rate in Honduras fell 36 percent from its high point of 86.5 per 100,000 in 2011.[136]

Dominican Republic

In the Dominican Republic, as in Central America, the armed forces regularly act in support of the police. Indeed, in June 2013, the newly elected government of Danilo Medina deployed 1,400 soldiers to the streets of the nation's capital, Santo Domingo, in response to increasing violence there.[137] As in El Salvador and Guatemala, the military in the Dominican Republic cannot perform arrests, save for detaining persons witnessed as committing flagrant criminal acts. In such cases, the military is expected to promptly turn the person over to the police, along with the relevant evidence. Beyond direct participation in operations against criminals, the Dominican armed forces do support operations against criminal organizations in other important ways. Military personnel, for example, provide part of the staffing to the nation's anti-drug organization, the *National Counter-Drug Command (DNCD)*.

Colombia

In Colombia, the military operate in a law enforcement capacity in select areas, but only occasionally in coordinated operations with the police. Indeed, in operations potentially involving actions against criminal groups, the Colombians have traditionally preferred to take representatives from the criminal investigation agency (*CTI*) of the attorney general's office, rather than Colombian national police personnel, because Colombian military-police relations were not strong. More recently, the Colombian national police provide special investigation units (*GOIEC*) to military battalions, which are generally used rather than the *CTI*.[138] As in most Central American countries, the Colombian military has authority to make arrests only when a member has directly observed the "flagrant" commission of a crime in the course of their other duties. The Colombian military is also developing its own capabilities to perform law-enforcement-like functions. A number of such unites already exist, as an outgrowth of efforts by the armed forces to combat the criminal activities of terrorist groups during the nation's civil war. Some of the most prominent examples include the *Gaula*, a specialized unit to fight kidnapping, a counter-narcotrafficking brigade (*BRANCA*) and a brigade created in 2015 to counter illegal mining.

The Colombian military has also begun to operate directly against criminal groups, bombing of an encampment belonging to the criminal *Gulf Clan* in November 2015.[139] Indeed, in recognition of the current and future importance of such operations, the Colombian military has developed new guidelines, including Decree 15 and 16 of the Colombian Ministry of Defense, regulating actions "armed organized groups" (*GAO*). The decrees provide guidance and supporting processes regarding which groups can potentially be combatted through the application of military force, consistent with international law. As of October 2016, groups so named include the previously mentioned *Gulf Clan*, the *Pelusos*, and the *Puntilleros*.[140]

In the context of the November 2016 peace accord formally ending the fighting between the Colombian government and the FARC, guidelines such as Decree 15 and 16 signals that the Colombian government contemplates expanding the use of the military to combat criminal groups which present a significant threat to the state, even if those groups are not explicitly seeking to overthrow the government. Nonetheless, as in other cases discussed in this work, Colombians consulted off-the-record for this work suggested that the armed forces are concerned about the legal framework within which they would be asked to conduct such operations.

Peru

In Peru, Legislative Decree 1095 gives the armed forces conditional legal authority to operate domestically with the police in areas such as the *VRAEM*.[141] In addition, as noted previously, prior to 2016, Peru's military exercised control over the region as a special district. Nonetheless, Peru's armed forces have been relatively cautious in focusing their efforts against *Shining Path*, as a terrorist group, rather than against the criminal groups that operate on the national territory. In part, this reflects the historical legacy of the *Shining Path* as the principal internal threat to the Peruvian state, and in part, because no single one of the numerous criminal family clans operating in Peru posed a threat to the Peruvian state.

Nonetheless, on various occasions, the Peruvian military has been called upon to provide security when activities by criminal groups or protesters have overwhelmed the capabilities of local and national police authorities. The most prominent recent example is the December 2015 deployment of the military to the port of Callao and surrounding neighborhoods when a turf war between rival gangs led the government to declare a state of emergency in response to the explosion of violence there.[142]

Despite the limited nature of the activities by the Peruvian military against organized crime groups, as in Mexico and elsewhere in the region, multiple Peruvian officials interviewed by the author have expressed concern whether the legal framework under which the Peruvian armed forces operate adequately protects them from criminal prosecution from actions arising from the exercise of their military duties.[143]

Brazil

The Brazilian armed forces, like their counterparts in most of the rest of the region, generally do not view operations against criminals within the national territory as their principal mission.

By contrast to other countries in Latin America, Brazil's military has special authority under the nation's 1988 constitution, in special circumstances (which it has been reluctant to put to the test), to take actions within the country as necessary to preserve the domestic order. The constitution authorizes the Brazilian military, to conduct domestic law enforcement operations in a specific place for a limited duration of time, when requested by one of Brazil's states. Within Brazil, such operations are referred to as "Guarantee of Law and Order Operations" (GLO), and Brazilian officials emphasize that such activities are conducted only on an "episodic" basis when the requirement exceeds the capabilities of the police and other authorities responsible for domestic law enforcement, but that the presence of the military, per the wording of the constitution, cannot be a permanent or regular supplement to the police.[144]

The involvement of Brazil's military in domestic law enforcement since the end of military rule in 1985 has included deployments to the slums of Rio de Janeiro, including Alemão in 2010, Rocinha in 2011, Maré in 2014, and again to Rocinha in 2017 to control violence and criminality there. It also has included deployments to urban areas during the 2014 World Cup and 2016 Olympics in Rio de Janeiro during the 2016 Olympics. The military was also deployed in January 2017 after deadly prison riots in multiple overcrowded facilities including Monte Cristo in Roraima state,[145] and Alcacuz in Natal.[146] It was also deployed to the states of Espiritu Santo when local police went on strike there in February 2017,[147] and to Rio de Janeiro later the same month when they threatened to go on strike.[148] The military was also deployed briefly to the capital, Brasilia, when large-scale protests threatened to get out of control and police forces in adjacent states were not available, sparking some political concern in the moment.[149]

While Brazil's military has exercised some police powers in its interventions in urban areas, it generally operates independently from both the investigative police, as well as the state military police forces (UPP) stationed in the favelas on a semi-permanent basis, and other law enforcement such as the police special forces unit BOPE (*Batalhão de Operações Policiais Especiais*).[150] On an unofficial basis, the Brazilian military, like others in the region, is profoundly uncomfortable with its participation in domestic security activities.

Finally, although the Brazilian federal police are the principal force in charge of border control, as discussed previously, the military has special police authorities in the strip within 150 kilometers of the nation's land borders, and also participates in exercises such as Agata and Amazon Log, and other operations to secure its frontiers.

As in other nations, despite authority within the constitution to conduct such internal operations, many in Brazil are uncomfortable with the role, and the potential vulnerability of individual members of the military for legal action in domestic courts stemming from such actions.[151]

Argentina

Since the end of military rule in Argentina in 1983, the nation's military has played a very limited role in law enforcement. Indeed, the use of the military against Argentine nationals within the country is a sensitive political matter in the country, owing to human rights abuses during the "dirty war" of the 1970s against Communist insurgents. Reflecting these concerns, as noted previously, the 1988 National Defense Law prohibits the military from a role in internal security, delegating such functions strictly to the national and provincial-level police forces, and the national militarized police, the *Gendarmerie*.

Due to such concerns and legal provisions, the military is not used to augment the national police in operations against criminal groups, or even to control land borders, as it is in other parts of the region. Such restrictions notwithstanding, the perceived threat from narcotrafficking other transnational criminal challenges within the country led the incoming Macri administration to declare a national emergency against drugs in January 2016, with Decree 228 authorizing the use of the military as a tool in that struggle.[152]

As noted previously, the principal role of the military in that fight has been to support "Operation Northern Shield" by providing radar coverage, and to conduct flights to patrol for and intercept potential enemy aircraft.

The military has also been called on to contribute in other ways to the fight against domestic criminality, but has responded cautiously. In December 2016, for example, the National Security Ministry called upon President Macri to sign a new decree authorizing the use of the military to protect critical infrastructure, which it was estimated would free up an estimated 1,500 *Gendarmerie* currently defending those assets, to be deployed into urban areas. The decree was, however, never approved.[153]

INSTITUTIONAL REFORM WITHIN LAW ENFORCEMENT

In the majority of countries within the region, combatting organized crime, perceived high levels of corruption within police and other law enforcement institutions has led to important efforts to reform those institutions, even while simultaneously pursuing other options, such as the use of the military to supplement police forces.[154]

In general, corruption affecting law enforcement varies widely across the region. Chile, for example, leads Latin America in the perceived lack of corruption in its institutions, with a score of 70/100 in the 2015 Transparency International corruption index. By contrast, Venezuela ranks 158th with a score of 17.[155]

In countries such as Chile where corruption is limited, the problems created by transnational organized crime actors can arguably be combatted from within the system, using existing mechanisms. In other cases, such as Venezuela the state may be so thoroughly penetrated by criminal actors at the highest level, actively and effectively protecting the corrupt, that a combination of sweeping political change, and the purging and reconstruction of law enforcement institutions may ultimately be required. In the middle, in some cases such as Colombia, Honduras, and Guatemala, corruption may be combatted with a combination of systemic reforms, external support, and technical means, although the process may be extended, controversial, and politically and economically disruptive.

The vulnerability of law enforcement officials throughout the region to corruption and intimidation is a significant challenge. In part because of low salaries, law enforcement personnel and their families often live in the same poor neighborhoods as the criminals that they fight against. Although most countries in the region make efforts not to assign police to operations in the neighborhoods where they live, and while police routinely have protocols to hide their identity during operations, such procedures do not fully eliminate the risks to them and to their families over time, where they face persistent, well-resourced criminal organizations with networks spanning from the areas that they operate to the zones where they, and their families, live.

With respect to technical solutions, efforts to combat corruption specifically in law enforcement include expanded use for vetting and monitoring personnel, such as polygraphs and background checks at the beginning of an individual's career, including upon entry to service academies, and on a periodic basis thereafter. To be effective, such efforts must be supported by reliable databases, and transparent, legally sound procedures that allow problem personnel to be quickly identified and eliminated. Indeed, in many cases, the success of law enforcement reform in the region has been impeded by organizational rules protecting the personnel themselves, political top cover, and distrust of such technical means among judges and others responsible for the elimination of personnel. Often, faced with such obstacles, it has been easier to simply reassign questionable personnel, rather than to fire them, with the risk that those dismissed could mount an expensive and time-consuming appeal, or even put the deciding official and his family in danger.

Maintaining a nationally accessible database of such dismissal actions, and taking timely actions to prosecute dismissed personnel where appropriate, is an equally important but often overlooked step of maintaining the integrity of law enforcement organizations. Frequently, in Latin America, purges of the police have been undermined by the ability of the terminated individual, now desperate and embittered, to obtain a new position with a different law enforcement organization, or to use his or her knowledge of the workings of police organizations in the service of a criminal entity.

Mexico

Mexico has made significant efforts to reform its police, including implementing a "unified command" (*mando unico*), a process of consolidating the nation's 1,800 municipal police forces under the control of Mexico's thirty-two state governments.[156] This effort is an attempt to combat corruption in the face of cases in which some small-town police forces had become completely co-opted by narcotraffickers.

Historically, local governments in Mexico have resisted efforts to put local police under state control because local autonomy was a tradition, and appointments to the police force were a form of patronage. Because of such factors, resistance to such initiatives has been particularly strong where the dominant political party in the locality was different than that in the state which would absorb the force. Although the Peña Nieto government was unable to secure a law to put local police forces under state control, it obligated the municipalities to do so through the federal funding to states and localities. A key instrument in this regard was the public security fund (*SUBSEMUN*) provided by the federal government to assist local governments in security matters.[157]

During the process of consolidation, there were multiple high-profile cases of local officials resisting integration, including that of Cuatemoc Blanco, the mayor of Cuernavaca, as well as Gisela Mota, the mayor of Timixco, in the state of Morelos, who was assassinated in front of her family, allegedly for supporting the initiative.[158]

The result of efforts to achieve "unified command" has been achievement of state control over municipal police forces to some degree, but with important differences in the way that states have implemented it, or left items in local hands such as administration, salaries, and confidence testing. The initiative is regarded as a relative success in some states, such as the relatively wealthy Nuevo Leon,[159] as well as in the state of Mexico, where 118 of 125 municipalities agreed to the initiative.[160] Nonetheless, despite such significant, if uneven, advances, the Mexican public does not fully perceive the reform to be complete. In a 2016 poll conducted by the respected Mexican Newspaper *El Universal* only 17 percent of Mexico's 1,800 municipalities were perceived to have implemented unified command.[161]

Beyond Mando Unico, at the federal level, as in other countries in the region, the federal police have expanded confidence testing and internal purges to combat corruption within its ranks. Nonetheless, Mexican security professionals still continue to regard it as inefficient, corrupt, and profoundly infiltrated by organized crime.[162] Another part of Mexico's attempt to reform its police is the failed experiment to work with self-defense groups (and even incorporate them into police forces in some cases) to respond to the crisis in public security. In Michoacán, the federal government cautiously accepted such groups, created in the state largely in response to the activities there of the criminal organizations *La Familia Michoacana* and *Knights' Templar*. The government attempted to regulate the group, and ultimately put them under the supervision of the Mexican Army. Yet elements of the organizations were engaged in criminal activities,[163] with some even covertly backed by the cartel *Jalisco Nueva Generación*, which hoped to use them to displace their rivals from

Michoacán.[164] In the end, the government officially gave the self-defense groups the choice of incorporating themselves into the regular police (with associated controls and oversight), or remaining outside of the law, which a substantial portion did.

Perhaps the greatest reform for Mexican law enforcement was the transition of the judicial system to an adversarial system of justice. Although the first oral trials under the new system began in Mexico City in January 2015,[165] the process of certifying individual jurisdictions throughout the country to change over to the new system continues. While Mexico's law schools, judges, lawyers, and institutions are struggling with the transition, the government reportedly hopes that the new system will facilitate the resolution of minor cases more efficiently, help to lower the backlog of people in pre-trial detention, and allow a greater focus on more serious offenders.[166]

Guatemala

In Guatemala, during the administrations of Otto Perez Molina and Jimmy Morales, the government has made important progress in professionalizing the national police and combatting corruption within its ranks, although much work remains to be done. The contemporary problems with the Guatemalan national police are related, in part, to the dismantling of its predecessor organization following the 1996 peace accords that ended that nation's thirty-six-year-long civil war. The difficulties were further complicated by the flawed reconstruction of the police based on the model of the Spanish Civil Guard, which was not entirely appropriate to the Guatemalan experience. The result was the creation of a new national police entity with limited professionalization, and a vulnerability to the expansion of narcoviolence in the early 2000s.[167]

During the administration of Otto Perez Molina, the Interior Ministry of Guatemala instituted a more structured police career path in an effort to improve police professionalism and fight corruption. The reforms included expanding police professional education requirements; the ministry, for example, created a year-long education program in police sciences to become an officer, supplemented by master's degrees in police forensics and criminal investigation.[168]

The government also expanded the program for screening new entrants into the national police, and regularly administering confidence tests for police officers thereafter, as well as expanding efforts to impose legal charges against them for criminal wrongdoing through existing channels, rather than just firing them. Although some criticized the reforms for moving too slowly and working within the existing system, those responsible for the effort consulted for this study argue that the process helped avoid the costs of numerous appeals from expelled police officers, as well as preventing the putting of large numbers of corrupt fired police onto the streets, where they might turn their bitterness and desperation to criminal activities, leveraging their knowledge of the Guatemalan police system and its personnel.[169]

In addition to educational reforms and screening, the Guatemalan government has also provided the PNC with more and better technology, such as tools to connect the officers who interact with suspects on the street, with police and other databases that allow them to identify whether persons they are detaining are wanted on criminal charges. Doing so not only alerts the officer to the potential risk and opportunity to detain a wanted criminal, but also, by recording who has made the inquiry, making it more difficult for him or her to allow the suspect to go free by bribing the official.

While the Guatemalan national police is also hampered by a lack of resources, the situation is improving. Overall, the organization has been expanded from less than thirty thousand persons, to thirty-five thousand, with plans to grow by another six thousand as it replaces the previously mentioned "Citizen Security Brigades" (which are comprised principally of former military personnel) with civilian police. At the political level, above administrative reforms within the PNC, some of the most important blows against corruption, both technically and symbolically, have come from the Commission Against Impunity in Guatemala (CICIG). At its core, its success comes from leveraging actors external to the national political system, to empower the CICIG within Guatemala, to take forward legal actions against powerful elites in a form that is too visible, and perceived as too legitimate, to be easily stopped by those elites.

In Guatemala the CICIG, backed by the United Nations and under the leadership of Colombian judge Ivan Velasquez, successfully brought charges against, and secured the removal of both Vice President Roxana Baldetti and President Otto Perez Molina.[170] By 2017, it not only had elaborated a series of cases against Baldetti, Perez Molina, and other senior leaders, but also had begun to pursue cases against local politicians such as Antigua mayor Edgar Francisco Ruiz Paredes and other local-level officials.[171] Throughout 2017, CICIG continued to demonstrate that no one was too well-connected to be beyond its reach, when it arrested both the son and brother of Guatemala's new president, Jimmy Morales, for influence peddling,[172] was investigating matters involving the president himself, and successfully blocked an associated attempt by the president in September 2017 to terminate its mandate.[173] Despite its considerable accomplishments, the power of the CICIG goes beyond its legal authority, insofar as that it has fundamentally altered expectations among normal Guatemalans that the wealthy and politically powerful can be brought to account through the application of law and concerted political action.

Honduras

In Honduras, under the administration of President Juan Orlando Hernandez, the country has made a series of increasingly effective efforts to purge corrupt elements from its police force. In the early days of the Hernandez administration, with the support of the US, the Honduran national police implemented a new system of controls, including widespread screening through polygraph tests. The government used Spanish-speaking personnel from Colombia, supplied through a program with the US, to help administer the test.

Unfortunately, early efforts ran into multiple problems. On one hand, the number of officers who failed the tests was far greater than anticipated, presenting the dilemma of how to deal with the large number who had failed the test, without effectively dismantling the police force. The ability to remove officers who had failed the test was also made difficult by protections afforded to them under the basic law governing the police. Compounding such obstacles, many judges were reportedly reluctant to accept the failure of a polygraph test as a reason for depriving a police officer of his livelihood.[174]

To avoid the difficulties associated with firing police officers, those failing the polygraph tests or otherwise suspected of corruption were too often simply transferred to another part of the force. In addition, for those who were indeed dismissed, the lack of a national database on police officers meant that they could easily obtain a police or security sector job elsewhere, without their new employer knowing the reason they had previously been fired.

In recognition of the shortcomings of the initial attempt to clean up the police, the Hernandez government created a new police reform commission. The new body evaluated police personnel across the force, and demonstrated a willingness to act against senior police officials where there was evidence of wrongdoing. By January 2017, the new commission had evaluated over 4,900 officers, and had fired over 2,500 of them. In total, the government dismissed 18 percent of the entire police force, with 28 percent of those fired being senior-level personnel.[175] In January 2017, in an encouraging gesture, the Hernandez administration renewed the commission to continue its work for another year.[176] In October 2017, the campaign against police corruption also resulted in the arrest of former police commissioner Jorge Alberto Barralaga through Operation Perseus, providing further evidence that action against police corruption in Honduras was reaching senior levels, at least in some cases.[177]

Colombia

In Colombia, the national police has long had an extensive system of internal controls, balanced against extensive corrupting forces, particularly against organizations such as the police counternarcotics directorate (DIRAN). The police reportedly administer some four thousand polygraphs per year, for example, yet the force has grown so quickly in recent years that even such controls have been insufficient.[178]

TARGETING THE FINANCIAL RESOURCES OF TRANSNATIONAL ORGANIZED CRIME

As noted previously, the ability of transnational criminal groups to repatriate and legitimize earnings from their illicit activities is one of the centers of gravity in the war against such groups. The importance of focusing on this money trail has received increasing recognition within the region in recent years.[179] The large informal sectors in the economies of the region have made such efforts difficult. In Peru, for example, almost three-fourths of the population of the country are believed to be employed outside in unregistered employment.[180] In the informal sector, the absence of tax recordkeeping and the reliance of cash facilitates the laundering of money and the legitimation of illicitly generated wealth by transnational organized crime groups.

For their part, a number of countries in the region have imposed new laws and regulations for better monitoring and controlling financial flows, in order to restrict the space in which illicit groups can operate. They have passed more stringent regulations and oversight governing banking and foreign currency transactions, including in money changing houses.

An important advance in recent years has been the establishment or enhancement of "Financial Intelligence Units," (FIUs) in multiple countries of the region, although the level of success, to date, has been uneven. Such advances have also been assisted by the Edgemont Group, a global society of FIUs, established to promote standardized practices, enhanced collaboration, and secure communications between its members. In Latin America and the Caribbean, the Edgemont Group has thirty-five members.[181] Complimenting FIUs on the US side, the Treasury Department and its Financial Action Task Force (FATF) has been an important tool.

Mexico

In Mexico, the Treasury Department (Secretaria de *Hacienda y Crédito Publico*) has established a FIU, although the organization is relatively small and, at the time of this writing, its coordination with the US Treasury Department and other relevant financial institutions around the world was limited.[182]

In 2014, Mexico passed a law limiting bank deposits in dollars. Although the law made money laundering more difficult, it caused difficulty for some residents and businesses.[183] Despite such laws, however, the Mexican government's control over the financial sector remains limited.[184]

Honduras

Honduras, like the majority of other nations in the region, has a Financial Intelligence Unit, accepted into the Edgemont Group in June 2005. The principal institution is the National Commission of Banking and Securities (*Comisión Nacional de Bancos y Seguros*). As with other FIUs in the region, it is a member of the International Financial Action Group of Latin America (*GAFILAT*), which conducts periodic inspections of the intuition and makes recommendations, with the last major inspection being June 2015.[185]

With respect to actions against economic elites, in 2015, the government took the bold step of arresting Jaime Rosenthal, arguably the leading businessman in the country, and extraditing him to the United States to face trial.[186] As part of the same case, based in part on intelligence and a request from the US Treasury Department, the Honduran government shut down Continental Bank, the most important financial institution in the country, for its ties to narcotraffickers.

With respect to the fight against gang money, during the course of 2016, the Honduran government conducted the multi-phase "Operation Avalanche," which included sixty operations and seized over 1,500 gang assets in October 2016 alone.[187]

Guatemala

In Guatemala, the state's principal tool to uncover and combat financial crimes is the "Special Verification Unit" (*IVE*), located within the nation's banking supervisory organization, the *Superintendencia de Bancos de Guatemala*. Its efforts are complimented by specialized organizations within the national police for making arrests and seizing assets, and a similarly specialized organization for prosecuting financial crimes within the Public Ministry (*Ministerio Publico*), as well as capabilities within the nation's tax organization, the SAT (*Superintendencia de Administración Tributaria*).

The IVE, established by the money laundering law of 2001 (77–2001), is unique among entities for combatting financial crimes within the region, with respect to its organizational location within the organization for banking supervision, rather than existing as an independent FIU. Nonetheless, the IVE is considered adequately independent, and is regarded as one of the most capable such organizations in the region, according to a 2016 review by *GAFILAT*. Indeed, the IVE has provided inputs to sister organizations across the region, including those in Panama and Honduras regarding best practices. The IVE further shares information and best practices with other nations through its membership in the Edgemont Group, of which it has been a member for more than a decade.

As a compliment to the efforts by the IVE and related organizations, the government has passed a series of regulations building on Guatemala's 2001 anti-money laundering law, in order to more effectively control potentially illicit flows passing through banks, cooperatives, cash transfer companies, and other financial, as well as non-financial institutions. One such regulation, for example, was resolution 108–2010 restricting the amount of deposits denominated in dollars that banks can accept, and imposing requirements to report such transactions.

Dominican Republic

The Dominican Republic has a financial intelligence unit within its counternarcotics organization, the *DNCD*. The unit reportedly is supported by military personnel, and has good external ties to organizations such as the US Drug Enforcement Administration. The Dominican Republic has been working to improve the performance of its financial intelligence unit and reduce corruption, so that the country can be re-admitted into the Edgemont Group.

Colombia

Like many of the other countries in the region, Colombia has a FIU, but the organization is located in the Ministry of the Economy and restricted to reporting only to the attorney general, impeding to some degree coordination with other organizations. Colombia also has organizations that collect financial intelligence within the police, armed forces,[188] and attorney general's office. Yet the ability of such organizations to coordinate is reportedly limited, and the only entity with the ability to access and examine bank accounts is the FIU within the Ministry of the Economy.

Argentina

Argentina has an independent Financial Intelligence Unit, but in 2015, the US Treasury's Financial Crimes Enforcement Network (FINCEN) suspended cooperation with the organization after evidence that information that it had collected was used against political opponents of Argentina's previous government. In 2016, with the arrival of the new government of Mauricio Macri, and the giving of appropriate assurances to the US government, FINCEN renewed its cooperation.[189]

PRISON CONTROL AND REFORM

Effective control of penitentiary systems is a key element in the fight against transnational organized crime in Latin America and the Caribbean, and one of its most significant challenges. Throughout the region, penitentiaries too often do not effectively control the incarcerated, and frequently present an environment in which criminal leaders can consolidate control over group members incarcerated within the prisons themselves, and even run or coordinate criminal operations on the outside of its walls. In many cases, through a combination of bribes and credible threats, the incarcerated leaders of the criminal organizations come to effectively dictate decisions to prison administrators and workers.

The crisis of prison systems varies by country in Latin America, as well as between national-level facilities versus those administered at the sub-national level (e.g., by the governments of states, departments and localities). The problem generally reflects a mutually reinforcing combination of corruption, poor conditions, and inadequate control within the prisons themselves, as well as failure to fully isolate the incarcerated from their criminal associates on the outside.

In many prison systems in Latin America and the Caribbean, particularly those involving the gangs of Central America, the bond of obedience of those outside prisons to those inside is maintained because group members outside expect that they will eventually be incarcerated, where any lack of obedience to the gang leaders while on the outside will be punished once the gang members are subject to them on the inside. Such chains of obedience are also self-reinforcing; if someone on the "outside" defies a leader on the "inside," that leader can instruct someone else on the outside to punish him or her.

A critical element of the relationship between those inside and outside of prison in the region, as suggested in the preceding paragraph, is the ability to communicate beyond the control of authorities. As an illustration of just how far controls over such communication have broken down, a substantial number of extortion calls made by telephone in the Northern Triangle come from within the nation's prisons.[190]

Much has been written about the relative ease by which cell phones, satellite phones and other communication devices can be smuggled into prisons, or messages passed to family members and other visitors of the incarcerated. As seen previously, the ability to communicate is a mutually reinforcing cycle; the ability to obtain communication devices, as well as to pass messages (like the ability to obtain a range of formally prohibited goods and privileges) is a function of the ability of those incarcerated to bribe and intimidate the administrators, guards, and other prison personnel, which, in turn, relies on their ability to communicate with the outside.

Prison overcrowding, which is common across Latin America and the Caribbean, contributes to this cycle. Such overcrowding not only creates frequently inhumane conditions, but also makes it more difficult for administrators to effectively control and separate groups within the penitentiaries. Guatemala's jails, for example, are at almost 300 percent capacity,[191] and those of Honduras are at 200 percent capacity. Often pre-trial detention facilities are far more overcrowded than facilities for the long-term detention of convicted criminals.

Different countries in the region have adopted a range of postures to address the challenge of prison control as one part of the struggle against transnational organized crime.

Mexico

In Mexico, despite (and in part because of) multiple highly publicized escapes from federal prison by Sinaloa Cartel head *El Chapo* Guzman, the federal penitentiary system has made important advances, including completion of new prisons to alleviate overcapacity, and the implementation of modern prisoner control technologies in approximately half of the twenty-one penitentiaries in the federal system. Mexico has also reportedly established new organizations to professionalize the system of prison administration.[192]

State-level prisons, on the other hand, have received less attention and funding than their federal counterparts. The serious problems in Mexico's state prison system were illustrated by the death of forty-nine persons in February 2016 in a riot in Topo Chico, an overcrowded state-level facility in Nuevo Leon,[193] and sixteen deaths a year later in a riot in the Cadereyta prison in the same state in March 2017.[194]

Guatemala

As in other parts of the region, The Guatemalan government is working to reform the nation's prison system. Since the 1970s, the country has had 22 penitentiaries with a total capacity of seven thousand inmates. Yet without an increase in that capacity, the prison population has increased from roughly four thousand prisoners in the 1970s to almost twenty-one thousand by 2016.[195] Overcrowding is even worse for those in pre-trial detention. As of late 2016, according to Guatemalan officials interviewed for this work, 8,538 persons were being held in a pre-trial detention system designed for 2,485. Compounding the problem, because the conviction rate is very low in Guatemala, the majority of detainees held under such overcrowded conditions, sometimes for years, are ultimately turned loose.[196]

As part of its effort to reform the system, Guatemala is working with the Dominican Republic to implement a version of the latter's "model penitentiary" approach. Yet to date, only one small facility has been transformed under that effort—a one hundred-person jail for women with children, the old, and the terminally ill. Even this effort has been beset by obstacles, including resistance to its construction by residents of Villa Nueva, the neighborhood where the facility is to be built.[197]

El Salvador

In El Salvador, like many countries in the region, the shortcoming of the government in combatting criminal groups such as the Mara Salvatrucha and Barrio 18 street gangs is not putting their leaders in prison, but rather, breaking the bond between gang leaders and members, with their incarcerated leaders. The Salvadoran government has imprisoned an estimated 42 percent of the country's gang population without effectively controlling the gangs themselves.[198]

In 2016, the Salvadoran government of Salvador Sánchez Cerén made retaking control of the nation's prisons a cornerstone of a new series of initiatives against street gangs. As part of those efforts, it announced the intention to construct three new minimum-security prisons, and three rural prisons to move sixteen thousand personnel out of higher-security facilities to free up space for higher risk inmates in existing penitentiaries.[199] The Salvadoran government also transferred both inmates and prison workers between prisons to break up corruption networks. It further announced that it was activating military reservists, in order to deploy more military personnel into the prisons. Although the Salvadoran government had long used the military forces of *San Carlos Command* to control contraband goods entering the prisons, the government of Mauricio Funes had agreed to withdraw the military to the perimeter of the penitentiaries, as part of a truce between El Salvador's street gangs in 2012. When the military returned to establish a presence in the interior of the nation's prisons in 2016, it agreed to use combined teams of military, police, and penitentiary system personnel to perform joint inspections, in order to avoid accusations of abuses previously made against the military by inmates.

As a further assertion of control over the prisons, the government announced that it would work with local cell phone service providers to more effectively deny cell phone coverage to the penitentiaries.[200]

Honduras

The challenges of prison overcrowding and a lack of control in Honduras are similar to those faced in El Salvador and Guatemala. At the height of the problem in November 2014, the Honduran prison system had 14,805 inmates, an increase of 25 percent over the previous year, with only eleven thousand beds.[201] A 2013 report on Honduras's prisons by the Interamerican Commission on Human Rights found that virtually all of the nation's twenty-four federal penitentiaries were characterized not only by squalid conditions and overcrowding, but also by inmates effectively running the facilities on the inside, including everything from handing out food, issuing fines and punishments, to charging "rent" to other inmates for the use of beds.[202] The report concluded that "internal control of the prisons has been ceded into the hands of the prisoners themselves."[203]

Although widely known inside of Honduras, the widespread problems within Honduran prisons[204] was brought into the international spotlight by a fire in a prison in Comayagua in February 2012 which killed more than three hundred inmates.[205] Following the incident and reports such as the previously cited findings by the Interamerican Commission on Human Rights, the Honduran government began taking steps to expand, modernize, and reform its prison system, including closing the main penitentiary in San Pedro Sula, and constructing two large new maximum security prisons, El Poza and La Tolva.[206] The Honduran government also began pardoning lesser offenders in an attempt to address a system which was holding almost twice as many people as for which it was designed. The first of the new Honduran facilities was opened in the Honduran department of Santa Barbara in September 2016.[207]

Despite efforts to reform the prison system, the escape of sixty-five prisoners from three facilities over a fifteen-day period from April to May 2017 highlighted that much work remains to be done to reassert control over the Honduran prison system.[208]

Brazil

In Brazil, as in other parts of the region, a series of events in the second half of 2016 shed light on the overcrowding of, and lack of control in, the nation's prisons. On October 16, 2016, a clash between inmates belonging to the *PCC* and the *Red Command* in the Agricola de Monte Cristo Prison in Boa Vista, capital of the Brazilian state of Roraima, killed ten persons. The following day, a clash broke out between the two groups in a state penitentiary in Porto Velho, capital of the state of Rondonia, killing another eight in the resulting fire.[209]

In January 2017, an even more widespread series of riots broke out in prisons across the north of Brazil, including in another major riot in Monte Cristo,[210] one in the Alcacuz prison in Natal,[211] one in the Puraquequara prison in Manaus, and one in the Jobim prison in Amazonas. As an illustration of how out-of-control conditions had become in the Jobim prison, during the riot in that facility, 112 prisoners escaped through sixteen tunnels which they had built under the prison.[212] In total,

140 people were killed across the country in prison rioting during January 2017.[213]

INTERNATIONAL COOPERATION AGAINST ORGANIZED CRIME

Authors frequently lament that governments are limited by national frontiers in their fight against criminal groups, while those groups themselves are not. In reality, as shown previously, in their organizations and transactions, such groups are far more impacted by borders than is recognized in the popular literature. More importantly, to a limited degree, governments in the region are indeed cooperating internationally against organized crime. Such cooperation and coordination includes activities among geographically contiguous neighbors, cooperation within regional organizations, support from broader international organizations, intelligence sharing, and the providing of resources and other support from extra-regional actors such as the United States, Russia, and even China.

Border Control Cooperation

States in Latin America and the Caribbean increasingly cooperate with respect to securing common borders. Examples include Mexico's coordination with Guatemala and Belize, with encouragement and resource contributions from the United States. Similarly, as noted previously, Honduras and Guatemala have formed a joint task force, *Maya-Chorti*, for patrolling their own common border.[214]

Despite ideological differences, Honduras and Nicaragua reportedly coordinate regularly to stem the flows of illicit drugs through their shared border.[215] Colombia similarly cooperates with its southern neighbors, Peru and Brazil, regarding the impacts of its peace accord with the FARC, and with respect to expanding narcotics production in its southern departments such as Putumayo and Nariño, creating possible spillover effects south of the Putumayo river in Peruvian territory, as well as with respect to Colombia's border with Brazil. Brazil similarly collaborates with Paraguay regarding the difficult-to-control land border between both countries.[216]

One important vehicle for cooperation in the control of frontiers, as noted previously, has been the establishment of binational frontier committees, referred to as *Combifrons*. Brazil, for example, has established committees with Colombia and Argentina, while Ecuador has *Combifrons* with both of its neighbors, Peru and Colombia. Such coordinating bodies facilitate the struggle against organized crime by establishing protocols for the handling of incidents at the border, and institutionalizing regular meetings in which information between officials on both sides may be exchanged.

Despite such coordination, controlling the flows of people and illicit substances across borders in the region occasionally generates frictions. During mid-2016, Costa Rica's relationship with Nicaragua to its north and Panama to its south became strained over the flow of Cuban immigrants through the region.[217] Similarly, Ecuadorans perceive themselves prejudiced by the spillover effects of narcotrafficking and guerilla activity from Colombia onto Its Side of the Border,[218] while Colombians have complained of guerillas fighting against the Colombian state, taking refuge in the territory of its neighbors, Ecuador and Venezuela.[219]

International cooperation against transnational organized crime is further visible in individual agreements between member states. In September 2016, the three states of the northern triangle announced a security pact to cooperate against organized crime. The agreement was focused principally on collaboration against urban gangs such as Mara Salvatrucha and Barrio 18, which member states perceived as the leading security challenge in the sub-region.[220] Nonetheless, the accord included elements useful in combatting other narcotrafficking flows more broadly, including the establishment of new binational security forces to control shared borders, and expanded intelligence sharing on transnational criminal actors between member states. Nonetheless, the pact was criticized by some for not doing more to cooperate on other aspects of the common challenge, such as domestic crime, corruption, and money laundering.[221]

Multilateral Facilitation Mechanisms

With respect to regional organizations, groups within the interamerican system, such as the Conference of Central American Armed Forces (CFAC), the Central American Integration System (SICA), and the Conference of American Armies, contribute to coordination and/or building capacity in the struggle against organized criminal activities in the Americas, principally through training, professional military education, and information exchange activities.

Arguably, the Conference of Central American Armed Forces (CFAC) is one of the best examples of how multilateral collaboration mechanisms have facilitated cooperation against transnational organized crime in the region. The CFAC has been instrumental in setting up trimestrial meetings of the intelligence chiefs and operational heads of the Central American armed forces to exchange data, facilitating the establishment of joint border patrols such as the task force *Maya-Chorti* on the Honduras–Guatemala border, *Lenca-Sumpul* on the Honduras–El Salvador Border, and the joint task force *Morazon-Sandino* on the Nicaragua–Honduras border. The CFAC was also instrumental in establishing regular meetings between commanders of brigades on opposite sides of national borders to exchange information and plan for future coordinated activities such as coinciding patrols. The CFAC also was the instrument for setting up regional training centers, such as the regional center for training against organized crime and terrorism (CCTRACCT) in San Salvador.[222]

The best known international organization active in the region in the fight against organized crime is Interpol, which provides police around the world with targeted training, investigative support, data, and secure communications channels.[223] It has offices in forty-four nations and dependencies throughout the Western Hemisphere. While known for its international notices, including "Red Notices" obliging member nations "to seek the location and arrest of wanted persons with a view to extradition or similar lawful action,"[224] Interpol also provides a range of other services, including translators and information to facilitate police coordination between countries in the region in the fight against transnational organized crime.

United States

As is widely understood, but not always explicitly recognized, the most important source of international support in the fight against organized crime in the Latin America and the Caribbean besides the countries themselves is the resources, training, and intelligence of the United States, although the support of other extra-hemispheric actors such as Russia and China is also increasingly relevant.

The principle US-led programs in the region in recent years include *Plan Colombia, Plan Merida* (in support of Mexico), *the Central American Regional Security Initiative* (CARSI), the *Caribbean Basin Security Initiative* (CBSI), and most recently, the *Alliance for Prosperity,* focused on the states of the Northern Triangle. The US has also channeled funds for combatting organized crime in the region through multilateral bodies, such as the Central American Integration System (SICA).[225]

While much US assistance in the fight against organized crime has been channeled through these programs, other cooperation has come in the form of bilateral assistance, or support for individual military and other activities in the region. The United States has historically provided an array of support in the fight against transnational criminal organizations, including detection and interdiction of narcotics in the Pacific, Caribbean, and in some cases, national territories in coordination with local governments. A leading example is Operation Martillo, conducted with Central American partner nations, which seized 581 aircraft and watercraft, and almost seven hundred tons of cocaine, as well as other illicit goods and bulk cash from its inception in January 2012 through August 2016.[226]

The US has also operated a number of important forward operating locations in the region in support of these activities. These include Joint Interagency Task Force South (JIATF-S) in Key West, Florida, which serves as a clearinghouse for data on narcotics and other criminal activity in the region, fusing input from multiple US government sources and international partners.

Within the military realm, Joint Task Force Bravo (JTF-B) in Soto Cano Airbase, Honduras, serves as a hub for US military cooperation with Honduras and other partners in Central America and the Caribbean in the fight against transnational organized crime, as well as exercises, disaster relief, and other security support activities for the region.[227]

In addition, the US also helps multiple partners in the region to combat criminal groups through intelligence sharing, selective direct intervention where permitted by the laws of the partner nations. It also provides partner nations with material support, including equipment, logistics, and training, as well as programs to strengthen institutions and fight corruption. The previously mentioned August 2016 agreement between the US and the nations of the Northern Triangle to expand cooperation in the fight against transnational organized crime, for example, included a provision to work more closely with the US-based Center against Transnational Gangs (CAT).[228]

In many cases, such US programs include only a minor security component, with significant spending on institutional and developmental issues. Major programs in recent years include Plan Colombia, Plan Merida, in support of Mexico, the Caribbean Basin Security Initiative, and the Central America Regional Security Initiative (CARSI), and the Alliance for Prosperity in Central America.[229] In addition, however, the US has also provided significant direct support to many of the countries in the region.

The US military has provided training to an estimated thirteen thousand counterparts in the region. As one component, US Joint Combined Exchange Training teams (JCETS), which conduct activities in the region to simultaneously train US and host nation personnel, have expanded their presence in the region from twelve in 2007 to thirty-six in 2014.[230]

Russia

In addition to the US, other extra-regional actors have also played a role in the support against organized crime. While European governments have primarily provided assistance primarily in support of development, Russia, in recent years, has been increasingly active in the region in counterdrug and other law enforcement support activities. Such activities include intelligence cooperation between the Russian Federal Drug Control Service (FSKN) and Peru, Brazil, and other nations of the region, as well as the operation of Russian law enforcement training facilities in Lima, Peru and Managua, Nicaragua (the Marshall Zhukov Center).[231] While Russia is impacted by the flow of cocaine and other drugs from

Andean region source-zone countries, such activities have also allowed it to maintain a security presence in Latin America.

People's Republic of China

As transpacific crime has expanded as a challenge in the region, as noted in previous chapters, the PRC has also supported law enforcement activities against Chinese criminal groups with ties in Latin America. Such cooperation includes the sending of a law enforcement agent to Argentina to build a case against Chinese mafias operating in that country, including the organization Pixue,[232] as well as cooperation in transpacific money laundering cases involving Chinese banks. Indeed, in Argentina, Chinese police reportedly maintain a presence in that nation's embassy in Buenos Aires to assist with ongoing transpacific organized crime cases involving Chinese criminals.[233] Following Panama's diplomatic recognition of the People's Republic of China, Panama and the PRC were reportedly discussing police cooperation between their countries as well.[234]

CONCLUSIONS

Each of the eight areas of comparison in this chapter regarding the approaches of different governments in the region toward combatting transnational organized crime highlight ideas and innovations that merit consideration by others, as appropriate to their national situations.

The widespread examination of "whole-of-government" solutions by Latin American and Caribbean countries suggests that most generally understand the importance of coordinating the efforts and resources of different parts of the government, and not simply confronting transnational organized crime as a police or security problem.

A critical element for success appears to be the presence of a strategic concept of how to attack the challenge in systemic terms, recognizing the integral relationship between the criminal actors, and the economic, social, and political context in which they operate, including the commercial, financial, transportation, and other infrastructures upon which they depend. Examples such as Colombia suggest that the success of a systemic strategic concept is strengthened by an actively engaged, hands-on leader with the authority to overcome the obstacles of bureaucratic divisions, and who is able to conduct an ongoing monitoring of the situation to exploit success, correct what is not working, and shift effort as the situation evolves.

With respect to interdiction, binational coordination regarding shared frontiers, such as that seen in task forces *Maya-Chorti* and *Lenca-Sumpul*, as well as the Sandino-Morazán operations, are positive steps that merit further study.

Aerial interdiction is another area which deserves greater sharing of experiences. With seven countries in the region having some type of aerial "shoot-down" law against unauthorized flights, supported by radars and interceptor aircraft, such activities are increasingly a realty. Information sharing between countries regarding best practices will help to ensure that such aerial interdiction can be performed in the safest, most effective fashion possible, while minimizing hazards to civilian aircraft.

With respect to targeting high-value assets, such as the leaders or senior financial officers of transnational criminal organizations, the approach has arguably been effective in disabling a broad range of groups, with governments leveraging multi-source intelligence and international cooperation to identify and take down such leaders. The application of similar approaches to street gangs such as Mara Salvatrucha and Barrio 18, as well as the leadership of narcotrafficking and other criminal groups, similarly appears promising, particularly when targeting financial assets of the groups, and especially when the ability of criminal leaders in prison to communicate with their organizations can be effectively limited. While new leaders often rise up to assume the roles of those killed or jailed, their organizations are nonetheless transformed and degraded, creating windows of opportunity for the government, albeit only temporarily.

While the targeting of high-value assets by governments has proven more impactful than is commonly acknowledged, the violence continually and predictably unleashed by such actions suggests that the states acting against the groups still do not effectively plan for the ultimate effects of those actions, including the splintering of the groups targeted, and new competition between them. While taking down the leadership of criminal groups is an inexact science, there is arguably room for improvements, to conduct operations selectively, and in a fashion that best produces effects which support the strategic goals of the nation acting and the region.

With respect to the use of the military to support law enforcement, this chapter has illustrated a range of experiences, challenges, and lessons learned. Argentina, in the southern cone, has chosen to rely principally on specialized police forces, the Gendarmerie, although the Macri administration has created discomfort in the military by using the armed forces to interdict drug flights.

Despite the differences in each nation's legal framework, there are clearly opportunities for countries to learn from the solutions adopted by the others. Honduras's experience in integrating the police and military within FUSINA, for example, arguably provides insights for El Salvador in military support to the police such as those of Command *Zeus* or the FERES.

In virtually every case examined in this chapter, the military was deeply uncomfortable regarding the legal framework that it was operating in, when conducting operations inside the national territory, including both current and future legal challenges against its members in the conduct of their assigned missions.

At a philosophical level, the debate in the region over use of the military in support of domestic operations against criminal groups highlights the deeper need for a re-thinking of the role of national militaries versus police forces in confronting the transnational challenges of the twenty-first century. The traditional distinction between the armed forces as the defender of the nation against external threats versus the police as the guardian of internal order reflects a largely bygone era when the line between foreign and domestic challenges was not so blurred. Although Latin American and Caribbean armed forces were employed during the twentieth century to fight insurgent threats within the national territory, today's transnational flows of goods, information, capital, and people further cloud the historic distinction between the roles of the military and police. Today, transnational flows allow groups operating both within and outside of national territories to present a serious threat to the state, even if not formally challenging the state's claim to govern the national territory.

In this framework, the debates over whether the military should conduct operations against a nation's own citizens within the national territory highlight the difficulty of using an "internal versus external" dichotomy to simultaneously legitimize and limit the role of the military. At a deeper level, it suggests the need to advance a philosophical basis for the role of the military, versus the police, appropriate to an era where borders have ever less relevance in the discourse on security.

With respect to police reform, in multiple cases, the ability to purge police and other organs of corrupt personnel has been limited by the hurdles presented by laws enabling law enforcement organizations and protecting the arbitrary dismissal of their personnel. The problem has been compounded by the reluctance of judges to accept technical evidence, such as the failure of a polygraph test, as the reason for depriving a person of his or her livelihood. As a result, in many countries, it has often been easier to transfer a person who comes under question, rather than firing them.

The discussion of law enforcement reform in this chapter highlights the importance of planning reforms from a whole-country perspective. Attempting to purge the police force of bad individuals by rapidly firing a large number of persons not only undermines the effectiveness of the organization, but also potentially puts corrupt, desperate, and embittered persons on the street, pushing them into the hands of criminal groups, bringing with them their insider knowledge of their former government organization.

With respect to combatting the finances of criminal groups, this chapter highlights the promise of financial intelligence units and similar entities, as well as the advances that many countries are making in laws that make it harder to launder money, and easier to identify the illicit earnings of criminal groups. In some cases, the FIUs have been quasi-independent organizations, while in other cases, they are located within the attorney general's office or the Finance Ministry. In general, greater institutional independence seems to facilitate resistance to corruption and the ability of the organization to coordinate with multiple other government entities.

This chapter has also highlighted the importance in controlling and reforming national penitentiary systems as a key, albeit often overlooked, part of the struggle against transnational criminal groups. Such reform is fundamental in breaking the destructive cycle in which criminal leaders continue to manage their organizations from within prison through having ready access to cell phones, visitors, and other means of communication from inside the facilities.

The discussion of prison reform also highlights the negatively reinforcing nature of communication between those on the inside and outside of penitentiaries; the ability to communicate with others on the outside of the prison allows them to obtain resources to bribe prison officials, and to threaten actions against their families outside the prisons. Such threats and bribes, in turn, make it very difficult for penitentiary leadership to control the access of prisoners to cell phones, reinforcing the negative cycle.

In El Salvador, a combination of cell phone jamming, the use of military personnel inside the prisons to augment controls, isolation of prisoners, and transfers of both prisoners and prison officials produced promising results in at least temporarily breaking the communication-corruption cycle. Such partial successes deserve further study, to see if there are lessons that can be applied by other prison systems with similar challenges.

Finally, this chapter highlights the importance of international coordination in combatting organized crime groups as a transnational threat. Types of collaboration identified in this section that have proven useful in the region include intelligence collaboration in actions against criminal entities, financial collaboration in identifying and going after group resources, bi-national cooperation in interdiction and controlling frontiers, and in some cases, joint operations within national territory where permitted by local legal frameworks. It highlighted that, while the US plays an important role in the region's fight against organized crime, other actors such as Russia and the PRC are also increasingly interacting with the region in this fight.

NOTES

1. See, for example, Jonathan D. Rosen and Hanna S. Kassab, *Fragile States in the Americas* (Lanham, MD: Lexington Books, 2016).
2. See, for example, Bruce Bagley, "Drug Trafficking and Organized Crime in the Americas," Woodrow Wilson Center, August 1, 2012, https://www.wilsoncenter.org/publication/drug-trafficking-and-organized-crime-the-americas-major-trends-the-twenty-first-century.
3. See, for example, Michael Allison, "Justice Deferred: Rule of Law in Central America," *World Politics Review*, November 11, 2014, http://www.worldpoliticsreview.com/articles/14415/justice-deferred-rule-of-law-in-central-america.
4. See Sonja Wolf, "El Salvador's Pandilleros Calmados: The Challenges of Contesting Mano Dura through Peer Rehabilitation and Empowerment," *Bulletin of Latin American Research* 31, no. 2 (2012): 190–205. See also Sonja Wolf, *Mano Dura: The Politics of Gang Control in El Salvador*, (Austin: University of Texas Press, 2017). See also Mo Hume, "Mano Dura: El Salvador Responds to Gangs." *Development in Practice* 17, no. 6 (2007): 739–751.
5. See, for example, David E. Spencer, *Colombia's Road to Recovery: Security and Governance 1982–2010* (Washington D.C.: National Defense University Press, 2012).
6. Winifred Tate, *Drugs, Thugs, and Diplomats: US Policymaking in Colombia* (Stanford, CA: Stanford University Press, 2015).
7. *Plan Nacional de Desarrollo 213–2018*, Government of Mexico, Official Website, accessed March 1, 2016, http://pnd.gob.mx/.
8. Mexico also has a national defense policy and a defense "White Book" which were reportedly written some years ago, but never formally accepted by the presidency and published.
9. Interview with Mexican defense officials, Mexico City, February 2016.
10. See, for example, Francisco Reséndiz, Elena Michel, and Ricardo Gómez, "Peña Nieto entrega plan de cambios en secretarías," *El Universal*, November 14, 2012, http://archivo.eluniversal.com.mx/notas/883003.html.
11. "50ª Reunión Ordinaria de la Conferencia Nacional de Gobernadores," Presidencia de Mexico, Official Website, February 29, 2016, http://www.gob.mx/presidencia.
12. R. Evan Ellis, "Strategic Insights—Mexico: New Directions, Continuity, and Obstacles in the Fight against Transnational Organized Crime," US Army War College Strategic Studies Institute, March 31, 2016. http://strategicstudiesinstitute.army.mil/index.cfm/articles/Mexico-New-Directions-Continuity-Obstacles/2016/03/31.
13. Ellis, "Strategic Insights—Mexico."
14. Claire Ribando Seelke and Kristin Finklea, "US-Mexican Security Cooperation: The Mérida Initiative and Beyond," *Congressional Research Service*, July 29, 2017, https://fas.org/sgp/crs/row/R41349.pdf.
15. See Jorge Chabat, *La Iniciativa Mérida y la relación México-Estados Unidos: en busca de la confianza Perdida* (Mexico City: Centro de Investigación y Docencia Ecónomicas [CIDE], División de Estudios Internacionales, 2010). See also Jorge Chabat, "La seguridad en la política exterior de Calderón," *Foro Internacional* (2013): 729–749. See also Eric L. Olson and Christopher E. Wilson, "Beyond Mérida: The Evolving Approach to Security Cooperation," Woodrow Wilson International Center for Scholars (2010).
16. The Guatemalan system also includes the National Disaster Management Agency (CONRED) and the Guatemalan Secret Service (SAAS), although their heads do not sit on the NSC.
17. Interview with Guatemalan security officials, Guatemala City, October 2016.
18. "Cabecilla prófugo migró a Guatemala a extorsionar," *La Prensa Grafica*, October 13, 2016, http://www.laprensagrafica.com/2016/10/13/cabecilla-profugo-migro-a-guatemala-a-extorsionar.
19. Ellis, "Honduras: A Pariah State."

20. Ellis, "Honduras: A Pariah State."

21. Rosa Maria Pastrán, "Presentan anteproyecto de impuesto a la telefonía," *La Prensa Grafica*, September 18, 2015, http://www.laprensagrafica.com/2015/09/18/presentan-anteproyecto-de-impuesto-a-la-telefonia.

22. Beatriz Calderón, "Consejo de Seguridad presenta Plan 'El Salvador Seguro,'" *La Prensa Grafica*, January 15, 2015, http://www.laprensagrafica.com/2015/01/15/consejo-de-seguridad-presenta-plan-el-salvador-seguro#sthash.ti6VfKkE.dpuf

23. "Barrio Seguro está cambiando la vida a más de 4 mil jóvenes" Government of Panama, Official Website, January 8, 2016, https://www.presidencia.gob.pa/Noticias/Barrio-Seguro-esta-cambiando-la-vida-a-mas-de-4-mil-jovenes.

24. The zone initially covered just portions of the Ene and Apurimac river valleys (VRAE), but in 2012, was administratively expanded to include the Mantaro river valley as well, reflecting the importance of the zone as a trafficking route for cocaine and precursor chemicals, and correspondingly was renamed the "VRAEM." See "Peru Plans to Step Up Security, Inclusion in Coca Growing Region," *Peruvian Times*, June 29, 2012, http://www.peruviantimes.com/29/peru-plans-to-step-up-security-inclusion-in-coca-growing-region/16136/.

25. Ellis, "Crime-Terrorism Nexus in Peru."

26. "Vraem: PNP reasumirá control de lucha contra el narcotráfico," *El Comercio*, December 12, 2015, http://elcomercio.pe/sociedad/vraem/vraem-pnp-reasumira-control-lucha-contra-narcotrafico-noticia-1863086.

27. Ellis, "Crime-Terrorism Nexus in Peru."

28. Ellis, "Crime-Terrorism Nexus in Peru."

29. Ellis, "Crime-Terrorism Nexus in Peru."

30. "'Artemio' capturado," *IDL Reporteros*, February 12, 2012, https://idl-reporteros.pe/artemio-capturado/.

31. Julieta Pelcastre, "Peruvian Navy Brings Healthcare, Social Services to Amazon Region," *Dialogo*, December 14, 2015, https://dialogo-americas.com/en/articles/peruvian-navy-brings-healthcare-social-services-amazon-region.

32. Ellis, "Organized Crime in Peru."

33. Interview with Argentine defense official, by email, February 2017.

34. Peter Andreas, "The Transformation of Migrant Smuggling across the US-Mexican Border," in *Global Human Smuggling: Comparative Perspectives* (2001): 107–25. See also Peter Andreas, *Smuggler Nation: How Illicit Trade Made America* (Cambridge: Oxford University Press, 2013).

35. Ted Gallen Carpenter, *Bad Neighbor Policy: Washington's Futile War on Drugs in Latin America* (New York: St. Martin's Press, 2014).

36. Interview with senior Guatemalan navy personnel, Guatemala City, October 2016.

37. Interview with senior Guatemalan military officers, Guatemala City, October 2016.

38. Ellis, "Honduras: A Pariah State."

39. Ellis, "Honduras: A Pariah State."

40. "Panama Canal Sets New Monthly Tonnage Record," *Panama Canal Authority*, February 6, 2017, https://www.pancanal.com/eng/pr/press-releases/2017/02/06/pr616.html.

41. Interview with senior Panamanian security official, Bogota, Colombia, September 2016.

42. Julio Montes, "Panamá Crea la Fuerza Especial Antinarcóticos (FEAN)," *Defensa*, September 12, 2016, http://www.defensa.com/frontend/defensa/noticia.php?id_noticia=19283&id_seccion=339.

43. Ellis, "Organized Crime in Peru."

44. "Inauguration of the Xinca Task Force," US Embassy in Guatemala, August 31, 2017, https://gt.usembassy.gov/inauguration-xinca-task-force/.

45. Bonello, "Criminal Activity Spreading Fire."

46. Interview with Guatemalan security experts, Guatemala City, November 2016.

47. Interview with Guatemalan security experts, Guatemala City, November 2016.
48. "Honduran and Nicaraguan Armies Join Forces in Operation Morazán-Sandino," *Dialogo*, August 23, 2017, https://dialogo-americas.com/en/articles/honduran-and-nicaraguan-armies-join-forces-operation-morazan-sandino.
49. See R. Evan Ellis, "The New Offensive against Gangs in El Salvador," *Latin America Goes Global*, May 2, 2016, http://latinamericagoesglobal.org/2016/05/new-offensive-gangs-el-salvador/.
50. Ellis, "The Gang Challenge in El Salvador."
51. Ellis, "The New Offensive."
52. Interview with Salvadoran security official, San Salvador, El Salvador, May 2016.
53. Information on SENAFRONT is available through the organization's official website, http://www.senafront.gob.pa/index.html.
54. Interview with a Panamanian security personnel, Bogota, Colombia, September 2016.
55. Interview with Peruvian security personnel, Lima, Peru, May 2016.
56. Ellis, "Crime-Terrorism Nexus in Peru."
57. "¿Cómo está y que hacer en el Vraem?, por Rubén Vargas," *El Comercio*, April 17, 2016, http://elcomercio.pe/opinion/colaboradores/como-esta-y-que-hacer-vraem-ruben-vargas-noticia-1894782.
58. . R. Evan Ellis, "Brazil: Between Cooperation and Deterrence," *Global Americans*, December 18, 2017, https://theglobalamericans.org/2017/12/brazil-cooperation-deterrence/.
59. "Sisfron Technology Helps the Brazilian Armed Forces Secure Border Regions," *Dialogo*, November 21, 2014, https://dialogo-americas.com/en/articles/sisfron-technology-helps-brazilian-armed-forces-secure-border-regions.
60. "Border Sensor Program Gains Momentum in Brazil," *Defesanet*, March 21, 2017, www.defesanet.com.br/en/defense/noticia/24963/Border-sensor-program-gains-momentum-in-Brazil/.
61. "Brazil Deploys Troops to Secure Borders for World Cup," *Reuters*, May 10, 2014, https://www.reuters.com/article/us-brazil-worldcup-security/brazil-deploys-troops-to-secure-borders-for-world-cup-idUSBREA4908H20140510.
62. "US Military Personnel are Joining the Largest International Military Operation Ever Held in the Amazon," *Business Insider*, November 9, 2017, http://www.businessinsider.com/r-us-military-joins-brazil-army-exercises-in- amazon-2017–11.
63. Nelza Oliveira, "Brazil Promotes New Phase of Operation Ágata," *Dialogo*, July 15, 2016, https://dialogo-americas.com/en/articles/brazil-promotes-new-phase-operation-agata.
64. "Operação Ágata apreende armas, drogas e munição nas fronteiras do País," Government of Brazil, Official Website, June 25, 2016. http://www.brasil.gov.br/defesa-e-seguranca/2016/06/operacao-agata-apreende-armas-drogas-e-municao-nas-fronteiras-do-pais.
65. Ellis, "Brazil."
66. See John A. Cope and Andrew Parks, "Frontier Security: The Case of Brazil," Institute for National Strategic Studies (Washington, D.C.: National Defense University, August 2016).
67. Stan Lehman and Sarah DiLorenzo, "Military Police Begin Patrols in Paralyzed Brazilian State," *PBS News Hour*, February 11, 2017, http://www.pbs.org/newshour/rundown/military-police-patrols-brazil/.
68. "Brazilian Army Orders 9,000 Troops into the Streets of Rio de Janeiro," *EFE*, February 14, 2016, http://www.efe.com/efe/english/portada/brazilian-army-orders-9–000-troops-into-the-streets-of-rio-de-janeiro/50000260–3179613.
69. R. Evan Ellis, "Don't Cry for Mauricio Macri's Argentina," *Latin America Goes Global*, January 19, 2017, http://latinamericagoesglobal.org/2017/01/dont-cry-mauricio-macris-argentina/.

70. "Posture Statement."

71. The Peruvian government estimated that a quarter of the airstrips destroyed by the government in 2014 had been rebuilt—a process requiring less than twenty-four hours. See David Gagne, "24-Hour Turnaround to Rebuild Peru's Narco-Airstrips," *Insight Crime*, October 14, 2014, http://www.InsightCrime.org/news-briefs/6112-peru-vraem-narco-airstrips-rebuilt. See also "Interdicción de 'narcovuelos' en el VRAE," *IDL Reporteros*, December 17, 2013, https://idl-reporteros.pe/interdiccion-de-%e2%80%98narcovuelos%e2%80%99-en-el-vrae/.

72. Interviews with Guatemalan defense officials, Guatemala City, October 2016.

73. "Honduras compra radares a Israel por $30 millones," *El Economista*, December 19, 2013, http://www.eleconomista.net/2013/12/19/honduras-compra-radares-a-israel-por-30-millones.

74. "Honduras aprueba derribar aviones sospechosos de narcotráfico," *BBC*, January 18, 2014, http://www.bbc.com/mundo/ultimas_noticias/2014/01/140118_ult-not_honduras_autoriza_derribo_aviones_sospechosos_drogas_lav.

75. James Bargent, "US Halts Honduras Cooperation over Narco-Plane Shoot Down Law," *Insight Crime*, April 1, 2014, http://www.InsightCrime.org/news-briefs/us-halts-honduras-cooperation-over-narco-plane-shoot-down-law.

76. "Honduras: Fuerza Aérea halla narcoavioneta en La Mosquitia," *La Prensa*, March 24, 2014, http://www.laprensa.hn/inicio/626506-96/honduras-fuerza-aerea-halla-narcoavioneta-en-la-mosquitia.

77. "Mandatario panameño inicia instalación de primer radar contra narcotráfico," *La Prensa*, October 9, 2012, http://www.laprensa.com.ni/2012/10/09/internacionales/119406-mandatario-pameno-inicia-instalacion-de-primer-radar-contra-narcotrafico.

78. "Presenta amparo de garantías para anular parte de la investigación," *La Estrella*, July 1, 2016, http://laestrella.com.pa/panama/politica/presenta-amparo-garantias-para-anular-parte-investigacion/23948522.

79. Casado, "Autoridades indagan sobreprecio Super Tucano."

80. "Dominican Republic Military Has 3-D Radar Starting Today," *Dominican Today*, July 15, 2010, http://www.dominicantoday.com/dr/technology/2010/7/15/36321/Dominican-Republic-military-has-3-D-radar-starting-today.

81. Interview with senior military officer from the Dominican Republic, Bogota, Colombia, September 2016.

82. "Peru Declares No-Fly Zone in Its Most Lawless Coca-Growing Region," *Reuters*, February 4, 2015, http://www.reuters.com/article/2015/02/04/us-peru-drugs-idUSKBN0L82MU20150204.

83. The full name of the committee is the "Comisión de Defensa Nacional, Orden Interno, Desarrollo Alternativo y Lucha Contra las Drogas."

84. Peru ceased the program in 2001 following the accidental downing of a plane carrying US Baptist missionaries over the jungle near Iquitos, causing the death of a mother and her seven-month old child.

85. Ellis, "Crime-Terrorism Nexus in Peru."

86. Ellis, "Organized Crime in Peru."

87. "Decreto 228/2016," *Boletín Oficial de la República de Argentina*, January 21, 2016, https://www.boletinoficial.gob.ar/#!DetalleNorma/140329/20160122.

88. Conversation with Argentine defense official, Buenos Aires, Argentina, December 2016.

89. "Lucha contra el narcotráfico."

90. Interview with Argentine security official, Buenos Aires, Argentina, December 2016.

91. "Argentina—Air Force," *Janes Sentinel Security Assessment—South America*, November 8, 2016, https://janes.ihs.com/Janes/Display/1767023.

92. "Argentina: President Promises Change Amid National Turmoil," *NBC News*, March 2, 2016, http://www.nbcnews.com/news/latino/argentina-president-promises-change-amid-national-turmoil-n530311.

93. Interview with Argentine security official, Buenos Aires, Argentina, December 2016.
94. See, for example, "Drug Enforcement Administration 1991–1994," Drug Enforcement Administration Official Website, Accessed October 20, 2016, https://www.dea.gov/about/history/1990–1994.pdf.
95. See, for example, Victor D. Hyder, "Decapitation Operations: Criteria for Targeting Enemy Leadership," Fort Leavenworth, KS: School of Advanced Military Studies, United States Army Command and General Staff College, https://fedgeno.com/documents/military-decapitation.pdf.
96. See, for example, Austin Long, "Assessing the Success of Leadership Targeting," *Combatting Terrorism Center*, 2010, https://www.ctc.usma.edu/posts/assessing-the-success-of-leadership-targeting.
97. "Mexico Govt Refuses to Reveal Most Wanted List," *Insight Crime*, August 21, 2015, http://www.InsightCrime.org/news-analysis/mexico-govt-refuses-to-reveal-most-wanted-list.
98. "Diario Oficial," Procurador General de la Republica, Official Website, March 23, 2009, http://www.pgr.gob.mx/normatec/Documentos/a-123–09.pdf.
99. Interview with senior Guatemalan security official, Guatemala City, Guatemala, October 2016.
100. "Presentan a los hermanos Valle, capturados en Honduras," *La Prensa*, October 5, 2014, http://www.laprensa.hn/sucesos/754732–410/presentan-a-los-hermanos-valle-capturados-en-honduras. See also Ellis, "Honduras: A Pariah State."
101. "Estados Unidos detuvo a dos narcotraficantes hondureños, líderes del cártel Los Cachiros," *Infobae*, February 6, 2015, http://www.infobae.com/2015/02/06/1625362-estados-unidos-detuvo-dos-narcotraficantes-hondurenos-lideres-del-cartel-los-cachiros/.
102. "Cabecilla del cartel de los AA."
103. "Operación 'Sultán.'"
104. "Honduras: Operación Avalancha arremete contra bienes de la Mara Salvatrucha MS-13," *El Heraldo*, October 17, 2016, http://www.elheraldo.hn/pais/1009148–466/honduras-operación-avalancha-arremete-contra-bienes-de-la-mara-salvatrucha-ms-13.
105. "Se reactivó banda de narcotraficantes Los *Perrones*: FGR," *La Prensa Grafica*, July 31, 2014, http://www.laprensagrafica.com/2014/07/31/se-reactivo-banda-de-narcotraficantes-los-perrones-fgr.
106. "Asesinan a supuesto narcotraficante salvadoreño 'Chepe' Luna," *La Prensa Grafica*, June 29, 2014, http://www.laprensagrafica.com/2014/06/27/asesinan-a-supuesto-narcotraficante-salvadoreo-chepe-luna.
107. Christine Wade, "El Salvador's 'Iron Fist': Inside Its Unending War on Gangs," *World Politics Review*, June 6, 2016, http://www.worldpoliticsreview.com/articles/18982/el-salvador-s-iron-fist-inside-its-unending-war-on-gangs.
108. Marroquin and Lopez, "Fuerzas Especiales van tras 100 cabecillas de pandillas," 2016.
109. Ellis, "The New Offensive."
110. Interview with Colombian security expert, Bogota, Colombia, September 2016.
111. "Aceptan la Renuncia del Viceministro de Defensa Iván Vega," *Agencia de Noticias de Peru*, March 2013, http://www.agenciadenoticiasdelperu.com/2016/03/aceptan-renuncia-del-viceministro-de.html.
112. "Cómo murió 'William,'" 2012.
113. "Tras muerte de 'Alipio' y 'Gabriel': ¿Qué otros cabecillas tiene Sendero?" 2013.
114. In Peru, the presence of significant illegal mining operations in the Department of Madre de Dios, and its spread to neighboring departments such as Junin and Cusco created a special imperative for the government to incorporate the struggle against such activities as part of its campaign against organized crime. In January 2017, the Peruvian government incorporated illegal mining within a new organized crime law. "Objetivo es formalizar a 60,000 pequeños mineros en tres años," *El Peruano*, January

20, 2017, http://www.elperuano.com.pe/noticia-objetivo-es-formalizar-a-60000-pequenos-mineros-tres-anos-50386.aspx.

115. See Richard L. Millett and Orlando J. Pérez, "New Threats and Old Dilemmas: Central America's Armed Forces in the 21st Century," *Journal of Political and Military Sociology*, 33, No. 1 (2005): 59. See also Orlando J. Pérez, *Civil-military Relations in Post-conflict Societies: Transforming the Role of the Military in Central America*, Vol. 12 (New York: Routledge, 2015).

116. Eleno Michael and Ricardo Gómez, "Aprueban parco legal para el Ejercito," *El Universal*, April 28, 2010, http://archivo.eluniversal.com.mx/nacion/177343.html.

117. "México lanzó la operación Veracruz seguro," *Infobae*, October 4, 2011, http://www.infobae.com/2011/10/04/1034993-mexico-lanzo-la-operacion-veracruz-seguro/.

118. "Mexico envia el '25o Batallón de Caballería Motorizada' a la Frontera con EE.UU," *Infodefensa*, January 23, 2017, http://www.infodefensa.com/latam/2017/01/23/noticia-mexico-reubica-batallon-caballeria-motorizada-frontera.html.

119. Azam Ahmed and Eric Schmittmay, "Mexican Military Runs up Body Count in Drug War," *New York Times*, May 26, 2016, https://www.nytimes.com/2016/05/27/world/americas/mexican-militarys-high-kill-rate-raises-human-rights-fears.html?_r=0.

120. "Mexico: Investigate All Evidence in Killings of 22 by Soldiers," *Human Rights Watch*, August 22, 2014, https://www.hrw.org/news/2014/08/22/mexico-investigate-all-evidence-killings-22-soldiers.

121. Kirk Semple, "Missing Mexican Students Suffered a Night of 'Terror,' Investigators Say," *New York Times*, April 26, 2016, https://www.nytimes.com/2016/04/25/world/americas/missing-mexican-students-suffered-a-night-of-terror-investigators-say.html.

122. Kate Linthicum, "A Decade into Mexico's Deadly Drug War, Lawmakers Give the Military More Power," *Los Angeles Times*, December 15, 2017, http://www.latimes.com/world/mexico-americas/la-fg-mexico-military-law-20171215-story.html.

123. E. Eduardo Castillo and Mark Stevenson, "Gendarmería, nuevo cuerpo policial de México," *Huffington Post*, August 22, 2014, http://www.huffingtonpost.com/huffwires/20140822/amn-gen-mexico-gendarmeria/.

124. "Estado invierte Q158 millones anuales en nueve escuadrones de seguridad ciudadana del Ejército," *La Hora*, November 14, 2015, http://lahora.gt/estado-invierte-q158-millones-anuales-en-nueve-escuadrones-de-seguridad-ciudadana-del-ejercito/.

125. Interview with Guatemalan security official, October 2016.

126. Ellis, "The Struggle against Organized Crime in Guatemala."

127. Geovanni Contreras Corzantes, "Soldados van a vigilar dos mil kilómetros," *Prensa Libre*, January 23, 2017, http://www.prensalibre.com/guatemala/politica/soldados-van-a-vigilar-dos-mil-kilometros.

128. Interview with Guatemalan security officials, Guatemala City, October 2016.

129. Interview with Guatemalan security officials, Guatemala City, October 2016.

130. "PNC y FAES lanzan fase de recuperación de territorios en La Campanera," *La Prensa Grafica*, April 26, 2016, http://www.laprensagrafica.com/2016/04/26/pnc-y-faes-lanzan-fase-de-recuperacion-de-territorios-en-la-campanera.

131. See "Decreto No. 168–2013," *Gaceta Oficial*, No. 33, 211, August 24, 2013, http://www.tsc.gob.hn/leyes/Ley_Policia_militar_orden_publico_2013.pdf.

132. For a more detailed discussion of the PMOP, see Ellis, "Honduras: A Pariah State."

133. See, for example, "Honduras: Dictan detención judicial a la esposa de "Chepe" Handal," *El Heraldo*, March 21, 2015, http://www.elheraldo.hn/sucesos/824440–219/honduras-dictan-detenci%C3%B3n-judicial-a-la-esposa-de-chepe-handal.

134. Ellis, "Honduras: A Pariah State."

135. Ellis, "Honduras: A Pariah State."

136. "Presidente de Colombia resalta logros en seguridad del gobierno hondureño," Secretary of State of the Honduran Presidency, Official Website, April 6, 2016, http://

www.sep.gob.hn/sitio/historial-de-noticias/139-noticias-destacadas/ 1810-2016-04-07-20-59-16.

137. "Military Takes to the Streets in Fight against Crime in Dominican Republic," *Miami Herald*, June 16, 2016, http://www.miamiherald.com/news/nation-world/world/americas/article1952530.html.

138. Interview with Colombian security expert, Bogota, Colombia, September 2016.

139. "Primer bombardeo directo."

140. R. Evan Ellis, "The Post-Conflict and the Transformation of Colombia's Armed Forces," US Army War College Strategic Studies Institute, August 17, 2016, http://strategicstudiesinstitute.army.mil/index.cfm/articles/Colombias-Armed-Forces/2016/08/17.

141. Ana Lescano and Carlos Navea, "Fuerzas Armadas inician lucha contra inseguridad ciudadana," *Correo Semanal*, November 23, 2014, http://correosemanal.pe/actualidad/fuerzas-armadas-inician-lucha-contra-inseguridad-ciudadana/

142. "Callao: 5 cosas que tienes que saber sobre el estado de emergencia en esta region," *Peru 21*, December 13, 2015, http://peru21.pe/actualidad/callao-5-cosas-que-tienes-que-saber-sobre-estado-emergencia-esta-region-2234179.

143. Ellis, "Crime-Terrorism Nexus in Peru."

144. See Ellis, "Brazil."

145. "Brazilian Army Moves to Stem Prison Violence," *The Guardian*, January 28, 2017, https://guardian.ng/news/brazilian-army-moves-to-stem-prison-violence/.

146. "Police use shipping containers to separate Brazil prison gangs," *Yahoo*, January 21, 2017, https://www.yahoo.com/news/police-shipping-containers-separate-brazil-prison-gangs-214108311.html.

147. Stan Lehman and Sarah Dilorenzo, "Hundreds of Police Back on Duty in Paralyzed Brazil State," *ABC News*, February 11, 2017, http://abcnews.go.com/International/wireStory/striking-military-police-brazil-agree-return-work-45422063.

148. "Brazilian Army Orders 9,000 Troops into the Streets of Rio de Janeiro," 2017.

149. Simon Romero and Dom Phillips, "Brazil's President Deploys Federal Troops to Quell Protests," *New York Times*, May 24, 2017, https://www.nytimes.com/2017/05/24/world/americas/brazil-michel-temer-brasilia-protests.html.

150. Interview with Brazilian security official, Bogota, Colombia, September 2016.

151. Based on interviews off-the-record with Brazilian officials in Brasilia December 2017.

152. "Decreto 228/2016."

153. "Militares podrían custodiar las represas y centrales nucleares para que haya más gendarmes 'en lugares críticos,'" *La Nación*, December 12, 2016, http://www.lanacion.com.ar/1966244-militares-podrian-reemplazar-a-gendarmes-en-la-proteccion-de-represas-y-centrales-nucleares.

154. For an academic analysis of this, see John Bailey and Lucía Dammert, eds. *Public Security and Police Reform in the Americas* (Pittsburgh: University of Pittsburgh Press, 2005).

155. "Table of Results: Corruption Perceptions Index 2015," *Transparency International*, accessed October 19, 2016, http://www.transparency.org/cpi2015.

156. Mauricio Torres, "Mando único policial y otras 10 claves del nuevo plan de seguridad de Peña," *CNN Mexico*, December 3, 2014, http://mexico.cnn.com/nacional/2014/12/03/mando-unico-policial-y-otras-10-claves-del-nuevo-plan-de-seguridad-de-pena.

157. "Subsidio para la Seguridad en los Municipios (SUBSEMUN)," Secretaria de Gobernacion, Official Website, accessed October 19, 2016, http://secretariadoejecutivosnsp.gob.mx/en/SecretariadoEjecutivo/Subsemun.

158. James Bargent, "Mayor's Murder Could Impact Mexico Security Reforms," *Insight Crime*, January 4, 2016, http://www.InsightCrime.org/news-briefs/mayor-murder-could-impact-mexico-security-reforms.

159. Sandra Gonzalez, "Dejan militares mando único a Fuerza Civil." *Milenio*, September 4, 2015, http://www.milenio.com/region/Militares_Fuerza_Civil_mando_unico-Seguridad_NL-Fuerza_Civil_0_585541543.html.
160. "Mando Único entra al Estado de México," *Informador*, May 24, 2016, http://www.informador.com.mx/mexico/2016/662940/6/mando-unico-entra-al-estado-de-mexico.htm.
161. Marcos Muedano, "A seis años, Mando Único opera en 17.5% de municipios," *El Universal*, January 8, 2016, http://www.eluniversal.com.mx/articulo/nacion/seguridad/2016/01/8/seis-anos-mando-unico-opera-en-175-de-municipios.
162. Ellis, "Strategic Insights-Mexico: New Directions, Continuity, and Obstacles in the Fight against Transnational Organized Crime," 2016.
163. "Autodefensas procesados son porque cometieron un delito: Salvador Jara," *Milenio*, December 12, 2014, http://www.milenio.com/estados/proceso_contra_autodefensas-michoacan_y_autodefensas-amnistia_a_autodefensas_0_425957469.html
164. See, for example, Andres Becerril, "Autodefensas dan origen a otro cártel; nace en Michoacán La Tercera Hermandad o H3," *Excelsior*, May 6, 2016, http://www.excelsior.com.mx/nacional/2014/05/06/957619.
165. David Fuentes, "Inician juicios orales para delitos no graves," *El Universal*, January 16, 2015, http://archivo.eluniversal.com.mx/ciudad-metropoli/2015/impreso/inician-juicios-orales-para-delitos-no-graves-129295.html.
166. Interview with Mexican security official, February 2016.
167. Interview with Guatemalan security official, Guatemala City, October 2016.
168. Interview with Guatemalan security official, Guatemala City, October 2016.
169. Interview with Guatemalan security official, Guatemala City, October 2016.
170. For a good description of cases brought against former Guatemalan President Otto Pérez Molina, Roxana Baldetti, and other senior members of the Guatemalan government, see Michael Lohmuller, "Guatemala's Government Corruption Scandals Explained," *Insight Crime*, June 21, 2016, http://www.InsightCrime/com/news-analysis/guatemala-s-government-corruption-scandals-explained.
171. . David Gagne, "Ex-Mayor's Arrest Kicks off Guatemala Anti-Corruption Campaign," *Insight Crime*, January 22, 2016, http://www.InsightCrime.com/news-briefs/ex-mayor-arrest-kicks-off-guatemala-anti-corruption-campaign.
172. "'Sammy' y José Manuel Morales son enviados a prisión preventiva," *El Periodico*, January 19, 2017, http://elperiodico.com.gt/pais/2017/01/19/sammy-y-jose-manuel-morales-son-enviados-a-prision-preventiva/.
173. Rachel Schwartz, "Guatemala's President Tried to Expel the U.N. Commissioner Who Announced He Was under Investigation," *Washington Post*, September 6, 2017, https://www.washingtonpost.com/news/monkey-cage/wp/2017/09/06/guatemalas-president-tried-to-shut-down-a-u-n-commission-that-announced-it-was-investigating-him/?utm_term=.89d61ceda03c.
174. Interview with Honduran security official, Tegucigalpa, Honduras, July 2015.
175. . Elvin Diaz, "Comisión Depuradora: 28 por ciento de los depurados son oficiales de alto rango," *El Digital*, January 23, 2017, http://tiempo.hn/comision-depuradora-28-ciento-los-depurados-oficiales-alto-rango/.
176. Victoria Dittmar, "Honduras Extends Police Reform Commission until 2018," *Insight Crime*, January 24, 2017, http://www.InsightCrime.org/news-briefs/honduras-extends-police-reform-commission-until-2018.
177. Tristan Clavel, "As Honduras Tackles Police Corruption, Security Indicators Improve," *InsightCrime*, https://www.insightcrime.org/news/brief/as-honduras-tackles-police-corruption-security-indicators-improve/.
178. Interview with Colombian security official, Bogota, Colombia, September 2016.
179. See, for example, Celina B. Realuyo, "Leveraging the Financial Instrument of National Power to Counter Illicit Networks," Testimony before the Task Force to Investigate Terrorist Financing, Committee on Financial Services, US House of Repre-

sentatives, May 21, 2015, http://financialservices.house.gov/uploadedfiles/hhrg-114-ba00-wstate-crealuyo-20150521.pdf.
180. "El flagelo de la informalidad o el Perú que emerge a espaldas del Estado," *Gestion*, July 1, 2015, http://gestion.pe/economia/flagelo-informalidad-peru-que-emerge-espaldas-estado-2135974.
181. "The Edgemont Group of Financial Intelligence Units," Official Website, accessed October 18, 2016, http://www.egmontgroup.org/membership.
182. Ellis, "Strategic Insights-Mexico," 2016.
183. See, for example, Joel Olea Galindo, "Quedan restringidas las cuentas en dólares," *Tribuna de San Luis*, November 30, 2014, http://www.oem.com.mx/tribunadesanluis/notas/n3623648.htm.
184. Interview with Mexican security official, Mexico City, Mexico, February 2016.
185. "Honduras recibe la visita 'in situ' el próximo 1 de junio," Government of the Republic of Honduras, May 1, 2015, http://pplaft.cnbs.gob.hn/blog/2015/05/25/honduras-comienza-su-evaluacion-gafilat-el-proximo-2-de-junio/.
186. Dagoberto Rodríguez, "Solicitud de extradición de Jaime Rosenthal llega el lunes a la CSJ," *La Prensa*, January 2, 2016, http://www.laprensa.hn/honduras/916193-410/solicitud-de-extradici%C3%B3n-de-jaime-rosenthal-llega-el-lunes-a-la-csj.
187. "Honduras Seizes 50 Properties from Alleged Drug Gang," *Reuters*, August 18, 2014, http://www.reuters.com/article/us-honduras-drugs-idUSKBN0GI1VI20140818.
188. Financial intelligence against adversaries is collected in the armed forces by the financial intelligence committee.
189. "Argentina, US to Resume Sharing Financial Intelligence," *Reuters*, March 21, 2016, http://www.reuters.com/article/us-usa-argentina-crime-idUSKCN0WN1XU.
190. Alonso, "Guatemala Struggles to Prosecute."
191. "Guatemala," *World Prison Brief*, accessed September 1, 2016, http://www.prisonstudies.org/country/guatemala.
192. Interview with Mexican security official, Mexico City, February 2016.
193. Daniel Becerril, "Mexico Accuses Prison Officials of Homicide after Brutal Riot," *Reuters*, February 14, 2016, http://uk.reuters.com/article/uk-mexico-prison-idUKKCN0VN02M.
194. "Estalla motin en Cadereyta; chocan cifras de heridos," *El Universal*, March 28, 2017, http://www.eluniversal.com.mx/articulo/estados/2017/03/28/estalla-motin-en-cadereyta-chocan-cifras-de-heridos.
195. Interview with Guatemalan security official, Guatemala City, October 2016.
196. R. Evan Ellis, "Guatemala: Case Study of the Military in a Supporting Role in the Fight against Transnational Organized Crime," *Chilean Army War College*, June 2017.
197. Edwin Pitán, "Gobierno seguirá con plan para abrir cárcel pese a controversia," *Prensa Libre*, November 2, 2016, http://www.prensalibre.com/guatemala/comunitario/gobierno-seguira-con-plan-para-abrir-carcel-pese-a-controversia.
198. Ellis, "The Gang Challenge in El Salvador."
199. Ellis, "The New Offensive."
200. Seth Robbins, "El Salvador bloquea celulares en las prisiones en intento de reducir la extorsión," *Insight Crime*, May 21, 2014, http://www.france24.com/en/20160426-new-force-raids-el-salvador-gang-districts.
201. Mimi Yagoub, "Honduras Prisons Put Inmates at Risk, Fuel Gang Violence: OAS," *Insight Crime*, March 22, 2016, http://www.insightcrime.org/news-analysis/honduras-prisons-put-inmates-at-risk-fuel-gang-violence-oas.
202. . Catherine E. Schoichet, "Inmates Running the Asylum? In Honduras Prisons, That's No Joke," *CNN*, August 4, 2013, http://www.cnn.com/2013/08/04/world/americas/honduras-prisons/index.html.
203. "Report of the Interamerican Commission on Human Rights on the Situation of Persons Deprived of Liberty in Honduras," *Organization of American States*, March 18, 2013, http://www.oas.org/en/iachr/pdl/docs/pdf/HONDURAS-PPL-2013ENG.pdf.

204. Yagoub, "Honduras Prisons Put Inmates at Risk, Fuel Gang Violence: OAS," 2016.
205. Mariano Castillo and Elvin Sandoval, "More than 300 Killed in Honduras Prison Fire," *CNN*, February 16, 2012, http://www.cnn.com/2012/02/15/world/americas/honduras-fire-deaths/index.html.
206. "Reos más peligrosos de Honduras a megacárcel," *El Heraldo*, October 20, 2014, http://www.elheraldo.hn/alfrente/759995-331/reos-m%C3%A1s-peligrosos-de-honduras-a-megac%C3%A1rcel.
207. Tristan Clavel, "Honduras Takes First Step Toward Prison Overhaul with New Facility," *Insight Crime*, September 20, 2016, http://www.InsightCrime.org/news-briefs/honduras-first-step-prison-overhaul-new-facility.
208. Leonardo Goi, "Series of Escapes Underscores Weakness of Honduras Prison System," *Insight Crime*, May 15, 2017, https://www.insightcrime.org/news/brief/honduras-prisons-spotlight-65-escape-less-2-weeks/.
209. "UPDATE: Prison Gang Clashes Kill 18 in N. Brazil," *Xinhua*, October 17, 2016, http://news.xinhuanet.com/english/2016-10/18/c_135761526.htm.
210. "Brazilian Army Moves."
211. "Police Use Shipping Containers."
212. "Brazil Prison Knew about Escape Risk: Minister," *MSN*, January 5, 2017, http://www.msn.com/en-ca/news/world/brazil-prison-knew-about-escape-risk-minister/ar-BBxTXkW.
213. "Brazilian Army Moves."
214. Holger Alava, "Honduran and Guatemalan Armed Forces Cooperate to Improve Border Security through the Maya-Chortí Task Force," *Dialogo*, January 27, 2015, https://dialogo-americas.com/en/articles/honduran-and-guatemalan-armed-forces-cooperate-improve-border-security-through-maya-chorti-task-force.
215. Interview with Honduran defense official, Tegucigalpa, Honduras, July 2015.
216. See, for example, Marlinelza Batista de Oliveira, "Brazil and Paraguay Expand Military Cooperation," *Dialogo*, May 3, 2016, https://dialogo-americas.com/en/articles/brazil-and-paraguay-expand-military-cooperation.
217. Oswaldo Rivas, "Nicaragua Closes Border to Cuban Migrants, Rebukes Costa Rica," *Reuters*, November 15, 2015, http://www.reuters.com/article/us-nicaragua-cuba-idUSKCN0T502920151116.
218. See, for example, "Ecuador se convierte en 'Naciones Unidas' del crimen organizado, según la DEA," *El Universo*, May 10, 2011, http://www.eluniverso.com/2011/05/10/1/1355/cocaina-colombiana-peruana-pasa-traves-ecuador-segun-dea.html.
219. See, for example, "Uribe Accuses Venezuela of Backing FARC 'Genocide,'" *Financial Times*, March 4, 2008, https://www.ft.com/content/6576fd10-ea2a-11dc-b3c9-0000779fd2ac.
220. "Guatemala, Honduras y El Salvador firman acuerdo sobre pandillas," *Prensa Latina*, August 23, 2016, http://prensa-latina.cu/index.php?o=rn&id=21577&SEO=guatemala-honduras-y-el-salvador-firman-acuerdo-sobre-pandillas.
221. Mimi Yagoub, "Is the Northern Triangle's 'Historic' Security Pact Short-Sighted?" *Insight Crime*, August 24, 2016, http://www.InsightCrime.org/news-briefs/is-the-northern-triangle-historic-security-pact-short-sighted.
222. Ellis, "The New Offensive."
223. "Interpol," Official Website, accessed October 18, 2016, https://www.interpol.int/About-INTERPOL/Overview.
224. "Notices," Interpol, Official Website, accessed October 18, 2016, https://www.interpol.int/INTERPOL-expertise/Notices.
225. "USAID-SICA Regional Gang Prevention Activity Agreement," US Department of State, July 18, 2007, https://www.state.gov/p/wha/rls/89884.htm.
226. "Operation Martillo," US Southern Command, Official Website, August 22, 2016, http://www.southcom.mil/newsroom/Pages/Operation-Martillo.aspx.
227. "Joint Task Force Bravo," Official Website, accessed October 18, 2016, http://www.jtfb.southcom.mil/About-Us/.

228. Mike LaSusa, "Northern Triangle Policing Pact Limits Focus to Gangs," *Insight Crime*, August 15, 2016, http://www.InsightCrime.org/news-briefs/northern-triangle-policing-pact-limits-focus-to-gangs.

229. The US spent $1.2 billion on CARSI between 2008 and 2012. See *US Agencies Considered Various Factors in Funding Security Activities, but Need to Assess Progress in Achieving Interagency Objectives*, GAO-13–771, Washington DC: General Accounting Office, September 13, 2013, http://www.gao.gov/assets/660/658145.pdf.

230. Sarah Kinosian and Adam Isacson, "US Special Operations in Latin America: Parallel Diplomacy?" Washington Office on Latin America, August 30, 2016, https://www.wola.org/analysis/u-s-special-operations-latin-america-parallel-diplomacy/.

231. For a detailed discussion of Russian security assistance activities in Latin America and the Caribbean, see R. Evan Ellis, "The New Russian Engagement With Latin America: Strategic Engagement, Commerce, and Dreams of the Past," Carlisle Barracks, PA: US Army War College Strategic Studies Institute, June 2015, http://www.strategicstudiesinstitute.army.mil/pubs/display.cfm?pubID=1275.

232. "China-Argentina Security Cooperation Helps Reduce Crime," *Xinhua*, June 22, 2016, http://www.china.org.cn/world/2016–06/22/content_38717054.htm.

233. Interview with Argentine security official, Buenos Aires, Argentina, December 2016.

234. Off-the-record conversation with Panamanian security official, November 2017.

FIVE
The Path Forward

OVERVIEW

This chapter builds on the analysis of the proceeding four, to provide concrete recommendations for Latin American and US policymakers for working together to more effectively combat the challenge of transnational organized crime in the region. Proposed cuts to the US foreign aid budget, and delays in appointing an assistant secretary of state for the Western Hemisphere and key US ambassadors to the region suggests to some scholars that the Trump administration, like its predecessors, will not give significant priority to the region. Yet the president's attention to select countries such as Mexico,[1] Cuba,[2] and Venezuela,[3] and trips by multiple senior officials to the region[4] argue that, while the new administration's approach departs significantly from its predecessors, relative attention to the region is arguably greater. The question for decisionmakers in the security realm thus is the strategy and policy that are most appropriate for that engagement.

FOR POLICYMAKERS IN THE REGION

The eight areas of comparison presented in the preceding chapter provide an organizing framework through which policymakers in the region can learn lessons from both best practices and difficulties in the struggle against organized crime and terrorism, and as appropriate, selectively adapt such insights to their own legal frameworks and circumstances.[5] The present section, however, does not revisit those comparisons item-by-item, but rather, focuses on broader insights and recommended actions.

Expand the Focus on Systemic Concepts and Internationally Coordinated, Whole-of-Government Solutions

As seen in the previous chapter, most governments in the region have structures for developing and implementing policies and actions against organized crime that coordinate the principal government organizations involved, and work with relevant international partners and multilateral institutions. Most governments have executive-level cabinets and national security planning documents which represent, to some degree, the potential contributions and interests of government stakeholders.

Unfortunately, while those cabinets and policy documents coordinate the efforts of a range of stakeholders, their work is not always built around a clear strategic concept of how to face the challenge of transnational organized crime in systemic terms, recognizing the interdependence between the criminal groups, and the infrastructures and socioeconomic conditions which enable their activities and are, in turn, transformed by them. Too often, the lines of action and balance of effort between different government organizations in the fight against organized crime in individual countries simply reflect what those organizations do, rather than how their capabilities can best be leveraged to attack the problem.[6]

Decision makers in the region, supported by academics and others where appropriate, should do more, in formulating their strategies, to consider the dynamics of the relationship between criminal groups and society, including feedback effects by which corruption, economic need, large informal sectors, and deteriorated respect for law and the state contribute to the functioning of criminal organizations in the national territory.

Such reflection on the interdependence between criminal actors and structural conditions lead decision makers to a different set of questions regarding how to most effectively break negative reinforcing cycles between criminal activity and broken societies within the limited resources available to them, rather than merely how to take down individual bad actors. As part of such strategic thinking, decision-makers should do more to identify the key "centers of gravity" of criminal activities within their culture, such as group finance, or the cycle of corruption and impunity, in order to develop creative strategic concepts that leverage the capabilities of multiple organizations to affect such centers of gravity in systematic terms.

Such strategic concepts should be developed collaboratively, with inputs from the government organizations and other actors involved. The management of such activities should be supported by effective measures of performance, monitored by decision-makers to understand how the dynamics of the system are evolving in response to government actions and other phenomenon. In this process, it is particularly important to have engaged, empowered, informed leaders to identify what is working and what is not, and use their authority to overcome bureaucratic and other obstacles to implement the required fixes at both the national and local levels.

Strengthen Efforts and Share Best Practices for Interdiction and Territorial Control

Effective control of the national land territory, airspace, and waters continues to be a fundamental and necessary part of combatting the illicit flows that give resources to, and thus empower, criminal organizations. To work toward this goal, governments in the region can do more to share insights and best practices from activities such as bi-national patrols and the coordinating committees (*Combifrons*) that are used by many countries to manage issues of shared frontiers. Governments can also share best practices and lessons learned regarding the use of scanners and other technical mechanisms to control road and land border checkpoints. Other areas where governments can effectively share insights include community policing and the use of police forces with enhanced capabilities (such as the *Carbiñeros* in Chile and Colombia and the *Gendarmerie* in Argentina) that provide citizen security in difficult areas.

Governments can also fruitfully share the best practices and pitfalls regarding the use of the armed forces to support the police (where doing so is consistent with national law and tradition in that country). Multinational forums within the InterAmerican system such as the Conference of Central American Armed Forces (CFAC), the Central American Integration System (SICA), or the Conference of American Armies (CAA) provide useful venues for the sharing of such information and experiences which should be further mined.

With respect to airspace control, seven countries in the region have developed, or are developing, a combination of legal frameworks, detection and interception capabilities to contest unauthorized use of their airspace by narcotraffickers and other criminal actors.[7] Such activities create both the need and opportunity for expanded coordination between countries regarding the detection, tracking, and possible interception of unauthorized aircraft, as well as the sharing of best practices and lessons learned regarding issues such as interception protocols. In this manner, these governments can not only more effectively defend their national airspace, but also decrease the risk of incidents such as the mistaken downing of an innocent aircraft.

With respect to maritime control, numerous countries are acquiring new oceangoing and riverine naval assets to control their coasts and inland waterways, including adapting and incorporating boats confiscated from narcotraffickers for these purposes, as well as creating naval facilities in remote areas to provide better coverage of their coastlines and national waters.[8] As in other areas, governments in the region should look for opportunities to collaborate with respect to lessons learned in areas such as support to remote naval facilities, the use of "motherships" to extend patrol endurance, or the incorporation of assets seized from transnational criminal organizations into their inventories.

Improve Anticipation and Management of Collateral Effects in Targeting Criminal Group Leadership

For virtually all of the countries in the region, the targeting of the leaders and other key personnel in transnational criminal organizations is a key element of their efforts to take down the groups. Examples include Mexico's takedown of El Chapo Guzman (multiple times), La Tuta Gomez, Miguel Treviño, and Héctor Beltrán Leyva, the arrests of the leadership of smuggling organizations such as the Cachiros and Valle Valles in Honduras, the Mendoza, Lorenzana, Leon, and Lopez Ortiz families in Guatemala, and leaders of the *Shining Path* terrorist organization in Peru, including comrades Artemio, Hector, Alipio, Gabriel, and William.[9] As noted in this work, governments such as El Salvador and Honduras have also expanded targeting of the leadership of gang organizations such as Mara Salvatrucha and Barrio 18.

Operations against group leaders have frequently been successful at a tactical level, yet repeatedly, the arrest or killing of such leaders leads to a fracturing or re-organization of the group, as well as a struggle over the position of the group relative to its rivals, generating considerable uncertainty and violence.

The complexity and lack of knowledge regarding such groups, including the situations and calculations of their junior leaders, makes it tremendously difficult to anticipate how such dynamics will play out. Nonetheless, arguably far more can be done to incorporate consideration of possible consequences within the group, and among its rivals, when the government plans to take action against an organization's leaders. It may not be possible to avoid the violent second-order consequences of acting against such persons, yet through the use of strategic communication, psychological operations, and other actions, government forces may be able to channel the repercussions in a fashion more advantageous to the nation's interests and strategic objectives. At the very least, the deliberate analysis of such effects as a part of these operations may help to minimize the consequences, or help the governments involved prepare for them, thus saving lives.

Study and Incorporate Regional Best Practices and Lessons Learned in the Use of the Armed Forces to Support the Police

The majority of the countries in Latin America and the Caribbean use their armed forces to support the police and other authorities in some fashion, although the manner in which they do so varies greatly according to the constitutional and legal framework of each country, local needs, and traditions. In some cases, such as *Zeus* command and *FERES* in El Salvador, such collaboration is institutionalized. In rare cases, such as the *PMOP* in Honduras, special military units have arrest and other police powers under the national legal framework.[10] Such variation should be regarded as an opportunity by decisionmakers and law enforcement personnel to selectively draw on the innovations and mistakes of their neighbors.

Leverage Regional Best Practices in Including Technical Means Statutory Adjustment for Reforming the Police and Judicial System

Virtually every nation in the region is working in some fashion to combat corruption in police and judicial organs. Initiatives include screening procedures for applicants, confidence tests upon entry and on a regular basis thereafter, and monitoring of personnel, to include their financial situations and legal or personal problems. Nonetheless, removing personnel identified as potentially corrupted runs up against a series of obstacles, including organizational enabling laws which make it difficult to dismiss a police officer or other person who fails a confidence test, and the associated incentive to merely reassign the official in question. In addition, law enforcement organizations engaged in large-scale purges of corrupt or otherwise undesirable personnel must manage the effect placing large numbers of corrupt, bitter, and newly unemployed personnel on the street with connections to, and knowledge of, the practices of their prior organizations, even while such dismissals leave a temporary manpower gap in the law enforcement organization.

Law enforcement organizations in the region can better manage these challenges by sharing experiences and lessons learned from these activities, studying how their counterparts have implemented confidence tests, have overcome the difficulties in reassigning personnel, and have dealt with the side-effects of dismissing personnel from their organizations.

Expand Effort, Coordination, and Legal Tools for Attacking Criminal Group Finances

The ability of transnational criminal organizations to move, access, and legitimize illicitly earned income is a center of gravity for them, and an important opportunity for governments in their struggle against those groups. As seen previously, such flows are necessary enablers for every aspect of transnational criminal entities and activities, including their recruitment of personnel and construction of criminal organizations, their acquisition of arms, their payment of bribes to protect themselves and achieve their operational goals, and the money required for the operations that earn them revenues, including the expenses of producing, transforming, and transporting drugs and maintaining the infrastructure to do so, among other activities.[11]

In support of the fight against transnational organized crime financing, most Latin American and Caribbean states are strengthening financial intelligence capabilities, along with supporting laws, regulations, and institutions. The solutions adopted across the region vary. Some countries such as Ecuador and Argentina have independent financial intelligence organizations. In other countries, capabilities are embedded within or report to finance or economics ministries, as occurs in Colombia, or are split up within a range of organizations, creating challenges for the sharing of national intelligence. The degree to which laws and banking regulations support the ability to gather and analyze the data necessary to pursue criminal organizations also varies.[12] Studying organizational arrangements and enabling laws and regulations that are particularly effective in some countries may provide insights, as well as impetus for their adoption, in others.

Improve Control and Further Reform of Penitentiary Systems

In the majority of states in the region, overcrowding and dysfunctionality of the penitentiary system impedes the ability of the state to combat criminal groups by incarcerating their members and leaders. Particularly in countries of the Northern Triangle, the ability of penitentiaries to isolate criminals and thus protect society from them is inhibited by a reinforcing cycle of corruption and intimidation within the penitentiary itself. As seen in repeated cases in the previous chapter, jailed criminal leaders can often dictate terms to their jailers, leveraging the ability of those criminals to communicate with their counterparts on the outside to take action against families of guards and prison administrators if the latter do not agree to their demands. The effectiveness of those threats, in turn, is the enabler for prisoners on the inside to obtain access to visitors, cell phones, and other resources which facilitate those communications.

In an effort to break the cycle, states such as El Salvador have attempted a range of measures, including transferring prisoners, guards, and supervisors to other facilities, bringing the military in to help supervise select activities in the prisons, and working with local cell phone providers to block coverage in the vicinity of penitentiaries.

Countries such as Mexico have invested significant resources in their federal prisons to increase control through new physical and technical systems although follow-through of those efforts over time to ensure their success could be greater. As in other areas explored in this book, it is important for prison officials and others involved with national penal systems to share experience regarding what works and what doesn't, to break the cycle of corruption and intimidation that allows the criminals, not the government, to effectively control the nation's prisons.[13]

Expand Bilateral and Multilateral International Coordination Mechanisms

A common theme of this chapter has been the importance of the sharing of information and lessons learned regarding transnational organized crime between the governments of the region. To date, some of the international collaboration that has received the greatest attention includes financial and operational intelligence support from partners such as the US, interdiction support, and capacity-building. Multilateral cooperation, albeit less glamorous, is also important. Examples include coordination and the sharing of information through *Combifrons* and other entities that help manage shared borders, in addition to organizations such as the Conference of American Armies (CAA), the Central American Integration System (SICA), and the Conference of Central American Armies (CFAC), which have helped to facilitate multiple collaboration initiatives.

There are ample opportunities to expand US and other nations' intelligence and other support for operations against transnational organized crime in the region, always in a manner consistent with the laws and needs of the nations involved, as well as to comparatively study what aspects of that support are particularly effective and can be expanded upon, and what aspects are less effective and may be curtailed.

The expanded use of the OAS and other multilateral organizations within the InterAmerican system should be given particular consideration, insofar as the OAS includes all of the nations of the Americas, and has an in-place bureaucracy, legal mechanisms, and the tradition for conducting such cooperative efforts. Nonetheless, the effectiveness of the OAS requires the political will of each of its member states to be successful. As such, it is important to continue to emphasize the importance of working through the OAS, where possible, in conducting the discourse between governments on security across the region.

FOR US POLICYMAKERS

The US is arguably currently at a crossroads with respect to the fight against transnational organized crime. The administration of US president Donald Trump has implicitly recognized the impact of the region on

US security and prosperity through his emphasis on issues such a trade with and migration from Latin America. Yet the rhetoric from the administration in the early days of the Trump presidency, particularly with respect to Mexico and Cuba, raises serious concerns about whether the administration will be able to establish the type of partnerships of mutual respect and trust that effective security cooperation against transnational organized crime in the hemisphere requires.[14]

Below the level of the president, the administration is represented by highly competent and experienced leaders who understand both the region and the value of cooperative partnerships, including Secretary of State Rex Tillerson and National Security Council Chief Lieutenant General H. R. McMaster. Below those respected figures, however, as of 2017, the administration's team for Latin America, and the specifics of its policy toward the region, were still taking shape.

This section respectfully offers suggestions to the Trump administration regarding how to effectively engage with US partners in Latin America and the Caribbean with respect to the shared fight against transnational organized crime.

Dedicate More Resources and Leadership Attention, Invested More Intelligently

It is common for discussions of solutions to the challenge of transnational organized crime in Latin America and the Caribbean to begin with the argument that the United States needs to invest more to help its partners in the region. Indeed, discussions of US initiatives to assist the region, from Plan Colombia, to Plan Merida in Mexico, to the CBSI and CARSI and the Alliance for Prosperity,[15] frequently emphasize the inadequate amount of resources being spent.

The argument for the US to spend more on Latin America and the Caribbean is often explicitly or implicitly based on a presumed moral obligation, rooted in the argument that the US has substantially contributed to the problem through its demand for narcotics and other illicit substances,[16] and through its role as a supplier of the arms used in much of the criminal violence in the hemisphere.[17] From a more self-interested perspective, the security and prosperity of the US is directly impacted by transnational organized crime in the region. The US is strongly connected to Latin America not only in geographic terms, but also through bonds of economic interdependence and family.

With respect to geography, as noted previously in this work, the physical proximity of Latin America to the United States, including not only its land border with Mexico, but also the Caribbean as the maritime access route to the country, creates the risk that the direct and indirect effects of organized crime in the region will impact the citizens and territory of the United States. There has been much political discussion about the possibility of terrorists using the southern border to enter the United

States, and possibly even smuggle weapons of mass destruction into the country.[18] Yet the illicit networks used by transnational criminal organizations also create opportunities for terrorist groups such as Hezbollah to raise and launder money in the region in support of their global activities, as well as using the region for planning, training, and recruitment of personnel. The recruitment by the Islamic State of personnel from Latin America and the Caribbean to fight in Syria, Iraq, and elsewhere, and their return to their homes once radicalized, calls attention to some of the national security imperatives of this geographic interconnectivity.

Beyond Latin America and the Caribbean's geographic connection to the US, no other region is more fundamental to US economic well-being. Although US trade with the PRC receives significant attention, no other region of the world has a higher volume of trade with the United States than does Latin America and the Caribbean. Indeed, US bilateral trade with Latin America is not only greater than US trade with the PRC, but also greater than US trade with all of Asia combined. The United States has come to particularly rely on agricultural goods and manufactured products from Mexico since the formation of the North American Free Trade Agreement (NAFTA) in 1994. Its economic integration with Central America and the Dominican Republic have similarly strengthened significantly since the entry into effect of the Central American Free Trade Agreement (CAFTA-DR) in 2006.

Finally, there is no region of the world to which the US is more closely bound by ties of family than Latin America. Currently, more than 17 percent of US residents have their roots in the region. In short, what happens in the region increasingly affects those who residents in the US call family.

As a compliment to US interests in addressing the transnational organized crime challenge in the region, it is also clear that the region itself lacks the resources, and in some cases, the institutional strength, to take on the challenge itself. Some level of US assistance is clearly required. Whatever the moral argument that US leaders might make about the region solving its own problems, US security and prosperity will be increasingly put at risk if the US does not do more to help the region in the shared struggle against transnational criminal groups.

Nonetheless, simply spending money on the region, and creating new assistance programs, is not the answer. This work argues that what is most needed is internally and internationally coordinated whole-of-government solutions that address and target the challenge in systemic terms. Such solutions must start with the countries themselves, with targeted US and other international support where it is most needed, where it can make the greatest difference, and where it most makes sense.

Pursue Solutions Consistent with the Preferred Strategies and Approaches of Partners in the Region

In recent years, the US has too often sought to impose its preferred approach to combatting transnational organized crime on its partners, and has, for a variety of reasons, refused to work with those partners in the ways that they believe is most appropriate. Particularly in the area of military engagement, the US has declined to support military forces engaging in law enforcement missions in the region, seeking instead to force its own approach of leading with law enforcement personnel. A case in point is Honduras, where the US has largely refused to engage with the PMOP, a cornerstone of the Hernandez administration strategy to combat gangs and transnational organized crime, yet has insisted on principle in equipping and training an alternative force within the national police, the Tigres.

In multiple cases, including Honduras and Peru, the US has refused to provide radar data or other support to partner nation efforts to defend the sovereignty of their own airspace through intercepting suspicious aircraft. It has arguably withheld such support based on the concern that the partner will mistakenly down an aircraft carrying innocent civilians. Repeatedly, the US has insisted on "vetting" partner nation units before training or engaging with them, in order to avoid the appearance that the US was providing training to a unit tainted by accusations of human rights violations. On the other hand, under the Obama administration, the US has spent significant resources on programs largely of its own choosing, to strengthen partner nation institutions. Although the programs are valuable, they are not necessarily how the partner nations would choose to invest such resources if making the decision on its own. In other cases, such as Mexico, the US has committed to a support program, then shown itself to be an unreliable partner by withholding part of the aid over findings that its partner has not complied with an administrative or legislative condition that it has imposed.[19]

While it is appropriate for the US and its partners to maintain a dialogue about how best to balance the partner's needs with US preferences, the US approach too often goes beyond intellectually productive dialogues about how best to work together, and instead, seeks to impose pressure based on matters of principle, or worse yet, in order to prevent US policymakers from being tarnished by the mistakes or inadvertent abuses of its partner. Such a posture undermines the fight against organized crime by spending scarce US resources on programs that are not the greatest need of the host government, or do not have the most heartfelt backing of its partner. Moreover, doing so hurts the US relationship with its partners, and undermines the long-term US strategic position in the region by showing disrespect for its partner's choices and sovereignty.

Pursue Coordinated, System-Oriented Solutions from the Perspective of the US as a Part of the Region

US policymakers have become reasonably adept in interagency coordination, and, in their State Department and Defense Department outreach programs, actively seek to teach such coordination to their partners. In reality, the US has had numerous problems with coordinating its own security and development efforts in places like Afghanistan and Iraq. Similarly, in Latin America and the Caribbean, the coordination between the state, the defense department, and others in initiatives such as the previously mentioned Plan Colombia, CARSI, and CBSI have been problematic. Even within the US itself, coordination between federal, local, and state agencies in responding to disasters such as Hurricane Katrina has been wrought by difficulties.[20]

In fairness, the US does have a relatively well-defined and functional system for interagency coordination, including the National Security Council and the policy organizations within the Department of Defense and Department of State bureaucracies. Within each US embassy throughout the world, including those in Latin America and the Caribbean, the ambassador as the highest representative of the US government in the country, coordinates the activities of the multiple US agencies doing work in that country, to include having the final say on all US government personnel coming into and out of the country, and all US government programs realized therein. In theory, thus, through the Integrated Country Strategy (ICS), the US ambassadors in each Latin America and Caribbean state coordinate and integrate support from the US for it, consistent with the US objectives, and the desires of the partner.[21] In reality, however, the details and the ultimate level of support depend on a myriad of dynamics in the US government bureaucracies that shape the programs, and on Congress, which authorizes and appropriates the funds. Thus, the ambassador is often reduced to being a "traffic cop" coordinating the resources that are ultimately approved for the country, and trying to shape them, at least in appearance, into a coherent picture. The situation becomes even worse when there is no Senate-confirmed US ambassador, obliging the Deputy Chief of Mission (DCM) to perform this role. In the process, despite everything that the US tells its partners about interagency coordination, the support that the US provides the country is in practical terms, a laundry list of what each agency has managed to get approved, filtered by what it could get funded. Despite the often-heroic efforts of the US embassy team, thus, at the end of the day, the US support for its partners in the region in the struggle against transnational organized crime is not fully based on what make sense as the most effective manner to work with the US partner to combat organized crime in systemic terms. Nor, often, is there the flexibility to change the emphasis of the programs at the local level as the needs and situation shift. For its part, the local partner, in practical terms, adopts a posture of "taking what it can get" from the US and others, and integrating it with its own efforts in the best manner that it can.

The US needs to change this system to do better. With the arrival of a new secretary of state, and significant personnel change within the organization, the present may be the ideal time to do so. It is important for the US to design its support for partners in the region from the perspective of attacking transnational organized crime as a system, providing sufficient continuity of effort to allow long-range planning, but also allowing adaptation at the local level as the needs of the situation change. It should also do so in a form respectful to the wishes and situation of its partner.

Leverage the Experience of Latin American Governments with Interagency Coordination in US Partnerships and Activities Globally

While there are many important ways that the US can support its partners in Latin America and the Caribbean, and work together with them in the struggle against organized crime, there are also many ways in which the US can leverage and benefit from the significant experience of Latin American and Caribbean countries in its own partnerships and activities against transnational organized crime elsewhere in the world. For years, the US military had the lead in engagements with partners in Afghanistan and Iraq fighting against insurgent groups. The challenges of such missions resemble, in important ways, the activities of security forces in Latin America against transnational criminal entities, although also different in important ways.

With respect to similarities, US military forces in Afghanistan, for example, often had to work with their local military counterparts, as well as other Afghan police and security forces, in an environment in which some of those partners were corrupt and had complex loyalties. US military officers overseeing programs in the country thus had to labor continuously with the question of how to coordinate the efforts of their police, military, and other partners that they could not fully trust, and whom they believed to have multiple agendas, knowing that their providing of resources or cooperation could confer a particularistic benefit on one of the partners. Navigating such situations is arguably very familiar to US counterparts in Latin American countries such as El Salvador, Honduras, Colombia, and Peru, as seen in this work.

While it may not always be possible for US forces to directly consult their Latin American and other colleagues during such operations in other parts of the world, there are many opportunities to selectively incorporate Latin American partners with relevant knowledge and experience into decision processes as consultants, both at the Department of State and Department of Defense, and elsewhere.

Part of taking advantage of such opportunities involves simply educating US officers and other decision-makers about the potential utility of the experiences of their Latin American counterparts, to orient and motivate them to reach out through both formal and informal channels to seek such inputs. Moreover, for Latin American and Caribbean security forces, long accustomed to being treated as the "little brother" (or worse) by their US counterparts, such sincere and productive solicitation of inputs will likely produce the significant added benefit of strengthening the relationship between the US and those partners.

CONCLUSIONS

As this book has argued, transnational organized crime is the most significant threat to governance, stability, and prosperity in the region that is more directly linked than any other to US national security. The presence of Mexican cartels and Salvadoran street gangs in US cities from Washington, D.C., to Chicago to Los Angeles testify to the degree to which the cancer of criminal groups in the region is also infecting and affecting the United States in grave ways that are ever more difficult to ignore.

This work has emphasized the shared nature of the challenge presented by transnational organized crime, and the corresponding importance of working together in identifying and implementing effective solutions. As shown in chapter 2, there is an interdependency between the United States as a consumer nation for not only drugs, but also migrants and illicit goods, and Latin America and the Caribbean as a source and transit zone. The revenues generated in the United States pay for the operations that bring those goods and people through the region to supply US markets, as well as the guns that are bought in the United States to support the power struggles by transnational organized crime groups in the region. In turn those flows generate corruption and violence that displace refugees and gang members to the United States, creating significant economic and security challenges.

In a similar fashion, the transnational character of Mexican cartels and Central American and Caribbean gangs highlights the need for the US to continue to work together closely with its Latin American and Caribbean partners. Combatting Mara Salvatrucha and Barrio 18 in the United States requires collaboration with the nations of the Northern Triangle to understand their organization, activities, and motivations there. Similarly, working against Mexican groups like the Sinaloa Cartel and *Jalisco Nueva Generacion* in major US cities requires close collaboration with the Mexican government, in order to understand the organization's activities there.

As chapter 4 illustrated, combatting transnational organized crime is also a complex process in which it is imperative for the governments of the region to cooperate and learn from each other. Doing so includes everything from adopting each other's best practices for interagency planning, to leadership targeting, the use of the military, attacking group financing, sharing intelligence, and reforming the police and other law enforcement organizations, as well as the prisons of each nation.

In short, from the US perspective, a layered defense of healthy partner governments, cooperating against transnational criminal organizations, and becoming ever stronger and more reliable by sharing best practices, is far more effective, and less risky as a strategy, than attempting to isolate the United States behind a wall that is high enough to permit its residents to be indifferent concerning the conditions beyond it.

The bad actors in the community affect us all. Working together is the best way to ensure that the Western Hemisphere that we all share remains safe, prosperous, and well governed.

NOTES

1. Azam Ahmedjan, "Mexico's President Cancels Meeting with Trump over Wall," *New York Times*, January 26, 2017, https://www.nytimes.com/2017/01/26/world/mexicos-president-cancels-meeting-with-trump-over-wall.html.
2. Julie Hirschfeld Davis, "Trump Reverses Pieces of Obama-Era Engagement with Cuba," *New York Times*, June 16, 2017, https://www.nytimes.com/2017/06/16/us/politics/cuba-trump-engagement-restrictions.html.
3. "Trump Alarms Venezuela with Talk of a 'Military Option,'" *New York Times*, August 12, 2017, https://www.nytimes.com/2017/08/12/world/americas/trump-venezuela-military.html.
4. See, for example, "Vice President Mike Pence to Travel to Central and South America," The White House, Official Website, June 15, 2017, https://www.whitehouse.gov/briefings-statements/vice-president-mike-pence-travel-central-south-america/. See also Gardiner Harris and Kirk Semple, "Rex Tillerson Arrives in Mexico Facing Twin Threats to Relations," *New York Times*, February 22, 2017, https://www.nytimes.com/2017/02/22/world/americas/rex-tillerson-mexico-border-relations.html.
5. These recommendations are adapted and extended from those presented in R. Evan Ellis, "Collaboration and Learning in Latin America's Fight against Transnational Organized Crime and Terrorism," *Latin America Goes Global*, September 28, 2016, http://latinamericagoesglobal.org/2016/09/collaboration-learning-latin-americas-fight-transnational-organized-crime-terrorism/.
6. Adapted from Ellis, "Collaboration and Learning."
7. Adapted from Ellis, "Collaboration and Learning."
8. Adapted from Ellis, "Collaboration and Learning."
9. Adapted from Ellis, "Collaboration and Learning."
10. Adapted from Ellis, "Collaboration and Learning."
11. Adapted from Ellis, "Collaboration and Learning."
12. Adapted from Ellis, "Collaboration and Learning."
13. Adapted from Ellis, "Collaboration and Learning."
14. See R. Evan Ellis, "Effective Cooperation with Mexico Contributes More to US Security than Any Wall," *Financial Times*, January 30, 2017, https://www.ft.com/content/6f4b90fc-98aa-3fac-b858-2f24c58a56d8.

15. Francisco Palmeri, "Central America and the Alliance for Prosperity: Identifying US Priorities and Assessing Progress," US Department of State, April 19, 2016, http://www.state.gov/p/wha/rls/rm/255958.htm,

16. See, for example, the statement by former Mexican president Felipe Calderon in "México culpa a Estados Unidos de narco," *Hoy*, March 11, 2007, http://hoy.com.do/mexico-culpa-a-estados-unidos-de-narco/.

17. See, for example, "Si EU deja de dar armas; México dejará de dar droga: EPN," *Tiempo*, August 31, 2016, http://tiempo.com.mx/noticia/50923-que_eu_deje_de_dar_armas_mexic/1.

18. See, for example, "Potential Terrorist Threats: Border Security Challenges in Latin America and the Caribbean," Hearing before the Subcommittee on the Western Hemisphere of the Committee on Foreign Affairs House of Representatives One Hundred Fourteenth Congress, Second Session. March 22, 2016, http://docs.house.gov/meetings/FA/FA07/20160322/104726/HHRG-114-FA07-Transcript-20160322.pdf.

19. Elisabeth Malkin and Azam Ahmed, "US Withholds $5 Million in Antidrug Aid to Mexico as Human Rights Rebuke," *New York Times*, October 19, 2015, http://www.nytimes.com/2015/10/20/world/americas/us-withholds-5-million-in-antidrug-aid-to-mexico-over-human-rights.html?_r=0.

20. John E. O'Neill, "The Interagency Process—Analysis and Reform Recommendations," US Army War College, March 15, 2006, http://www.strategicstudiesinstitute.army.mil/pdffiles/ksil445.pdf.

21. "Integrated Country Strategy Guidance and Instructions," US Agency for International Development, accessed October 3, 2016, http://pdf.usaid.gov/pdf_docs/PBAAA879.pdf..

Bibliography

"¿Cómo está y que hacer en el Vraem?, por Rubén Vargas." *El Comercio*, April 17, 2016. http://elcomercio.pe/opinion/colaboradores/como-esta-y-que-hacer-vraem-ruben-vargas-noticia-1894782.
"'Artemio' capturado." *IDL Reporteros*, February 12, 2012. https://idl-reporteros.pe/artemio-capturado/.
"'Sammy' y José Manuel Morales son enviados a prisión preventiva." *El Periodico*, January 19, 2017. http://elperiodico.com.gt/pais/2017/01/19/sammy-y-jose-manuel-morales-son-enviados-a-prision-preventiva/.
"2016 Seizures Suggest CentAm Still Top Drug Corridor to US." *Insight Crime*, July 26, 2016. http://www.InsightCrime.org/news-briefs/2016-drug-seizures-suggest-centam-still-top-trafficking-corridor.
"50ª Reunión Ordinaria de la Conferencia Nacional de Gobernadores." Presidencia de Mexico. February 29, 2016. http://www.gob.mx/presidencia.
"A Lethal Location." *The Economist*, September 17, 2016. http://www.economist.com/news/americas/21707244-how-argentine-port-became-gang-war-zone-lethal-location.
"Aceptan la Renuncia del Viceministro de Defensa Iván Vega." *Agencia de Noticias de Peru*, March 2013. http://www.agenciadenoticiasdelperu.com/2016/03/aceptan-renuncia-del-viceministro-de.html.
"Al Qaeda Seeks Tie to Local Gang." *Washington Times*, September 28, 2004. http://www.washingtontimes.com/news/2004/sep/28/20040928–123346–3928r/.
"Alias 'Otoniel' y otros 1.500 hombres del Clan del Golfo se someterían a la justicia." *Caracol*, September 11, 2017. https://noticias.caracoltv.com/colombia/alias-otoniel-y-otros-1500-hombres-del-clan-del-golfo-se-someterian-la-justicia.
"Amigos dos Amigos." *Insight Crime*. Accessed August 30, 2016. http://www.InsightCrime.org/brazil-organized-crime-news/amigos-dos-amigos.
"Argentina—Air Force." *Janes Sentinel Security Assessment – South America*, November 8, 2016. https://janes.ihs.com/Janes/Display/1767023.
"Argentina, U.S. to Resume Sharing Financial Intelligence." *Reuters*, March 21, 2016. http://www.reuters.com/article/us-usa-argentina-crime-idUSKCN0WN1XU.
"Argentina: President Promises Change Amid National Turmoil." *NBC News*, March 2, 2016. http://www.nbcnews.com/news/latino/argentina-president-promises-change-amid-national-turmoil-n530311.
"As Cartels Renew battle, Violence in Border City of Ciudad Juarez Spikes Again." *Fox News*, November 4, 2016. http://www.foxnews.com/world/2016/11/04/as-cartels-renew-battle-violence-in-border-city-ciudad-juarez-spikes-again.html.
"Asesinan a supuesto narcotraficante salvadoreño 'Chepe' Luna." *La Prensa Grafica*, June 29, 2014. http://www.laprensagrafica.com/2014/06/27/asesinan-a-supuesto-narcotraficante-salvadoreo-chepe-luna.
"Autodefensas procesados son porque cometieron un delito: Salvador Jara." *Milenio*, December 12, 2014. http://www.milenio.com/estados/proceso_contra_autodefensas-michoacan_y_autodefensas-amnistia_a_autodefensas_0_425957469.html.
"Autorizan extradición a EUA de José Inocente Valle y esposa." *La Prensa*, November 13, 2014. http://www.laprensa.hn/inicio/767394–417/autorizan-extradición-a-eua-de-josé-inocente-valle-y-esposa.

"Barrio Seguro está cambiando la vida a más de 4 mil jóvenes." Government of Panama. January 8, 2016. https://www.presidencia.gob.pa/Noticias/Barrio-Seguro-esta-cambiando-la-vida-a-mas-de-4-mil-jovenes.

"Bolivia." Trafficking In Persons Report 2016, U.S. Department of State, 2016. https://www.state.gov/documents/organization/258878.pdf, 99–102.

"Border Sensor Program Gains Momentum in Brazil." *Defensanet*, March 21, 2017, www.defesanet.com.br/en/defense/noticia/24963/Border-sensor-program-gains-momentum-in-Brazil/.

"Brazil Army Deploys in Rio Slum as Drug-Related Violence Worsens." *Reuters*, September 22, 2017. https://www.reuters.com/article/us-brazil-violence/brazil-army-deploys-in-rio-slum-as-drug-related-violence-worsens-idUSKCN1BX2Z9.

"Brazil Deploys Troops to Secure Borders for World Cup." *Reuters*, May 10, 2014. https://www.reuters.com/article/us-brazil-worldcup-security/brazil-deploys-troops-to-secure-borders-for-world-cup-idUSBREA4908H20140510.

"Brazil Prison Knew about Escape Risk: Minister." *MSN*, January 5, 2017. http://www.msn.com/en-ca/news/world/brazil-prison-knew-about-escape-risk-minister/ar-BBxTXkW.

"Brazil, Colombia Warn FARC Renegades Could Fuel Crime." *Yahoo*, January 31, 2017. https://www.yahoo.com/news/brazil-colombia-warn-farc-renegades-could-fuel-crime-002149583.html.

"Brazil." *Trafficking in Persons Report 2016*, U.S. Department of State, 2016. https://www.state.gov/documents/organization/258878.pdf, 104–108.

"Brazilian Army Moves to Stem Prison Violence." *The Guardian*, January 28, 2017. https://guardian.ng/news/brazilian-army-moves-to-stem-prison-violence/.

"Brazilian Army Orders 9,000 Troops into the Streets of Rio de Janeiro." *EFE*, February 14, 2016. http://www.efe.com/efe/english/portada/brazilian-army-orders-9-000-troops-into-the-streets-of-rio-de-janeiro/50000260–3179613.

"Cabecilla del cartel de los AA está enmontañado." *El Heraldo*, November 5, 2015. http://www.elheraldo.hn/pais/898146-466/cabecilla-del-cartel-de-los-aa-est%C3%A1-enmonta%C3%B1ado.

"Cabecilla prófugo migró a Guatemala a extorsionar." *La Prensa Grafica*, October 13, 2016. http://www.laprensagrafica.com/2016/10/13/cabecilla-profugo-migro-a-guatemala-a-extorsionar.

"Cachiros." *Insight Crime*. Accessed August 30, 2016. http://www.InsightCrime.org/honduras-organized-crime-news/cachiros.

"Callao: 5 cosas que tienes que saber sobre el estado de emergencia en esta region." *Peru 21*, December 13, 2015. http://peru21.pe/actualidad/callao-5-cosas-que-tienes-que-saber-sobre-estado-emergencia-esta-region-2234179.

"Capturan a Walter Mendoza, presunto líder de estructura criminal." *La Hora*, April 6, 2016. http://lahora.gt/capturan-walter-mendoza-presunto-lider-estructura-criminal.

"Cartel de los Soles." *Insight Crime*. Accessed August 30, 2016. http://www.InsightCrime.org/venezuela-organized-crime-news/cartel-de-los-soles-profile.

"Carteles mexicanos en labores de reclutamiento en Honduras." *El Heraldo*, May 29, 2015. http://www.elheraldo.hn/alfrente/844491-209/carteles-mexicanos-en-labores-de-reclutamiento-en-honduras.

"Central America's Unresolved Migrant Crisis." *New York Times*, June 16, 2015. http://www.nytimes.com/2015/06/16/opinion/central-americas-unresolved-migrant-crisis.html?_r=0.

"Chile Has Fastest Growing Immigrant Population in South America." *Mercopress*, May 26, 2009. http://en.mercopress.com/2009/05/25/chile-has-fastest-growing-immigrant-population-in-south-america.

"China complacida por lucha del tráfico de personas en Ecuador." *El Universo*, November 14, 2008. http://www.eluniverso.com/2008/11/14/0001/626/77D77D68D2D646D091AF366AB0CD8B67.html.

"China-Argentina Security Cooperation Helps Reduce Crime." *Xinhua,* June 22, 2016. http://www.china.org.cn/world/2016-06/22/content_38717054.htm.

"Clan del Golfo recluta a guerrilleros de las Farc por $1,8 millones: Fiscal General." *El Heraldo,* January 25, 2016. http://www.elheraldo.co/colombia/clan-del-golfo-recluta-guerrilleros-de-las-farc-por-18-millones-fiscal-general-322884.

"Coca in the Andes." Office of National Drug Control Policy, U.S. Department of State. Accessed October 13, 2016. https://www.whitehouse.gov/ondcp/targeting-cocaine-at-the-source.

"Cocaine from South America to the United States." *United Nations Office on Drugs and Crime.* http://www.unodc.org/documents/toc/Reports/TOCTASouthAmerica/English/TOCTA_CACaribb_cocaine_SAmerica_US.pdf.

"Colombia FARC Rebels Start Demobilization Process." *Yahoo News,* January 31, 2017. https://www.yahoo.com/news/colombia-farc-rebels-start-demobilization-process-160029284.html.

"Colombia Freezes FARC Assets under Peace Deal." *Yahoo News,* February 23, 2017. https://www.yahoo.com/news/colombia-freezes-farc-assets-under-peace-deal-212015308.html.

"Colombia to Crack Down on Coca Crops." *BBC,* January 28, 2017. http://www.bbc.com/news/world-latin-america-38779685.

"Colombia: Abatieron a Luis Orlando Padierna Peña alias 'Inglaterra,' el número dos del Clan del Golfo." *InfoBae,* November 23, 2017. https://www.infobae.com/america/colombia/2017/11/23/colombia-abatieron-a-luis-orlando-padierna-pena-alias-inglaterra-el-numero-dos-del-clan-del-golfo/.

"Colombian Drug Cartels Used Hong Kong Banks to Launder More than US$5bn." *South China Morning Post,* September 12, 2015. http://www.scmp.com/news/hong-kong/law-crime/article/1857155/laundering-ring-pumped-billions-drug-money-through-hong.

"Colombian ELN Rebels 'Regret' Journalists' Kidnap." *BBC,* May 30, 2016. http://www.bbc.com/news/world-latin-america-36412101.

"Colombian FARC Rebels' Links to Venezuela Detailed." *BBC,* May 10, 2017. http://www.bbc.com/news/world-latin-america-13343810.

"Colombia's FARC Has Completed Disarmament, UN Says." *BBC,* June 27, 2017. http://www.bbc.com/news/world-latin-america-40413335.

"Cómo murió 'William.'" *IDL Reporteros,* September 6, 2012. https://idl-reporteros.pe/como-murio-william/.

"Continental hipotecó bienes de Los Cachiros." *El Heraldo,* October 19, 2015. http://www.elheraldo.hn/pais/892193-214/continental-hipotec%C3%B3-bienes-de-los-cachiros.

"Country Fast Facts: Colombia." *CBS News,* September 17, 2007. http://www.cbsnews.com/news/country-fast-facts-colombia-3268352/.

"Dangerous 'One Order' Concept Spreading, Says Senior Cop." *Jamaica Observer,* January 20, 2010. http://www.jamaicaobserver.com/news/One-order-concept-Wed--Jan-20--2010_7340287.

"Decreto 228/2016." *Boletín Oficial de la República de Argentina,* January 21, 2016. https://www.boletinoficial.gob.ar/#!DetalleNorma/140329/20160122.

"Decreto No. 168-2013." *Gaceta Oficial,* No. 33, 211, August 24, 2013. http://www.tsc.gob.hn/leyes/Ley_Policia_militar_orden_publico_2013.pdf.

"Derriban helicóptero de Sedena en Jalisco; mueren 3 militares." *Nacional,* May 1, 2015. http://diario.mx/Nacional/2015-05-01_7cfde641/derriban-helicoptero-de-sedena-en-jalisco-mueren-3-militares/.

"Descubren en República Dominicana un gran laboratorio soterrado de drogas." *El Mundo,* September 1, 2013. http://www.elmundo.es/america/2013/09/01/noticias/1378063613.html.

"Desmantelan campamento de pandillas en manglares." *La Prensa Grafica,* January 12, 2015. http://www.laprensagrafica.com/2015/01/12/desmantelan-campamento-de-pandillas-en-manglares.

"Diario Oficial." Procurador General de la Republica. March 23, 2009. http://www.pgr.gob.mx/normatec/Documentos/a-123–09.pdf.

"Digna Valle, la mujer que pone en jaque al cartel de Sinaloa." *La Prensa*, October 7, 2014. http://www.laprensa.hn/inicio/755263-417/digna-valle-la-mujer-que-pone-en-jaque-al-cartel-de-sinaloa.

"Dissident Faction Splits with El Salvador's Notorious MS-13 Gang." *Telesur*, May 2, 2017. https://www.telesurtv.net/english/news/Dissident-Faction-Splits-with-El-Salvadors-Notorious-MS-13-Gang-20170502-0015.html.

"Dominican Republic Military Has 3-D Radar Starting Today." *Dominican Today*, July 15, 2010. http://www.dominicantoday.com/dr/technology/2010/7/15/36321/Dominican-Republic-military-has-3-D-radar-starting-today.

"Dominican Republic." *2016 International Narcotics Control Strategy Report*, U.S. Department of State. No. 1 (2016). https://www.state.gov/j/inl/rls/nrcrpt/2016/vol1/253257.htm.

"Dozens Killed in Gang Violence at Brazilian Jail." *Reuters*, January 2, 2017. https://www.theguardian.com/world/2017/jan/02/dozens-killed-in-gang-violence-at-brazilian-jail-manaus.

"Drug Enforcement Administration 1991–1994." Drug Enforcement Administration. Accessed October 20, 2016. https://www.dea.gov/about/history/1990–1994.pdf.

"Economia Subterranea: El Caso de Paraguay." *ProDesarrollo Paraguay*, 4th Edition, November 2016. http://www.pro.org.py/wp-content/uploads/2016/11/ECONOMIA_SUBTERRANEA_2016.pdf.

"Ecuador se convierte en 'Naciones Unidas' del crimen organizado, según la DEA." *El Universo*, May 10, 2011. http://www.eluniverso.com/2011/05/10/1/1355/cocaina-colombiana-peruana-pasa-traves-ecuador-segun-dea.html.

"Ecuador y China eliminan visa para turismo." *El Universo*, June 14, 2016. http://www.eluniverso.com/noticias/2016/06/14/nota/5636385/ecuador-china-eliminan-visa-turismo.

"Ecuador, escala en tráfico de indocumentados chinos." *El Universo*, December 12, 2008. http://www.eluniverso.com/2008/12/12/1/1360/40F307FB4904484381C8C0F32D1FE45C.html.

"El 88% de la producción de oro de Colombia es ilegal, alertan." *Newsweek en Espanol*, August 2, 2016. http://nwnoticias.com/#!/noticias/el-88-de-la-produccion-de-oro-de-colombia-es-ilegal-alertan-mineros.

"'El cártel de Los Caballeros Templarios está totalmente desmembrado'." *Univision*, March 8, 2015. https://www.univision.com/noticias/noticias-de-mexico/el-cartel-de-los-caballeros-templarios-esta-totalmente-desmembrado.

"El flagelo de la informalidad o el Perú que emerge a espaldas del Estado." *Gestion*, July 1, 2015. http://gestion.pe/economia/flagelo-informalidad-peru-que-emerge-espaldas-estado-2135974.

"El Salvador cerrará 2012 con mitad de homicidios por tregua." *La Prensa*, December 12, 2012. http://www.prensa.com/mundo/Salvador-cerrara-mitad-homicidios-tregua_0_3546395343.html.

"ENFOQUE-Lucha contra minería ilegal de oro en Perú crea nueva ruta de contrabando por Bolivia." *Reuters*, November 25, 2014. http://lta.reuters.com/article/topNews/idLTAKCN0J91WL20141125?pageNumber=1&virtualBrandChannel=0.

"Es oficial: Termina era del glifosato en fumigaciones en Colombia." *El Tiempo*, May 15, 2015. http://www.eltiempo.com/politica/justicia/colombia-dejara-de-fumigar-con-glifosato/15757420.

"Estado invierte Q158 millones anuales en nueve escuadrones de seguridad ciudadana del Ejército." *La Hora*, November 14, 2015. http://lahora.gt/estado-invierte-q158-millones-anuales-en-nueve-escuadrones-de-seguridad-ciudadana-del-ejercito/.

"Estados Unidos detuvo a dos narcotraficantes hondureños, líderes del cártel Los Cachiros." *Infobae*, February 6, 2015. http://www.infobae.com/2015/02/06/1625362-estados-unidos-detuvo-dos-narcotraficantes-hondurenos-lideres-del-cartel-los-cachiros/.

"Estalla motin en Cadereyta; chocan cifras de heridos." *El Universal*, March 28, 2017. http://www.eluniversal.com.mx/articulo/estados/2017/03/28/estalla-motin-en-cadereyta-chocan-cifras-de-heridos.

"EUA tras cartel formado por jueces, militares, alcaldes y policías." *La Prensa*, October 11, 2016. http://www.laprensa.hn/honduras/1007292-410/eua-tras-cartel-formado-por-jueces-militares-alcaldes-y-polic%C3%ADas.

"FARC Denies Having Billions of Dollars, Colombia Has No Proof." *Telesur*, April 29, 2016. http://www.telesurtv.net/english/news/FARC-Denies-Having-Billions-of-Dollars-Colombia-Has-No-Proof-20160429-0026.html.

"FARC Dissidents Face Full Force of Colombia Military: President." *Reuters*, November 23, 2017. https://www.reuters.com/article/us-colombia-peace/farc-dissidents-face-full-force-of-colombia-military-president-idUSKBN1DN24A.

"Firearms in Central America." United Nations Office on Drugs and Crime. Accessed October 14, 2016. https://www.unodc.org/documents/toc/Reports/TOCTASouthAmerica/English/TOCTA_CACaribb_firearmssmuggling_within_CAmerica.pdf.

"Former Mexican Drug Cartel Leader Extradited to U.S.: Justice Department." *Reuters*, December 19, 2017. https://www.reuters.com/article/us-usa-mexico-drugs/former-mexican-drug-cartel-leader-extradited-to-u-s-justice-department-idUSKBN1EE01B.

"Guatemala decide extraditar a veterano narcotraficante a EEUU." *Reuters*, August 6, 2012. http://lta.reuters.com/article/domesticNews/idLTASIE87600320120807.

"Guatemala, Honduras y El Salvador firman acuerdo sobre pandillas." *Prensa Latina*, August 23, 2016. http://prensa-latina.cu/index.php?o=rn&id=21577&SEO=guatemala-honduras-y-el-salvador-firman-acuerdo-sobre-pandillas.

"Guatemala." *World Prison Brief*. Accessed September 1, 2016. http://www.prisonstudies.org/country/guatemala.

"Gustavo Gorriti: El drama de Kepashiato muestra la compleja y vulnerable situación del VRAE." *La Republica*, April 13, 2012. http://www.larepublica.pe/13-04-2012/gustavo-gorriti-el-drama-de-kepashiato-muestra-la-compleja-y-vulnerable-situacion-del-vrae.

"Guyana, Suriname Discuss Gold Smuggling, Exploitation of Natural Resources." *Kaieteur News*, February 13, 2013. http://www.kaieteurnewsonline.com/2013/02/13/guyana-suriname-discuss-gold-smuggling-exploitation-of-natural-resources/.

"Helicóptero da PM cai durante operação em favela do Rio." *Globo*, October 18, 2009. http://g1.globo.com/Noticias/Rio/0,,MUL1344807-5606,00-HELICOPTERO+DA+PM+CAI+DURANTE+OPERACAO+EM+FAVELA+DO+RIO.html.

"Helicopters Face High Risk of Attack in Peru's VRAEM Region." *IHS Jane's Intelligence Weekly*, October 29, 2014. http://www.janes.com/article/45176/helicopters-face-high-risk-of-attack-in-peru-s-vraem-region.

"Honduran and Nicaraguan Armies Join Forces in Operation Morazán-Sandino." *Dialogo*, August 23, 2017. https://dialogo-americas.com/en/articles/honduran-and-nicaraguan-armies-join-forces-operation-morazan-sandino.

"Honduras aprueba derribar aviones sospechosos de narcotráfico." *BBC*, January 18, 2014. http://www.bbc.com/mundo/ultimas_noticias/2014/01/140118_ultnot_honduras_autoriza_derribo_aviones_sospechosos_drogas_lav.

"Honduras compra radares a Israel por $30 millones." *El Economista*, December 19, 2013. http://www.eleconomista.net/2013/12/19/honduras-compra-radares-a-israel-por-30-millones.

"Honduras ha reducido un 98.11 % aterrizaje de avionetas con droga en 5 años." *El Nuevo Diario*, October 1, 2015. http://www.elnuevodiario.com.ni/internacionales/372236-honduras-ha-reducido-98-11-aterrizaje-avionetas-dr/.

"Honduras recibe la visita 'in situ' el próximo 1 de junio." Government of the Republic of Honduras, May 1, 2015. http://pplaft.cnbs.gob.hn/blog/2015/05/25/honduras-comienza-su-evaluacion-gafilat-el-proximo-2-de-junio/.

"Honduras Seizes 50 Properties from Alleged Drug Gang." *Reuters*, August 18, 2014. http://www.reuters.com/article/us-honduras-drugs-idUSKBN0GI1VI20140818.

"Honduras: Dictan detención judicial a la esposa de 'Chepe' Handal." *El Heraldo*, March 21, 2015. http://www.elheraldo.hn/sucesos/824440–219/honduras-dictan-detenci%C3%B3n-judicial-a-la-esposa-de-chepe-handal.

"Honduras: Fuerza Aérea halla narcoavioneta en La Mosquitia." *La Prensa*, March 24, 2014. http://www.laprensa.hn/inicio/626506–96/honduras-fuerza-aerea-halla-narcoavioneta-en-la-mosquitia.

"Honduras: Operación Avalancha arremete contra bienes de la Mara Salvatrucha MS-13." *El Heraldo*, October 17, 2016. http://www.elheraldo.hn/pais/1009148–466/honduras-operación-avalancha-arremete-contra-bienes-de-la-mara-salvatrucha-ms-13.

"Human Trafficking & Migrant Smuggling: Understanding the Difference." U.S. Department of State, July 27, 2015. http://www.state.gov/j/tip/rls/fs/2015/245175.htm.

"In Colombia, Peace Remains Elusive One Year On." *Deutsche Welle*." November 23, 2017, www.dw.com/en/in-colombia-peace-remains-elusive-one-year-on/a-41372941.

"Inauguration of the Xinca Task Force." U.S. Embassy in Guatemala, August 31, 2017. https://gt.usembassy.gov/inauguration-xinca-task-force/.

"Incautan 37,5 kilos de cocaína en Quijarro." *El Deber*, June 26, 2015. http://www.eldeber.com.bo/santacruz/incautan-37-kilos-cocaina-quijarro.html.

"Integrated Country Strategy Guidance and Instructions." U.S. Agency for International Development. Accessed October 3, 2016. http://pdf.usaid.gov/pdf_docs/PBAAA879.pdf.

"Interdicción de 'narcovuelos' en el VRAE." *IDL Reporteros*, December 17, 2013. https://idl-reporteros.pe/interdiccion-de-%e2%80%98narcovuelos%e2%80%99-en-el-vrae/.

"Interpol." Interpol. Accessed October 18, 2016. https://www.interpol.int/About-INTERPOL/Overview.

"Iquique como puedo pasar contrabando a Peru." *La Primera*, July 5, 2012. https://www.diariolaprimeraperu.com/online/entrevista/contrabando-el-enemigo-economico-peru-114732/.

"Jamaica Pushes Back Human Trafficking." *Jamaica Gleaner*, July 21, 2013. http://jamaica-gleaner.com/gleaner/20130721/focus/focus6.html.

"Jamaica." *2016 International Narcotics Control Strategy Report*, Department of State, 2016. https://www.state.gov/j/inl/rls/nrcrpt/2016/vol1/253277.htm.

"Joint Task Force Bravo." U.S. Southern Command. Accessed October 18, 2016. http://www.jtfb.southcom.mil/About-Us/.

"Leaders of Honduran Drug Cartel Face Federal Drug and Money Laundering Charges in the Eastern District of Virginia." Federal Bureau of Investigation. December 19, 2014. https://www.fbi.gov/washingtondc/press-releases/2014/leaders-of-honduran-drug-cartel-face-federal-drug-and-money-laundering-charges-in-the-eastern-district-of-virginia.

"Leones." Insight Crime. Accessed August 30, 2016. http://www.InsightCrime.org/guatemala-organized-crime-news/los-leones.

"Lorenzanas." Insight Crime. Accessed August 30, 2016. http://www.InsightCrime.org/guatemala-organized-crime-news/los-lorenzana.

"Los Escorpiones, terrible escolta de Tormenta." *El Universal*, November 5, 2010. http://archivo.eluniversal.com.mx/notas/721570.html.

"Los Rastrojos se están fortaleciendo en territorio venezolano, alerta la FIP." *El Espectador*, July 16, 2017. https://www.elespectador.com/noticias/judicial/los-rastrojos-se-estan-fortaleciendo-en-territorio-venezolano-alerta-la-fip-articulo-703454.

"Lottery Scam Taskforce Being Reintroduced." *Jamaica Observer*, September 26, 2016. http://www.jamaicaobserver.com/news/Lottery-Scam-Taskforce-being-reintroduced.

"Lucha contra el narcotráfico y derribo de aviones." *La Nacion*, February 9, 2016. http://www.lanacion.com.ar/1869405-lucha-contra-el-narcotrafico-y-derribo-de-aviones.

"Mandatario panameño inicia instalación de primer radar contra narcotráfico." *La Prensa*, October 9, 2012. http://www.laprensa.com.ni/2012/10/09/internacionales/

119406-mandatario-panameno-inicia-instalacion-de-primer-radar-contra-narcotrafico
"Mando Único entra al Estado de México." *Informador*, May 24, 2016. http://www.informador.com.mx/mexico/2016/662940/6/mando-unico-entra-al-estado-de-mexico.htm.
"Matan a 'Chepe' Luna; caen 4 de los sicarios y dos mueren." *La Tribuna*, June 27, 2014. http://www.latribuna.hn/2014/06/27/matan-a-chepe-luna-caen-4-de-los-sicarios-y-dos-mueren/.
"Mendozas." *Insight Crime*. Accessed August 30, 2016. http://www.InsightCrime.org/guatemala-organized-crime-news/los-mendoza.
"Mexican Cartel Smuggling Cocaine into Hong Kong amid Booming Demand for Drugs." *South China Morning Post*, February 2, 2014. http://www.scmp.com/news/hong-kong/article/1418852/mexican-cartel-smuggling-cocaine-hong-kong-amid-booming-demand-drugs.
"Mexican Drug Gangs Expand into Illegal Mining." *Reuters*, October 4, 2010. http://www.reuters.com/article/us-mexico-mining-idUSTRE69D04U20101014.
"México culpa a Estados Unidos de narco." *Hoy*, March 11, 2007. http://hoy.com.do/mexico-culpa-a-estados-unidos-de-narco/.
"Mexico envia el '25o Batallón de Caballería Motorizada' a la Frontera con EE.UU." *Infodefensa*, January 23, 2017. http://www.infodefensa.com/latam/2017/01/23/noticia-mexico-reubica-batallon-caballeria-motorizada-frontera.html.
"Mexico Govt Refuses to Reveal Most Wanted List." *Insight Crime*, August 21, 2015. http://www.InsightCrime.org/news-analysis/mexico-govt-refuses-to-reveal-most-wanted-list.
"México lanzó la operación Veracruz seguro." *Infobae*, October 4, 2011. http://www.infobae.com/2011/10/04/1034993-mexico-lanzo-la-operacion-veracruz-seguro/.
"Mexico: Investigate All Evidence in Killings of 22 by Soldiers." *Human Rights Watch*, August 22, 2014. https://www.hrw.org/news/2014/08/22/mexico-investigate-all-evidence-killings-22-soldiers.
"México: Matan a 15 policías en una emboscada en Jalisco." *BBC*, April 7, 2015. http://www.bbc.com/mundo/ultimas_noticias/2015/04/150407_ult-not_mexico_policias_mueren_emboscada_bd.
"Militares podrían custodiar las represas y centrales nucleares para que haya más gendarmes 'en lugares críticos'." *La Nación*, December 12, 2016. http://www.lanacion.com.ar/1966244-militares-podrian-reemplazar-a-gendarmes-en-la-proteccion-de-represas-y-centrales-nucleares.
"Military Takes to the Streets in Fight against Crime in Dominican Republic." *Miami Herald*, June 16, 2016. http://www.miamiherald.com/news/nation-world/world/americas/article1952530.html.
"Ministerio Público pone en marcha la Operación 'Sultán'." Honduran Government Public Ministry. November 28, 2016. https://www.mp.hn/index.php/author-login/48-noviembre/1019-ministerio-publico-pone-en-marcha-la-operacion-sultan.
"Narcos brasileños usan Uruguay de trampolín." *El Pais*, January 24, 2014. http://www.elpais.com.uy/informacion/narcos-brasilenos-uruguay-trampolin-crimen.html.
"Nation Was Fortunate Security Forces Repelled the Shower Posse." *The Jamaica Gleaner*, April 14, 2015. http://jamaica-gleaner.com/article/news/20150414/nation-was-fortunate-security-forces-repelled-shower-posse-attack-ellington.
"Notices." Interpol. Accessed October 18, 2016. https://www.interpol.int/INTERPOL-expertise/Notices.
"Nuevos ataques con granadas en puestos de la PNC." *La Prensa Gráfica*, March 31, 2015. http://www.laprensagrafica.com/2015/03/31/nuevos-ataques-con-granadas-en-puestos-de-la-pnc-1.

"Objetivo es formalizar a 60,000 pequeños mineros en tres años." *El Peruano*, January 20, 2017. http://www.elperuano.com.pe/noticia-objetivo-es-formalizar-a-60000-pequenos-mineros-tres-anos-50386.aspx.

"Operação Ágata apreende armas, drogas e munição nas fronteiras do País." Government of Brazil. June 25, 2016. http://www.brasil.gov.br/defesa-e-seguranca/2016/06/operacao-agata-apreende-armas-drogas-e-municao-nas-fronteiras-do-pais.

"Operation Martillo." U.S. Southern Command. August 22, 2016. http://www.southcom.mil/newsroom/Pages/Operation-Martillo.aspx.

"Panama Canal Sets New Monthly Tonnage Record." *Panama Canal Authority*, February 6, 2017. https://www.pancanal.com/eng/pr/press-releases/2017/02/06/pr616.html.

"Paraguay." *2016 International Narcotics Control Strategy Report*, U.S. Department of State, 2016. https://www.state.gov/j/inl/rls/nrcrpt/2016/vol1/253299.htm.

"Paraguay." *Trafficking in Persons Report 2016*, U.S. Department of State, https://www.state.gov/documents/organization/258881.pdf.

"Penas de 500 años a pandilleros por atentado." *La Prensa Grafica*, February 2, 2014. http://www.laprensagrafica.com/2014/02/12/penas-de-500-aos-a-pandilleros-por-atentado.

"Perrones." *Insight Crime*, November 7, 2015. http://www.insightcrime.org/el-salvador-organized-crime-news/perrones-profile.

"Peru Comes Out Strong in Fight against Shining Path." *Dialogo*, February 3, 2014. https://dialogo-americas.com/en/articles/peru-comes-out-strong-fight-against-shining-path.

"Peru declares no-fly zone in its most lawless coca-growing region." *Reuters*, February 4, 2015. http://www.reuters.com/article/2015/02/04/us-peru-drugs-idUSKBN0L82MU20150204.

"Peru Plans to Step Up Security, Inclusion In Coca Growing Region." *Peruvian Times*, June 29, 2012. http://www.peruviantimes.com/29/peru-plans-to-step-up-security-inclusion-in-coca-growing-region/16136/.

"PJ denunció utilización del "Tren de Aragua" para sabotear las primarias." *El Nacional*, September 12, 2017. http://www.el-nacional.com/noticias/politica/denuncio-utilizacion-del-tren-aragua-para-sabotear-las-primarias_203200.

"PNC y FAES lanzan fase de recuperación de territorios en La Campanera." *La Prensa Grafica*, April 26, 2016. http://www.laprensagrafica.com/2016/04/26/pnc-y-faes-lanzan-fase-de-recuperacion-de-territorios-en-la-campanera.

"Police Use Shipping Containers to Separate Brazil Prison Gangs." *Yahoo*, January 21, 2017. https://www.yahoo.com/news/police-shipping-containers-separate-brazil-prison-gangs-214108311.html.

"Posture Statement of Admiral Kurt W. Tidd, Commander, United States Southern Command, before the 114th Congress Senate Armed Services Committee." U.S. Southern Command. March 10, 2016. http://www.southcom.mil/newsroom/Documents/SOUTHCOM_POSTURE_STATEMENT_FINAL_2016.pdf.

"Potential Terrorist Threats: Border Security Challenges in Latin America and the Caribbean." Hearing before the Subcommittee on the Western Hemisphere of the Committee on Foreign Affairs House of Representatives One Hundred Fourteenth Congress, Second Session

"Presenta amparo de garantías para anular parte de la investigación." *La Estrella*, July 1, 2016. http://laestrella.com.pa/panama/politica/presenta-amparo-garantias-para-anular-parte-investigacion/23948522

"Presentan a los hermanos Valle, capturados en Honduras." *La Prensa*, October 5, 2014, http://www.laprensa.hn/sucesos/754732-410/presentan-a-los-hermanos-valle-capturados-en-honduras.

"Presidente de Colombia resalta logros en seguridad del gobierno hondureño." Secretary of State of the Honduran Presidency. April 6, 2016. http://www.sep.gob.hn/sitio/historial-de-noticias/139-noticias-destacadas/1810-2016-04-07-20-59-16.

"Presidential Executive Order on Enforcing Federal Law with Respect to Transnational Criminal Organizations and Preventing International Trafficking." The White House, February 9, 2017. https://www.whitehouse.gov/the-press-office/2017/02/09/presidential-executive-order-enforcing-federal-law-respect-transnational.

"Presidential Executive Order on Enforcing Federal Law with Respect to Transnational Criminal Organizations and Preventing International Trafficking." The White House. February 9, 2017. https://www.whitehouse.gov/presidential-actions/presidential-executive-order-enforcing-federal-law-respect-transnational-criminal-organizations-preventing-international-trafficking/.

"Primer bombardeo directo a banda criminal: mueren 12 del 'clan Úsuga'." *El Tiempo*, November 3, 2015. http://www.eltiempo.com/politica/justicia/clan-usuga-bombardeo-en-choco/16419814.

"Principal narcotraficante do Panamá é capturado, diz polícia." *Globo*, September 6, 2016. http://g1.globo.com/mundo/noticia/2016/09/principal-narcotraficante-do-panama-e-capturado-diz-policia.html

"Pure Third Command." *Insight Crime*. Accessed August 30, 2016. http://www.InsightCrime.org/brazil-organized-crime-news/pure-third-command.

"Rebel Leader Apologizes for Colombian Church Kidnapping." *CNN*, June 7, 1999. http://www.cnn.com/WORLD/americas/9906/07/colombia/.

"Red Command." *Insight Crime*. Accessed November 30, 2016. http://www.InsightCrime.org/brazil-organized-crime-news/red-command-profile.

"Renegade Colombia FARC Rebels in Deadly Clash." *The Guardian*, January 18, 2017. https://guardian.ng/news/renegade-colombia-farc-rebels-in-deadly-clash/

"Reos más peligrosos de Honduras a megacárcel." *El Heraldo*, October 20, 2014. http://www.elheraldo.hn/alfrente/759995-331/reos-m%C3%A1s-peligrosos-de-honduras-a-megac%C3%A1rcel.

"Report of the Interamerican Commission on Human Rights on the Situation of Persons Deprived of Liberty in Honduras." *Organization of American States*, March 18, 2013. http://www.oas.org/en/iachr/pdl/docs/pdf/HONDURAS-PPL-2013ENG.pdf.

"Report: 'El Chapo' Guzman's Sons Wounded in Cartel Attack." *ABC News*, February 9, 2017. http://abcnews.go.com/International/wireStory/report-el-chapo-guzmans-sons-wounded-cartel-attack-45363829.

"Roundup Weedkiller 'Probably' Causes Cancer, Says WHO Study." *The Guardian*, March 21, 2015. https://www.theguardian.com/environment/2015/mar/21/roundup-cancer-who-glyphosate-.

"Se confirma muerte de 10 personas en ataque terrorista en Vraem." *El Comercio*, April 11, 2016. http://elcomercio.pe/sociedad/vraem/vraem-confirman-muerte-diez-personas-ataque-terrorista-noticia-1893147.

"Se reactivó banda de narcotraficantes Los *Perrones*: FGR." *La Prensa Grafica*, July 31, 2014. http://www.laprensagrafica.com/2014/07/31/se-reactivo-banda-de-narcotraficantes-los-perrones-fgr.

"Si EU deja de dar armas; México dejará de dar droga: EPN." *Tiempo*, August 31, 2016. http://tiempo.com.mx/noticia/50923-que_eu_deje_de_dar_armas_mexic/1.

"Single-Handed." *The Economist*, September 12, 2015. http://www.economist.com/news/books-and-arts/21664050-how-ant-nio-francisco-bonfim-lopes-better-known-nem-rocinha-took-over-brazilian.

"Sisfron Technology Helps the Brazilian Armed Forces Secure Border Regions." *Dialogo*, November 21, 2014. https://dialogo-americas.com/en/articles/sisfron-technology-helps-brazilian-armed-forces-secure-border-regions.

"Smuggling Soars as Venezuela's Economy Sinks." *Reuters*, January 20, 2016. http://www.reuters.com/article/us-venezuela-smuggling-insight-idUSKCN0UY1IT.

"Strategy to Combat Transnational Organized Crime: Definition." The White House. Accessed September 6, 2016. https://www.whitehouse.gov/administration/eop/nsc/transnational-crime/definition.

"Subsidio para la Seguridad en los Municipios (SUBSEMUN)." Secretaria de Gobernacion. Accessed October 19, 2016. http://secretariadoejecutivosnsp.gob.mx/en/SecretariadoEjecutivo/Subsemun.

"Table of Results: Corruption Perceptions Index 2015." *Transparency International*. Accessed October 19, 2016. http://www.transparency.org/cpi2015.

"Terror on Flight 9463." *The Guardian*, April 27, 1999. https://www.theguardian.com/theguardian/1999/apr/28/features11.g23.

"The Edgemont Group of Financial Intelligence Units." Edgemont Group. Accessed October 18, 2016. http://www.egmontgroup.org/membership.

"Traficantes cambian la ruta de la marihuana." *El Pais*, January 17, 2017. http://www.elpais.com.uy/informacion/traficantes-cambian-ruta-marihuana-narcotrafico.html.

"Tras muerte de 'Alipio' y 'Gabriel': ¿Qué otros cabecillas tiene Sendero?" *El Comercio*, August 12, 2013. http://elcomercio.pe/peru/lima/muerte-alipio-ygabriel-que-otros-cabecillas-tiene-sendero-noticia-1616591.

"Treasury Sanctions Five Businesses Supporting Cartel De Jalisco Nueva Generacion." U.S. Department of the Treasury. September 17, 2015. https://www.treasury.gov/press-center/press-releases/Pages/jl0168.aspx.

"Treasury Targets 'Los Cachiros Drug Trafficking Organization in Honduras." U.S. Department of the Treasury, September 19, 2013. https://www.treasury.gov/press-center/press-releases/Pages/jl2168.aspx.

"Trial of Honduran Drug Kingpin Matta Opens." *Los Angeles Times*, October 6, 1990. http://articles.latimes.com/1990-10-06/local/me-1378_1_drug-kingpin.

"Trump Alarms Venezuela with Talk of a 'Military Option.'" *The New York Times*, August 12, 2017. https://www.nytimes.com/2017/08/12/world/americas/trump-venezuela-military.html.

"UPDATE: Prison Gang Clashes Kill 18 in N. Brazil." *Xinhua*, October 17, 2016. http://news.xinhuanet.com/english/2016-10/18/c_135761526.htm.

"Uribe Accuses Venezuela of Backing FARC 'Genocide.'" *Financial Times*, March 4, 2008. https://www.ft.com/content/6576fd10-ea2a-11dc-b3c9-0000779fd2ac.

"Urresti presentó 7.6 toneladas de cocaína incautadas en Trujillo." *Peru21*, September 1, 2014. http://peru21.pe/actualidad/droga-cocaina-dirandro-daniel-urresti-policia-nacional-trujillo-2197279.

"Uruguay." *Trafficking in Persons Report 2016*. U.S. Department of State, 2016. https://www.state.gov/documents/organization/258882.pdf.

"US Military Personnel Are Joining the Largest International Military Operation ever Held in the Amazon." *Business Insider*, November 9, 2017. http://www.businessinsider.com/r-us-military-joins-brazil-army-exercises-in- amazon-2017-11.

"US requests Colombia Urabeños 'Gang Leader' Extradition." *BBC*, December 29, 2012. http://www.bbc.com/news/world-latin-america-20862023.

"USAID-SICA Regional Gang Prevention Activity Agreement." U.S. Department of State, July 18, 2007. https://www.state.gov/p/wha/rls/89884.htm.

"Valles." *Insight Crime*. Accessed August 30, 2016. http://www.InsightCrime.org/honduras-organized-crime-news/lvalles.

"Venezuela." *2016 International Narcotics Control Strategy Report*, U.S. Department of State, 2016. https://www.state.gov/j/inl/rls/nrcrpt/2016/vol1/253323.htm.

"Vice President Mike Pence to Travel to Central and South America." The White House. June 15, 2017, https://www.whitehouse.gov/briefings-statements/vice-president-mike-pence-travel-central-south-america/.

"Victims Caught in Honduras Drugs Crossfire." *BBC*, July 16, 2012. http://news.bbc.co.uk/2/hi/programmes/hardtalk/9737563.stm.

"VRAEM: Ataque terrorista a base temporal deja un militar herido." *Peru.com*. November 18, 2014. http://peru.com/actualidad/nacionales/vraem-ataque-terrorista-base-temporal-deja-militar-herido-noticia-301927.

"Vraem: PNP reasumirá control de lucha contra el narcotráfico." *El Comercio*, December 12, 2015. http://elcomercio.pe/sociedad/vraem/vraem-pnp-reasumira-control-lucha-contra-narcotrafico-noticia-1863086.
2015 National Drug Threat Assessment Summary. U.S. Drug Enforcement Administration, 2015. https://www.dea.gov/docs/2015%20NDTA%20Report.pdf.
Ahmed, Azam, and Eric Schmittmay. "Mexican Military Runs up Body Count in Drug War." *The New York Times*, May 26, 2016. https://www.nytimes.com/2016/05/27/world/americas/mexican-militarys-high-kill-rate-raises-human-rights-fears.html?_r=0.
Ahmed, Azam. "Mexico's President Cancels Meeting with Trump over Wall." *The New York Times*, January 26, 2017. https://www.nytimes.com/2017/01/26/world/mexicos-president-cancels-meeting-with-trump-over-wall.html.
Alava, Holger. "Honduran and Guatemalan Armed Forces Cooperate to Improve Border Security through the Maya-Chortí Task Force." *Dialogo*, January 27, 2015. https://dialogo-americas.com/en/articles/honduran-and-guatemalan-armed-forces-cooperate-improve-border-security-through-maya-chorti-task-force.
Allison, Michael. "Justice Deferred: Rule of Law in Central America." *World Politics Review*, November 11, 2014. http://www.worldpoliticsreview.com/articles/14415/justice-deferred-rule-of-law-in-central-america.
Alvarado, Irvin. "Fiscalía: 'sabemos quién es el responsable de este atentado'" *La Prensa Grafica*, September 11, 2015. http://www.laprensagrafica.com/2015/09/11/fiscalia-sabemos-quien-es-el-responsable-de-este-atentado?rel=HomePrincipales#sthash.u01uAIIF.dpuf.
Andreas, Peter. "The Transformation of Migrant Smuggling across the US-Mexican Border." In *Global Human Smuggling: Comparative Perspectives*, edited by David Kyle and Rey Koslowski, pp. 107–125. Baltimore, MD: Johns Hopkins University Press, 2001.
Andreas, Peter. *Smuggler Nation: How Illicit Trade Made America*. Cambridge: Oxford University Press, 2013.
Andres Diaz, Fabio. "Will Colombia's Most 'Stubborn' Rebel Group Agree to Peace?" *Huffington Post*, February 7, 2017. http://www.huffingtonpost.com/the-conversation-global/will-colombias-most-stubb_b_14634604.html.
Arana, Ana. "How the Street Gangs Took Central America." *Foreign Affairs*, May/June 2005. https://www.foreignaffairs.com/articles/central-america-caribbean/2005-05-01/how-street-gangs-took-central-america.
Arauz, Sergio, Óscar Martínez, and Efren Lemus. "El Cartel de Texis." *El Faro*, May 16, 2011. http://elfaro.net/es/201105/noticias/4079/?st-full_text=0.
Arcia, José. "'Maras no operan en territorio panameño.'" *La Estrella de Panama*, July 15, 2016. http://laestrella.com.pa/panama/politica/maras-operan-territorio-panameno/23951030.
Avelar, Bryan. "El Salvador Vice President Engaged in 'Money Laundering Methods': Prosecutors." *InsightCrime*, April 18, 2017. https://www.insightcrime.org/news/analysis/el-salvador-vice-president-engaged-money-laundering-methods-prosecutors/.
Avelar, Bryan. "Fiscalía: Óscar Ortiz participó en "métodos de lavado." *Factum*, April 17, 2017. revistafactum.com/fiscalia-oscar-ortiz-participo-en-metodos-de-lavado-en-caso-chepe-diablo/.
Ávila, Laura. "AUC." *Insight Crime*. Last updated November 27, 2015. https://www.insightcrime.org/colombia-organized-crime-news/auc-profile/.
Ávila, Laura. "Brazil Gang in Uruguay Shows Country's Growing Role in Drug Trade." *Insight Crime*, January 27, 2017. http://www.InsightCrime.org/news-briefs/brazil-gang-uruguay-shows-growing-role-drug-trade.
Bagley, Bruce. *Drug Trafficking and Organized Crime in the Americas: Major Trends in the Twenty-First Century*. Washington, D.C.: The Woodrow Wilson Center for International Scholars, August 2012. https://www.wilsoncenter.org/sites/default/files/BB%20Final.pdf.

Bailey, John, and Jorge Chabat, eds., *Transnational Crime and Public Security: Challenges to Mexico and the United States*, Boulder, CO: Lynne Rienner, 2002.

Bailey, John, and Lucía Dammert, eds. *Public Security and Police Reform in the Americas*, Pittsburgh, PA: University of Pittsburgh Press, 2005.

Bailey, John. *The Politics of Crime in Mexico: Democratic Governance in a Security Trap*, Boulder, CO: Lynne Rienner Publishers, 2014.

Bargeant, Steve. "Ecuador Bulk Cash Smuggling Reflects New Laundering Trend." *Insight Crime*, April 11, 2013. http://www.insightcrime.org/news-analysis/rise-in-ecuador-cash-smuggling-reflects-wider-crime-trends.

Bargent, James. "Argentina Drug Law Reforms Target Cocaine Paste." *Insight Crime*, January 9, 2017. http://www.insightcrime.com/news-briefs/argentina-drug-law-reforms-target-cocaine-paste.

Bargent, James. "Mayor's Murder Could Impact Mexico Security Reforms." *Insight Crime*, January 4, 2016. http://www.InsightCrime.org/news-briefs/mayor-murder-could-impact-mexico-security-reforms.

Bargent, James. "US Halts Honduras Cooperation over Narco-Plane Shoot Down Law." *Insight Crime*, April 1, 2014. http://www.InsightCrime.org/news-briefs/us-halts-honduras-cooperation-over-narco-plane-shoot-down-law.

Batista de Oliveira, Marlinelza. "Brazil and Paraguay Expand Military Cooperation." *Dialogo*, May 3, 2016. https://dialogo-americas.com/en/articles/brazil-and-paraguay-expand-military-cooperation.

Becerril, Andres. "Autodefensas dan origen a otro cártel; nace en Michoacán La Tercera Hermandad o H3." *Excelsior*, May 6, 2016. http://www.excelsior.com.mx/nacional/2014/05/06/957619.

Becerril, Daniel. "Mexico Accuses Prison Officials of Homicide after Brutal Riot." *Reuters*, February 14, 2016. http://uk.reuters.com/article/uk-mexico-prison-idUKKCN0VN02M.

Belton, Lloyd. "Report Spotlights Drug Traffic at Santos Port, Brazil's Drug Policies." *Insight Crime*, July 20, 2016. http://www.InsightCrime.org/news-analysis/report-spotlights-drug-trafficking-at-santos-port-brazil-drug-policies.

Bertrand, Natasha. "This Mexican Town Is the Sex-Trafficking Capital of the World." *Business Insider*, February 10, 2015. http://www.businessinsider.com/this-mexican-town-is-the-sex-trafficking-capital-of-the-world-2015-2.

Bonello, Deborah. "Criminal Activity Spreading Fire in Guatemala's Maya Reserve." *Insight Crime*, July 1, 2016. http://www.InsightCrime.com/news-briefs/criminals-spread-fire-in-guatemala-maya-reserve.

Boraz, Steven C., and Thomas C. Bruneau. "Are the Maras Overwhelming Central America." *Military Review*, November–December 2006. http://usacac.army.mil/CAC2/MilitaryReview/Archives/English/MilitaryReview_20061231_art007.pdf.

Bristow, Matthew. "Colombia Hunts 300 FARC Dissidents Doing 'Pure Organized Crime.'" *Bloomberg*, January 26, 2017. https://www.bloomberg.com/politics/articles/2017-01-26/colombia-hunts-300-farc-dissidents-doing-pure-organized-crime.

Brown, Rachel. "The Boom in Chinese Smuggled Across the U.S. Border." *Newsweek*, July 24, 2016,

Caballero, Sergio. "En narcomantas, Los Zetas se atribuyen ataque al Blue Parrot." *El Proceso*, January 17, 2017. http://www.proceso.com.mx/470454/en-narcomantas-los-zetas-se-atribuyen-ataque-al-blue-parrot.

Calderón, Beatriz. "Consejo de Seguridad presenta Plan "El Salvador Seguro." *La Prensa Grafica*, January 15, 2015. http://www.laprensagrafica.com/2015/01/15/consejo-de-seguridad-presenta-plan-el-salvador-seguro#sthash.ti6VfKkE.dpuf

Calderon, Veronica. "Una ofensiva del narco en México derriba un helicóptero militar." *El Pais*, May 2, 2016. http://internacional.elpais.com/internacional/2015/05/01/actualidad/1430505154_355398.html.

Campos Garza, Luciano. "Hay 280 organizaciones criminales en México." *Proceso*, July 24, 2017. http://www.proceso.com.mx/496191/280-organizaciones-criminales-en-mexico-revela-alcalde-san-pedro-nl.

Casado, Teresa. "Autoridades indagan sobreprecio Super Tucano y montos seguros La Procuraduría investiga a varios legisladores que supuestamente habrían recibido dinero." *El Dia*, August 19, 2016. http://eldia.com.do/autoridades-indagan-sobre-precio-super-tucano-y-montos-seguros/.

Casey, Nicholas. "Colombia and FARC Sign New Peace Deal, This Time Skipping Voters." *New York Times*, November 24, 2016. https://www.nytimes.com/2016/11/24/world/americas/colombia-juan-manuel-santos-peace-deal-farc.html.

Castillo, E. Eduardo, and Mark Stevenson. "Gendarmería, nuevo cuerpo policial de México." *Huffington Post*, August 22, 2014. http://www.huffingtonpost.com/huff-wires/20140822/amn-gen-mexico-gendarmeria/.

Castillo, E. Eduardo. "Reportan hasta 80 carteles del narco en México." *Yahoo*, December 18, 2012. https://www.yahoo.com/news/reportan-hasta-80-carteles-del-narco-en-m-175244606.html.

Castillo, Mariano, and Elvin Sandoval. "More Than 300 Killed in Honduras Prison Fire." *CNN*, February 16, 2012. http://www.cnn.com/2012/02/15/world/americas/honduras-fire-deaths/index.html.

Chabat, Jorge. *La Iniciativa Mérida y la relación México-Estados Unidos: en busca de la confianza Perdida*. Mexico City: Centro de Investigación y Docencia Ecónomicas (CIDE), División de Estudios Internacionales, 2010.

Chabat, Jorge. "La seguridad en la política exterior de Calderón." In *Foro Internacional* (2013): 729–749.

Chávez, Suchit, and Nelson Rauda. "Traslados de pandilleros por atentados contra policías." *La Prensa Grafica*, January 20, 2015. http://www.laprensagrafica.com/2015/01/20/traslados-de-pandilleros-por-atentados-contra-poli-cias#sthash.VAYic3DN.dpuf.

Choque, Marilyn. "La FELCN encontró 1.000 pistas clandestinas en los últimos tres años." *La Razon*, June 5, 2016. http://www.la-razon.com/nacional/seguri-dad_nacional/FELCN-encontro-pistas-clandestinas-ultimos_0_2503549647.html.

Cisneros, Bernardo. "Pugna entre cartels de Jalisco y Sinaloa deja 5 muertos en Tijuana." *Milenio*, December 13, 2016. http://www.milenio.com/policia/muerte_tijuana-baja_california-cartel_sinaloa-jalisco_nueva_generacion-milenio_0_865113674.html.

Clavel, Tristan. "As Honduras Tackles Police Corruption, Security Indicators Improve." *InsightCrime*. https://www.insightcrime.org/news/brief/as-honduras-tack-les-police-corruption-security-indicators-improve/.

Clavel, Tristan. "Barrio 18 Wants to Join Possible Talks with El Salvador Govt: Report." *Insight Crime*, January 17, 2017. http://www.InsightCrime.org/news-briefs/barrio-18-wants-to-join-possible-talks-with-el-salvador-govt-report.

Clavel, Tristan. "Bolivian Children Sold for $300 on Argentina Border." *Insight Crime*, September 7, 2016. http://www.InsightCrime.org/news-briefs/bolivian-children-sold-for-300-on-argentina-border.

Clavel, Tristan. "Honduras Takes First Step toward Prison Overhaul with New Facility." *Insight Crime*, September 20, 2016. http://www.InsightCrime.org/news-briefs/honduras-first-step-prison-overhaul-new-facility.

Condori, Ivan. "Miembros del Comando Vermelho intentaron sacar droga de Bolivia." *La Razon*, September 4, 2015. http://www.la-razon.com/nacional/seguri-dad_nacional/Gobierno-miembros-Comando_Vermelho-intentaron-sacar-droga-Bolivia_0_2338566180.html.

Contreras Corzantes, Geovanni. "Soldados van a vigilar dos mil kilómetros." *Prensa Libre*, January 23, 2017. http://www.prensalibre.com/guatemala/politica/soldados-van-a-vigilar-dos-mil-kilometros.

Cooper, Helene, and Marc Lacey. "In a Coup in Honduras, Ghosts of Past U.S. Policies." *New York Times*, June 29, 2009. http://www.nytimes.com/2009/06/30/world/americas/30honduras.html?_r=0.

Cope, John A., and Andrew Parks. "Frontier Security: The Case of Brazil." Institute for National Strategic Studies. Washington, D.C.: National Defense University, August 2016.

Correa-Cabrera, Guadalupe. *Los Zetas Inc.: Criminal Corporations, Energy, and Civil War in Mexico.* Austin: University of Texas Press, 2017.

Crooks, Nathan. "Venezuela Shakes up Cabinet, Appoints Drug-Indicted General." *Bloomberg,* August 2, 2016. https://www.bloomberg.com/news/articles/2016-08-03/venezuela-s-maduro-replaces-perez-abad-as-his-economy-czar.

Cruz, José Miguel. "Central American Maras: From Youth Street Gangs to Transnational Protection Rackets." *Global Crime* 11, no. 4 (2010): 379–398.

Daniel Uria, "Venezuelan First Lady's 'Narco Nephews' Jailed for Drug Trafficking." *UPI,* Dec. 14, 2017. https://www.upi.com/Top_News/World-News/2017/12/14/Venezuelan-first-ladys-Narco-Nephews-jailed-for-drug-trafficking/4611513304357/.

Daugherty, Aaron. "Murder Draws Attention to Paraguay-Uruguay Marijuana Trade." *Insight Crime,* February 11, 2016. http://www.insightcrime.org/news-briefs/murder-draws-attention-to-paraguay-uruguay-marijuana-trade.

Daughterty, Aaron. "Has Colombia's Next Narco Boss Emerged?" *Insight Crime,* November 2, 2015. http://www.InsightCrime.org/news-briefs/colombia-next-narco-boss-puntilla-pachon.

De Cordoba, Jose, and Juan Forero. "Venezuelan Officials Suspected of Turning Country into Global Cocaine Hub." *Wall Street Journal,* May 18, 2015. https://www.wsj.com/articles/venezuelan-officials-suspected-of-turning-country-into-global-cocaine-hub-1431977784.

Desmond Arias, Enrique. *Drugs and Democracy in Rio de Janeiro: Trafficking, Social Networks, and Public Security.* Chapel Hill: University of North Carolina Press, 2009.

Desmond Arias, Enrique. "Faith in Our Neighbors: Networks and Social Order in Three Brazilian Favelas." *Latin American Politics and Society* 46, no. 1 (2004): 1–38.

Desmond Arias, Enrique. "Trouble en Route: Drug Trafficking and Clientelism in Rio de Janeiro shantytowns." *Qualitative Sociology* 29, no. 4 (2006): 427–445.

Diaz, Elvin. "Comisión Depuradora: 28 por ciento de los depurados son oficiales de alto rango." *El Digital,* January 23, 2017. http://tiempo.hn/comision-depuradora-28-ciento-los-depurados-oficiales-alto-rango/.

Dittmar, Victoria. "Honduras Extends Police Reform Commission until 2018." *Insight Crime,* January 24, 2017. http://www.InsightCrime.org/news-briefs/honduras-extends-police-reform-commission-until-2018.

Dominguez, Alejandro. "Estrategias en Michoacán comenzaron en 2006 y siguen." *Milenio,* January 13, 2014. http://www.milenio.com/politica/seguridad-estrategias_Michoacan-Calderon_Michoacan-Pena_Nieto_Michoacan-violencia_0_226177863.html.

Drash, Wayne. "Driven to Death by Phone Scammers." *CNN,* October 7, 2015. http://www.cnn.com/2015/10/07/us/jamaica-lottery-scam-suicide/index.html.

Dudley, Steven. "Guatemala Authorities Capture Ex-Military Turned Drug Trafficker." *Insight Crime,* May 2, 2016. http://www.InsightCrime.com/news-briefs/guatemala-authorities-capture-ex-military-turned-drug-trafficker.

Echevarria II, Antulio J. "Clausewitz's Center of Gravity: Changing Our Warfighting Doctrine—Again!" Carlisle Barracks, PA: U.S. Army War College, 2002. http://www.strategicstudiesinstitute.army.mil/pdffiles/PUB363.pdf.

Ellis R. Evan, and Roman D. Ortiz. "*Un acuerdo entre interrogantes.*" *Foreign Affairs Latinoamérica,* vol. 17, no. 1 (2017): pp. 93–100. www.fal.itam.mx.

Ellis, R. Evan. "The Post-Conflict and the Transformation of Colombia's Armed Forces." U.S. Army War College Strategic Studies Institute, August 17, 2016. http://strategicstudiesinstitute.army.mil/index.cfm/articles/Colombias-Armed-Forces/2016/08/17.

Ellis, R. Evan. "Anticipating the Collapse of Venezuela." *Latin America Herald Tribune,* May 8, 2016. http://laht.com/article.asp?CategoryId=13303&ArticleId=2411674.

Ellis, R. Evan. "Brazil: Between Cooperation and Deterrence." *Global Americans,* December 18, 2017. https://theglobalamericans.org/2017/12/brazil-cooperation-deterrence/.

Ellis, R. Evan. "Chinese Organized Crime in Latin America." *Prism*, 4, no. 1 (2012): 67–77.

Ellis, R. Evan. "Collaboration and Learning in Latin America's Fight against Transnational Organized Crime and Terrorism." *Latin America Goes Global*, September 28, 2016. http://latinamericagoesglobal.org/2016/09/collaboration-learning-latin-americas-fight-transnational-organized-crime-terrorism/.

Ellis, R. Evan. "Don't Cry for Mauricio Macri's Argentina." *Latin America Goes Global*, January 19, 2017. http://latinamericagoesglobal.org/2017/01/dont-cry-mauricio-macris-argentina/.

Ellis, R. Evan. "Effective Cooperation with Mexico Contributes More to US Security Than Any Wall." *Financial Times*, January 30, 2017. https://www.ft.com/content/6f4b90fc-98aa-3fac-b858-2f24c58a56d8.

Ellis, R. Evan. "El nexo evolutivo entre el crimen transnacional y el terorismo en Peru, y su importancia estratgica para EE.UU y la region." *Academia de Guerra Naval*, March 7, 2016. http://www.acanav.mil.cl/agn/documentos/temas_seleccionado/2016/Tema_Seleccionado_01.pdf.

Ellis, R. Evan. "Guatemala: The Military in a Supporting Role in the Fight against Transnational Organized Crime." *Ensayos Militares*, vol. 3, no. 1 (2017): pp. 39–60. http://www.ceeag.cl/wp-content/uploads/2017/09/REM2017.pdf.

Ellis, R. Evan. "New Developments in Organized Crime in Peru." *The Cipher Brief*, May 20, 2016. https://www.thecipherbrief.com/column/strategic-view/new-developments-organized-crime-peru-1091.

Ellis, R. Evan. "Suriname and the Chinese: Timber, Migration, and the Less-Told Stories of Globalization." *SAIS Review*, 32, no. 2 (Summer-Fall 2012): 85–97.

Ellis, R. Evan. "The Evolution of Transnational Organized Crime in Peru." *Latin America Goes Global*, May 4, 2017. http://latinamericagoesglobal.org/2017/05/evolution-transnational-organized-crime-peru/.

Ellis, R. Evan. "The Evolving Transnational Crime-Terrorism Nexus in Peru and its Strategic Relevance for the U.S. and the Region." *PRISM*, 5, no. 4 (2016): 189–205. http://cco.ndu.edu/Portals/96/Documents/prism/prism_5-4/Evolving%20Transnational%20Crime-Terrorism.pdf,

Ellis, R. Evan. "The Gang Challenge in El Salvador: Worse than You Thought." *War on the Rocks*, December 16, 2015. http://warontherocks.com/2015/12/the-gang-challenge-in-el-salvador-worse-than-you-can-imagine/.

Ellis, R. Evan. "The New Offensive Against Gangs in El Salvador." *Latin America Goes Global*, May 2, 2016. http://latinamericagoesglobal.org/2016/05/new-offensive-gangs-el-salvador/.

Ellis, R. Evan. "The New Russian Engagement with Latin America: Strategic Engagement, Commerce, and Dreams of the Past." Carlisle Barracks, PA: U.S. Army War College Strategic Studies Institute, June 2015. http://www.strategicstudiesinstitute.army.mil/pubs/display.cfm?pubID=1275.

Ellis, R. Evan. "The Strategic Importance of the Western Hemisphere – Defining U.S. Interests in the Region." Testimony to the Subcommittee on the Western Hemisphere, U.S. House of Representatives Foreign Affairs Committee, February 3, 2015. http://docs.house.gov/meetings/FA/FA07/20150203/102885/HHRG-114-FA07-Wstate-EllisE-20150203.pdf.

Ellis, R. Evan. "The Struggle against Organized Crime in Guatemala." *Latin America Goes Global*, November 10, 2016. http://latinamericagoesglobal.org/2016/11/struggle-organized-crime-guatemala/.

Ellis, R. Evan. "What Panama's Recognition of China Means for America's Backyard." *World Politics Review*, October 5, 2017. https://www.worldpoliticsreview.com/trend-lines/23316/what-panama-s-recognition-of-china-means-for-america-s-backyard.

Ellis, R. Evan. "Colombia: Preparing for the Post-Agreement,' Not the 'Post-Conflict.'" *Latin America Goes Global*, March 15, 2016. http://latinamericagoesglobal.org/2016/03/2755/.

Ellis, R. Evan. "Honduras: A Pariah State, or Innovative Solutions to Organized Crime Deserving U.S. Support?" Carlisle Barracks, PA: U.S. Army War College Strategic Studies Institute, June 2016. http://www.strategicstudiesinstitute.army.mil/pubs/display.cfm?pubID=1315.

Ellis, R. Evan. "Strategic Insights—Mexico: New Directions, Continuity, and Obstacles in the Fight against Transnational Organized Crime." Carlisle Barracks, PA: U.S. Army War College Strategic Studies Institute, March 31, 2016. http://strategicstudiesinstitute.army.mil/index.cfm/articles/Mexico-New-Directions-Continuity-Obstacles/2016/03/31.

Farah, Douglas. "Transnational Organized Crime, Terrorism, and Criminalized States in Latin America: An Emerging Tier-One National Security Priority." Carlisle Barracks, PA: U.S. Army War College Strategic Studies Institute, August 2012. http://strategicstudiesinstitute.army.mil/pubs/display.cfm?pubID=1117.

Fernanda Boidi, María, Rosario Queirolo, and José Miguel Cruz. "Cannabis Consumption Patterns among Frequent Consumers in Uruguay." *International Journal of Drug Policy* 34 (2016): 34–40.

Fernando Alonso, Luis. "30 Buses Burned in Honduras This Year as Result of Extortion." *Insight Crime*, August 25, 2016. http://www.insightcrime.org/news-briefs/30-buses-burned-in-honduras-this-year-as-result-of-extortion.

Fernando Alonso, Luis. "Guatemala Struggles to Prosecute Extortion in Capital." *Insight Crime*, June 28, 2016. http://www.InsightCrime.com/news-briefs/guatemala-struggles-to-prosecute-extortion-in-capital.

Ferri, Pablo, and Jose Luis Pardo. "Paraguay's Marijuana Trade: The Bitter Green Smell of the Red Land." *Insight Crime*, August 4, 2014. http://www.insightcrime.org/news-analysis/inside-paraguay-marijuana-trade-to-brazil.

Fiegel, Brenda. "Venezuela, Military Generals, and the Cartel of the Suns." *Small Wars Journal*, June 27, 2015. http://smallwarsjournal.com/jrnl/art/venezuela-military-generals-and-the-cartel-of-the-suns.

Fiezer, Ezra. "Drug Use Soars in Dominican Republic." *The Star*, August 24, 2011. https://www.thestar.com/news/world/2011/08/24/drug_use_soars_in_dominican_republic.html.

Figueredo Ruiz, Cándido. "Identifican a supuesto alto 'jefe' del PCC en Paraguay." *ABC Color*, August 3, 2014. http://www.abc.com.py/edicion-impresa/judiciales-y-policiales/identifican-a-supuesto-alto-jefe-del-pcc-en-paraguay-1272485.html.

Final Report. Peru Truth and Reconciliation Commission. August 28, 2003. http://www.cverdad.org.pe/ingles/ifinal/index.php.

Finnegan, William. "Silver or Lead: The Drug Cartel La Familia Gives Local Officials a Choice: Take a Bribe or a Bullet." *The New Yorker*, May 31, 2010. http://www.newyorker.com/magazine/2010/05/31/silver-or-lead.

Fowks, Jacqueline. "Tres policías peruanos mueren en una emboscada de narcoterroristas." *El Pais*, March 18, 2017. https://elpais.com/internacional/2017/03/18/america/1489871093_445014.html.

Fuentes, David. "Inician juicios orales para delitos no graves." *El Universal*, January 16, 2015. http://archivo.eluniversal.com.mx/ciudad-metropoli/2015/impreso/inician-juicios-orales-para-delitos-no-graves-129295.html.

Gagne, David. "2000 Illegal Weapons Cross US-Mexico Border Per Day: Report." *Insight Crime*, January 22, 2015. http://www.InsightCrime.org/news-analysis/2000-illegal-weapons-cross-us-mexico-border-every-day.

Gagne, David. "24-Hour Turnaround to Rebuild Peru's Narco-Airstrips." *Insight Crime*. October 14, 2014. http://www.InsightCrime.org/news-briefs/6112-peru-vraem-narco-airstrips-rebuilt.

Gagne, David. "CentAm Authorities Break up Massive Migrant Smuggling Ring." *Insight Crime*, June 30, 2016. http://www.InsightCrime.com/news-analysis/centam-authorities-break-up-massive-migrant-smuggling-ring.

Gagne, David. "Lucrative Cocaine Trade Fuels Gang Presence in Brazil's Amazon." *Insight Crime*, January 13, 2017. http://www.insightcrime.com/news-briefs/lucrative-cocaine-trade-fuels-gang-presence-brazil-amazon.
Gagne, David. "Who Are the Urabeños Leaders Indicted by the U.S.?." *Insight Crime*, June 24, 2015. http://www.insightcrime.org/news-analysis/us-indicts-17-leaders-of-colombia-urabenos.
Gagne, David. "Despite Colombia Accord, a New Rebel Threat Emerges." *Insight Crime*, September 14, 2016. http://www.InsightCrime.org/news-analysis/despite-colombia-accord-new-rebel-threat-emerges.
Gagne, David. "Ex-Mayor's Arrest Kicks Off Guatemala Anti-Corruption Campaign." *Insight Crime*, January 22, 2016. http://www.InsightCrime.com/news-briefs/ex-mayor-arrest-kicks-off-guatemala-anti-corruption-campaign.
Galen Carpenter, Ted. *Bad Neighbor Policy: Washington's Futile War on Drugs in Latin America*. New York: St. Martin's Press, 2014.
Gallegos, Zorayda. "Un policía y tres atacantes mueren en un tiroteo contra la Fiscalía de Cancún." *El País*, January 18, 2017. http://internacional.elpais.com/internacional/2017/01/18/mexico/1484696156_746631.html.
Garcia, Eduardo. "Abatido alias Gavilán,segundo al mando del Clan del Golfo." *El Heraldo*, August 31, 2017. https://www.elheraldo.co/colombia/abatido-alias-gavilan-segundo-al-mando-del-clan-del-golfo-398185.
Garcia, Jacobo G. "'El 'Chapo Guzmán' podría encontrarse en Honduras'." *El Mundo*, November 20, 2013. http://www.elmundo.es/internacional/2013/11/19/528bbd5261fd3d914e8b457a.html.
Gast, Phil, Catherine E. Shoichet, and Evan Perez. "Extradited 'El Chapo' Guzman Arrives in US; Hearing Set for Friday." *CNN*, January 20, 2017. http://www.cnn.com/2017/01/19/us/el-chapo-guzman-turned-over-to-us/index.html.
Gayle, Barbara. "Stone Crusher Gang Leader Bailed." *Jamaica Gleaner*, March 9, 2012. http://jamaica-gleaner.com/power/35795.
Glenny, Misha. *Nemesis*. New York: Alfred A. Knopf, 2016.
Goi, Leonardo. "Series of Escapes Underscores Weakness of Honduras Prison System." *Insight Crime*, May 15, 2017. https://www.insightcrime.org/news/brief/honduras-prisons-spotlight-65-escape-less-2-weeks/.
Gonzalez, Sandra. "Dejan militares mando único a Fuerza Civil." *Milenio*, September 4, 2015. http://www.milenio.com/region/Militares_Fuerza_Civil_mando_unico-Seguridad_NL-Fuerza_Civil_0_585541543.html.
Gordón Guerrel, Ismael. "Informe de Fiscalía reporta unas 204 pandillas en Panamá." *La Estrella de Panama*, April 7, 2016. http://laestrella.com.pa/panama/nacional/informe-fiscalia-reporta-unas-204-pandillas-panama/23932442.
Graham, David A. "What Is Mossack Fonseca, the Law Firm in the Panama Papers?" *The Atlantic*, April 4, 2016. http://www.theatlantic.com/international/archive/2016/04/panama-papers-mossack-fonseca/476727/.
Granada, Carlos. "Los Invisibles de la Quiaca." *Foro de Periodismo Argentina*, September 5, 2016. http://www.investigacionesfopea.com/trata-personas-jujuy/#11.
Grillo, Ioan. "Jamaican Organized Crime after the Fall of Dudus Coke." *Combatting Terrorism Center*, January 15, 2014. https://www.ctc.usma.edu/posts/jamaican-organized-crime-after-the-fall-of-dudus-coke.
Grillo, Ioan. *El Narco: En el corazón de la insurgencia criminal Mexicana*. Mexico City: Tendencias, 2012.
Grinberg, Emanuella, and Rafael Romo. "Official: Son of 'El Chapo' Has Been Kidnapped." *CNN*, August 17, 2016. http://www.cnn.com/2016/08/16/americas/el-chapo-son-kidnapped-official-says/index.html.
Guerrero, Kay, Claudia Dominguez, and Catherine E. Shoichet. "Venezuelan President Nicolas Maduro's Family Members Indicted in U.S. Court." *CNN*, November 12, 2015. http://www.cnn.com/2015/11/11/americas/venezuela-president-family-members-arrested/index.html.

Harris, Gardiner and Kirk Semple. "Rex Tillerson Arrives in Mexico Facing Twin Threats to Relations." *New York Times*, February 22, 2017. https://www.nytimes.com/2017/02/22/world/americas/rex-tillerson-mexico-border-relations.html.

Hernandez, Daniel. "Calderon's War on Drug Cartels: A Legacy of Blood and Tragedy." *Los Angeles Times*, December 1, 2012. http://articles.latimes.com/2012/dec/01/world/la-fg-wn-mexico-calderon-cartels-20121130.

Hirschfeld Davis, Julie. "Trump Reverses Pieces of Obama-Era Engagement With Cuba." *New York Times*, June 16, 2017. https://www.nytimes.com/2017/06/16/us/politics/cuba-trump-engagement-restrictions.html.

Hume, Mo. "Mano dura: El Salvador responds to gangs." *Development in Practice* 17, no. 6 (2007): 739–751.

Hyder, Victor D. "Decapitation Operations: Criteria for Targeting Enemy Leadership." Fort Leavenworth, KS: United States Army Command and General Staff College. https://fedgeno.com/documents/military-decapitation.pdf.

Jachimoowicz, Maia. "Argentina's Economic Woes Spur Emigration." *Migration Policy Institute*, July 1, 2003. http://www.migrationpolicy.org/article/argentinas-economic-woes-spur-emigration/.

Jacky, Alejandro. "Hip Hop Is Not Dead: The Emergence of Mara Salvatrucha Rap as a Form of MS-13 Expressive Culture." *Alternativas*, Spring 2014. http://alternativas.osu.edu/en/issues/spring-2014/essays1/jacky.html.

Jones, Nathan P. *Mexico's Illicit Drug Networks and the State Reaction*. Washington, D.C.: Georgetown University Press, 2016.

King, Quenton. "$350 Billion Lost to Corruption in Venezuela: Expert." *Insight Crime*, March 22, 2016. http://www.insightcrime.org/news-briefs/350-billion-lost-to-corruption-venezuela-official.

Kinosian, Sarah, and Adam Isacson. "U.S. Special Operations in Latin America: Parallel Diplomacy?" Washington Office on Latin America, August 30 2016. https://www.wola.org/analysis/u-s-special-operations-latin-america-parallel-diplomacy/.

Koop, Fermin. "Argentine Cash Deposits in Uruguay Grow 13%." *Buenos Aires Herald*. http://www.buenosairesherald.com/article/187215/argentine-cash-deposits-in-uruguay-grow-13.

LaSusa, Mike. "Northern Triangle Policing Pact Limits Focus to Gangs." *Insight Crime*, August 15, 2016. http://www.InsightCrime.org/news-briefs/northern-triangle-policing-pact-limits-focus-to-gangs.

Leali, Francisco. "Polícia Federal aponta elo entre facção brasileira e Hezbollah." *O Globo*, September 11, 2014. http://oglobo.globo.com/brasil/policia-federal-aponta-elo-entre-faccao-brasileira-hezbollah-14512269#ixzz4NjTVRVQf .

Leguizamón, Iván. "Un 'general' del Comando Vermelho en Paraguay." *ABC Color*, December 29, 2014. http://www.abc.com.py/edicion-impresa/suplementos/judicial/un-general-del-comando-vermelho-en-paraguay-1320957.html.

Lehman, Stan and, Sarah DiLorenzo. "Military Police Begin Patrols in Paralyzed Brazilian State." *PBS News Hour*, February 11, 2017. http://www.pbs.org/newshour/rundown/military-police-patrols-brazil/.

Lehman, Stan, and Sarah Dilorenzo. "Hundreds of Police Back on Duty in Paralyzed Brazil State." *ABC News*, February 11, 2017. http://abcnews.go.com/International/wireStory/striking-military-police-brazil-agree-return-work-45422063.

Lescano, Ana, and Carlos Navea, "Fuerzas Armadas inician lucha contra inseguridad ciudadana." *Correo Semanal*, November 23, 2014. http://correosemanal.pe/actualidad/fuerzas-armadas-inician-lucha-contra-inseguridad-ciudadana/

Lessing, Benjamin. *The Logic of Violence in Criminal War: Cartel-State Conflict in Mexico, Colombia, and Brazil*. PhD Thesis. Berkeley: University of California Press, 2012. https://escholarship.org/uc/item/03m9r44h.

Linthicum, Kate. "A Decade into Mexico's Deadly Drug War, Lawmakers Give the Military More Power." *Los Angeles Times*, December 15, 2017. http://

www.latimes.com/world/mexico-americas/la-fg-mexico-military-law-20171215-story.html.
Lohmuller, Michael. "Guatemala's Government Corruption Scandals Explained." *Insight Crime*, June 21, 2016. http://www.InsightCrime/com/news-analysis/guatemalas-government-corruption-scandals-explained.
Long Austin. "Assessing the Success of Leadership Targeting." *Combatting Terrorism Center*, 2010. https://www.ctc.usma.edu/posts/assessing-the-success-of-leadership-targeting.
Lopez, Jaime. "Maras intentan infiltrar PNC, Academia y Ejército." *El Salvador.com*, February 4, 2017. http://www.elsalvador.com/articulo/sucesos/maras-intentan-infiltrar-pnc-academia-ejercito-140038.
Lopez, Julie. "Los Lorenzana se quedan sin Patriarca. ¿Quién tomará su lugar?" *Soy502*, March 18, 2014. http://www.soy502.com/articulo/extraditan-waldemar-lorenzana-quien-era-y-quien-lo-sucedera.
Malkin, Elisabeth, and Azam Ahmed. "U.S. Withholds $5 Million in Antidrug Aid to Mexico as Human Rights Rebuke." *New York Times*, October 19, 2015. http://www.nytimes.com/2015/10/20/world/americas/us-withholds-5-million-in-antidrug-aid-to-mexico-over-human-rights.html?_r=0.
Mander, Benedict. "Venezuela Accused of Becoming 'Narco State.'" *Financial Times*, April 12, 2011. https://www.ft.com/content/85701a1c-652d-11e0-b150-00144feab49a.
Martin, Sabrina. "Brazil Evaluates Measures against Influx of Venezuelan Refugees." *PanamPost*, October 16, 2016. https://panampost.com/sabrina-martin/2016/10/20/brazil-evaluates-measures-against-influx-of-venezuelan-refugees/.
Martínez D'Aubuisson, Juan José. "International Terror and the Gangs of Douglas Farah." *Insight Crime*, February 26, 2016. https://www.insightcrime.org/news/analysis/international-terror-douglas-farah-gangs-ms13-barrio18/.
Martínez Pizarro, Jorge, Verónica Cano Christin, and Magdalena Soffia Contrucci. "Tendencias y patrones de la migración latinoamericana y caribeña hacia 2010 y desafíos para una agenda regional." New York: Economic Commission for Latin America and the Caribbean, October 2014.
Martinez, Carlos, and Roberto Valencia. "MS-13 pide diálogo al gobierno y pone sobre la mesa su propia desarticulación." *El Faro*, January 9, 2017. http://elfaro.net/es/201701/salanegra/19747/MS-13-pide-diálogo-al-gobierno-y-pone-sobre-la-mesa-supropia-desarticulaciÛn.htm.
Massé, Frédéric. "La entrega del Erpac." *El Espectador*, December 21, 2011. https://www.elespectador.com/noticias/judicial/entrega-del-erpac-articulo-318004.
McDermott, Jeremy. "Colombia's BACRIM Count More Than 3400 Fighters." *Insight Crime*, September 8, 2014. http://www.insightcrime.org/news-briefs/colombia-bacrim-count-more-than-3400-fighters.
McDermott, Jeremy. "What Does Colombia Peace Deal Mean for Cocaine Trade?" *Insight Crime*, August 24, 2016. http://www.InsightCrime.org/news-analysis/what-does-colombia-peace-deal-mean-for-cocaine-trade.
McDonnell, Patrick J., Kate Linthicum, and Del Quentin Wilber. "Drug Lord 'El Chapo' Extradited to the United States." *Los Angeles Times*, January 19, 2017. http://www.latimes.com/world/la-fg-el-chapo-extradition-20170119-story.html.
McKinley, James C. "U.S. Is Arms Bazaar for Mexican Cartels." *New York Times*, February 5, 2009. http://www.nytimes.com/2009/02/26/us/26borders.html.
Melgar, Ana. "Narcotraficante hondureño señala a hermano de presidente Juan Orlando Hernández." *CNN*, March 17, 2017. http://cnnespanol.cnn.com/2017/03/17/narcotraficante-hondureno-senala-a-hermano-de-presidente-juan-orlando-hernandez/.
Michael, Eleno, and Ricardo Gómez. "Aprueban parco legal para el Ejercito." *El Universal*, April 28, 2010. http://archivo.eluniversal.com.mx/nacion/177343.html.
Millett, Richard L., and Orlando J. Pérez. "New Threats and Old Dilemmas: Central America's Armed Forces in the 21st Century." *Journal of Political and Military Sociology*, 33, no. 1 (2005): 59.

Miroff, Nick. "Colombia is again the World's Top Coca Producer. Here's Why That's a Blow to the U.S.." *The Washington Post,* November 10, 2015. https://www.washingtonpost.com/world/the_americas/in-a-blow-to-us-policy-colombia-is-again-the-worlds-top-producer-of-coca/2015/11/10/316d2f66-7bf0-11e5-bfb6-65300a5ff562_story.html?utm_term=.4707114c9d4c.

Moloney, Anastasia. "Sex Trafficking 'Staggering' in Illegal Latin American Gold Mines: Researchers." *Reuters,* March 30, 2016. https://www.reuters.com/article/us-latam-trafficking-mines/sex-trafficking-staggering-in-illegal-latin-american-gold-mines-researchers-idUSKCN0WW21U.

Montes, Julio. "Panamá Crea la Fuerza Especial Antinarcóticos (FEAN)." *Defensa,* September 12, 2016. http://www.defensa.com/frontend/defensa/noticia.php?id_noticia=19283&id_seccion=339.

Mosso, Ruben. "Invade cartel de Jalisco ocho estados y el DF." *Milenio,* April 20, 2015. http://www.milenio.com/policia/PGR-predominante_cartel_de_Jalisco_Nueva_Generacion-carteles_del_narcotrafico_0_503349665.html.

Movilla, Martin. "MS-13 habría recibido entrenamiento militar en El Salvador." *Radio Canada Internacional,* March 17, 2014. http://www.rcinet.ca/es/2014/03/17/ms-13-habria-recibido-entrenamiento-militar-en-el-salvador/.

Muedano, Marcos. "A seis años, Mando Único opera en 17.5% de municipios." *El Universal,* January 8, 2016. http://www.eluniversal.com.mx/articulo/nacion/seguridad/2016/01/8/seis-anos-mando-unico-opera-en-175-de-municipios.

Muga M., Ricardo. "In Chile, Cocaine Consumption Is on the Rise." *Santiago Times,* April 25, 2010. http://santiagotimes.cl/2010/04/15/in-chile-cocaine-consumption-is-on-the-rise/.

Naim, Moises. *Ilicit: How Smugglers, Traffickers, and Copycats Are Hijacking the Global Economy,* New York: Anchor Books, 2005.

Neumann, William. "Defying U.S., Colombia Halts Aerial Spraying of Crops Used to Make Cocaine." *The New York Times,* May 14, 2015. https://www.nytimes.com/2015/05/15/world/americas/colombia-halts-us-backed-spraying-of-illegal-coca-crops.html?_r=0.

Nolan, Stephanie. "Crack Cocaine Is King in Brazil: What Sao Paulo Is Doing about It." *The Globe and Mail,* April 26, 2014. http://www.theglobeandmail.com/news/world/crack-is-king-in-brazil-what-sao-paulo-is-doing-about-it/article18232957/.

O'Neill, John E. "The Interagency Process—Analysis and Reform Recommendations." U.S. Army War College, March 15, 2006. http://www.strategicstudiesinstitute.army.mil/pdffiles/ksil445.pdf.

Olea Galindo, Joel. "Quedan restringidas las cuentas en dólares." *Tribuna de San Luis,* November 30, 2014. http://www.oem.com.mx/tribunadesanluis/notas/n3623648.htm.

Oliveira, Nelza. "Brazil Promotes New Phase of Operation Ágata." *Dialogo,* July 15, 2016. https://dialogo-americas.com/en/articles/brazil-promotes-new-phase-operation-agata.

Olson, Eric L. and Christopher E. Wilson. "Beyond Mérida: The Evolving Approach to Security Cooperation." Washington, D.C.: Woodrow Wilson International Center for Scholars, 2010.

Otis, John. "The FARC and Colombia's Illegal Drug Trade." The Wilson Center, November 2014. https://www.wilsoncenter.org/sites/default/files/Otis_FARCDrugTrade2014.pdf.

Pachico, Elyssa. "Guatemala Arrests Alleged Leader of Mendoza Criminal Clan." *Insight Crime,* April 6, 2016. http://www.InsightCrime.com/news-briefs/guatemala-arrests-alleged-leader-of-mendoza-criminal-clan.

Pachico, Elyssa. "Guatemala Military Brigade to Fight Poppy Production Near Mexico." *Insight Crime,* January 3, 2013. http://www.InsightCrime.org/news-briefs/guatemala-military-poppy-production-mexico.

Palma, Claudia. "Guatemala. Ministerio de Gobiernación vi desafío en ataque de las maras." *Kaosenlared*, March 15, 2016. http://kaosenlared.net/guatemala-ministro-de-gobernacion-ve-desafio-en-ataques-de-marasministro-de-gobernacion-ve-desafio-en-ataques-de-maras/.

Palmeri, Francisco. "Central America and the Alliance for Prosperity: Identifying U.S. Priorities and Assessing Progress." U.S. Department of State, April 19, 2016. http://www.state.gov/p/wha/rls/rm/255958.htm.

Panoussian, Florence. "Colombia Seeks 'Complete Peace' at ELN Talks." *Yahoo News*, February 7, 2017. https://www.yahoo.com/news/colombia-seeks-complete-peace-eln-talks-022328664.html.

Park, Madison. "Mexico's Most Notorious Drug Cartels." *CNN*, August 18, 2016. http://www.cnn.com/2016/08/18/americas/mexican-drug-cartels/.

Pastrán, Rosa Maria. "Presentan anteproyecto de impuesto a la telefonía." *La Prensa Grafica*, September 18, 2015. http://www.laprensagrafica.com/2015/09/18/presentan-anteproyecto-de-impuesto-a-la-telefonia.

Payne, Ed. "Report: Many Weapons Used by Mexican Drug Gangs Originate in U.S." *CNN*, June 4, 2011. http://www.cnn.com/2011/US/06/14/mexico.guns/index.html.

Paz Paniego, Maria. "El paco avanza: en las villas, ya lo consumen desde los 10 años." *La Nacion*, August 11, 2016. http://www.lanacion.com.ar/1926815-el-paco-avanza-en-las-villas-ya-lo-consumen-desde-los-10-anos.

Pelcastre, Julieta. "Los Perrones Collaborate with 'El Chapo' in Central America." *Dialogo*, September 26, 2013. https://dialogo-americas.com/en/articles/los-perrones-collaborate-el-chapo-central-america.

Pelcastre, Julieta. "Peruvian Navy Brings Healthcare, Social Services to Amazon Region." *Dialogo*, December 14, 2015. https://dialogo-americas.com/en/articles/peruvian-navy-brings-healthcare-social-services-amazon-region.

Pérez Salazar, Juan Carlos. "Los *Perrones*, el poderoso grupo criminal que pocos conocen." *BBC*, August 28, 2014. http://www.bbc.com/mundo/noticias/2014/08/140820_el_salvador_perrones_transportistas_cocaina_jcps.

Pérez, Orlando J. *Civil-Military Relations in Post-Conflict Societies: Transforming the Role of the Military in Central America*, Vol. 12. New York: Routledge, 2015.

Perú: Monitoreo de Cultivos de Coca 2012, United Nations Office on Drugs and Crime, September 2013. http://www.unodc.org/documents/crop-monitoring/Peru/Peru_Monitoreo_de_Coca_2012_web.pdf.

Philips, Dom. "With Nearly 100 Dead in Prison Riots, Brazil's Government Faces Crisis." *New York Times*, January 8, 2017. https://www.nytimes.com/2017/01/08/world/americas/brazil-prison-riots-michel-temer.html?_r=0.

Phillips, Dom, and Júlio Carvalho. "Brazil's Army Returns to Rio Favela amid Clashes between Gangs and Police." *The Guardian*, September 22, 2017. https://www.theguardian.com/world/2017/sep/22/brazils-army-deployed-to-rio-favela-amid-clashes-between-gangs-and-police.

Pitán, Edwin. "Gobierno seguirá con plan para abrir cárcel pese a controversia." *Prensa Libre*, November 2, 2016. http://www.prensalibre.com/guatemala/comunitario/gobierno-seguira-con-plan-para-abrir-carcel-pese-a-controversia.

Plan Nacional de Desarrollo 213–2018. Government of Mexico. Accessed March 1, 2016. http://pnd.gob.mx/.

Prada, Paulo. "5 Days of Violence by Gangs in São Paulo Leaves 115 Dead before Subsiding." *New York Times*, May 17, 2006. http://www.nytimes.com/2006/05/17/world/americas/17brazil.html?_r=0.

Primera, Maye. "El tráfico de cocaína hacia EE UU y Europa se hace fuerte en la ruta del Caribe." *El Pais*, April 15, 2014. http://internacional.elpais.com/internacional/2014/04/15/actualidad/1397517496_768647.html.

Realuyo, Celina B. "Leveraging the Financial Instrument of National Power to Counter Illicit Networks." Testimony before the Task Force to Investigate Terrorist Financing, Committee on Financial Services, U.S. House of Representatives, May 21,

2015. http://financialservices.house.gov/uploadedfiles/hhrg-114-ba00-wstate-crealuyo-20150521.pdf.

Rebando Seelke, Claire, Liana Sun Wyler, and June S. Beittel. "Latin America and the Caribbean: Illicit Drug Trafficking and U.S. Counterdrug Programs." Congressional Research Service, April 30, 2010. http://fpc.state.gov/documents/organization/142364.pdf.

Reséndiz, Francisco, Elena Michel and Ricardo Gómez. "Peña Nieto entrega plan de cambios en secretarías." *El Universal*, November 14, 2012. http://archivo.eluniversal.com.mx/notas/883003.html.

Ribando Seelke, Claire, and Kristin Finklea. "U.S.-Mexican Security Cooperation: The Mérida Initiative and Beyond." *Congressional Research Service*, July 29, 2017. https://fas.org/sgp/crs/row/R41349.pdf.

Ribando Seelke, Claire. "Gangs in Central America." Washington, D.C.: Congressional Research Service, August 29, 2016.

Ribeiro, Bruno. "PCC envia dinheiro do tráfico para Estados Unidos e China." *O Estado de S. Paulo*, January 15, 2015. http://sao-paulo.estadao.com.br/noticias/geral,pcc-envia-dinheiro-do-trafico-para-estados-unidos-e-china,1619985.

Riesenfeld, Loren. "Peru Shoots Down Narco Plane Heading to Bolivia." *Insight Crime*, March 2, 2015. http://www.InsightCrime.org/news-briefs/peru-shoots-down-narco-plane-heading-to-bolivia.

Rivas, Oswaldo. "Nicaragua Closes Border to Cuban Migrants, Rebukes Costa Rica." *Reuters*, November 15, 2015. http://www.reuters.com/article/us-nicaragua-cuba-idUSKCN0T502920151116.

Robbins, Seth. "El Salvador bloquea celulares en las prisiones en intento de reducir la extorsión." *Insight Crime*, May 21, 2014. http://www.france24.com/en/20160426-new-force-raids-el-salvador-gang-districts.

Robbins, Seth. "Guyana Is Becoming a 'Narco-State': Ex-Military Commander." *Insight Crime*, April 10, 2014. http://www.insightcrime.org/news-briefs/guyana-is-becoming-a-narco-state-ex-military-commander.

Robinson, Melia. "It's 2017: Here's Where You Can Legally Smoke Weed Now." *Business Insider*, January 8, 2017. http://www.businessinsider.com/where-can-you-legally-smoke-weed-2017-1.

Rodríguez, Dagoberto. "Solicitud de extradición de Jaime Rosenthal llega el lunes a la CSJ." *La Prensa*, January 2, 2016. http://www.laprensa.hn/honduras/916193-410/solicitud-de-extradici%C3%B3n-de-jaime-rosenthal-llega-el-lunes-a-la-csj.

Rodriguez, Manuel. "Ex-agente de la DEA: Reverol es líder en el Cártel de los Soles." *Noticias Venezuela*, August 2, 2016. http://noticiasvenezuela.org/2016/08/02/ex-agente-de-la-dea-reverol-es-lider-en-el-cartel-de-los-soles/.

Rojas, Pablo. "Cierran pistas ilegales para frenar 'fiesta' narco." *Costa Rica Hoy*, July 7, 2016. http://www.crhoy.com/archivo/cierran-pistas-ilegales-para-frenar-fiesta-narco/nacionales/.

Romero, Simon, and Dom Phillips. "Brazil's President Deploys Federal Troops to Quell Protests." *The New York Times*, May 24, 2017. https://www.nytimes.com/2017/05/24/world/americas/brazil-michel-temer-brasilia-protests.html.

Rosen, Jonathan D. and Hanna S. Kassab, eds. *Fragile States in the Americas*. Lexington, KY: Lexington Books, 2016.

Rosen, Jonathan. *The Losing War: Plan Colombia and Beyond*, Albany, NY: SUNY University Press, 2014.

Royster, Michael. "Opinion: Rio's Evil Export." *Rio Times*, January 6, 2017. http://riotimesonline.com/brazil-news/opinion-editorial/opinion-rios-evil-export/.

Sánchez-Garzoli, Gimena. "December Update: Colombia Social Leaders Face Imminent Security Threat from Illegal Armed Groups." *Washington Office on Latin America*. https://www.wola.org/analysis/december-update-social-leaders-face-imminent-security-threat-illegal-armed-groups/.

Schoichet, Catherine E. "Inmates Running the Asylum? In Honduras Prisons, That's No Joke." *CNN*, August 4, 2013. http://www.cnn.com/2013/08/04/world/americas/honduras-prisons/index.html.

Schwartz, Rachel. "Guatemala's President Tried to Expel the U.N. Commissioner Who Announced He Was under Investigation." *Washington Post*, September 6, 2017. https://www.washingtonpost.com/news/monkey-cage/wp/2017/09/06/guatemalas-president-tried-to-shut-down-a-u-n-commission-that-announced-it-was-investigating-him/?utm_term=.89d61ceda03c.

Semple, Kirk. "Missing Mexican Students Suffered a Night of 'Terror,' Investigators Say." *New York Times*, April 26, 2016. https://www.nytimes.com/2016/04/25/world/americas/missing-mexican-students-suffered-a-night-of-terror-investigators-say.html.

Shadboldt, Peter. "Philippines Raid Reveals Mexican Drug Cartel Presence in Asia." *CNN*, February 25, 2014. http://www.cnn.com/2014/02/24/world/asia/philippines-mexico-sinaloa-cartel/index.html.

Shirk, David A. *The Drug War in Mexico: Confronting a Shared Threat*. New York: Council on Foreign Relations, 2011.

Silva Ávalos, Héctor, "El Salvador Mayor's Arrest." *Insight Crime*, June 1, 2017. https://www.insightcrime.org/news/brief/shadow-perrones-looms-el-salvador-mayor-arrest/.

Silva Ávalos, Héctor, and Suchit Chávez, "Montecristo, la sociedad que unió a un capo y al vicepresidente Ortiz." *Factum*, April 5, 2016. http://revistafactum.com/montecristo-la-sociedad-unio-capo-al-vicepresidente-ortiz/.

Silva Ávalos, Héctor. "In About-Face, El Salvador Govt Reopens 'Chepe Diablo' Case." *Insight Crime*, December 7, 2016. http://www.insightcrime.org/news-analysis/in-about-face-el-salvador-govt-reopens-chepe-diablo-case.

Solis Lerici, Alessandro. "Detrás de la economía de las maras salvadoreñas." *Nacion*, January 15, 2017. http://www.nacion.com/ocio/revista-dominical/Detras-economia-maras-salvadorenas_0_1609839033.html

Spencer, David E. *Colombia's Road to Recovery: Security and Governance 1982–2010*. Washington, D.C.: National Defense University Press, 2012.

Stevenson, Mark. "Mexican Drug Cartels Are Now Involved in Lucrative Illegal Mining Operations." *Business Insider*, November 29, 2013, www.businessinsider.com/mexican-drug-cartels-mining-2013-11.

Strategy to Combat Transnational Organized Crime: Addressing Converging Threats to National Security, The White House, July 2011. https://www.whitehouse.gov/sites/default/files/microsites/2011-strategy-combat-transnational-organized-crime.pdf.

Tabory, Sam. "Arrests Add to Murky Picture of Crime-Politics Links in Honduras." *Insight Crime*, August 19, 2015. http://www.InsightCrime.com/news-briefs/arrests-add-murky-honduras-picture-crime-political-relationship.

Tate, Winifred. *Drugs, Thugs, and Diplomats: US Policymaking in Colombia*. Stanford, CA: Stanford University Press, 2015.

The White House, "Executive Order: Border Security and Immigration Enforcement Improvements." January 25, 2017. https://www.whitehouse.gov/the-press-office/2017/01/25/executive-order-border-security-and-immigration-enforcement-improvements.

Thompson, Ginger. "U.S. Suspends $30 Million to Honduras." *New York Times*, September 3, 2009. http://www.nytimes.com/2009/09/04/world/americas/04honduras.html.

Torres, Mauricio. "Mando único policial y otras 10 claves del nuevo plan de seguridad de Peña." *CNN Mexico*, December 3, 2014. http://mexico.cnn.com/nacional/2014/12/03/mando-unico-policial-y-otras-10-claves-del-nuevo-plan-de-seguridad-de-pena.

Trafficking in Persons Report. U.S. Department of State, June 2016. http://www.state.gov/documents/organization/258876.pdf.

Transnational Organized Crime in Central America and the Caribbean: A Threat Assessment, U.N. Office on Drugs and Crime (UNODC), September 2012. http://

www.unodc.org/documents/data-and-analysis/Studies/
TOC_Central_America_and_the_Caribbean_english.pdf.
Trucco, Florencia, and Alanne Orjoux. "Colombia's government reaches ceasefire deal with ELN." *CNN*, September 4, 2017, www.cnn.com/2017/09/04/americas/colombia-eln-ceasefire/index.html.
U.S. Agencies Considered Various Factors in Funding Security Activities, but Need to Assess Progress in Achieving Interagency Objectives, GAO-13–771. Washington DC: General Accounting Office, September 13, 2013. http://www.gao.gov/assets/660/658145.pdf.
United Nations Office on Drugs and Crime. "Global Overview of Drug Demand and Supply." *World Drug Report, 2017.* New York: United Nations, 2017.
United States of America-Mexico Binational Criminal Proceeds Study, Washington D.C.: Department of Homeland Security, 2016. https://www.ice.gov/doclib/cornerstone/pdf/cps-study.pdf.
Valdés Castellanos, Guillermo. *Historia del Narcotrafico en Mexico*. Mexico City: Penguin-Random House, 2015.
Valdez, Al. *Gangs: A Guide to Understanding Street Gangs*. San Clemente, CA: Law Tech Publishing Company, 2000.
Valencia, Andre. "Cartel Jalisco Nueva Generación va por 'territorios' de Los Zetas en Tamaulipas ante caída del Z42." *Blog del Narco*, March 2015. http://www.blogdelnarco.mx/2015/03/cartel-jalisco-nueva-generacion-va-por.html.
Vyas, Kjal, and John Forero. "Top Venezuelan Bodyguard Defects to U.S." *Wall Street Journal*, January 27, 2015. https://www.wsj.com/articles/top-venezuelan-bodyguard-defects-to-u-s-1422406536.
Wade, Christine. "El Salvador's 'Iron Fist': Inside Its Unending War on Gangs." *World Politics Review*, June 6, 2016. http://www.worldpoliticsreview.com/articles/18982/el-salvador-s-iron-fist-inside-its-unending-war-on-gangs.
Walker, Karyl. "Lotto Scammers Living Large." *Jamaica Observer*, May 13, 2012. http://www.jamaicaobserver.com/news/Lotto-scammers-living-large_11448149.
Wee, Sui-Lee. "China Deflects Blame for Opioid Crisis as Trump Visit Nears." *New York Times*, November 3, 2017. https://www.nytimes.com/2017/11/03/world/asia/china-opioid-fentanyl-trump.html.
Wolf, Sonja "Mara Salvatrucha: The Most Dangerous Street Gang in the Americas?" *Latin American Politics and Society* 54, no. 1 (2012): 65–99.
Wolf, Sonja. "El Salvador's Pandilleros Calmados: The Challenges of Contesting Mano Dura through Peer Rehabilitation and Empowerment." *Bulletin of Latin American Research* 31, no. 2 (2012): 190–205.
Wolf, Sonja. *Mano Dura: The Politics of Gang Control in El Salvador*. Austin: University of Texas Press, 2017.
Wolf, Sonja. "Street Gangs of El Salvador." in *Maras: Gang Violence and Security in Central America*, edited by Thomas Bruneau, Lucía Dammert, and Elizabeth Skinner, pp. 43–70. Austin: University of Texas Press, 2011.
Woody, Christopher. "Colombia Has a New Deal to End a 52-Year War, but Violence and Uncertainty Still Loom over It." *Yahoo*, November 25, 2016. https://www.yahoo.com/news/colombia-deal-end-52-war-211559588.html.
Woody, Christopher. "'El Chapo' Guzmán's key role in the global cocaine trade is becoming clearer." *Business Insider*, August 6, 2015. http://www.businessinsider.com/the-sinaloa-cartel-and-colombian-cocaine-2015-8.
Woody, Patrick. "There's a Sinister Theory for Why the Mexican Government Can't Take Down Fugitive Drug Lord 'El Chapo' Guzmán." *Business Insider*, December 21, 2015. http://www.businessinsider.com/mexican-government-sinaloa-cartel-cooperation.
World Drug Report, 2014. New York: United Nations Office on Drugs and Crime, 2014. http://www.unodc.org/documents/wdr2014/World_Drug_Report_2014_web.pdf.
World Drug Report, 2016. New York: United Nations Office on Drugs and Crime, 2016. http://www.unodc.org/wdr2016/.

Yagoub, Mimi. "Colombia Protests Bad Sign for Post-Conflict Coca Reduction." *Insight Crime*, August 24, 2016. http://www.InsightCrime.org/news-analysis/colombia-protests-cast-doubts-over-post-conflict-coca-reduction.

Yagoub, Mimi. "Colombia's Eastern Plains up for Grabs after Drug Lord Capture." *Insight Crime*, March 1, 2016. http://www.InsightCrime.org/news-briefs/colombia-eastern-plains-up-for-grabs-after-drug-lord-capture.

Yagoub, Mimi. "Honduras Prisons Put Inmates at Risk, Fuel Gang Violence: OAS." *Insight Crime*, March 22, 2016. http://www.insightcrime.org/news-analysis/honduras-prisons-put-inmates-at-risk-fuel-gang-violence-oas.

Yagoub, Mimi. "Is the Northern Triangle's 'Historic' Security Pact Short-Sighted?" *Insight Crime*, August 24, 2016. http://www.InsightCrime.org/news-briefs/is-the-northern-triangle-historic-security-pact-short-sighted.

Yagoub, Mimi. "Peru's Shining Path is Making a Comeback, Analyst Says." *Insight Crime*, August 25, 2016. http://www.InsightCrime.org/news-briefs/peru-shining-path-making-a-comeback.

Zamost, Scott, Drew Griffin, Kay Guerrero and Rafael Romo. "U.S. Calls Venezuela's Vice President an International Drug Trafficker." *CNN*, February 13, 2017. http://www.cnn.com/2017/02/13/world/us-sanctions-venezuela-vice-president/.

Zavaleta, Noe. "Espiral de violencia en Veracruz: Narcofosas, balaceras, secuestros." *El Proceso*, July 4, 2014. http://www.proceso.com.mx/376645.

Zukerman Daly, Sarah. *Organized Violence after Civil War*. New York: Cambridge University Press, 2016.

Index

Ábrego, Juan Garcia, 57
Acción Integral, 106
air interdiction, 158; Argentina with, 125–126; Brazil with, 125; Dominican Republic with, 124; Guatemala with, 122–123; Honduras with, 123; Latin American with, 122; Panama with, 123; Peru with, 124
airstrips (clandestine), 122
Amazon Rain Forest, 2
Andreas, Peter, 112
Arab Spring, 3
Arellano Felix organization, 59
Argentina: air interdiction in, 125–126; consumption zone, 37; financial resources in, 148; land interdiction in, 121; military use in, 139–140; narcoflights in, 37; role of, 36–38; transit zone of, 36; whole-of-government solutions in, 112
Asia: extra-hemispheric zone of, 40; immigrants from, 14; Latin America and, 40; migrants from, 40
Atlantic Cartel, 72
authoritarian governments, 2

BACRIM. *See* drug cartels and criminal bands
Baja California, 59
Baldetti, Roxana, 144
Barrio 18, 5, 23, 69, 158; in Central America, 81; gang of, 85; organization of, 85
Beltrán-Leyva organization (BLO), 61–62
Bolivia: government of, 68; human trafficking in, 36; role of, 35–36; source zone of, 35

border control, 4; Brazil for, 153; Colombia for, 153; cooperation for, 153–154; Honduras for, 153
border wall, 1
Brazil: air interdiction in, 125; border control for, 153; consumption zone as, 34; gangs in, 35, 88; land interdiction in, 120–121; military use in, 138–139; prison systems reform in, 152; role of, 34–35; transit zone of, 34
Brazilian Amazon, 115
Brazilian military, 121

CAA. *See* Conference of American Armies
Cachiros, 70
CAFTA-DR. *See* Central American Free Trade Agreement
Calderón, Felipe, 9, 17, 126
Cali Cartel, 27
Calle Serna, Javier Antonio, 66
Calor Calor, 86
Camarena, Enrique, 17, 54
Caribbean, 1, 51; economic activity in, 13; gangs in, 80–90; maritime transit zone of, 24–26; money laundering through, 25; naval interdiction in, 115; policymakers in, 173–179; transnational crime in, 3, 6
Caribbean Basin Security Initiative (CBSI), 155
Carpenter, Ted Gallen, 112
Carrillo Fuentes, Amado, 60
Carrillo Fuentes organization, 60, 61
CARSI. *See* Central American Regional Security Initiative
Cartel of the Suns, 29, 68–69
cartels, 27; drug trafficking for, 5; gangs and, 15; intermediary groups

and, 67–68. *See also* Cartel of the Suns; Guadalajara Cartel; Gulf Cartel; Jalisco Nuevo Generation Cartel; Medellin Cartel; Mexican cartels; Milenio Cartel; Sinaloa Cartel; Texis cartel; Tijuana Cartel
CAT. *See* Center against Transnational Gangs
CBSI. *See* Caribbean Basin Security Initiative
Center against Transnational Gangs (CAT), 156
Central America: Asian immigrants through, 14; Barrio 18 in, 81; criminal organizations in, 6; CV in, 89; gangs in, 81–83; geography of, 19–24; immigrants from, 19; MS-13 in, 81, 83; narcotrafficking through, 20; organized crime leaders in, 127
Central American Free Trade Agreement (CAFTA-DR), 181
Central American Integration System (SICA), 7, 154, 175
Central American Regional Security Initiative (CARSI), 155
CFAC. *See* Conference of Central American Armed Forces
Chavez, Hugo, 29, 68
Chile, 38, 39
China, 14, 31, 40, 157
CICIG. *See* Commission Against Impunity in Guatemala
Citizen Security Squadrons, 133
cocaine, 28, 32, 54, 64
coca plants, 28, 33
Coke, Dudus, 26, 87
Colombia, 7; BACRIM in, 27; border control for, 153; civil war in, 27; corruption in, 105; Dominican Republic and, 25; financial resources in, 148; guerrillas in, 29; Gulf Clan and, 64; Honduras bridge with, 19; illegal mining in, 28; institutional reform in, 145; Medellin Cartel in, 27; Mexican cartel and, 63; military use in, 137; narcotrafficking in, 27; organize crime groups of, 63–64; organize crime leaders of, 129; Rastrojos in, 66; as source zone, 27–29; war on drugs and, 106; whole-of-government solutions for, 105–106
Colombian Revolutionary Anti-Subversive Army (ERPAC), 66
commercial ports: importance of, 33; Quetzal as, 114; Rosario port as, 37; smugglers and, 33
Commission Against Impunity in Guatemala (CICIG), 144
Conference of American Armies (CAA), 7, 154, 175
Conference of Central American Armed Forces (CFAC), 7, 116, 118, 154, 175
consumption zone: Argentina as, 37; Chile as, 38; Europe as, 39; transit zone countries with, 15; Uruguay of, 38; US as, 16–17
corruption, 4; in Colombia, 105; combating of, 141; with criminal organizations, 103; institutional reform and, 141; law enforcement and, 140; perceived impunity and, 8–9; in Venezuela, 30, 69
Costa Rica, 24, 86
criminal flows, 112–126, 116
criminal investigation agency (CTI), 137
criminal organizations, 186; corruption with, 103; governments against, 92; in Honduras, 21; international borders and, 4; in Mexico, 18; regional response to, 6–7; self perpetuating aspect of, 5; smuggling in, 15; whole-of-government approach to, 6. *See also* organized crime groups
criminal patterns, 41
CTI. *See* criminal investigation agency
CV. *See* Red Command; *Red Command*

DEA. *See* Drug Enforcement Administration
Defense Institutional Reform Initiative (DIRI), 108
Díaz González, Martín Farfán (Pijarbey), 67
domestic law enforcement, 130–140

Index

Dominican Republic: air interdiction in, 124; Colombia and, 25; financial resources in, 148; gangs in, 87; military use in, 136; transit zone of, 25–26
Don Mario. *See* Herrera, Daniel Rendón
drug cartels and criminal bands (BACRIM), 27, 64
Drug Enforcement Administration (DEA), 25
drug markets, 35
drug trafficking, 5
drug use, 16

ECLAC. *See* Economic Commission for Latin America and the Caribbean
economic activity, 13, 157. *See also* socioeconomic issues
Economic Commission for Latin America and the Caribbean (ECLAC), 39
Ecuador, 31–32, 111
ELN. *See* National Liberation Army
El Salvador, 117, 160; gangs in, 23, 84; land interdiction in, 118; military use in, 134–135; MS-13 in, 84; organized crime leaders in, 129; prison systems reform in, 151; smugglers through, 23; transit zone of, 22–23; transportations groups based in, 75; violence in, 23; whole-of-government solutions for, 109; *Zeus* Command for, 118
ERPAC. *See* Colombian Revolutionary Anti-Subversive Army
Escobar, Pablo, 19, 27
Europe, 33, 39
extortion, 13, 27, 82, 84
extra-hemispheric zone, 39–40, 40

La Familia Michoacana (LFM), 61, 62
FARC. *See* Revolutionary Armed Forces of Colombia
FATF. *See* Financial Action Task Force
FERES. *See* Specialized Reaction Force of El Salvador
Financial Action Task Force (FATF), 146

Financial Intelligence Units (FIUs), 146, 160
financial resources: in Argentina, 148; in Colombia, 148; in Dominican Republic, 148; financial intelligence units and, 160; in Guatemala, 147; in Honduras, 147; laws and regulations for, 146; targeting of, 146–148; tools against, 177–178
firearms, 16
First Capital Command (PCC), 88–89, 89
FIRT. *See* Territory Recuperation Force
FIUs. *See* Financial Intelligence Units
Forward-Looking Infrared Radar (FLIR), 122
Friends of Friends, 90
Fujimori, Alberto, 79
FUSINA, 109, 117, 158

Gallardo, Angel Felix, 59
gangs, 53, 67; Barrio 18 as, 85; Brazil and, 35, 88; in Caribbean, 86; cartels and, 15; in Central America, 81–83; of CV, 89; in Dominican Republic, 87; in El Salvador, 23, 84; Friends of Friends as, 90; immigrants and, 81; in Jamaica, 87; in Latin America and Caribbean, 80–90; military members in, 82; MS-13 as, 83–85; of northern triangle, 23; in Panama, 86; of PCC, 88–89; of TCP, 90; Los Zetas with, 58. *See also* urban gangs
gangster rap culture, 81
Gendarmerie, 121, 139, 140, 175
global warming, 2
governments: Bolivia form of, 68; corruption strategies for, 103; against criminal organizations, 92; institutional reform within, 142; interdiction by, 112; law enforcement and, 145; military and, 104; against organized crime leaders, 127; Sinoloa Cartel influence on, 54
Granger, David, 30
Grupo Continental, 9
Guadalajara Cartel, 17, 19, 54, 57

Guatemala: aircraft for, 123; air interdiction in, 122–123; Citizen Security Squadrons in, 133; domestic military use in, 132–134; financial resources in, 147; institutional reform in, 143–144; intermediary groups in, 68; land interdiction in, 116–117; military capabilities of, 21; narcoflights in, 22; narcotrafficking in, 22, 83; naval interdiction in, 113–114; NSC and, 108; organized crime leaders in, 127–128; police screening in, 143; prison systems reform in, 150; transit zone of, 21–22
Guatemalan Aire Force, 122
guerrilla groups, 29, 78–79, 79–80
Guillen, Osiel Cardenas, 57, 58
Gulf Cartel, 17, 56, 57, 58–59, 62, 66
Gulf Clan, 64, 65, 119, 137
Gulf of Mexico, 131
Guyana, 30
Guzman, Abimael, 79, 91
Guzman, Joaquín "El Chapo", 53, 127, 176; capture of, 54; Juarez Cartel against, 60; kidnapping of, 55; in Sinaloa Cartel, 40; Sinoloa Cartel leader of, 54–55

Hernandez, Juan Orlando, 70, 117, 135, 145, 182
heroin, 16, 54, 66
Herrera, Daniel Rendón (Don Mario), 64
Honduran Navy, 114
Honduras, 9; air interdiction in, 123; border control for, 153; CFAC for, 118; Colombia bridge with, 19; criminal organizations in, 21; financial resources in, 147; institutional reform in, 145; land interdiction in, 117–118; law enforcement in, 145; narcotrafficking in, 21, 114; naval interdiction in, 114–115; organized crime leaders in, 128; other groups in, 71–72; prison system reforms in, 151–152; smuggling key for, 70; transportistas based in, 69

Huistas, 74
human smuggling, 14
human trafficking, 36, 51; in Bolivia, 36; in Chile, 39; human smuggling distinction between, 14; international sex trade and, 35

ICS. *See* Integrated Country Strategy
ideologically-oriented groups, 76–80, 91
IIRIRA. *See* Illegal Immigrant Reform and Immigrant Responsibility Act
illegal drugs, 19
Illegal Immigrant Reform and Immigrant Responsibility Act (IIRIRA), 19
illegal immigration, 1
illegal logging, 2
illegal mining, 2, 14, 51; in Colombia, 28; in Mexico, 18; Peru with, 32, 34, 165n114
illicit materials, 14, 15, 19
illicit networks, 180
immigrants, 39, 110; from Central America, 19; deportation of, 81; gangs and, 81; problems for, 14–15
income sources, 51
institutional reform: in Colombia, 145; corruption and, 141; within government, 142; in Guatemala, 143–144; in Honduras, 145; within law enforcement, 140–145; in Mexico, 141–143
Institutional Revolutionary Party (PRI), 107
Integrated Country Strategy (ICS), 183
interdiction: best practices for, 175–176; challenge of, 112; of criminal flows, 112–126; by government, 112; joint task forces and, 117; of US, 113. *See also* air interdiction; naval interdiction
intermediary group, 75, 75–76, 91
intermediary groups: business relationships for, 67; Cachiros as, 69; cartels and, 67–68; in Guatemala, 68; Huistas as, 74; smuggling with, 67; Valle Valles as, 69
international borders, 4

Index

international sex trade, 35
Interpol, 7

Jalisco Nuevo Generation Cartel (CJNG), 142, 185; Carrillo Fuentes organization and, 61; Mexican cartel of, 55–56; Milenio Cartel and, 56; violent acts by, 56; Los Zetas rivals with, 56
Jamaica, 26, 87
Jamaica Labor Party (JLP), 87
JCETS. *See* Joint Combined Exchange Training teams
JIATF-S. *See* Joint Interagency Task Force South
JLP. *See* Jamaica Labor Party
Joint Combined Exchange Training teams (JCETS), 156
Joint Interagency Task Force South (JIATF-S), 24, 113, 155
joint task forces, 117
Juarez Cartel, 60
judicial system, 177

Key West, 24, 113
kidnapping, 51; of El Chapo, 55; extortion and, 27; heroin and, 66
Knights Templar, 18, 61, 142

land interdiction: in Argentina, 121; in Brazil, 120–121; in El Salvador, 118; in Guatemala, 116–117; in Honduras, 117–118; meaning of, 116; military and, 120; narcotrafficking and, 119; in Panama, 119; in Peru, 119–120
Latin America, 1, 51; air interdiction in, 122; Asia and, 40; economic activity in, 13; gangs in, 80–90; ideologically-oriented groups in, 76–80; naval interdiction in, 113; policymakers in, 173–179; prison systems in, 149; terrorism in, 3; transnational crime in, 3, 6; US partnerships with, 184–185; whole-of-government in, 104
law enforcement, 159; criticisms against, 104; government and, 145; in Honduras, 145; institutional reform within, 140–145; judicial system and, 177; in Mexico, 143; military use with, 139, 177; reform for, 159, 182; in VRAEM, 138; vulnerable officials in, 141. *See also* domestic law enforcement
law enforcement patterns, 15
Leones group, 73–74
LFM. *See* La Familia Michoacana
Lobo, Pepe, 21, 70
Lopez Ortiz Family, 74
Lorenzans group, 73

Maduro, Nicholas, 29
Makled, Walid, 29
Mara Salvatrucha (MS-13): in Central America, 81; in El Salvador, 84; extortion by, 82, 84; gang of, 83–85; organization of, 84; terrorism and, 84
marijuana, 38, 54
maritime transit zone, 24–26, 180
Matta, Juan Ramon, 19
Mauricio, Oscar, 66
Medellin Cartel, 19, 27, 63
Mendozas, 72–73
Merida Plan, 107
Mexican Armed Forces, 131, 132
Mexican cartels, 185; BLO as, 61–62; of CJNG, 55–56; Colombian government and, 63; evolution of, 52; groups of, 52–53; narcotrafficking for, 53; of Sinaloa Cartel, 54–55; small groups of, 128; splintering of, 53; supply and demand and, 53; Los Zetas as, 58–59
Mexico: criminal organizations in, 18; defense in, 161n8; domestic military use in, 131; FIU in, 146; geography of, 17–18; illegal mining in, 18; institutional reform in, 141–143; law enforcement in, 143; military and, 107; narcotrafficking in, 17; organized crime in, 142; organized crime leaders in, 126–127; prison systems reform in, 150; as transit zone, 17, 18; war against the cartels by, 17–18; for whole-of-government solutions, 106–107

Mexico City, 56
Mexico-US border, 18
Middle East, 3
migrants: Asia with, 40; Mexico-US border and, 18; Mexico with, 18; in North America, 16
Milenio Cartel, 55, 56
militarized police, 139
military: *Acción Integral* within, 106; Argentina use of, 139–140; Brazil use of, 138–139; Colombia use of, 137; in domestic law enforcement, 130–140; Dominican Republic use of, 136; ELN and, 105; El Salvador use of, 134–135; FUSINA integration with, 109, 158; gangs members in, 82; governments and, 104; Guatemala use of, 132–134; internal security role of, 130; land interdiction and, 120; law enforcement use with, 139, 177; Mexico and, 107, 131; Peru use of, 138; for security, 133; against Shining Path, 80; used of, 159. *See also* Brazilian military; Mexican Armed Forces
Military Police for Public Order (PMOP), 118, 135
militias, 63
money laundering, 5, 24, 25
Morales, Jimmy, 108, 143
Moreno González, Nazario (El Chayo), 61–62
MS-13. *See* Mara Salvatrucha

NAFTA. *See* North American Free Trade Agreement
narcoflights, 22, 37
narcosubmarines, 31
narcotrafficking, 37; BLO and, 61; Cachiros for, 70; Central America with, 20; Colombia with, 27; Costa Rica with, 24; Dominican Republic with, 25; FARC and, 77; financial institutions and, 147; Guatemala with, 22, 83; Honduras with, 21, 114; in Jamaica, 26; land interdiction and, 119; for Mexican cartels, 53; Mexico with, 17; Milenio Cartel with, 55; Panama with, 24; with PCC, 89; Peru with, 32; source zone for, 13; transit zone for, 13; Valle Valles with, 71; Venezuela with, 29. *See also* illicit materials
National Liberation Army (ELN), 5, 76, 78–79, 91, 105
National Security Council (NSC), 4–6, 108
naval interdiction, 113–116
Norte del Valle Cartel, 65
North American Free Trade Agreement (NAFTA), 181
Northern Triangle, 19, 23, 82, 104, 133, 178
NSC. *See* National Security Council

Obama, Barack, 16, 122, 182
Office of Foreign Assets Control (OFAC), 68
Operation Agamemnon, 65
organize crime leaders, 129, 176
organized crime: border control and, 154; China against, 157; complexity of, 41; economic activity and, 157; in Europe, 39; international cooperation against, 153–157; JIATF-S against, 155; in Mexico, 142; multilateral facilitation mechanisms against, 154–157; Russia against, 156; socioeconomic and, 104; US against, 155–156
organized crime groups, 160; of Colombia, 63–64; fight against, 108; income generation for, 8; income sources for, 51; law enforcement patterns for, 15; in Panama, 24, 86; in societies, 8; with systemic centers of gravity, 8–9; systems within systems for, 7; targeting leaders of, 126–130; varieties of, 51
organized crime leaders: Central America and, 127; in El Salvador, 129; government successes against, 127; in Guatemala, 127–128; in Honduras, 128; Mexico and, 126–127; in Peru, 130
Ortiz, Lopez, 74
Oseguera, Nemesio, 55

Otoniel. *See* Úsuga, Dario Antonio
Pacific coast, 22
Panama: air interdiction in, 123; Costa Rica and, 24; gangs in, 86; land interdiction in, 119; money laundering in, 24; narcotrafficking in, 24; naval interdiction in, 115; organized crime groups in, 24, 86; whole-of-government solutions for, 109
Panama Canal, 115
Panama Coast Guard, 115
Paraguay, 36
PCC. *See* First Capital Command
Peña Nieto, Enrique, 106, 126
People's National Party (PNP), 87
perceived impunity, 8–9
Perez Molina, Otto, 143
Los Perrones cartel, 22
Perrones group, 75
Peru: air interdiction in, 124; cocaine production in, 32; coca plants farmed in, 33; criminal clans in, 5; Europe imports from, 33; illegal mining in, 32, 34, 165n114; land interdiction in, 119–120; military use in, 138; narcotrafficking in, 32; naval interdiction in, 115–116; organized crime leaders in, 130; Shining Path in, 79, 138; source zone of, 32–34; whole-of-government solutions for, 110
Plan Colombia, 183
PMOP. *See* Military Police for Public Order
PNP. *See* People's National Party
policymakers: better resources for, 180–181; in Caribbean, 173–179; decision making by, 174; in Latin America, 173–179; for US, 179–185
PRI. *See* Institutional Revolutionary Party
prison systems: Brazil reform, 152; cellphone jamming in, 160; El Salvador reform in, 151; Guatemala reform in, 150; Honduras reforms, 151–152; in Latin America, 149; Mexico reform of, 150; overcrowding in, 150; reform and, 149–152, 160, 178–179; security for, 151
Los Puntilleros, 66–67

Quintero, Rafael Caro, 54

Rastrojo, Diego, 65
Rastrojos, 64, 65–66
Red Command (CV), 36, 89, 152
Revolutionary Armed Forces of Colombia (FARC), 24, 63, 91; Ecuador and, 31; Gulf Clan and, 65; as ideologically-oriented group, 77–78; members of, 77; narcotrafficking and, 24, 27–28, 77; reduction of, 105
Rio de Janeiro, 121
Rosario port, 37
Rosenthal, Jaime, 9, 70
Rozo, Pachón, 66
Russia, 156

Sánchez Cerén, Salvador, 151
Santos, Juan Manuel, 105
SENAN, 115
Shining Path, 5, 32, 76, 91, 111, 176; as guerrilla groups, 79–80; military against, 80; in Peru, 79, 138; take down of, 80
The Shower Posse, 26
SICA. *See* Central American Integration System
Sinaloa Cartel, 4, 25, 32, 60; BLO alliance with, 61; Guzman, J., in, 40; Mexican cartel of, 54–55; size of, 54
Sinoloa Cartel, 54, 54–55
smugglers, 33, 39, 87; beginning of, 73; of cocaine, 64; commercial ports and, 33–34; through El Salvador, 23
smuggling, 67, 70, 72
socioeconomic issues, 104, 106, 110
source zone: Bolivia as, 35; Colombia as, 27–29; drug raw materials in, 14; for narcotrafficking, 13; Peru as, 32–34
South America, 27
Specialized Reaction Force of El Salvador (FERES), 118

street gangs. *See* gangs
supply and demand, 53
synthetic drugs, 40
systemic centers of gravity, 8–9, 9
system-oriented approach, 7–9, 183–184

TCP. *See* Third Pure Command
Territory Recuperation Force (FIRT), 118
terrorism, 2; funding for, 2; in Latin America, 3; MS-13 and, 84; transnational crime as, 2
terrorists, 29
Texis cartel, 22, 75–76
Third Pure Command (TCP), 90
Tidd, Kurt, 2
Tijuana, 59
Tijuana Cartel, 59
Tillerson, Rex, 180
Torres, Camilo, 78
transit zone: Argentina as, 36; Brazil as, 34; Central America as, 19; consumption zone countries with, 15; Dominican Republic as, 25–26; Ecuador as, 31; El Salvador as, 22–23; groups in, 14; Guatemala as, 21–22; Jamaica as, 26; Mexico as, 17, 18; for narcotrafficking, 13; Paraguay as, 36. *See also* maritime transit zone
transnational organized crime. *See specific topics*
transportistas groups, 5, 73–74, 75
Trevino, Miguel, 59
Trump, Donald, 1, 16, 179

United Nations Office on Drugs and Crime (UNODC), 82
United States (US): challenges for, 2; cocaine in, 16; as consumption zone countries, 16–17; defense and, 186; drug use in, 16; firearms sourced by, 16; heroin in, 16; interdiction of, 113; Latin America partnerships with, 184–185; national security in, 1–2; against organized crime, 155–156; policymakers for, 179–185; system-oriented approach and, 183–184;

Tijuana gateway to, 59; trade partners of, 3
United States-Mexico Bi-National Criminal Proceeds study, 16
UNODC. *See* United Nations Office on Drugs and Crime
urban gangs, 35
Uribe, Álvaro, 4, 63, 105
Uruguay, 38
US. *See* United States
US Coast Guard, 114
US national security, 1
US Southern Command, 3
Úsuga, Dario Antonio (Otoniel), 64
Úsuga, Juan de Dios, 64

Valle Valles, 69, 71
Valley and the Apurimac, Ene and Mantauro river valleys (VRAEM), 110, 111, 138
Varela, Wilber, 30
Venezuela: Cartel of the Suns and, 68–69; corruption in, 30, 69; narcotrafficking in, 29; Rastrojos in, 66; role of, 29–30; terrorists in, 29
Venezuelan military, 69
VRAEM. *See* Valley and the Apurimac, Ene and Mantauro river valleys

war on drugs, 106
whole-of-government solutions: in Argentina, 112; Colombia with, 105–106; coordination solutions for, 104–112; criminal organizations approach of, 6; in Ecuador, 111; for El Salvador, 109; examination of, 157; expansion of, 174–175; in Latin America, 104; meaning of, 6–7; Mexico for, 106–107; for Panama, 109; for Peru, 110; VRAEM and, 111

Zelaya, Manuel, 21, 70
Los Zetas, 17, 56, 62; CJNG rivals with, 56; gangs of, 58; Gulf Cartel and, 57, 58–59; history of, 58; LFM war against, 62; Mexican cartel of, 58–59
Zeus Command, 118

About the Author

Dr. Evan Ellis is research professor of Latin American studies at the U.S. Army War College Strategic Studies Institute with a focus on the region's relationships with China and other non-Western Hemisphere actors, as well as transnational organized crime and populism in the region.

Dr. Ellis has published over two hundred works, and has presented his work in a broad range of business and government forums in twenty-six countries on four continents. He has given testimony on Latin America security issues to the US Congress on multiple occasions, has discussed his work in various radio and television programs, and is cited regularly in the print media in both the US and Latin America.

Dr. Ellis holds a PhD in political science with a specialization in comparative politics.

Made in the USA
Middletown, DE
13 August 2022